Situations and Attitudes

JON BARWISE and JOHN PERRY

A Bradford Book

The MIT Press

Cambridge, Massachusetts
London, England

Fourth printing, 1986

Copyright © 1983 by
The Massachusetts Institute of Technology

Library of Congress Cataloging in Publication Data

Main entry under title:

Situations and attitudes.

"A Bradford book."
Bibliography: p.
Includes index.
1. Semantics (Philosophy)   I. Barwise, Jon, 1942–
II. Perry, John, 1943–
B840.S53   1983   149'.946   82–24985
ISBN 0-262-02189-7

Typographic design by David Horne
Composition by Horne Associates, Inc.,
West Lebanon, New Hampshire.
This book was printed and bound
in the United States of America.

Situations and Attitudes

∃**L** *Bradford Books*

Edward C. T. Walker, Editor. Explorations in THE BIOLOGY OF LANGUAGE. 1979. The M.I.T. Work Group in the Biology of Language: Noam Chomsky, Salvador Luria, et alia.

Daniel C. Dennett. BRAINSTORMS: Philosophical Essays on Mind and Psychology. 1979.

Charles Marks. COMMISSUROTOMY, CONSCIOUSNESS AND UNITY OF MIND. 1980.

John Haugeland, Editor. MIND DESIGN. 1981.

Fred I. Dretske. KNOWLEDGE AND THE FLOW OF INFORMATION. 1981.

Jerry A. Fodor. REPRESENTATIONS: Philosophical Essays on the Foundations of Cognitive Science. 1981.

Ned Block, Editor. IMAGERY. 1981.

Roger N. Shepard and Lynn A. Cooper. MENTAL IMAGES AND THEIR TRANSFORMATIONS. 1982.

Hubert L. Dreyfus, Editor, in collaboration with Harrison Hall. HUSSERL, INTENTIONALITY AND COGNITIVE SCIENCE. 1982.

John Macnamara. NAMES FOR THINGS. A Study of Human Learning. 1982.

Natalie Abrams and Michael D. Buckner, Editors. MEDICAL ETHICS: A Clinical Textbook and Reference for the Health Care Professions. 1983.

Morris Halle and G. N. Clements. PROBLEM BOOK IN PHONOLOGY: A Workbook for Introductory Courses in Linguistics and in Modern Phonology. 1983.

Irvin Rock. THE LOGIC OF PERCEPTION. 1983.

Elliott Sober, Editor. READINGS IN THE PHILOSOPHY OF BIOLOGY. 1983.

Jerry A. Fodor. MODULARITY OF MIND: An Essay on Faculty Psychology. 1983.

George D. Romanos. QUINE AND ANALYTIC PHILOSOPHY. 1983.

Robert Cummins. THE NATURE OF PSYCHOLOGICAL EXPLANATION. 1983.

Jon Barwise and John Perry. SITUATIONS AND ATTITUDES. 1983.

TO MARY ELLEN AND FRENCHIE

Contents

Preface

What do a logician working on model theory and a philosopher working on memory and personal identity have in common? When we began working together three years ago, we shared the conviction that the Fregean tradition in logic and philosophy within which we grew up was seriously flawed. Initially we traced the problems to a technical decision made by Frege to take the reference of a sentence to be a truth-value, thereby smuggling a sort of semantic holism into the heart of logic, and depriving logicians and logically oriented philosophers of situations, a tool we found most useful.

It now seems to us that the problem concerns not just Frege's technical decision but also one of man's oldest questions: *What and where is meaning?* Not just the meaning of a word or a sentence but the meaning of a loved one's raised eyebrows, and meaning quite generally. Descartes doubted everything but the meaning of his own thoughts. Locke solidified this view, locating meaning in the mind of man, or the heads of people. Frege realized that there was a world of difference between the mind of man and the heads of individuals, and that this difference required a more abstract, objective view of meaning. He located meaning not in the external world, nor in the psychological, but in a third realm, of sense and meaning. It is this view of meaning that is built into the very foundations of modern logic. It is El Camino Real of modern philosophy.

In recent years a different perspective, one we associate with Thomas Reid, has been revitalized by the work of the psychologist J. J. Gibson and a famous paper by Hilary Putnam, "The meaning of 'Meaning.'" Gibson, studying the coordinated perception and action of animals, found much more information in the environment (and so less work to be done by the animal brain, or mind) than the traditional view of perception admitted; and Putnam's paper, we think, shows that there is much more meaning and information in the world and less in the head than the traditional view of meaning assumed. From these two complementary movements a new realism has emerged, Ecological Realism, a view that finds meaning located in the interaction of living things and their environment. What began for us as an exercise in technical philosophy, reworking Frege, undoing his mistake, led us step by inevitable step to working out the beginnings of a theory of meaning implicit in this new realism.

The present book is divided into four parts. Part A is introductory. In Chapter 1 we outline our picture of a world full of meaning and information for living organisms, the picture that underlies the theory we develop later. In Chapter 2 we present central facts about human language that must be accounted for in a theory of meaning as it applies to language. The picture that emerges is one in which meaning arises out of recurring relations between situations. It is a common-sense view that we recently found foreshadowed in a remark of Franklin Delano Roosevelt: "Eternal truths will be neither true nor eternal unless they have fresh meaning for every new . . . situation."

In Part B we develop a theory of situations within which we make more precise this view of meaning and information. The main notions are situation, course of event, event-type, and constraint. Constraints between types of situations are actual and give rise to meaning—relations that allow one situation to contain information about another.

The book began with Part C, on the semantics of natural language. We had become convinced that the standard view of logic derived from Frege, Russell, Tarski, and work in mathematical logic is completely inappropriate for many of the uses to which it had been put by philosophers, linguists, computer scientists, and others—full of ideas appropriate for mathematics (even there we have our doubts) but inappropriate for more ordinary uses of language. In Part C we present an alternative that we call "situation semantics." We seek to explain the main ideas of the situation semantics within the context of a larger theory of mind and meaning, skipping over many formal details and ignoring all but the most simple linguistic constructions. In a sequel, *Situation Semantics*, we plan to present a rigorously developed semantics for a large fragment of English, with little attention to philosophical issues. But the technical details and the larger perspective seem intimately connected; the ideas we needed to make our theory of language work seem grounded in the larger picture of meaning we have tried to articulate.

Any semantic theory of language and underlying theory of meaning must sooner or later run the gauntlet of the attitudes by giving an account of the meanings of statements made using verbs like SEE, KNOW, BELIEVE, and ASSERT which describe cognitive states and activities. This is where one expects the greatest difficulty for a realist account. And so Part D is devoted to an account of the attitudes.

Part D is slightly schizophrenic. After our earlier paper "Situations and Attitudes," we felt that there were two approaches we could take to the attitudes, a hard-line approach which treated them as reporting relations to situations and left the rest to "pragmatics," and a more fine-grained approach that took them as indirect classifications of mental states and activities. We found it difficult to be clear in our own thinking about the relative merits of the two approaches without working out the hard-line approach first, finding its deficiencies, and using them as motivation for the more refined theory. So this is the way we have structured Part D. Chapters 8 and 9 develop a theory that takes the attitudes as reporting relations to alternative situations, ending with a list of shortcomings. Chapter 10 develops a theory of images, ideas, beliefs, and the like which we think is compatible with our realism but can nevertheless provide a rich vocabulary for talking about the mind.

In connection with Parts C and D, we feel compelled by past experience to offer a reminder to our friends—philosphers, logicians, linguists, and computer scientists alike. It sometimes happens in science that the vocabularly of a particular theory becomes so ingrained that the scientist starts confusing the empirical data with its theory-laden description. If the categories of the theory cut across the grain of actual phenomena, then artificial problems are created, problems whose solutions cannot be given until a new framework is adopted. One is simply missing the properties of things and relations between things that really matter.

Because we think that this is the case in the study of semantics of natural language, we ask the reader to remember that notions like:

logical form
logical constant
proper name
quantifier

variable
quantifier scope
opaque and transparent contexts
de dicto and *de re* readings
sense and reference
intension and extension
meaning postulate
possible world
rigid designator
truth conditions and T-sentences
tense operator

are all technical or pseudo-technical notions introduced by philosophers and logicians. They are not part of the data of natural language. It just might be that some or all of them cut across the grain of the phenomena in unnatural ways, generating artificial problems and constraining the space of possible solutions to the genuine puzzles that language presents. We believe this to be the case. Few of these notions appear in our theory, and those which do are conceived in somewhat different ways. The reader who opens to Part C or D and tries to understand what we are saying in terms of these traditional notions is likely to misunderstand what we are up to.

That makes it sound as though we developed our theory from scratch, but this isn't so. Problems with the traditional approach and insights about how to deal with them have been accumulating for years, in the work of logicians, philosophers, linguists, and computer scientists. Usually these insights either were couched in ever more complex reworkings of the traditional framework, bringing in some of the notions listed above, or were thought of as at odds with the spirit of a model theoretic approach, or were simply left unconnected with such an approach. We do see our approach as radical, in that we see the need for change in the very roots of the tradition, the holism that came from Frege, and the mishandling of what we call *efficiency* by both Frege and Russell. But we want to conserve these recent insights and the powerful methods of traditional model theoretic analysis.

To be a bit more specific, we see our work as building upon a host of recent developments, in addition to that of ecological realism, mentioned above, some of which have been thought of as opposed to one another. Kaplan's work on the logic of demonstratives has had a profound influence on us. Insights from the "new theory of reference" in the work of Kripke, Donnellan, Wettstein, and others has been very important. Castaneda's work on the epistemological significance of indexicals and demonstratives, which seems in quite a different tradition, has also had a profound influence on our views. So has Austin's theory of truth as gounded in historical situations. David-son's theories of language and action, with its emphasis on events, has helped liberate us from traditional ideas. The details of our theory of situations is more in the spirit of the approach of Brandt, Gold-man, and Kim, however. The theory of speech acts of Austin, Grice, and Searle, usually seen as at odds with model theory, has been im-portant. Our emphasis on information rests heavily on the work of Dretske. The use of partial functions, which is so crucial to our ac-count of information, though not common in model theory, is old hat in recursion theory, since Kleene introduced them in the late 1930's. Computations rest on finite amounts of information, and partial functions are needed to keep track of this. The move from sets to properties is a move back to Russell motivated by the demands of ecological realism. Our approach to the mind seems to us in the spirit of some of the recent work by Smart, Armstrong, Lewis, Fodor, and Grice. The revolution in the conception of the relation between linguistic evidence and theory promoted by Grice's theory of con-versational implicature has played a large role in our thinking.

Kripke's possible-worlds semantics for modal logic provided a tool that has been used to develop Frege's theory of meaning into a model theory of natural language. We do not believe that there are other possible worlds in the sense demanded of them by this theory, only other ways this world of ours might have been and might be. But we owe a great deal to the work of those in this tradition. The work of Jaakko Hintikka on the logic of the attitudes anticipates many of the ideas in Chapter 9; we should add that there is a distinctly non-Fregean cast to his version of possible-worlds semantics. Richard Montague and his followers have refocused attention on developing a genuine semantics for natural language, rather than some artificial language invented by logicians. Montague argued that it should be possible to develop a mathematical theory of linguistic meaning. Our goal in parts C and D is to further this aim by trying to develop a model theoretic semantics that takes recent work in the philosophy of language to heart.

We offer this book to all who have bumped up against inadequacies in the received view of logic. At the very least, it will provide some new inadequacies to cope with. But of course we hope for much more, even that the book will, in some small way, contribute to a rethinking of the relation of people to the world around them, a world full of constraints and meaning, both for people and for the other beings with whom they share it.

ACKNOWLEDGMENTS

Because this book is the product of interaction between two people and with many others, in addition to the obligations we have listed above there are a host of more personal debts that we are proud to acknowledge.

Parts of the book are written in the first-person singular because examples that stress the efficiency of language by using "I" are too important to give up, even if the book is co-authored. Pick one of the authors as the speaker and interpret the examples accordingly. Then read it again using the other author as speaker. Looked at this way, this book is a bargain, two for the price of one, which agree on theoretical issues but differ in examples. The simultaneous appearance of two books with so much agreement must be reckoned as striking evidence for the common ideas. But for now we must shed our cloak of common identity.

Barwise's Acknowledgments:

I spent 1975–76 as a Sloan Fellow at UCLA, where I taught a course in the history of mathematics. In this course, and in discussions with Michael Makkai and Yiannis Moschovakis, I was struck forcibly by the inadequacy of what logicians, including myself, had to say about the nature of mathematical activity. Since the mid 1960's I had worked on the model theory of languages that are stronger than the first-order predicate calculus, but like others I had side-stepped the difficult issue of where the notions in mathematics that go beyond first-order logic come from. On returning to Madison, a friend, James Gustafson, discovering that I admired the novels of Walker Percy, gave me a. collection of essays on language (Percy, 75). I was amazed at the parallel between the puzzle I faced and the puzzle Percy saw in human language. In fact, it seemed to me the same puzzle. So I turned to see what linguists had to say about meaning.

It was my good luck that the Linguistics Department of the University of Wisconsin–Madison had just hired Robin Cooper, with whom I have worked and talked during the years since. He has been an extremely patient informant, guiding me through the confusing literature and ideas in linguistics, and encouraging and contributing to this work at all stages.

An early discovery was that Percy was right about the neglect of meaning by linguists. The only formal theory of meaning for natural language was the one developed by a logician, the late Richard Montague; its pursuit was just beginning, by a small but dedicated group of linguists that included Barbara Partee, Stanley Peters, Lauri Karttunen, and Robin Cooper, to name those who have had the greatest impact on my own work. As interesting as this theory was, however, it left me feeling unsatisfied on two counts. In the first place, it was set within possible-worlds semantics, a theory that has never had much to say about mathematics. Montague grammar does not shed any light at all on the question that had prompted my interest—where mathematical notions come from. In the second place, the model theory that went along with the theory was computationally hopeless, even at the most elementary level, because of the use of total functions of arbitrary finite type. I toyed with the idea of reworking the theory, using hereditarily consistent partial functions as they are used in higher recursion theory, but I quickly found the holism implicit in possible-worlds semantics incompatible with the use of partial functions to represent partial information.

I decided to take a different tack by finding a simple construction in English that goes beyond first-order logic and seeing where its semantics led. I stumbled on the NI-perception sentences (discussed in Chapter 8) in an article of Chomsky's—I no longer remember which one—and was struck by the clear semantic intuitions that go with those sentences in spite of their not being expressible in first-order logic in any straightforward way. Investigating the model theory of such sentences, I was led to partial structures, for what we see are limited parts of the world. In 1979–80 I gave a logic seminar on the model theory of natural language at the University of Wisconsin, where I presented these ideas. I also presented them in colloquia in the U.W.–Madison Philosophy Department, at the University of Illinois at Chicago Circle, and at the University of Texas, Austin. The discussions at this seminar and following these presentations led to significant changes in the final product. Not everyone agrees that they were improvements.

In 1979 I moved to Stanford University and gave a course on the semantics of perceptual reports, where I presented the semantics of

NI-perceptual reports and attempted to extend it to SEE THAT reports. It was an exciting seminar for me because I was constantly challenged by visitors who presented problems for my account. I remember Paul Benacerraf, Michael Bratman, Daniel Dennet, Dagfin Follesdal, Janet Fodor, Pat Hayes, Philip Johnson-Laird, John McCarthy, Robert Moore, Julius Moravcsik, and John Perry asking especially tough questions. I also remember Willard Quine turning up once and answering a tough question for me. It was at lunch on the last day of this seminar that Perry and I started working together on Barwise and Perry (81a). And it was John Perry that eventually made me see that my account of the semantics of SEE THAT was doomed unless I admitted that there are properties and relations in the world, not just things and names of sets. My paper (Barwise, 81b) came out of that seminar, and I am very grateful to these people for their challenges and encouragement.

I was a fellow at the Center for Advanced Study in the Behavioral Sciences for 1981–82, though for reasons connected with my return to Wisconsin, I was able to be at the Center only from January through July; but John Perry was a Fellow there in 1980–81, and I was present almost every day of that year. If this book is the product of an interaction, then the crucible for the interaction is the Center. I owe a tremendous debt of gratitude to Gardner Lindzey, Director of the Center, and to its staff, for providing an amazing environment in which to work. And if the Center was the crucible, then money from foundations was the catalyst. My own time at the Center was supported by the University of Wisconsin Research Fund, by the National Science Foundation (BNS76–22943), and by the Systems Development Foundation. More recent NSF support (MCS–8201940) has also helped to bring this book to completion. I am very grateful to acknowledge this support. The book would never have come into being without it.

My time at the Center was spent away from my family. I must thank Mary Ellen both for putting up with my absence and then for putting up with my presence during the six months of finishing the book. I don't dare ask her which was hardest. I promised her about eight years ago that I wouldn't write another book for eleven years. I naively thought that co-authoring a book would be half the work and so count as half a book in this regard.

The time away from my family was made more bearable by the exciting intellectual environment of the Center and the presence there

of many people interested in language and meaning: Manfred Beir-
wisch, Johan van Benthem, May Brodbeck, Hector-Neri Castaneda,
Robin Cooper, Elisabet Engdahl, David Evans, Dagfin Follesdal,
Hans Kamp, Lauri Karttunen, Richard Larson, Stan Peters, Richard
Watson, and Arnold Zwicky. Each of these Fellows and Associates
contributed in some way to the theory that follows.

There were others at the Center and in the Bay area that also
added to the sense of intellectual excitement and provided encouragement during that period. Besides my co-author and his family, I think
especially of Susan Castagnetto, Lewis Kornhauser, Helen Nissenbaum, and Brian Cantwell Smith. The support of these friends and
their willingness to discuss situation semantics meant and means a
great deal to me.

Since returning to Madison, I have given a course on this book, or
some combination of this and previous versions of the book, and have
discussed related topics with colleagues in a philosophy discussion
group and with friends. The final draft has profited greatly from
these interactions. I would especially like to thank Mike Byrd, Robin
Cooper (yet again), Berent Enc, Fred Dretske, Susan Millar, Terry
Millar, Dennis Stampe, Mary Tait, and Palle Yourgrau.

Perry's Acknowledgments:

In 1975–76 I had a sabbatical from Stanford and a fellowship from
the Guggenheim Foundation, and I thought I was going to write a
book on personal identity. I thought I had a pretty plausible theory
on most issues, but knew I would have to do some thinking about
problems of self-knowledge of the sort that Sidney Shoemaker and
Hector-Neri Castaneda had been discussing. I had a hunch that Kaplan's work on the logic of demonstratives would prove helpful in im-
plementing the insights of Castaneda and Shoemaker in a way that
would mesh with more general theories of the propositional attitudes.
But things did not go smoothly. Kaplan's theory seemed semantically
plausible, although I did not like the possible-worlds framework within which it was developed. But when it came to analyzing the attitudes and the way we report them, it wasn't at all easy to see how
things should go. So I spent the year trying to work out a coherent
view of self-knowledge, digging deeper into problems in the philosophy of language. Weekly discussions with Michael Bratman, Keith
Donnellan, Alvin Goldman, and Holly Smith were instrumental in
seeing how successive attempts to solve the problem didn't work, as

were occasional discussions with Tyler Burge and David Kaplan. I read an early version of Perry (79) at Stanford and UCLA, and comments from a number of philosophers at both places were helpful. In particular Julius Moravcsik made a number of important and penetrating suggestions, including one—the observation that my claim that Frege could not handle the problems I raised—needed to be made at length. This led to Perry (77), which was read at a conference organized by Moravcsik in the winter of 1979. Comments from Kaplan, Moravcsik, Jaakko Hintikka, and, particularly, Kenneth Olson were extremely helpful. These papers leaned heavily on Kaplan (79a, b) and Castaneda (66, 68), and Kaplan and Castaneda were both encouraging and helpful. A version of Perry (79) was read at Indiana University, and conversations with Romane Clark and Michael Pendlebury raised a number of important points as did the discussion in a paper drawn from Pendlebury's dissertation (Pendlebury, 80). I also read Perry (79) as part of an APA Symposium, at which very useful comment was received from Tyler Burge and Hugh Chandler. Burge's very plausible view and persuasive arguments about the irreducibility of "*de re* belief," along with more conversations with Kaplan, stimulated interest in the problems discussed in Perry (80), a version of which was read at the Oberlin Colloquium, where very helpful comments were given by John Heinz. During this period I became more and more convinced that the Fregean tradition went badly astray in its treatment of properties as senses, and that these mistakes were built firmly into possible-worlds semantics. I'm sure that earlier conversations with Wade Savage, Michael Tooley, and Nancy Cartwright left me open for this conversion to realism; but I had no conception of what an alternative semantics might be like until Barwise and I began working together. He commented on a later version of Perry (80), and in the last draft I incorporated a few of our ideas about situations.

I was a Fellow at the Center in 1980–81, and it was here that Barwise and I started the first version of a book. Gardner Lindzey and the staff of the Center were extraordinarily accommodating to the needs of our collaboration. My year at the Center was supported by a sabbatical from Stanford, the National Endowment for the Humanities, and the Mellon Foundation. During this year Barwise and I discussed larger issues of psychology regularly with Michael Turvey, and came to see an important connection between our approach and that of ecological psychologists like Gibson, Shaw, and Turvey. Lynn Gale was a participant in these discussions, helping us to clarify our ideas. She also drew the illustrations for this book, for which we are particularly indebted.

Throughout the time when our theory was developing and this book was being written, I have chaired the Philosophy Department at Stanford. The patience of colleagues and staff, in particular Nancy Steege, with the various derelictions of duty that work on situation semantics entails is much appreciated. The Dean of Humanities and Sciences should also be thanked for providing an extra sabbatical. I have not yet finished the book on personal identity; so this is my first opportunity to thank four philosophers who gave me a lot of help while I was getting started in philosophy: Robert Browne, Merton French, Wilson Wade, and Darryl Williams.

Joint Acknowledgments:

We began working together in the interval between the winter and spring quarters of the 1979–80 academic year. Perry's seminar in the fall, on Frege and the attitudes, and Barwise's in the winter, on the logic of perception, each ended with a brief consideration of what we now call the slingshot, an argument that claims to pose problems for the ideas presented in each seminar, yet is easily seen to be defective in the light of these ideas. Perry attended Barwise's seminar, noted the coincidence, and suggested a joint paper on the argument. At first we thought that paper could be written during the week between quarters, but we quickly found that our ideas not only had the rejection of the slingshot in common, but also were complementary in a variety of ways. Yet when we mixed them, there was a much more explosive reaction than we had anticipated; in fact, a new theory emerged. This theory, to vary the metaphor again, though clearly a child of the old ideas, did not always honor its parents. We have spent three years trying to understand and partially tame this theory.

During the spring and summer of 1980 we wrote Barwise and Perry (80) for Barwise to present at a workshop on semantics in Oslo, organized by Jens-Eric Fenstad. The excitement of the early ideas can still be felt in that paper in its intemperate tone and overextended claims. Reaction to it from a wide range of sources, including many of the people mentioned above, has helped us to see many problems with those early ideas, and has encouraged us to improve them. Later, Richmond Thomason and Jaako Hintikka, who commented on our paper "Situations and Attitudes" at an APA Symposium, helped us to see problems with a somewhat more mature set of ideas.

Graduate students who met with us during the years at the Center were extremely helpful in many ways. Ken Olson contributed some healthy skepticism at the beginning—good ideas and criticisms, when he was working on modality and situations, and more recently a historical perspective—with his work on the rise, fall, and, we hope, reemergence of facts as an important notion in philosophy. Susan Castagnetto has been a constant source of encouragement, prodding for clarification, a healthy skeptic, a critic of both style and content, and has helped us see the relation of our approach to Reid's realism.

Two deserve much more than sincere appreciation: John Etchemendy and Helen Nissenbaum. John was working on his dissertation on the philosophy of semantics and talking to us frequently during the early days of this work. In the first stages of our collaboration he forced us to confront some basic issues it would have been easy to avoid. His insights into some of the problems with standard model theoretic semantics have, we hope, been absorbed into our work. John also read the final draft of the book with great care and made countless substantive and stylistic suggestions. We feel that this is a much better book because of his efforts. Helen Nissenbaum was working on her dissertation on the emotions and the language we use to talk about emotions, and talking to at least one of us almost daily. Her pointed objections and suggestions led to significant changes in our theory. Indeed, certain aspects of our theory of constraints and of our treatment of functional uses of definite descriptions stem from Helen's thinking about how these function with emotion verbs.

This book was written three times. Our original plan was to collect some papers that we had written individually and together on the topics of the attitudes, and add some new material to put the work into the perspective provided by the theory that had emerged. But the transitions grew and the theory kept developing in spite of our best efforts to quiet it, and the old papers came to seem dated and inadequate, although they are probably still a good guide to our dissatisfactions with other approaches. There are probably not more than five paragraphs in this book drawn from these papers. A second draft was completed in the spring of 1982.

The second draft was read by a number of friends from whom we received a host of suggestions, including Johann von Bentham, Alice ter Meulen (who had long encouraged us to consider the Partee problem), Julius Moravcsik, Howard Wettstein, Michael Bratman, Pat Suppes, Brian Smith, and David Israel. Barbara Partee, Scott Soames, and Robert Stalnaker gave it a particularly close reading, at the behest of our publisher, Harry Stanton, and provided us with an overwhelming number of counterexamples, objections, and suggestions concerning substance, organization, and style. They, together with a series of discussions between Brian Smith and Barwise in the Boundary Waters Canoe Area in early August, provided both the motivation and the encouragement to embark on a complete rewrite. Throughout this whole process Harry and Betty Stanton have been patient and encouraging, while insisting that whatever other perfections a book might have, existence is an important one.

The summer of 1982 was a particularly crucial period, as we worked out the ideas embodied in the final draft. During part of this period we were supported at the Center by the Systems Development Foundation. The opportunity to talk with Kamp about his theory of discourse representation and to develop our theory in a way that could deal with his insights was particularly valuable. So too were the discussions about the relation of syntax, semantics, and logical form with Robin Cooper and Stanley Peters.

Over the past two years, the authors have spent a great deal of time separated, Barwise having temporarily returned to the University of Wisconsin. Communication proceeded through a computer network, and John McCarthy, Pat Suppes, Larry Landweber, the U.W. Computer Sciences Department, and the National Science Foundation are to be thanked for making this possible in various ways.

In keeping with the realist perspective of this book, most of the individuals referred to are family or friends. We owe an incalculable debt to the Barwises—Mary Ellen, Melanie, Jonny, Jackie, and Scruffy—and to the Perrys—Frenchie, Jim, Sarah, Joe, and Molly—not only for providing examples, but for putting up with distracted, disorganized, and basically obsessed husbands and fathers for the past several years. The length of time is attested by the fact that the Jonny of the book has grown into Jon, and Jim and Melanie changed from teenagers into quite pleasant adults.

Ruth Marcus, Stan Peters, and Barbara Partee were among the earliest to spot something promising about situation semantics and to communicate their enthusiasm to the authors in various ways over a number of years. More recently, encouragement from Brian Smith has been especially important to us. We hope the result is not too disappointing to all of you who have encouraged and aided us in this undertaking.

The reader will discover the problems about the nature of mathematical activity and about the nature of self-knowledge and personal identity which led us into situation semantics are not explicitly discussed in this book. Although there are hints about these topics, their development will have to take place elsewhere.

Madison, Wisconsin
Palo Alto, California
January 1983

PART A
Introduction

CHAPTER ONE

Meaningful Situations

Semantics, the study of linguistic meaning, is a notoriously slippery business. Though it is tautological that meaningful expressions are just that, meaningful, it has proven extremely difficult to say much more about this property of meaning. But it seems clear that a test for a theory of meaning and a key to its development is the fact that meaningful expressions can be used to convey information (and mis-information), both about the external world and our states of mind. In this book we present a theory of meaning that passes this test—or so we think.

Suppose you say, "It is raining out." If you are right, I can learn something about the weather by believing you. But I can also learn something about you: that you have the information that it is rain-ing. And even if you are wrong, I can still learn that you believe it is raining. If I were not convinced of the latter, then I wouldn't take what you said as an indication of what the weather was like.

If expressions were not systematically linked with kinds of events, on the one hand, and states of mind, on the other, their utterance would convey no information; they would be just noises or scribbles, without any meaning at all. These systematic links are essential to meaning, and for this reason essential to any *theory* of meaning as well. Indeed, the ability of language to classify minds and events can be turned back on language itself; we can classify expressions by the way they classify us and the world. And this is just what a theory of meaning does.

Some theories stress the power of language to classify minds, the mental significance of language, and treat the classification of events as derivative. Thus John Locke held that words, in their primary signification, stand for ideas. They stand for objects in the world derivatively, since the ideas stand for those objects. One problem with this sort of theory is that we have no good way to classify the ideas that expressions stand for. Another is that it simply pushes the problem of external significance from expressions to ideas. For unless there is to be a regress, the ideas words stand for must stand for objects without the further mediation of another layer of ideas.

A second approach is to focus on the *external* significance of language, on its connection with the described world rather than the describing mind. Sentences are classified not by the ideas they express, but by how they describe things to be. The standard extensional model-theory of first-order logic is usually seen as a development of this strategy.

But there seem to be two fatal problems with this approach, problems pointed out by Frege (60c). First of all, meanings are more fine-grained than the objects expressions stand for. THE MORNING STAR IS IN THE SKY and THE EVENING STAR IS IN THE SKY both describe the same state of affairs, for THE MORNING STAR and THE EVENING STAR both designate Venus. But the sentences don't mean the same thing. And second, there are meaningful expressions, expressions like THE PLANET CLOSER TO THE SUN THAN MERCURY, that don't designate anything at all.

Frege adopted a third strategy. He postulated a third realm, a realm neither of ideas nor of worldly events, but of senses. Senses are the "philosophers' stone," the medium that coordinates all three elements in our equation: minds, words, and objects. Minds grasp senses, words express them, and objects are referred to by them.

Frege never really developed a theory of senses, either of their structure or of the way they interact with the other realms. But one way of regarding the crucial notion of intension in possible worlds semantics is as a development of Frege's notion of sense. This approach, in the hands of theorists like Carnap, Hintikka, Kaplan, Kripke, Lewis, Montague, and others, has been the most fruitful approach to the semantics of natural language.

Situation semantics is our attempt to work out a new theory following the second strategy, one that incorporates insights into the nature of language that have come to light since first-order model theory came to be, and one that exploits the ideas and techniques of those working in possible worlds semantics. More precisely, we think of ourselves as pursuing the second strategy while exploiting insights of the third, in a way that explains the motivations behind

EFFICIENT DISAGREEMENT

I'm right, you're wrong.

I'm right, you're wrong.

the first. We develop a theory for classifying events, our Theory of Situations, and then use it as the basis for our semantics.

The bane of such a theory has always been attitude reports, like MELANIE BELIEVES THAT JONNY IS ASLEEP, and for just the reasons Frege mentioned. The embedded sentence, JONNY IS ASLEEP, is being used to classify Melanie's mind, and this seems to require a more fine-grained meaning than a semantics based on external significance can provide. But the theory of meaning we develop overcomes Frege's challenges, because of the dividends of taking situations and the efficiency of language seriously.

By the *efficiency of language* we mean this: expressions used by different people, in different space-time locations, with different connections to the world around them, can have different interpretations, even though they retain the same linguistic meaning. This description uses technical terms we haven't explained yet, but the point can be made with an example. When you say, "I am right, you are wrong," talking to me, and I use the same words, talking to you, we disagree. We make different claims about the world. What you said will be true if you are right and I am wrong, while what I said will be true if you are wrong and I am right. These different claims are the different interpretations our utterances have. But the meaning of the sentence we both used did not change. It is the same; the interpretations are different. That's what we are calling *efficiency.*

One can imagine nonefficient sentences, sentences that make the same claim about the world no matter who says them and when. These are (roughly) what Quine calls *eternal sentences.* They contain no indexicals like I, no demonstratives like THIS, no tense. One can imagine such sentences, but with the possible exception of sentences from mathematics it is not easy to produce examples. In spite of this, eternal sentences have served as the paradigm of a meaningful expression. We see meaning as a far more ubiquitous phenomenon than is commonly acknowledged in present-day philosophy. Once this possibility is taken seriously, it becomes clear that the efficient unit of meaning (whether expressions or something else) is the norm. Modern philosophy of language has, then, done two things: taken nonefficient expressions as the paradigm of linguistic meaning, and forgotten that things besides expressions can be meaningful.

The interpretation of an utterance depends on the meaning of the expressions used and on various additional facts about the utterance. The truth of an utterance depends, in turn, on whether its interpretation fits the facts. Facts about the world thus come in twice on the road from meaning to truth: once to determine the interpretation, given the meaning, and then again to determine the truth value, given the interpretation. This insight we owe to David Kaplan's important work on indexicals and demonstratives (Kaplan, 77, 79a, 79b), and we believe it is absolutely crucial to semantics.

But we think that one further step must be made if a theory is to take efficient expressions as the paradigmatic carriers of meaning. That step is an appreciation of situations. Using situations, one can separate cleanly the two parts of reality that intervene between meaning and truth, the facts about the utterance, and the facts about the *described situation,* i.e., those relevant to the truth and falsity of the utterance as interpreted. When I say, "You are sitting," facts about me, who I am and who I am talking to, determine the interpretation of my utterance. But facts about you determine whether my utterance is true or false. The notion of a situation allows the articulation of what we will call *the relation theory of meaning*: meaning in general, and linguistic meaning in particular, is a relation between situations.

The importance of situations has been obscured by another tradition stemming from Frege, a tradition we might call *semantic holism.* This is the idea that in the reference of a sentence, as Frege put it, "all that is specific is lost." This idea has been projected into the very definitions of logical notions that philosophers and linguists grow up with. It has led some to a perplexing condescension toward most sentence-embedding constructions of language (Quine, 66a, 66d) and has made the very possibility of a semantics based on situations seem suspect.

Our strategy can be summarized very succinctly. We develop a theory of situations and of meanings as relations between situations. While focusing on the external significance of language, and on meaning in general, our theory provides an alternative philosopher's stone. It does not provide a third realm, a realm of objects interacting with language, mind, and external world, but rather a classificatory scheme, a system of abstract objects that allow us to describe the meaning both of expressions and of mental states in terms of the information they carry about the external world. And so it is that we account for the attractiveness of Locke's approach. Mental states *have* meanings but they aren't themselves meanings. This puts rather crudely our version of a familiar idea, one that underlies much recent philosophy of mind. But it is an idea that we think requires the relation theory of meaning to be really plausible.

In the remainder of this chapter we describe the general philosophical perspective within which we work, as well as, in an informal way, the main points of our theory. We do not really argue for the philosophical perspective, but try to state it clearly enough for readers to understand how we view situation semantics as fitting into the larger scheme of things. Those who reject our metaphysics and epistemology may still find value in the formal theory developed below in Parts B, C, and D.

BASIC IDEAS OF SITUATION SEMANTICS

Situations

Reality consists of situations—individuals having properties and standing in relations at various spatiotemporal locations. We are always in situations; we see them, cause them to come about, and have attitudes toward them. The Theory of Situations is an abstract theory for talking about situations. We begin by pulling out of real situations the basic building blocks of the theory; individuals, properties and relations, and locations. These are conceived of as invariants or, as we shall call them, *uniformities* across real situations; the same individuals and properties appear again and again in different locations. We then put these pieces back together, using the tools of set theory, as *abstract situations*. Some of these abstract situations, the *actual situations*, correspond to the real ones; others do not.

Individuals are uniformities in that they persist through some course of events, having properties and standing in relations. They are usually extended in space and time, unlike the points of mathematics, and often have parts that are also objects. Words are also objects, uniformities across utterances, though perhaps rather odd objects, since they appear in various remote situations at the same time.

Properties (like that of being edible, threatening, or red) are properties of things, and are important to the classification of situations. More generally, we have relations (like being in, on, or under; kicking or being mother of) between or among objects, relations that hold for some period of time, usually at some place or other. Places are uniformities in that different things can happen at the same place at different times. Times are uniformities because different things can be going on at the same time at different places.

Our abstract situations are built from locations and *situation-types*. Suppose Molly barked this morning, and that she barked yesterday morning too; both times in my backyard. What do these two locations, my backyard yesterday morning and my backyard this morning, have in common? Intuitively, they have in common what is going on in them: Molly barking. In our theory, what they share is a common situation-type, a partial function from n-ary relations and n individuals to the values 0 ("false") and 1 ("true"). In official set-theoretic notation, a situation-type s in which Molly barks and Jackie doesn't would be described by:

s (barks, Molly) = 1
s (barks, Jackie) = 0.

The numbers 0 and 1, unlike the individuals Molly and Jackie, are just tools we use to build up our system of classifying real situations.

We will use a somewhat different notation in this book however—one that seems a bit more perspicuous, and perhaps less intimidating:

in *s*: barks, Molly; yes
   barks, Jackie; no.

By calling 0 and 1 "no" and "yes" respectively we suggest how they work.

Situation-types are partial. They don't say everything there is to say about everyone, or even everything about the individuals appearing in the situation-type. Molly was certainly doing more than barking; she must have been breathing and been next to something and five feet from something else, and so forth. The situation-type *s* is silent on these things. That's why we need the 0's and 1's; a situation-type's leaving a question open must not be confused with its giving a negative answer.

A *course of events* is a function from locations to situation-types. Like a situation-type, it is partial; a course of events may tell us about what is going on at one location, or at a hundred, or even at all of them, assuming there is a totality of locations. A course of events that is defined on just one location we call a *state of affairs.*

Since a course of events *e*, at a location *l* on which it is defined, gives us a situation-type, we can use a modification of the notation recently introduced:

In *e*, at *l*: barks, Molly; yes
   at *l'*: shouts at, Mr. Levine, Molly; yes
   at *l''*: barks, Molly, no

So *e* is a course of events that has Molly barking at one location, Mr. Levine shouting at her at another location, and her being silent at a third. If these locations are close together, we have an episode of successful shouting. But for all that's been said so far, the locations could be years and miles apart.

All of these entities are abstract set-theoretic objects, built up from the individuals, properties, relations, and locations abstracted from real situations. They play no role in the causal order. People don't grasp them, see them, move them, or even know or believe them. But as semanticists we can use them to classify real situations. Then, by assigning our classifiers of real situations to expressions and to mental states, we study their property of meaningfulness.

The Relation Theory of Meaning

The situations we perceive and participate in are always limited, a small part of all that has gone on, is going on, and will go on. Situations overlap in time and space in complicated ways, but each situation is unique unto itself, no one quite the same as any other. And in this uniqueness resides a puzzle. For if living things are to survive, they must constantly adapt to the course of events in which they find themselves, to ever changing, fleeting, and unique situations. But how can a living thing make any sense out of something unique and instantaneous?

Not only must a living organism cope with the cascade of new situations that make up its course of events, it must also anticipate the course events will take. It must prepare for the future, run to escape its predators, and catch its prey. To accomplish this it must be able to pick up information about one situation from another. A smell, sound, or shadow may alert it to the presence of a predator or prey. From smoke pouring out a window it may learn that its house is on fire. From an X-ray the doctor learned of the break in Jackie's leg. And from the doctor's utterance "She has a broken leg" Jonny learned that his dog Jackie had a broken leg.

At bottom, things just are the way they are, a heterogeneous reality. Yet parts of this reality have a capacity for perception, for acquiring information from other parts, and an accompanying capacity for acting on still others. Those parts having the capacity for perception and action we call *organisms*.

To maneuver successfully through an extended course of events, an organism must be attuned to similarities between situations, what we have called *uniformities*, and to relationships that obtain between these uniformities, those significant to its well-being. Whether this attunement comes about through biological endowment, learning, or divine providence is largely beside the point here. We need only note that even the simplest creatures are attuned to the uniformities in their environment that are important to their well-being. Indeed, it is by categorizing situations in terms of some of the uniformities that are present, and by being attuned to appropriate relations that obtain between different types of situations, that the organism manages to cope with the new situations that continually arise.

Imagine an organism whose needs are vastly different from our own, say a giant sea tortoise or a praying mantis. These organisms will be attuned to quite different uniformities across situations, uniformities that may be invisible to us as humans. That is what makes it so challenging to try to discover how the sea tortoise finds its way across thousands of miles of ocean to its breeding grounds, or how the praying mantis, which grows by startling spurts, still knows precisely how far it must reach to grab a prey. The uniformities primitive to one organism may go quite unnoticed by another, may even be invisible except as reflected in the actions of the first. The organisms inhabit the same heterogeneous reality but differentiate it in widely divergent ways. (The view of information arising out of animal/environment interaction forms the basis of J. J. Gibson's theory of perception and the school of ecological realism that has followed him; Gibson, 79; Michaels and Carello, 81). We might imagine a Martian visiting Earth for the weekend, with perceptual abilities, needs, and capacities for action quite distinct from our own. The Martian would still inhabit the same reality we do, but might well have a hard time understanding how or why we humans do the things we do. It might have a hard time, that is, if it noticed us at all. The Martian might, in effect, rip reality apart at entirely different seams, seams that we would not recognize, and vice versa.

Happily, though, we do not need to know what uniformities sea tortises, praying mantisses, or Martians are attuned to. Since our task is that of understanding how humans use the simpler parts of their language, we need only concern ourselves with the basic uniformities that human beings recognize. We are attuned to the use of language and it provides the guide. Humans recognize objects, properties, and relations, and categorize situations as ones in which certain objects have certain properties and stand in certain relations.

The emphasis here has been on how the organism differentiates its environment, on the sorts of uniformities it recognizes from situation to situation. Different organisms can rip the same reality apart in different ways, ways that are appropriate to their own needs, their own perceptual abilities and their own capacities for action. This interdependence between the structure its environment displays to an organism and the structure of the organism with respect to its environment is extremely important. For while reality is there, independent of the organism's individuative activity, the structure it displays to an organism reflects properties of the organism itself.

Take, for example, Joe's dog, Molly. Whenever Molly hears the voice of someone in the family, she wags her tail furiously. But when she hears the voice of anyone else, she barks as though being attacked. For Molly there is a property of people that we might call "pro," and another, opposite, property that we might call "con." These are properties of things, very real to Molly. They are systematically linked to her perception of people and her actions in their presence. But they are only one side of the coin. The other side takes place in the dog. Molly goes into one state, say *pro*, when she perceives pros, and another, say *con,* when she sees cons. These states are uniformities across situations involving the dog, just as the properties of pro and con are uniformities across the situations the dog confronts. The properties and corresponding states are like two sides of the same coin.

Notice that there is no reason to consider these states of the dog as anything like words in some internal dog language. Indeed, there is good reason not to. For language is a symbolic system, a non-natural carrier of meaning, and nothing could be more natural than the act of an organism individuating its environment for its own well being.

The act of classifying situations according to uniformities is the act of a cognitive agent, for it presupposes the ability to break down the heterogeneous reality of which situations are composed in a way significant to the well being of the agent. Philosophically, this ripping apart of a situation into, say, objects having properties and standing in relations at some space-time location, may in some sense do violence to the way things "really" are. But it also gives rise to meaningful relations, relations that can be exploited to pick up information about one part of reality from factors present in another. Some concrete divergent examples of meanings might help clarify this point.

(i) *Smoke means fire.* There is a lawlike relation between smoke and fire. Situations where there is smoke are, by and large, close to situations where there is fire. And it is attunement to this relation that enables us to learn about fires from smoke. Being attuned to this relation does not presuppose language, only the ability to detect smoke, to respond in some way appropriate to fire, and to do the latter on the occasion of the former.

(ii) *Kissing means touching.* Suppose the issue is whether Mary has ever touched Bill. If you learn somehow or other that Mary has kissed Bill, then you have the information available to conclude that Mary has touched Bill. This has nothing to do with language per se; kissing and touching are uniformities across situations recognized by human beings in this culture—relational activities. And it falls out of our recognition of these uniformities that kissings are touchings. Kissing is just a more fine-grained uniformity than touching.

This relation between relations is not a natural law that has to be discovered, but rather an automatic consequence of differentiating the relations in the first place. And it is this relation between relations that allows the information that Mary kissed Bill to contain the information that Mary touched Bill.

(iii) *The ringing bell means class is over.* The school bell rings and the students learn that it is time for class to end. A certain type of sound, one they hear on different days, is systematically related to a certain type of situation, the end of class. It is this relation between different types of situations that the students become attuned to, and thereby learn that the sound of the bell means that it is time for class to end. Thus the sound of the bell, on any particular occasion, conveys the information about the end of class.

In this example the conventional nature of the relation brings in an important wrinkle. The convention may break down, maybe because the bell itself is broken, or because the principal gets fed up and decides class should go on after the bell rings. In this case the bell might be taken as a sign that it is time for class to end when in fact it isn't. Conventional relations bring in the possibility of a situation conveying *mis*-information.

(iv) COOKIE *means cookie.* Mommy saying "cookie" means that there is a cookie available to Brynn. The word COOKIE is itself a uniformity across situations, a feature which is common to utterances containing the word. Similarly, the property of being a cookie is common to all situations in which a cookie is present. Language is conventional in that COOKIE stands only for cookies because we use it that way. But as long as mommy is dependable, systematically linking utterances of the word with situations in which there is a cookie, it might as well be a natural sign for all Brynn cares. And it is this systematic relation between uniformities, between the word COOKIE and the property of being a cookie, that the child must learn to exploit if she is to know the meaning of COOKIE, to come when mommy calls "cookie," and to demand "Cookie!" when she wants a cookie.

As in the previous example, the relationship can be abused. If Brynn becomes attuned to this relation, she can be frustrated, believing that there are cookies present when there aren't. Or, if the relation is abused before she learns it, she may simply not learn the meaning of the word. She might, for example, come to think that COOKIE means egg.

What we take these examples and countless others to show is this: One situation s can contain information about another situation s' only if there is a systematic relation M that holds between situations sharing some configuration of uniformities with s and situations that share some other configuration of uniformities with s'. These uniformities may be physical objects, abstract objects like words, physical or abstract properties or relations, places, or times, or other uniformities we will discuss in due course. But in any case, it is the relationship M that allows us to say that the first situation means the second.

The point here might be summarized by the rather opaque slogan: *a meaning is a relation M between different types of situations.* The type of a situation is determined, of course, by uniformities that occur in it. We call this the *Relation Theory of Meaning.* Our task in Part B is to spell out this theory in greater detail.

On this view, the various uniformities across situations (objects, properties, etc.) and the relations between them that give rise to meaning stem directly from an organism's need for efficient ways to cope with the stream of situations it encounters, ways that will serve the organism not just once but in a variety of different but similar situations.

Event Meaning versus Event-type Meaning

Efficiency is not just a feature of linguistic meaning, but is crucial to all meaning. My utterance "I am right, you are wrong" means what it does about you and me because of the efficient meaning of the expression I AM RIGHT, YOU ARE WRONG. Similarly, that smoke pouring out of the window over there means that that particular building is on fire. Now the specific situation, smoke pouring out of that very building at that very time, will never be repeated. The next time we see smoke pouring out of a building, it will be a new situation, and so will in one sense mean something else. It will mean that the building in the new situation is on fire at the new time. Each of these specific smoky situations means something, that the building then and there is on fire. This is what we mean by *event meaning.*

The two meaningful situations had something in common, they were of a common type, smoke pouring out of a building, a type that means fire. This is what we call *event-type meaning.* This is what we become attuned to when we learn that smoke means fire, and it is what allows us to learn about a fire from a specific smoky situation. What a particular case of smoke pouring out of a building means, what it tells us about the wider world, is determined by the meaning of smoke pouring out of a building and the particulars of this case of it.

This is just the pattern we called *efficiency* above. A fresh footprint means a bear has been by recently. That's what a fresh bear footprint always means. But this case of a fresh footprint, the one we examine here and now, means that a bear was by here not too long before now. The case we examined over there last week meant something quite different, that a bear had been by there, not too long before.

Organism/Environment Duality

Now that we have isolated what is required for one situation to contain information about another situation, we can take a second look at the relation that obtains between an organism and its individuated environment. In doing so we get a first hint as to why cognitive states have meaning.

Why does my seeing a football on the lawn mean that there is a football there? That is, how is it that my perceptual state has meaning about the situation in front of me? Roughly, because of the intimate relation between the property of being a football and the state people are in when they individuate a football as a football. The relationship between a uniformity and the state of the organism that corresponds to its individuation by the organism is about as intimate a relation as you can have. A situation with the uniformity present causes the organism to be in the corresponding state. That is why being in that state can contain the information that the uniformity is present.

We shall have a great deal more to say about this in Chapter 10. Our point now, though, is just to reassure those who are used to thinking of meaning as residing in cognition that we are not forgetting that cognitive states have meaning. Far from it. What we are trying to do is to see why they have meaning by seeing what meaning is more generally.

We have been speaking of an organism, but of course we are really thinking of an organism as part of a species, a collection of organisms with similar needs, perceptual abilities, and capacities for action. One supposes, almost without thinking about it, that roughly the same uniformities are individuated by different organisms, so that different organisms in the species have roughly the same states corresponding to these uniformities. Of course this is only roughly true, because individuals do learn and they learn different things depending on their experience and capacities. When we come to human language, we will be thinking not of an individual or of a species but of something in between: a linguistic community.

Linguistic Meaning

Meaning's natural home is the world, for meaning arises out of the regular relations that hold among situations—bits of reality. We believe linguistic meaning should be seen within this general picture of a world teeming with meaning, a world full of information for organisms appropriately attuned to that meaning.

C. S. Peirce emphasized the distinction between signs and symbols, between "natural" and "conventional" or "non-natural" carriers of information. According to Peirce, smoke is a sign of fire while the word FIRE is not. The latter stands for fire, but obviously not in the same way that smoke does. Similarly, an X-ray picture can be a sign of a broken leg, but A BROKEN LEG is not a sign of a broken leg. It is something else, something that has the meaning it does because people use it to talk about broken legs and not about sea tortoises. While X-rays of broken legs could never serve as signs of sea tortoises, our language, which is a system of symbols, could have developed differently. We could, for example, have used the phrase "a broken leg" to talk about a sea tortoise.

Peirce's distinction between sign and symbol, between natural and non-natural meaning, is an important one—one that will have its place in any reasonable theory of meaning and information. But it should not be forgotten that the distinction is between species of a common genus. From the point of view of a theory of meaning, a theory that aims to account for the flow of information, the two turn out to be very much the same. Consider the case of Jonny's dog Jackie, who is limping badly. Jonny takes her to the vet. The vet X-rays Jackie's leg, sees that it is broken, comes out, and says to Jonny, "She has a broken leg." Both the vet and Jonny have learned that Jackie has a broken leg; one from a sign, a natural carrier of information, and one from a symbol, a conventional carrier of information.

The point we want to emphasize is the variety of relations that enable information to flow from one situation to another, even in interactions as commonplace as the one imagined. The X-ray provides information about Jackie's leg, thanks to a regular relation between features of such photographs and broken legs. This is a meaning relation to which the doctor is attuned, though Jonny is not. But the

The Flow of Information

doctor's utterance provides Jonny with the same information. To accomplish this, the doctor exploits a meaning relation to which Jonny, as a speaker of English, is also attuned. The flow of information that uses linguistic meaning is part and parcel of the general flow of information that uses natural meaning.

On our view, then, the meaning of a human language consists of an intricate relation M between utterance events and other aspects of objective reality, a relation entirely determined by the way the linguistic community uses the language. To know the language is to be able to exploit this relation, in tandem with other available resources, to give and receive information about the world.

This characterization applies not just to humans and the language they use, but to any community of living things that recognize the same uniformities in their environment and have a way of communicating information about them. So it is with the flap of a beaver's tail or the warning bark of a mother dog. But there is an important difference here. While a beaver may know instinctively what sort of situation is related to the flap of another beaver's tail, while he may, in other words, know what the flap means, there is no reason to suppose that he recognizes the relationship itself. What seems unique to humans is their recognition of the meaning relation M itself as a uniformity.

Children use words to convey information about their wants and needs long before they are conscious of words as words. They can ask for a cookie by using the word COOKIE long before becoming consciously aware of the relation that makes this an effective strategy. But at a certain point they come to appreciate the relation and may even state "COOKIE means cookie." To do so they must recognize meaning as a relationship between words and parts of their environment. Some philosophers have seen in this explicit recognition of meaning the very essence of what it is to be human. Whether or not this is the case, it is surely a significant development. If nothing else, it is the start of semantics and so the dawn of our profession.

Once meaning relations are themselves recognized as uniformities, we can short cut a lot of experience by finding out what one word means in terms of what other words mean. This is one of the principal functions of a dictionary. But a dictionary is no good at all without a substantial knowledge of the language and an explicit recognition of meaning. And of course any attempt to define linguistic meaning as, say, that which is characterized by a dictionary would be circular.

A meaning relation that arises out of the use a certain community makes of certain symbols, that is, a relation which reflects a convention, does not constrain the course of events in the same way as a relation with natural meaning. The latter constrains the way things can fall out; the former only constrains the way things fall out when the convention is not violated. This fact gives rise to an important difference between the bearers of conventional meaning and the bearers of natural meaning.

If people said only what they knew to be the case, then we would never notice truth as a property of some utterances and not others. It is because people sometimes violate the conventions of language, inadvertently or otherwise, that we come to recognize truth as a uniformity across certain utterance situations. Obviously, if truthful assertions were not an important part of our life, and if we did not possess a fairly good ability to recognize them, utterances would not carry information for us, and so language would not be meaningful. This is why semantics focuses on truth conditions, as a way of understanding linguistic meaning.

Truth is only one constraint placed on speakers by linguistic meaning, a constraint on the legitimate use of simple declarative statements.

It is just as much a violation of these conventions to say "Close the door" when you don't want the door closed, or to ask "Which leg is broken?" when you don't want the information requested, as it is to say something false. Austin and later writers on speech acts have forced us to realize that, important as truth is to understanding language, there is more to a theory of linguistic meaning than an account of the truth conditions of utterances. But it is on that first step that we shall concentrate.

Situation Semantics

The leading idea of situation semantics is that the meaning of a simple declarative sentence is a relation between utterances and described situations. The interpretation of a statement made with such a sentence on a specific occasion is the described situation.

Consider the sentence I AM SITTING. Its meaning is, roughly, a relation that holds between an utterance u and a situation e just in case there is a location l and an individual a such that in u, a is speaking at l, and in e, a is sitting at l. In notation that we will introduce in Chapter 6, this will be expressed as follows:

$$u [\![\text{I AM SITTING}]\!] e$$
$$\text{iff}$$

There is a location l and an individual a, such that

    in u: at l: speaks, a; yes

    in e: at l: sits, a; yes.

The extension of this relation will be a large class of pairs of abstract situations.

Now suppose we fix certain facts about the utterance. Fred is the speaker, and the location is a particular spacetime region l. Then *any* situation that has Fred sitting at l will be an interpretation of the utterance. An utterance usually describes lots of different situations, or at any rate partially describes them. Because of this, it is sometimes useful to think of the interpretation as the class of such situations. Then we can say that the situations appearing in the interpretation of our utterance vary greatly in how much they constrain the world. There is the situation that has Fred sitting at l and nothing more. There is one that has Fred sitting at l and many other folks doing various things at other locations. And there may be one that is a maximal event, telling us what everyone is doing at every location.

When uttered on a specific occasion, our sentence constrains the described situation to be a certain way, to be like one of the situations in the interpretation. Or, one might say, it constrains the described situation to be one of the interpretations. Now what do the parts of the sentence do? Basically, they help build up this constraint, either by contributing subject matter, that is, the individuals, properties, and locations that appear in the described situation, or by showing how the contributed subject matter fits together. Thus the meaning of a simple noun phrase will typically be a relation between an utterance and an individual, and the meaning of a verb, a relation between an utterance and a property. This is the basic idea behind the semantics worked out in Chapter 6.

To get a better feel for the theory, in the next chapter we'll look at how it handles six features of natural language that we put forward as *semantic universals,* semantic features shared by all natural languages. Of course, at this point we are merely saying how we claim our theory works; later on, when more details have been set out, the reader can check that we have lived up to our promises.

CRITICISMS AND COMPARISONS

As will become obvious, we think our theory lends itself to a wide range of important applications. But narrowly considered, as a technical tool in semantics, the chief advantage over more traditional approaches lies in the way we treat the interpretation of statements. In this section we will explain this a bit more, and discuss an influential argument that purports to show that any view like ours is incoherent. While we refute this argument, the issues raised will show how crucial the treatment of the attitudes is for a view like ours, hence why the attitudes form a central topic of this book.

In this section we will by and large ignore matters of the efficiency of language. We will use the term *statement* for a specific assertion of a declarative sentence. As the distinction between statements and sentences isn't crucial here, we will also use *statement* in describing the view with which we are contrasting our own.

Interpretation and Reference

Frege has been criticized for talking about the *reference* of statements. If all that is meant here is that our ordinary use of the word REFERENCE does not correspond well to Frege's technical use of BEDEUTUNG, then we agree. We think that, in fact, the ordinary English word REFERS captures rather well an important semantical notion. Through utterances people refer to people, things, times, and places, and the reference of these acts is relevant to the interpretation of the utterances. But reference in this ordinary sense really doesn't agree very well with Frege's theoretical notion of *Bedeutung*.

Still, any semantic theory will need some notion that plays the role that reference does in Frege's theory. This is just the semantic property of an expression that is relevant to the truth of statements in which it occurs. Intuitively, the truth of STAN IS SITTING is determined by who STAN stands for, and by the condition that IS SITTING identifies. These are roughly what Frege calls the reference of the proper name and the reference of the predicate. They are also approximately what we have in mind with the notion of the interpretation of such expressions. Thus the statement STAN IS SITTING will be true if the reference (interpretation) of STAN satisfies the reference (interpretation) of IS SITTING.

Since statements themselves occur as parts of other statements, they, too, must have a reference or interpretation. Consider the simple attitude report,

JONNY BELIEVES THAT JACKIE IS HUNGRY

Suppose we take Jonny to be the reference or interpretation of JONNY, and the condition of believing that Jackie is hungry to be the reference or interpretation of the predicate,

BELIEVES THAT JACKIE IS HUNGRY

The statement as a whole will be true if Jonny satisfies the condition expressed by this predicate. But the predicate itself breaks down into constituents, one of which happens to be a sentence:

JACKIE IS HUNGRY

At this point we need to say how the condition we assign to the predicate depends on the statement it embeds. But this just means that we need a reference or interpretation for the statement, one that is determined in turn by the statement's parts. It is here that interpretation veers off from reference, that situation semantics parts company with Fregean semantics. Frege chose, as the reference of statements, their truth-value. We choose the described situations.

In our opinion, Frege's choice at this juncture exhibits a confusion between the interpretation of a statement and its evaluation, whether or not it is true. This confusion is closely connected to one we discuss in the next chapter, the confusion of meaning with interpretation. Indeed, the latter promotes the former. But for now we are not interested in why Frege made the choice he did, but merely in establishing that it was a poor choice, and that ours is a viable alternative.

Truth Values and Subject Matter

"If now the truth value of a sentence is its reference, then on the one hand all true sentences have the same reference and so, on the other hand, do all false sentences. From this we see that in the reference of the sentence all that is specific is obliterated" (Frege, 60c). Frege is certainly right about this, and the very point he makes is our principal objection to his decision.

Given the principle of compositionality that Frege assumed (and which we will discuss in the next chapter), substitution of statements with the same truth value in a larger expression should preserve the reference of that larger expression. But of course, this just doesn't happen. Compare the predicates,

BELIEVES THAT JACKIE IS A NICE DOG

BELIEVES THAT CARSON CITY IS WEST OF LOS ANGELES.

The statements embedded in those predicates happen to have the same truth-value. So given that the reference of a statement is its truth value, the two predicates above should refer to the same condition. But there is no reason to suppose that they do, to suppose that those who believe that Jackie is a nice dog are just those who believe that Carson City is west of Los Angeles.

Of course Frege was aware of this problem and thought he had a solution to it. The solution involved his realm of sense, and the mechanism of indirect reference. According to Frege's theory the embedded sentences in our examples do not refer to truth values, since they occur as complements to BELIEVES. Frege claimed that sentences occurring in such contexts have indirect reference; they refer to the thoughts they usually express, not to their truth values.

Much of this book can be viewed as criticism of this feature of Frege's theory, but our aim is the construction of an alternative. For now, though, we just want to point out that positing the mechanism of indirect reference is a partial admission of our point. For a wide range of perfectly ordinary expressions it is silly to think that the reference (or interpretation) of the statements embedded in them is their truth value. One must either treat all of these as special cases, as Frege did, or abandon the doctrine that the reference of a sentence is a truth value. We advocate the latter.

The inadequacy of truth value as the reference of an embedded statement is the rule, not the exception. There are almost no statement-embedding contexts in which the reference of the whole may plausibly be regarded as determined solely by the truth value of the embedded statement. Consider, for example, causal explanations. Suppose I am right that Henry made Mary move. Does it follow that Henry made Hitler invade Poland? One assumes not, though this would indeed follow if Mary moved and the embedded statement stood for its truth value. Or consider perception reports. If Jim saw Melanie bake a pie, did Jim see Ruby shoot Oswald? Once again, it doesn't follow at all.

The intuitive response to either of these cases is that the inferences obviously fail because the subject matter has changed completely. What Henry did to Mary has nothing to do with Hitler and Poland. And a report about Jim's seeing Melanie baking a pie is no evidence at all for a report about Jim seeing something that happened years ago in Texas (Ruby's shooting Oswald, for our younger readers).

We believe that in each of these cases, the natural thing to say is that the embedded statement describes a certain situation, and that the larger embedding sentence describes a larger situation which the first helps to identify. For example, Mary's moving was one situation, and it was in turn part of a larger one. This more encompassing situation is the one reported by the sentence HENRY MADE MARY MOVE.

In these examples we have regarded MARY MOVE and MELANIE BAKE A PIE as tenseless sentences, the syntactic result of combining a noun phrase with a tenseless verb phrase. There are various reasons we think this is a proper analysis. For example, they are naturally treated as having a truth value. Thus one might deny our report of what Jim saw by remarking, "But Melanie didn't bake a pie." But in any event, the same observation can be made without resorting to constructions that embed tenseless sentences. Even the most cursory survey uncovers such contexts as IT IS IMPORTANT THAT, IT IS RELEVANT THAT, and IT IS PROBABLE THAT. And of course there are also all of the more traditional attitude constructions. Each of these contexts embeds a garden variety sentence; but for none is it plausible to think that the contribution of the embedded statement is only its truth value. For all of these, then, the Fregean theory must invoke the mechanism of indirect reference.

In a later chapter we will argue that even Frege's realm of sense cannot provide satisfactory references for the embedded statements in attitude reports, and many of the arguments we use will apply equally to other statements-embedding contexts as well. But at present we merely want to emphasize how far reaching the exceptions must be, if we are to retain the doctrine that a statement refers to its truth value. This alone should give the reader some motivation for following our attempt to work out an alternative.

The Slingshot

There is an historically important piece of reasoning which, if correct, would show that the whole idea of semantics based on situations can't work. We call this argument the slingshot, for reasons buried in the early history of situation semantics. A number of distinguished philosophers have used versions of the argument, including Church (43, 56), Davidson (67a, b) and Quine (66c). We have treated the argument in some detail elsewhere (Barwise and Perry, 81b). But a brief look at it here will help make clear some important ways in which situation semantics differs from more traditional approaches, and why these approaches have diverted philosophers from what we feel is the most natural and intuitive account of the attitudes.

For the time being we will play down our emphasis on the relational nature of meaning, as well as such related issues as efficiency. Imagine a language all of whose expressions are inefficient. We can then say, without being too misleading, that in situation semantics sentences stand for situations. This means, of course, that sentences with the same truth value may stand for quite different things. But the argument in question aims to show that this is impossible. It purportedly shows that any two sentences with the same truth value must stand for the same thing if what they stand for is determined by what their parts stand for.

Here is a standard version of the argument, one that uses definite descriptions. We will begin with two arbitrary sentences, R and S, which just happen to have the same truth value. The conclusion will be that R and S must refer to the same thing. If they are both true we might call this common reference Reality, or The True; if they are both false, we might call it The False. The names, of course, are irrelevant.

The argument will turn on two critical assumptions: first, that *logically equivalent sentences have the same reference* and second, that *the reference of a sentence does not change if a component singular term is replaced by another with the same reference.*

For any sentence Q let t_Q be the definite description:

THE NUMBER THAT IS 1 IF Q, AND IS 0 IF NOT-Q

Notice that this construction guarantees that Q will be logically equivalent to the sentence ($t_Q = 1$). For if Q is true, then t_Q denotes 1, while if Q is false, t_Q denotes 0.

Now let us consider the sentences R and S, which we will suppose are both true. If the critical assumptions are correct, R and S must have the same reference. For, on these assumptions, each sentence in the following list has the reference of the one before it, for the reason displayed.

> R
> $t_R = 1$ (by logical equivalence)
> $1 = 1$ (by substitution of co-referring singular terms)
> $t_S = 1$ (by substitution of co-referring singular terms)
> S (again by logical equivalence)

If both R and S are false, the argument is the same, except that the line "$1 = 1$" is replaced by "$0 = 1$", since in that case both t_R and t_S will denote 0.

This argument has no force for the semanticist who thinks the subject matter of a sentence figures in its reference. The first sentence might be about Jackie biting Molly, the third about the number 1 and the identity relation, and the fifth about Hitler invading Poland. The problem with the argument, in all of its forms, is this. Once we seriously entertain the possibility that sentences stand for entities like situations, entities built up from what the parts of the sentence stand for, *neither critical assumption is the least bit reasonable.* We will defer our explanation of why the second assumption is not reasonable until we discuss noun phrases. For now, we will just look at the first assumption, the principle that logically equivalent sentences have the same reference.

Sentences are logically equivalent if they are true in the same models. A model is an assignment of appropriate set-theoretic entities to the terms and relations of the language involved. Thus the sentences,

> JOE IS EATING

and

> JOE IS EATING AND SARAH IS SLEEPING OR SARAH ISN'T SLEEPING

are logically equivalent. Every way of assigning individuals and sets to appropriate expressions of the language will make the second conjunct of the second sentence true. Because of this, the models in which the second sentence is true will be just those in which the first sentence is true.

If we think that sentences stand for situations, or indeed for any entity that does not lose track of subject matter, then we will not be at all inclined to accept the first principle required in the slingshot. The two logically equivalent sentences just given do not have the same subject matter, they do not describe situations involving the same objects and properties. In situation semantics, the first sentence will stand for all the situations in which Joe is eating, the second sentence for those situations in which Joe is eating and Sarah is sleeping plus those in which Joe is eating and Sarah isn't sleeping. Sarah is present in all of these. Since she is not present in many of the situations that JOE IS EATING stands for, these sentences, though logically equivalent, do not stand for the same entity. Sarah is part of the subject matter of the latter statement, but not the former. And in situation semantics we do not lose track of the subject matter in the reference of a sentence, or rather in its interpretation as we prefer to call it.

The assumption that logically equivalent sentences refer to the same thing seems reasonable if we already accept Frege's doctrine that the reference of a sentence is its truth value. Of course, if we already accepted this decision, we wouldn't need the slingshot at all. But historically, Frege's original decision seems to have been far more important than is usually realized; the decision is, itself, an important part of the picture that ends up being exploited to justify that same decision.

If one thinks that sentences stand for truth values, then logical equivalence will seem to be an extremely important relation. This may explain why, of all the equivalence relations among sentences, logical equivalence has been given the honorific title 'logical equivalence'. But of course it wasn't simply the authority of Frege that led philosophers to focus on the relation we call logical equivalence. There were a number of factors, some having to do with the purposes for which mathematical semantics was first developed, others having to do with conceptions, largely derived from those early aims, concerning what the evidence for a semantic theory should be. We turn now to discuss briefly some of these issues.

CHAPTER TWO

Evidence for a Theory of Linguistic Meaning

Semantics is the study of linguistic meaning, of the relationships that hold between expressions of language and things in the world. This study can be conducted in a precise way using the tools of modern mathematics. The approach is generally called "model-theoretic semantics," since model theory is the part of logic concerned with the relation between the linguistic expressions of mathematics and the mathematical structures they describe.

Sometimes this approach to semantics is called "formal semantics," presumably because it looks very formal to those outside the tradition. It is an unfortunate expression, since it suggests a connection with Formalism, Hilbert's philosophy of mathematics. Hilbert tried to reduce talk about mathematical objects to talk about mathematical expressions, in hopes that the problematic questions about mathematical objects might reduce to less problematic questions about finite mathematical expressions. Had this program succeeded, it would have reduced mathematical activity to a purely formal activity, to the manipulation of expressions by formal rules. And nothing could be more out of the spirit of genuine semantics. In any event, the enterprise was doomed from the start, as we have all learned from Gödel's Theorem.

Model theory does not study linguistic expressions *per se,* but the relationships that hold between linguistic expressions and parts of the world. It is usually judged by how well it accounts for entailments between sentences, why it is that a sentence like SOCRATES IS MORTAL follows from ALL MEN ARE MORTAL and SOCRATES IS A MAN. As such, the field is one of the success stories of modern philosophy. It has greatly clarified many formerly obscure issues in both logic and mathematics, such as those surrounding the relationship between proof and truth.

But the heritage of model theory, however illustrious, is a mixed blessing. For the founders of modern logic—Frege, Russell and Whitehead, Gödel, and Tarski—were preoccupied with the language of mathematics. Because of this preoccupation, many assumptions and attitudes about this language were built into the very heart of model theory, and so came to be assumptions about the nature of language in general. These assumptions have made it increasingly difficult to adapt the ideas of standard model theory to the semantics of natural languages.

In this chapter we argue that there is much more evidence than just entailments for which a semantic theory must account, evidence that in fact causes us to look with some skepticism on the very idea of entailments between sentences. The evidence consists of insights of philosophers of language and linguists into the way natural languages work. We call these insights *six semantic universals of human languages.* Most of these universals are at odds with assumptions built into standard model theory. We take these phenomena as central to an adequate semantic theory, not just minor headaches to be explained by amending the semantics of first-order logic, a theory that evolved before their ubiquity was recognized.

The six universals are, in order of treatment: the external significance of language, the productivity of language, the efficiency of language, the perspectival relativity of language, the ambiguity of language, and, finally, the mental significance of language. We have already mentioned several of these features in Chapter 1. In the chapters that follow we will explain how our theory deals with each of them.

THE EXTERNAL SIGNIFICANCE OF LANGUAGE

It is a fact that we use language to convey information about the world, and that much of what we as individuals know, we learned by being told. Take again the very simple example from the last chapter. Jonny takes his dog Jackie to the vet because she is limping badly. The doctor takes an X-ray, examines it, and tells Jonny "She has a broken leg." His utterance contains information about Jackie, that she has a broken leg.

On a simple-minded account, such as the one we adopt, the

doctor's utterance describes a certain state of affairs, that of Jackie's having a broken leg. The parts of the sentence—SHE, HAS, A, BROKEN, and LEG—have meanings because of the way they are used in English. As a result of these meanings, in tandem with various facts about the doctor's particular utterance, these expressions describe situational elements and put them together into a simple situation. We call this situation the *interpretation* of the statement, and propose to identify the external significance of the statement by means of it.

It is clear that the external significance of statements so identified must be explained by a genuine semantic theory. We further claim that a clear explanation of what situations a statement describes and how it achieves this provides a key that can be used to unlock the mystery of linguistic meaning.

There are some serious problems that must be faced by such a claim. We list some here.

The Priority of Information

The first problem is a problem for any model theoretic account of the information-carrying capacity of language. The information conveyed by the doctor's utterance was not the sentence used, for the sentence

SHE HAS A BROKEN LEG

by itself isn't even about Jackie. Nor is the vet's utterance, even considered as a whole, information about Jackie, though it's getting closer. The utterance *conveyed* information about Jackie, the same information that was conveyed to the vet by the X-ray, that her leg was broken. Information can be carried by language but information is not language; in fact, information is prior to language. If the whole incident had taken place in a different linguistic community, the doctor would have used a different expression, in a different language, to convey this same piece of information. If our theory of language is going to capture this ability of utterances to convey a piece of information we must have the information there to be conveyed.

This means that we must have a way of representing the way the world is, one that is independent of the language whose meanings we are trying to study. In this regard, standard model theory is woefully inadequate, for the structures it uses to represent the world all presuppose some specific language.

Let's put the matter a different way. Imagine the vet's saying of

Jackie, "She has a broken leg," when in fact she has a sprained leg. There are two (currently relevant) different mistakes the vet might have made, two different empirical, contingent facts he might have gotten wrong. Most likely the vet would be wrong about Jackie, thinking she has a broken leg, when in fact it is only sprained. But he might have been wrong about the meaning of BROKEN, thinking that it meant sprained. An omnipotent being interested in making sure the vet was always right could have rectified things in two ways; by breaking Jackie's leg, or by changing the meaning of BROKEN. The first would be to change the world so as to make accurate what was conveyed by the utterance; the second would be to change the language so that the utterance conveys different information. A theory that can't tell the difference between two such changes is not going to capture the relation between language and information.

The Underdetermination of Information by Interpretation

Having seen that the information a statement conveys is independent of the language used to make the statement, we might be tempted to try identifying the information contained in a statement with the situation it describes—that is, with its interpretation. But there are problems associated with that assumption also. For example, there can be different sentences, describing the same situation but carrying different information. If the vet had said either "Jackie has a broken leg" or "Your dog has a broken leg," the interpretation would have been the same, the state of affairs of Jackie having a broken leg. However, the statements carry different information. For from the different statements a third party (or Jonny) could have learned that Jackie was (a) female, (b) named Jackie, or (c) Jonny's dog. They are facts that the vet can exploit to describe a certain state of affairs; they are not part of the described state of affairs; but neither should they be lost in the informational account of the utterance.

Another problem to be considered is that there are all kinds of information in a statement in addition to facts about the situations it describes. For example, the vet's statement conveys information about his beliefs, about the language he speaks, information about how far away he is, and so on.

This raises a related issue. There are all kinds of utterances that don't describe situations at all: questions, commands, jokes, requests, promises, and so on. But all kinds of utterances convey information, about what the questioner wants to know, what the commander commands or the requester requests, or what the promiser intends to do. Our focus on information and the interpretation of utterances really amounts to both a claim and a methodological strategy.

Our claim is that the primary function of language is to convey information and that the meanings of expressions are what allow them to convey the information they do. Our strategy is to investigate the linguistic meanings of indicative sentences and their parts by exploring the ability of statements made using them to convey information.

THE PRODUCTIVITY OF LANGUAGE

One of the most remarkable (and most remarked upon) features of human language is our ability to use and understand expressions never before uttered. Out of a finite stock of words we are able to understand any of a potentially infinite list of expressions. For example, out of the five words BIT, DOG, THE, THAT, and MOLLY, we can form, among others, the following meaningful expressions:

MOLLY

THE DOG THAT BIT MOLLY,

THE DOG THAT BIT THE DOG THAT BIT MOLLY,

THE DOG THAT BIT THE DOG THAT BIT THE DOG THAT BIT MOLLY,

and so on. One senses that there is a fixed mechanism at work here, that what each of these successive expressions refers to depends on the reference of the previous one; or perhaps it is the case that the meaning of each depends on the meaning of its predecessor in some systematic way.

Frege assumes that both are the case, that the sense of a complex expression is a function of the senses of its parts, and that the reference of the whole is a function of the reference of its parts. In fact he uses this as a working assumption to figure out what the reference of an expression is when it isn't obvious. This is what led him to the conclusion that the reference of a sentence had to be a truth value.

The assumption that the meaning of a whole is a function of the meanings of its parts is called the *Principle of Compositionality.* It obviously expresses an intuition that people have about their language, however vaguely understood. It is something to be made precise in a semantic theory, to state how the meaning of an expression depends on those of its parts and vice versa.

Our own theory distinguishes between the meaning of an expression and its interpretation in a particular utterance. We will see that a version of compositionality holds of meanings, but not of interpretations. But the matter is impossible to discuss cogently until we know exactly what linguistic meanings are. It is a matter we discuss at some length in Chapter 6 and return to implicitly throughout the book.

THE EFFICIENCY OF LANGUAGE

The productivity of language has often been considered to be essential to the learnability of language. In fact, though, there is another phenomenon on which productivity is dependent, but which is usually accorded much less respect. Productivity emphasizes the possibility of using ever more complex expressions to describe things around us. But what is important, after all, is the fact that expressions, whether simple or complex, can be recycled, can be used over and over again in different ways, places, and times and by different people, *to say different things.* This is what we mean by the *efficiency* of language.

A preoccupation with the language of mathematics, and with the seemingly eternal nature of its sentences, led the founders of the field to neglect the efficiency of language. In our opinion this was a critical blunder, for efficiency lies at the very heart of meaning.

There are at least three ways a language can squeeze different interpretations out of a fixed unambiguous expression. It is clear that for this to happen at all, the interpretation of an expression must be a product of factors some of which are fixed solely by language, and others which vary with the expression's use. The former we call the linguistic meaning of the expression, the latter its context of use. The context needs to be broken down into three further factors, features of the context that are exploited in different ways in getting from the linguistic meaning of an expression to what it happens to signify on a particular occasion of use. We call these the discourse situation, connections, and resource situations.

Indexicality: Exploitation of the Discourse Situation

One of the most important and pervasive forms of efficiency arises from one of the simplest facts about human language: an utterance must be made by someone, someplace, and sometime. That is, an utterance always takes place in a *discourse situation,* and so the facts about the discourse situation can always be exploited to get from the meaning of the expression used to whatever information is to be conveyed.

Consider the sentence:

JACKIE IS BITING ME.

This sentence has a fixed linguistic meaning, independent of the context of use. But the information (or misinformation) conveyed by an utterance of this sentence will depend crucially on who the speaker is and when the utterance takes place. If I were to say it now, my utterance would describe a situation involving me, now. This is an obvious point but extremely important. Note, for example, that even if I believe I am Napoleon and that the date is January 8, 1797, my utterance of "Jackie is biting me" is still about me, now. It is not about Napoleon in 1797. Or, to take another example, suppose Rip van Winkle said when he awoke on October 20, 1823, after a twenty-year nap, "Today is October 20, 1803" (Castaneda, 68; Kaplan, 77; Perry, 77). What he said is wrong. His use of TODAY picks out October 20, 1823, no matter how firmly he believes it to be 1803.

The dependence of the interpretation of an utterance on facts about the discourse situation is usually referred to as indexicality. For historical reasons, it is often suggested that indexicality is not really a semantic phenomenon but belongs instead to the "pragmatic" side of language use. Another ploy, dating back to Russell, is to suppose that indexicals are disguised descriptions. For example, my use of TODAY might be considered shorthand for any of the numerous definite descriptions of the day I have in mind.

But the examples above show that this idea is wrong. In the first place I can use TODAY to refer to today without having any idea what day it is. In the second place, as the Rip van Winkle case shows, the fact that I have a description in mind does not suffice to get me from TODAY to the day I have in mind. Similarly, my use of I and ME can only pick out me.

The way a speaker exploits the discourse situation is not limited to a few isolated words like I, ME, NOW, HERE, TODAY, and YOU. Thus every tensed indicative statement exploits the time when it was uttered, though this is often obscured by the choice of examples like SNOW IS WHITE or THE EARTH MOVES. These are statements whose truth is largely independent of the time of utterance. But consider the sentence:

RONALD REAGAN IS PRESIDENT.

Again, this sentence has a fixed meaning, independent of when it is used. This fixed meaning is what allows us to say different things with it at different times. If used today it expresses something true. Said yesterday it expressed something quite different, namely that Reagan was president then. It is, indeed, a fact that he was president yesterday, but a different fact than that he is president today. And, of course, if uttered in 1979, it would have expressed something false.

Indexicality is extremely important to the information-carrying capacity of language. For example you, the reader, have no doubt picked up the fact that we wrote the previous paragraph during Reagan's presidency. Of course in writing "Reagan is president" we don't say anything about myself or about the writing, but you can pick this information up from knowledge of the way linguistic meaning and discourse situations interact.

Speaker Connections and Reference

When the doctor came out of the examination room and said, "She has a broken leg," he was referring to Jackie. As would commonly be said, the doctor's use of SHE was *made with reference to* her. In general, a speaker's perceptual experience (past and present), gives him connections to objects, properties, places, and times, connections that he can exploit in referring to these things. There are many examples; we will discuss three at this point.

Uses of names. I tell you "Sandy is asleep" and thereby tell you something about Sandy by using the name SANDY. But which Sandy have I told you something about? Sandy Denis, Sandy Koufax, or some other Sandy? There are many Sandys in the world. My experience of the world—through people I know and through the things I have seen, heard and read—places me in a position to refer to some of these Sandys by using the name SANDY. Similarly, my utterance JACKIE IS BITING ME was about a certain dog named JACKIE. But again there are many Jackies, and the meaning of the name is not sufficient to pick out my dog. Still, it is a fact about my particular utterance of JACKIE that it successfully referred to that particular dog.

The tradition in logic has been to pretend that the move from a name to the thing named is a function, that distinct things have distinct names. This pretense obscures an important way in which the use of a name by a speaker may convey information. For the use of a name may provide information not just about the object named but indirectly about the speaker's connections to that object. If someone comes up to me and says, "Melanie said to tell you that she would be late getting home," I learn that the speaker has some sort of connection to Melanie, however indirect. That is why it would be appropriate for me to ask, "Did you talk to her?"

Deictic uses of pronouns. The sentence SHE HAS A BROKEN LEG has a certain meaning, one that enabled the doctor to use it to convey information to Jonny about Jackie. But the very same sentence has been used on a number of occasions to convey different information, information about different females. In the present case, the meaning of SHE plus the doctor's perceptual connections to a particular female allowed him to use the word to refer to Jackie.

Demonstratives like THIS and THAT function similarly. When I said "That's my wife", I used THAT to refer to a particular person. Of course the meaning of the word THAT is not my wife. Rather, the meaning of the word gives me a way to refer to various things I am connected to.

Referential uses of tense. Logicians have usually treated all forms of the past tense as quantification over times past. Reichenbach was a notable exception. He realized that certain forms of the past tense involve direct reference to a past time. If I say, "Jackie was biting Molly," my statement refers to a specific time in the past.

When we say that my use of JACKIE WAS BITING MOLLY refers to some particular past time, we do not suggest that I could accurately identify or describe that time, say by offering some definite description. This involves a mistake analogous to thinking that Rip van Winkle's use of TODAY presupposed an ability to identify the date, or that to use SHE requires an ability to specify the female in question by some definite description. Rather, it is just that the meaning of JACKIE WAS BITING MOLLY requires that I be speaking about some particular past time, one with which I am somehow connected. Thus if Jackie has bitten Molly on many occasions, the statement can only be about one of them. This contrasts with my saying, "Jackie has bitten Molly," which doesn't describe any particular past biting of Molly by Jackie. Since the past is determined by the time of discourse, the referential use of tense also exploits the discourse situation.

In this book we take a very simple-minded approach to tense, emphasizing the deictic uses, as opposed to "quantificational" uses, as in the present perfect, or combinations of the two, as in the past perfect. A much fuller discussion of tense and aspect based on ideas in Chapter 11 will appear in our book *Situation Semantics.*

Exploitation of Resource Situations

A third form of efficiency stems from a speaker's ability to exploit one state of affairs in order to convey information about another. For example, if we wanted to describe Jackie's biting Molly but did not know Jackie's name, we might say something like "The dog that just ran past the window is biting Molly," or, perhaps, "Jonny's dog is biting Molly." Here we exploit one fact to get at another; we exploit the fact that Jackie just ran past the window, or the fact that she belongs to Jonny, to describe her biting Molly. Similarly, if my wife says "The dog needs to go out," she is exploiting the fact that we have only one dog in order to say something about that dog. This state of affairs, our having one and only one dog, is a resource situation that members of our family can and frequently do use in order to refer to her.

Resource situations can become available for exploitation in a variety of ways, including the following:

(i)   by being perceived by the speaker,

(ii) by being the object of some common knowledge about some part of the world,

(iii) by being the way the world is,

(iv) by being built up by previous discourse

and, somewhat controversially:

(v)   by being the way the speaker or listener or both mistakenly take some situation to be, or even just mutually pretend it to be. (Donnellan, 66, 68)

We leave it as an exercise for the reader to spot examples of each of these.

The three forms of efficiency described above all involve the exploitation of the speaker's and listener's place in the world. But the forms work rather differently in our theory, which is why we break them into three categories. Taken together, though, they provide ample evidence for a central fact about natural language: *The linguistic meaning of an expression in general greatly underdetermines its interpretation on a particular occasion of use.* Or, for short, *meaning underdetermines interpretation.*

Just as we cannot identify the information conveyed by an utterance with its interpretation, so we cannot identify it with the meaning of the expression used. The sentence SHE HAS A BROKEN LEG is an efficient carrier of meaning, and that meaning allows it to convey information, but the information is not the meaning. The meaning of the sentence doesn't get at anything about Jackie or anyone else.

However, we will argue that the relation theory of meaning, the theory that sees meaning as systematic relations between types of situations, allows us to account for all the ways an expression can carry information. Here are some examples of ways the phrase MY WIFE, with its meaning, can be used to convey information. All of these should be explainable by any semantic theory worth its salt. Imagine that I am going to a costume party dressed so as not to be recognizable to anyone but the host.

Case 1. I come to the party alone and say to the host, a good family friend, "My wife will be late." Since the host knows who I am and knows who my wife is, my utterance conveys to him the information that she will be late, information about a particular person.

Case 2. Someone else, a stranger, overhears my remark to the host. To her my utterance conveys the information that I am a married male, as well as the information that my wife, whoever she is, is going to be late. Notice that it does not convey to her information about any particular person other than me, since she does not know who my wife is.

Case 3. I am talking to the stranger when my wife enters. I say, simply, "That's my wife." This utterance, simple as it is, conveys to the stranger the information that the woman indicated is my wife.

Case 4. Now suppose I am talking not to a stranger, but to someone who knows my wife and me quite well, but who has not yet seen through my disguise. If my wife walks up and my interlocutor recognizes her, then my utterance of "That's my wife" will convey entirely different information—namely, information about who I am.

Case 5. Suppose it is midnight and costumes have been thrown aside. I see one of my ex-wives and, being a good sport, go over to talk to her. She asks "When did you start drinking martinis?" "When you were my wife," I reply. Here the phrase MY WIFE somehow manages to identify a period of time.

As we will explain in Chapter 7, our theory predicts a total of sixteen different ways in which the utterance of a simple indicative sentence containing MY WIFE can convey information. For now, we leave it to the reader to find some of the other eleven ways to use this phrase. The point, though, is simply this: the phrase MY WIFE, all by itself, has a certain linguistic meaning. That meaning allows speakers of English to convey many different kinds of information by utterances containing the phrase. We believe that an adequate account of the meaning of this phrase squares with all of them.

In situation semantics, we handle efficiency and information through the relation theory of meaning. An expression can be used over and over again with the same meaning, a meaning learned once and for all by the members of the linguistic community. But its interpretation may be new each time, determined by the unchanging meaning and the varying circumstances of utterance.

The sources of efficiency we have described correspond to three very general sorts of facts about utterances, what we call the *discourse situation,* the *connections,* and the *resource situations.* The discourse situation has to do with public facts about the utterance, like who the speaker is, and when it occurs. Connections have to do with the way the speaker (or listeners) are connected with the larger world. We have in mind here the sorts of causal connections emphasized by writers like Donnellan (70, 74), Kaplan (69), Kripke (72), Putnam (75), and others. We think our idea of connections is pretty accurately reflected in the ordinary use of the English term REFERS. The meaning of the expressions used, and the facts of the sort we call the discourse situation, still underdetermine interpretation. Connections fill this gap.

Construing the meaning of an expression as a multi-placed relation is what lets us account for information, since information is available about any or all of the coordinates, not just about the coordinate that gives the interpretation. The idea that all the information in an utterance must come from its interpretation we call the *fallacy of misplaced information.*

Connections play an important role in our theory, a role that some will find should be broken up further. We will have connections tying uses of proper names to their interpretations, uses of deictic pronouns to their interpretations, and uses of tensed verbs and common nouns to their interpretations. In each of these cases, the meaning of the expressions used, and the facts of the discourse situation, still leave the interpretation underdetermined. But even with this in common, these phenomena are doubtless still importantly different in many ways. There is certainly nothing in our theory that precludes a finer analysis of these factors.

THE PERSPECTIVAL RELATIVITY OF LANGUAGE

We have seen that language can exploit aspects of one situation to get at elements of another. And we are all in different situations with different resources to exploit. This is very important, for while there are many ways of saying the same thing, not all of them are available to all of us all the time. Hence, speakers are forced to adopt a strategy which gets at the right interpretation from the contextual milieu they find themselves in, from their "perspective." We call this the perspectival relativity of language.

Each of the three forms of exploitation gives rise to its own form of perspectival relativity. (a) Different speakers are always in different discourse situations, since one of the facts of a discourse situation is who is speaking. I would say, "Jackie is biting you" to describe what you would describe by saying, "Jackie is biting me." (b) Different people may have different causal connections to the world. Someone looking at Jackie can refer to her with THAT DOG, whereas someone who has never seen or heard of her cannot. (c) Different people usually have different resource situations available to them. Thus, for example, different people may use different descriptions to get at the same thing, say THE MORNING STAR and THE EVENING STAR to designate Venus because they have different resource situations by virtue of knowing different things about Venus.

THE AMBIGUITY IN LANGUAGE

Unlike the artificial languages used by logicians and computer scientists, natural languages are always ambiguous. That is, a given expression may have more than one meaning. First of all there are words that have more than one meaning, like BANK and BAND. And second, even if none of the individual words in an expression is ambiguous, the expression as a whole may be. In English, for example, we have sentences like the following:

MY SON'S TEAM DIDN'T LOSE ONE GAME.

Said one way, this sentence means the team didn't lose any games at all; said another, it means they somehow failed to lose at least one game. When I used the sentence, it unfortunately had this second meaning.

MELANIE BELIEVES THAT SHE DROPPED A BOOK.

Said one way, this sentence means that Melanie believes, of herself, that she dropped a book; with this meaning it might be used to explain why Melanie is looking around the hall. But said the other way, it means that Melanie believes of a particular female that she dropped the book, and so might explain why Melanie is asking Jim to give the book to Sally.

TWO PHILOSOPHY STUDENTS STALKED TWO LINGUISTS.

This might mean several different things. It might mean that there were two linguists, each being stalked by a student. Or it could mean that each linguist was stalked by a pair of students. Or finally it might mean that there were two students, each stalking a pair of linguists.

Ambiguities of this sort have always been a bane to logicians and have seemed to call for regimentation of some kind. Ambiguity has always been excluded from artificial languages. This paradigm of a regimented, unambiguous language has been carried over to the study of natural languages in various ways. One is the postulation of logical form, an underlying level of unambiguous representation. Another is Montague's ploy (Montague, 74b,d): while there is no separate level of unambiguous representation, an ambiguous expression is still assigned multiple syntactic structures.

Our approach to meaning suggests a different way of looking at ambiguity—as another aspect of the efficiency of language. Expressions are, after all, just uniformities across certain kinds of situations, utterances. That an expression can be used in more than one way is just another feature of that expression. Of course, in order for an utterance to have objective significance, the expression employed has to be used in a certain way. And which way it is used is a fact about the utterance. If I say something using MELANIE BELIEVES SHE DROPPED A BOOK, what I say depends on how I used the expression, and this is a fact about the utterance, not about the expression.

That raises a new issue and recalls an issue we slighted earlier. The new issue is how we will represent ambiguity in our theory, whether by appeal to some sort of "logical form" or by appeal to some other device. We will address this issue further in Chapter 6. The other issue is what to make of all the factors that are part of what determines an utterance, factors like who the speaker is referring to with a pronoun, what resource situation the speaker is exploiting, and the contextual facts which go toward getting a unique interpretation out of an ambiguous expression. If there is really this much slack in language, how do we ever understand what people are saying?

The answer is obvious: There are just an enormous number of features about language use, features like intonation patterns, gestures, eye-movement, and the place of an utterance in a larger conversational or social setting, that help us interpret an utterance. And, of course, sometimes we misinterpret what people say to us. All of this is part of a full theory of linguistic meaning. Its intricacy may be discouraging to the logician used to ignoring all contextual elements, but there is no getting away from the fact that natural language is an intricate device. And rather than give up the whole endeavor, we can make a start by isolating some of the relevant phenomena in a formal way, and by exploring how the remainder depends on these. Obviously, many gaps will remain open for future study.

THE MENTAL SIGNIFICANCE OF LANGUAGE

"A bear is coming this way," yells Melanie, a good observer, and not given to lying. From her utterance we learn two things. First, we learn that a bear is coming this way. Second, we learn something about Melanie's state of mind, that she has a certain belief. If we thought Melanie was sincere but extremely myopic, we might learn the second, but not the first. Melanie's utterance, like utterances in general, can give us information about two quite different situations. One is our situation, vis-à-vis bears in the neighborhood. The other is Melanie's situation, vis-à-vis what she believes. In regard to this second situation, we are led to expect Melanie to behave in certain ways, the ways fairly small people usually act when they believe a bear is approaching them, like climbing a tree. If she doesn't act this way, then we suspect she is not sincere.

Normally, we would first focus on the former, more threatening situation. But if we discover that there is no bear in the vicinity, we might focus on the second, on why Melanie believed what she did. Her myopia, and the large dog at the edge of camp, might provide an explanation. And her belief might in turn explain her subsequent behavior: what she said to us, and the fact that she climbed a tree.

Melanie's words, we might say, have mental significance as well as external significance. And this fact, it seems, must surely be the key to understanding how sentences of the following sort function:

MELANIE SAW THAT A BEAR WAS COMING TOWARD US.

MELANIE BELIEVED THAT A BEAR WAS COMING TOWARD US.

There can be no doubt that the mental significance of sentences is an important attribute, and that an account of this attribute will be central to any good theory of language.

It is obvious that these two features of language, its mental significance and its external significance, are closely related. The behavior Melanie exhibited when she believed a bear was approaching was just the sort of behavior we would expect of a person who saw that a bear was approaching her. It is natural to expect that the mental significance of A BEAR IS COMING TOWARD US is explained by its external significance, given a reasonable theory of mind.

That is a central claim of this book, one we call the Priority of External Significance: *the mental significance of language, including the role of sentences embedded in attitude reports, is adequately explained by their external significance, properly understood.*

This is not a new claim; a tally of its advocates would make a long and impressive list. However, many equally impressive theorists, including Frege and Locke, had a different view, taking the connection of language to some other realm as prior. Locke gave this privileged status to ideas, Frege gave it to senses, and many more recent authors have given it to mental representations, in various construals of that slippery term.

Locke took the primary significance of an expression to be an idea, with the external significance derivative on this, determined by what the idea is an idea of, if anything. Frege, on the other hand, posited the existence of a realm of senses for minds to grasp, senses that determine reference in the world, if any. It is to contrast our theory with such theories that we make the Priority of External Significance explicit.

There are several potential pitfalls for any theory like ours that assumes the Priority of External Significance. One such problem area is belief reports where the embedded sentence is false, as in

JOE BELIEVED THAT MOLLY WAS A BORDER COLLIE.

Here there seems to be no external significance to the embedded sentence MOLLIE WAS A BORDER COLLIE because Molly is and always was a mutt, not a border collie. Russell, striving to save the Principle of

External Significance, gave up compositionality, so that the parts MOLLY could refer to Molly, BORDER COLLIE, could refer to the property of being a border collie, with the whole standing for a complex relation between Joe, Molly, and the property of being a border collie, without assuming there was any situation for the embedded sentence to describe. Frege took the other move, of preserving compositionality but giving up the idea that the words in the embedded sentence refer to real things, assuming rather that in that context they refer to senses, thoughts. Problems like these make the attitudes a major testing ground for any semantic theory and account for the attention we give them in this volume.

EVIDENCE FOR A SEMANTIC THEORY

Logicians usually take entailments between sentences to be the primary data to be accounted for by a semantic theory—for example, why it is that "Socrates is mortal" follows from "All men are mortal" and "Socrates is a man" but does not follow from "Socrates is a Greek" and "Some Greeks are mortal." That is, what we are supposed to account for are *valid arguments.*

There is obviously something right about this. What is right is that in accounting for entailment relations, we provide a partial account of the external significance of language. If you are told that all men are mortal and that Socrates is a man then it does seem that you have the information that Socrates is mortal. But, as the reader may by now realize, there is also something profoundly misleading about the traditional concern over entailments between sentences. For one thing, their concern obscures the efficiency of language, and it is this efficiency that is central to meaning. For example, the *sentence*

SOCRATES IS SPEAKING

does not follow from the *sentences*

EVERY PHILOSOPHER IS SPEAKING

SOCRATES IS A PHILOSOPHER

even though this argument has the same "logical form" (on most accounts of logical form) as the earlier example. In the first place, there is the matter of tense. At the very least the three sentences would have to be said at more or less the same time for the argument to be valid. Sentences are not true or false; only statements made with indicative sentences, utterances of certain kinds, are true or false.

Again, it was a preoccupation with the seemingly eternal sentences of mathematics that led logicians to ask what makes one *sentence* follow from other *sentences.* For they were confronting real problems about the nature of the consequences of axioms, problems even about their very consistency. These questions are not, presumably, a function of where and when the expressions are used. But once we move to natural language, where efficiency shows itself as one of the most crucial semantic features, we must give up this assumption.

At the very least, then, our theory will seek to account for why the truth of certain *statements* follows from the truth of other *statements.* This move has several important consequences. For one thing, we see that there is a lot more to the subject than is traditionally supposed. For example, if you say to me, "You are wrong," then the truth of your statement entails the truth of my subsequent utterance of "I was wrong" and of someone else's utterance of "He was wrong." But of course it would also ensure the truth of my utterance "You were speaking."

There is a lot of information available from utterances that is simply missed in traditional accounts—accounts that ignore the relational aspect of meaning. If someone comes up to me and says, "Melanie saw a bear," I may learn not just that Melanie saw a bear, but also that the speaker is somehow connected to Melanie in a way that allows him to refer to her using MELANIE. And I learn that the speaker is somehow in a position to have information about what Melanie saw. A semantic theory must go far beyond traditional "patterns of inference" to account for the external significance of language.

A rather startling consequence of this is that there can be no syntactic counterpart, of the kind traditionally sought in proof

theory and theories of logical form, to the semantic theory of consequence. For consequence is simply not a relation between purely
syntactic elements.

A semantic theory must account for how language fits into the
general flow of information. The capturing of entailments between
statements is only one aspect of a real theory of the information in
an utterance. We think the relation theory of meaning provides the
proper framework for such a theory. By looking at linguistic meaning as a relation between utterances and described situations, we can
focus on the many coordinates that allow information to be extracted
from utterances, information not only about the situation described,
but also about the speaker and her place in the world.

A Theory of Situations

CHAPTER THREE

Abstract Situations

In situation semantics utterances are assigned *interpretations* in virtue of the *meanings* of the expressions used and other factors about the utterances. The interpretation of an utterance is a collection of situations; the meaning of the expression used is a binary relation, between utterances, situations of one kind, and described situations. To get the project off the ground we need to be serious about what situations are, about their structure and internal constituents. That is the main job of this chapter. Once we have settled this, we can discuss which kinds of relations between situations correspond to meanings. That will be taken up in Chapter 5.

THE KINDS OF SITUATIONS

In ordinary language the term "situation" is used in a very general way, both for static situations, called *states of affairs,* and more dynamic situations, called *events.* In this book we use the term in the same general way. A different sort of distinction is between *real situations* (parts of the world) and *abstract situations,* abstract mathematical objects used in situation semantics to represent real situations.

Here, then, is a chart with the major categories of situations and the sorts of variables we will use to range over them.

SITUATIONS

	States of Affairs	Courses of Events
Real	s, s', s"...	e, e', e" ...
Abstract	s, s', s"...	e, e', e"...

Abstract situations are subdivided into what we call the *actual,* *factual,* and *non-factual* situations. The actual situations exactly "correspond" to real situations. The factual situations correctly "classify" real situations as far as they go. The ones that get something wrong are non-factual. In this chapter we explain each kind of situation as well as how the abstract ones are constructed from the primitive invariants found among real situations.

A CHOICE OF PRIMITIVES

From both a metaphysical and an epistemological point of view we think of real situations as basic, with objects, properties, relations, and space-time locations arising as uniformities across them. This is not meant to be an exhaustive list of the uniformities humans individuate but a list of the most basic. In particular, it is a list of the uniformities that arise in the interpretation of the more basic parts of language—the parts that convey information by describing a situation or event in terms of uniformities internal to it. Thus we follow the lead of language and take the individuation of objects, properties, relations, and space-time locations as given and restrict our study, for the time being, to those parts of language where we can get by with complex objects that can be built out of these sorts of primitives.

Individuals. We use *a, b,* ... as variables over the collection *A* of individuals. These individuals should not be thought of as idealized points or atoms but as real things. Some individuals have parts that are also recognized as individuals. John's arm is a part of John. It seems likely that the individuation of individuals is in some sense dependent on the properties they have, but that is not an issue we go into here.

We will introduce the term "object" as a technical term so that it is not synonymous with "individual." Individuals are among our primitives. Objects can be complex as well as simple.

Relations. We are given collections of *n*-place (*n*-ary) relations for each $n \geq 0$. The 1-ary relations are called *properties,* like the property of being asleep. They are not words or sets, but properties of the kind recognized by human beings. The 2-ary relations are called *binary relations* and include things like the relational activity of kicking or the relation of being the mother of. The 0-ary relations are called *situational states,* and include, for example, states like the state a location is in when it is raining or when it is noon. We use $\mathcal{R}_n$ for the collection of n-ary relations, and $\mathcal{R}$ for the collection of all relations, that is $\cup_n \mathcal{R}_n$. We use $r, r',...$ to range over the collection $\mathcal{R}$. Note that when we refer to relations, this includes properties as a special case.

Space-time locations. The simpler parts of language do not refer explicitly to instants of time or points of space, but rather refer indirectly, through tense, to connected 4-dimensional regions of time and space. We let L be the collection of all space-time locations, connected regions of space-time.

There are many relations that hold between these space-time locations, relations that human beings recognize. For example, locations may overlap in time or space, or one location may wholly precede another in time. While relativity theory tells us that many of these relations are not absolute, we are going to assume that they are, or that the semanticist stands at some idealized frame of reference. This is not necessary, but it greatly simplifies matters. We will leave it to others to study the effects on semantics of travel near the speed of light. Thus we assume that the spatiotemporal relations are extensional and that there is a fixed fact of the matter about which relations hold of which locations.[1]

We use $l, l',...$ as variables over spatiotemporal locations. We assume that among the extensional spatiotemporal relations are the three relations mentioned above, and use the following notation for them:

$l \prec l'$ l wholly temporally precedes l'
$l \circ l'$ l temporally overlaps l'
$l @ l'$ l spatially overlaps l'

Whitehead and Russell argued that "points" of space and "instants" of time are more abstract than the events that have spatiotemporal duration, and showed how to reconstruct these abstracts out of events.[2] Once carried out, one could then identify each location l with a set of pairs $\langle p, t \rangle$ where p is a point of space and t is an instant of time. It is then possible to define other relations between locations, like:

$l \subseteq_t l'$ l is temporally included in l'
$l \subseteq_s l'$ l is spatially included in l'
$l \subseteq l'$ l is temporally and spatially included in l'.

We will use these relations among locations as well.

For technical reasons we will assume the existence of a largest space-time location l_u (for "universal location"), one that contains every location both spatially and temporally. This is largely a convenience and could be dispensed with.

Putting Things Together: Our Metatheory

We take individuals, relations and locations as primitive, and see how far we can push the theory using only complex objects that can be built out of them. These complexes will be used to classify reality. To carry out this project we must use, either implicitly or explicitly, a metatheory about what kinds of complexes there are and what their nature is. Like most of modern mathematics, our metatheory is a theory of sets and our complexes are set-theoretic complexes. Thus in addition to the above primitives, we will allow sets of such primitives, sets of sets of such, and so forth. Abstract situations will appear along the way, as well as other abstract objects.

When we use the term "set" we are presupposing an underlying set theory, a theory about what kinds of sets exist. We want to use a theory that does not assume the existence of infinite sets (nor make the contrary assumption), so that everything we say about sets will be true when interpreted as being about *finite* sets of primitives, finite sets of these finite sets, and so on.

We do this for two reasons. First, it is an interesting constraint on the theory, one that allows us to see how much we can interpret without using infinite collections of the primitives we have on hand. Or, to put it the other way around, it interests us to see just where in language we have to abandon this constrained metatheory and assume the existence of infinite objects. Second, since the human mind is presumably finite, the situations it perceives should be characterizable in finite terms, one would expect. Thus it would seem that a psychologically plausible theory of simple language use should have an interpretation in terms of finitary objects. We have repeatedly found that this constraint has forced us to confront problems that we would rather have ignored, but the solutions to which turned out to be crucial turning points in the theory.

A word of warning is necessary. While the situations we recognize are small, finite at least, the world is large. There is no reason to suppose, for example, that the collection L of space-time regions is finite. Thus this collection may itself not constitute a set. This is why we have been careful to use the term "collection" in describing A, $\mathfrak{R}$, and L. Our theory must distinguish between sets and collections too large to be countenanced as sets.[3] There are three ways for the reader to approach these issues. One is not to worry about the set-theoretic metatheory, to leave that to us. Another is to think of the word "set" as short for "finite set," "function" short for "finite function," and similarly for all set-theoretic terms. A third, more sophisticated, approach is to work in a metatheory like the theory KPU (of Kripke-Platek admissible set-theory with urelements), one that admits an interpretation in terms of finite objects. It makes little difference here, but the latter is what we have in mind for developing the theory at a more formal level.[4]

ABSTRACT SITUATIONS

At this point our primitives are singled out, but they are in a rather sorry state. We have no way to represent the connection between a real situation and its constituents. Similarly, there is no way to discuss similarities between situations, say all those in which I am sitting. What we need is a means of characterizing a situation in terms of its internal structure. For this we will introduce the notion of a situation-type.

Situation Types

It is important to realize that many situations can be of the same type, that among the invariants across situations are not just objects and relations, but also congeries of such. The relation I now have to my chair, that of sitting on it, is one I have often had in the past and plan to have again in the future. To provide the link between actual situations and their constituents, and to capture the fact that two unique situations can be of more or less the same type, we characterize the internal structure of a situation in terms of its location and what we call its situation-type.

Situation-types enable us to represent the way things stand in a situation, abstracting away from the where and when. Formally, we define a *constituent sequence* to be a sequence $y = \langle r, x_1,...,x_n \rangle$, where r is an n-ary relation ($r \in \mathcal{R}_n$) and $x_1,...,x_n$ are objects. A *situation-type* is an extensional relation s between constituent sequences $\langle r, x_1,...,x_n \rangle$ and 0 and 1, that is a set of pairs $\langle y, i \rangle$ where y is a constituent sequence and i is 0 or 1. We use the informal notation introduced in Chapter 1, where

$s := r, a, b$; yes
r', a, c; no

indicates the relation s:

$\{\langle\langle r,a,b\rangle,1\rangle, \langle\langle r',a,c\rangle,0\rangle\}$.

That is, we use the ": =" notation to spell out exactly what "facts" are in s. By contrast we use the "in" notation,

in s: r,a,b; yes
r',a,c; no

to indicate that the above set of pairs is a subset of s. We use

in s: r,b,a; undefined

to indicate that neither pair $\langle\langle r,b,a\rangle,1\rangle$ nor $\langle\langle r,b,a\rangle,0\rangle$ is in s. For example, if

in s: hungry, Jackie; yes
sleeping, Jackie; no
sleeping, Molly; yes
hungry, Molly; undefined

then s will correctly classify any situation s in which Jackie is hungry and Molly is sleeping but Jackie isn't, regardless of whether or not Molly is hungry. Such a situation might well have preceded one in which Jackie bit Molly.

A situation-type s is *coherent* if the following three conditions are met:

(i) s does not assign two values to any constituent sequence, that is, not both,

in s: $r, x_1,...,x_n$; yes
in s: $r, x_1,...,x_n$; no.

(ii) s does not represent two different objects as being the same, that is, in s: same, a, b; yes implies $a = b$.

(iii) s does not represent anything as being different from itself, that is, not

in s: same, a, a; no.

If (i), (ii), or (iii) fail, s is incoherent. Situation-types s and s' are *compatible* if their union is coherent. The Law of Noncontradiction, a basic "structural constraint," states that actual situations are coherent. But we are getting a bit ahead of ourselves, since structural constraints aren't discussed until later.

In the early days of situation semantics, when we ignored matters of tense, situation-types played a central role.[5] However, as the general theory of meaning emerged, it became clear that we could not give a real account of meaning without accounting for relations between situations that hold at different spatio-temporal locations. So now situation-types play only an auxiliary role, as ways to help characterize situations. They could be dispensed with entirely which would allow us to reserve "situation-type" for what we call in this book event-type.

States of Affairs

A pair $s = \langle l, s_0 \rangle$ of a location l and a situation-type s_0 is a *state of affairs*. The pair $\langle l, s_0 \rangle$ represents a state of affairs in which the facts represented by s_0 hold somewhere in the space of l throughout the time spanned by l. So, intuitively, the state of affairs s is *factual* if

(a) if in s: $r, a_1, ..., a_n$; yes
    then at l, $a_1, ..., a_n$ stand in the relation r;

(b) if in s: $r, a_1, ..., a_n$; no,
    then at l, $a_1, ..., a_n$ fail to stand in the relation r.

Note that this definition does not require a factual state of affairs to have in it everything that is happening at its location. It need only be right as far as it goes; it doesn't have to be exhaustive. In contrast, for the state of affairs s to be *actual* we must have, in addition:

(c) if at l, $a_1, ..., a_n$ stand in the relation r,
    then in s: $r, a_1, ..., a_n$; yes;

(d) if at l, $a_1, ..., a_n$ fail to stand in the relation r,
    then in s: $r, a_1, ..., a_n$; no.

A state of affairs s is *part of* a state of affairs s' if s and s' have the same location and the type of s is contained in the type of s'. Note that the use of "contained in" in this definition just means set theoretical inclusion ($\subseteq$), since situation types are sets of sequences. But "part of" is not inclusion, it is something defined especially for states of affairs.

Among states of affairs there is a special kind that will be particularly important for our purposes, those we call *discourse situations*. A discourse situation is a state of affairs s with exactly one speaker, that is, with exactly one individual b that is saying something. We will give a more extensive definition later. We let $\mathfrak{D}$ be the collection of discourse situations, and use $d, d', ...$ to range over $\mathfrak{D}$. We use a_d for the speaker of d and l_d for the location of d, called the *discourse location*.

Courses of Events

States of affairs are static situations, situations that hold throughout some stretch of time. In general we need to represent change to get at the ever changing course of events that give rise to meaning. We represent these by means of abstract objects we call courses of events.

A *course of events* (*coe,* for short) is a set e of triples $\langle l, y, i \rangle$ where l is a spatiotemporal location, y is a constituent sequence $\langle r, x_1, ..., x_n \rangle$ as above, and i is 0 or 1. A course of events e with $\langle l, \langle \text{biting, Jackie,} \text{Molly} \rangle, 1 \rangle$ in it represents an event where Jackie is biting Molly at the spatiotemporal location l. We use ε for the collection of *coe*'s and use the variables $e, e', ...$ to range over ε.

There is a ploy that is used frequently in set theory, that of representing (extensional) relations as partial functions taking sets as values. We can adopt this ploy here and think of a course of events e as a partial function from locations to situation-types. Namely, give e as a set of triples, let e^* be the function defined by

$l \in$ domain (e^*) iff $\langle l, y, i \rangle \in e$ for some y, i

and for $l \in$ domain (e^*)

$e^*(l) = \{ \langle y, i \rangle : \langle l, y, i \rangle \in e \}$

Thus $e^*(l)$ is a situation type (if defined). In this way we can think of a course of events as a (partial) function from the collection L of spatiotemporal locations to the collection of situation-types. Since a function is a set of ordered pairs, we can also think of it as a set of states of affairs, at most one for any location.

If e_0 and e_1 are *coe*'s, thought of as sets of triples, with e_0^* and e_1^* their associated functions, then e_0 is a subset of e_1 if and only if each state of affairs in e_0^* is part of some state of affairs in e_1^*. Thus we say that e_0 is *part of* e_1, and write $e_0 \subseteq e_1$, if these equivalent conditions hold. This is a notion that will come up repeatedly.

"Course of event" is an official term of the theory, not a purported analysis of the term "event." There is nothing in our definition that ensures that a *coe* really coheres the way an ordinary event like a baseball game does. We don't want to be construed as making a claim about what kinds of events there are in the world. For although every ordinary event can be seen as corresponding to a course of events, there are obviously many disjointed *coe*'s that we would not ordinarily call events, say one that had Russell sitting at a certain location in 1920, me sitting here now, and nothing else. Nevertheless, we will often simply say "events" when we really should say "course of events."

The definition of "course of events" is deceptively simple, for a course of events can itself have incredibly rich structure. Its locations can nest and overlap in complicated ways, and what is going on at the sundry locations can vary in equally complicated ways.

We extend the terminology and notation used for situation types in obvious ways. For example, the course of events e in which Molly was hungry at l, eating at a later l' where Jackie was sleeping, and not hungry at a still later l'' would be defined by:[6]

e: = at l: hungry, Molly; yes
  at l': eating, Molly; yes
     sleeping, Jackie; yes
  at l'': hungry, Molly, no.
  $(l \prec l' \prec l'')$

The following e_0 is part of this e according to the definition of "part of" given above:

e_0: = at l; hungry, Molly; yes
  at l'; eating, Molly, yes

Two *coe*'s are *compatible* if the situation-types assigned to any location common to their domains are compatible. A *coe* is coherent if it is compatible with itself, that is, if it only assigns coherent situation types to the locations in its domain.

SITUATIONS: ABSTRACT AND REAL

Semantics studies the relation between language and the world. Mathematical semantics, or model theory, does this by bringing in mathematical structures (various kinds of abstract objects) that, on the one hand, represent certain aspects of the world, and, on the other, bear certain relations to expressions of the language being studied. It is fairly common practice in mathematical semantics simply to identify the world with the structure that represents it. But this identification hides an important aspect of the whole endeavor, and so we resist it here. This is why we explicitly distinguish real situations from abstract ones that accurately *classify* real situations.

An abstract state of affairs or course of events is a set. It is not perceived, does not stand in causal relations to other abstract situations, and does not occur in nature.[7] Abstract situations have whatever status sets of contingently existing objects have, a topic we will not discuss in this book beyond the negative remarks just made. Real situations are not sets, but parts of reality. They are perceived and stand in causal relations to one another. They comprise what might be called the causal order.

We view *real* situations as metaphysically and epistemologically prior to relations, individuals, and locations. But relations, individuals and locations are metaphysically and epistemologically prior to *abstract* situations. The latter are built out of the former as sets of various kinds. It is important, then, not to confuse real situations with their abstract counterparts. On the other hand, it is also important to understand the theoretical relationship between real and abstract situations. In this section we will introduce certain notions that help clarify this relationship.

First let us recall the primary role abstract situations will play in our theory: they will be assigned to utterances as interpretations. Our theory classifies utterances according to the claims they make about the world, and abstract situations are a tool for identifying and classifying these claims. They are helpful for this purpose to the extent that they have a clear structure themselves and a clear relation to reality.

To promote the use of any system of classification, one must explain how certain abstract objects are to be assigned to real individuals, locations, etc., according to the system. For example, with a system of measurement, say the metric system, one must explain how numbers are to be assigned to individuals. This sort of explanation is what we try to provide in this section. In connecting the system of abstract situations with real situations, we are not defining relations between two parts of our formal theory, but simply explaining how we intend the formal theory to fit onto the world. Of course such an operation carries with it certain presuppositions that are part of the underlying metaphysics. In the case of measurement by grams and liters, these presuppositions are there but not obvious because they are so widely shared and so familiar. People assume that there really are bodies and quantities of liquid and the like to be measured.

Not everyone will share our belief in real situations. We don't offer much in the way of argument for them, beyond whatever overall satisfactoriness the reader may find in our way of looking at things. We

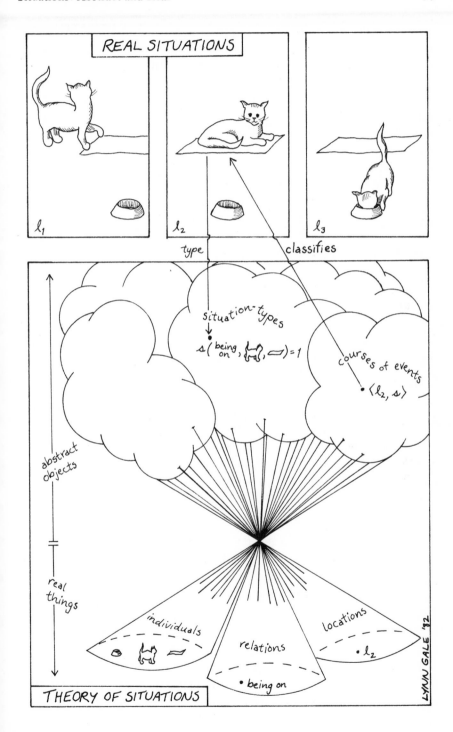

are only claiming to find this view of the world embedded in natural language, not to discover how the world really is, even if we do happen to think the world is the way we describe it.

It is worth noting that for the purpose of this section all that is required is belief in one big situation. Call it "Reality." The need for other situations, parts of Reality, will be spelled out in the section on individuating situations. But it should also be pointed out that one could turn the tables and express skepticism about Reality so long as one admits real situations with certain properties that we will describe. On this view, Reality is only a projection of the real situations we find ourselves in, a projection into one grand idealized situation. Of the two forms of skepticism, the latter seems more reasonable to us, but we won't press the issue here.

In the next subsection we are going to define what we mean by a situational structure, or structure of situations. Of the various situational structures that one can study, some will correspond to the view that there is a maximal real situation, a Reality; others will correspond to the contrary view, that there is no such maximal real situation. Among the former some will in fact have only one situation that is actual. Thus we simply leave the issue open.

Structures of Situations

The following definition is our substitute for the traditional definition of a model-theoretic structure. We will explain the various clauses following the definition.

A *structure* $\mathfrak{M}$ *of situations* consists of a collection M of courses of events with a non-empty subcollection M_0 satisfying the following conditions:

1. Every $e \in M_0$ is coherent
2. If $e \in M_0$ and $e_0 \subseteq e$ then $e_0 \in M$.
3. If X is a subset of M then there is a *coe* e in M_0 such that every *coe* in X is a part of e.
4. If C is any constraint in M then M respects C.

The *coe*'s in M_0 are called the *actual coe*'s of the structure $\mathfrak{M}$, those in M the *factual* coe's of the structure. The last condition (4) will be explained informally below and in detail in Chapter 5.

There are a number of equivalent ways of giving this definition. Notice, for example, that every factual *coe* is part of some actual *coe*, by (3). Also note that every pair e and e' in M are compatible, since by (3), e and e' are part of some actual e'', e'' is coherent by (1), so e and e' cannot conflict. Finally, notice that there might be only one actual situation, though there will always be as many factual situations as there are parts of actual situations. So in general, there are lots of factual situations.

To understand where we imagine these structures coming from, we suppose that there is a nonempty collection E_0 of real situations and a relation *classifies* that holds between abstract courses of events, on the one hand, and real situations, on the other. Objects, relations, and locations provide the connection between real situations and abstract situations. They are uniformities across the former and constituents of the latter. Intuitively, e classifies e if and only if

> if, in e, at l, r, $a_1,...,a_n$; yes,
> then, in e, at l, $a_1,...,a_n$ stand in the relation r;

and

> if, in e, at l, r, $a_1,...,a_n$; no;
> then, in e, at l, $a_1,...,a_n$ do not stand in the relation r.

And we say that e is *factual* if it classifies some real situation e.

By contrast, we say that e *(exactly) corresponds* to e if e classifies e and every e' that classifies e is part of e. In other words, e corresponds to e if it gets everything right that is going on in e. We say that e is *actual* if it corresponds to some real situation.

It should be obvious from this informal account of factual and actual events that conditions (1) and (2) are satisfied, i.e. that every actual event is coherent, and that every part of an actual event is factual. The third condition is a generalization of the intuition that any two factual events are parts of some bigger actual event. Just how strong an assumption the condition turns out to be depends on the underlying set theory. If we take all sets to be finite, then the condition follows from the assumption that every two factual events are part of some actual event.

The last condition is more complex. A realistic account will admit things like natural laws, and natural laws correspond to states of affairs. Such states of affairs we call *constraints*. The point of (4) is that any actual constraint must be respected by what is actually going on. Just how to state this precisely is a bit of a problem, one we solve in Chapter 5.

Reality

We have assumed that there is at least one actual *coe* but have not assumed that there is a largest actual *coe*. If the collection M_0 of actual events is not too large, that is, if it is actually a set, then it will follow from (3) that there is a largest actual event. There are other circumstances that will also guarantee this.

A *coe* w in a structure $\mathfrak{M}$ is *a world (of $\mathfrak{M}$)* if every *coe* of $\mathfrak{M}$ is part of w. Notice that if $\mathfrak{M}$ has a world, it is unique, and a member of M_0 so we call w *the* world (of $\mathfrak{M}$). We do not assume that every structure of situations has a world, though the reader is welcome to make this assumption if it seems appealing. The notion of a world is the mathematical analogue of what we have been calling Reality, the maximal real situation.

We are using an intuitive account of real situations and classification to motivate the formal notion of an actual course of events within a structure of situations. Notice that quite different collections of real situations can give rise to the same factual situations. For, a particular abstract situation may accurately classify two real situations, but exactly correspond to only one of them. Consequently, these different collections would be distinguishable only by which factual situations are also *actual*. Later, when we discuss the individuation of situations, we will see to what extent we are forced to admit more than one real situation.

Persistence

To sharpen intuitions about *coe*'s, to get a glimpse as to how our theory of meaning goes, and to discover some of the problems we have to solve, we introduce some notions that will get analyzed more fully below.

For the time being, think of e_1 being a part of e_2, $e_1 \subseteq e_2$, as meaning that e_2 contains all the information contained in e_1 and maybe more. We'll have to refine this a bit later. Given a collection P of *coe*'s, we say that P is *(simply) persistent* provided:

$e \in P$ and $e \subseteq e'$, implies $e' \in P$.

Information is usually simply persistent. Consider, for example, the interpretation P of my current utterance "I am sitting," odd as it sounds to my wife as she hears me say it to myself. Let me be a and the present location be l.

$P = \{e \mid \text{in } e \text{ at } l: \text{sitting}, a; \text{yes}\}$

This collection is simply persistent. It includes incompatible courses of events, and it includes *coe*'s that get larger and larger, both in the sense of how many locations they are defined on, and how much detail they depict at each location. Some e in P will have everything in World War II just right, where another one will have everything in the history of the world, save for my sitting here, completely wrong.

Further examples of persistent collections can be obtained from the following observations:

1. If e is any *coe*, then the collection of all e' of which e is a part is persistent.
2. The intersection of persistent collections is persistent.
3. The union of persistent collections is persistent.
4. The empty set and the set of all *coe* are persistent.

The reader can easily check these claims. The facts (2)–(4) imply that the persistent collections form what mathematicians call a "topology," a family closed under unions, finite intersections, containing the empty collection and the collection of all *coe*'s. We call this *the topology of partial information.*

We want to apply the notion of persistence not just to the interpretation of utterances but to the interpretation of any meaningful event. In accord with the relation theory of meaning outlined in Chapter 1, let MO be some binary relation on some collection MF of *coe*'s—i.e., MO is a collection of ordered pairs of *coe*'s. We say that MO is *informational* on a situation structure $\mathfrak{M}$ if for each factual $e \in M \cap MF$ there is some factual $e' \in M$ such that $e\, MO\, e'$. (We use "MF" for "meaningful" and "$e\, MO\, e'$" for "e' is a meaningful option from e".)

Examples:

1. Take MF to be the collection of smoky situations and MO the relation that holds between a smoky situation e and a fire e' that would cause the smoke, $e\, MO\, e'$.
2. Take MF to be the collection of assertive utterances and MO the relation that holds between an accurate assertion e and the situations e' it describes, $e\, MO\, e'$.

One of the puzzles we must solve is where these informational relations on structures come from. For now, though, simply take one as given. We can use such a relation to interpret an event e as giving us information, namely that one of the e' such that $e\, MO\, e'$

must be factual if e is. Thus we assign to each $e \in MF$ the collection

$$[\![e]\!]_{MO} = \{e' : e \, MO \, e'\}.$$

We leave off the subscript if no confusion can arise. MO is informational on $\mathfrak{M}$ if $e \in M \cap MF$ implies $[\![e]\!] \cap M$ is non-empty.

When we say that information is persistent, what we have in mind is that $[\![e]\!]_{MO}$ should be persistent.

Examples:

1. Consider an event u, an utterance, in which Sarah says to Jonny, "A dog is biting Molly," conveying information about an actual event e', one where Jackie is biting Molly at a present location l. Here the relation MO is that of Example 2 above. Then $[\![u]\!]$ consists of all those e'' such that for some a

   in e'': at l: biting, a, Molly; yes

                 dog, a; yes

   The actual event e' is one of these, and $[\![u]\!]$ is simply persistent.

2. Contrast Sarah's utterance u with a different event u_1, Joe saying "Jackie is biting Molly." This event has interpretation $[\![u_1]\!]$ which consists of those e such that

   in e: at l: biting, Jackie, Molly; yes

   This collection is also simply persistent. It is more specific about the biter but it doesn't contain the information that she is a dog. So neither $[\![u]\!]$ nor $[\![u_1]\!]$ is contained in the other, though e' is a member of each.

3. Now consider yet a third utterance, Jim's utterance u_2 of JACKIE, A DOG, IS BITING MOLLY. The interpretation of u_2 is the intersection of the interpretations of u and u_1 and so is simply persistent. It contains more information about e' than either u or u_1.

Information is always persistent in some intuitive sense. When this appears not to be the case, it is because our notion of simple persistence is too weak.

Consider the real situation here in my study, now, for example. There is only one dog here and she (call her b) is asleep. Consider the following collections P and Q, candidates for the interpretation of my utterance "The dog is asleep":

    P = the collection of e such that
    in e: at l: dog, b; yes,
                  sleeping, b; yes,

while

Q = the collection of e in P for which b is the only x such that in e at l: dog, x; yes.

The reader can easily check that P is simply persistent, but Q isn't. For there is one very small coe e_0 that contains just two facts, b being a dog and sleeping, but there are situations e of which e_0 is a part where there are dogs other than b and so are not in Q.

P seems inadequate because it doesn't convey the uniqueness. Q conveys the uniqueness, but doesn't seem to qualify as information, since it is not simply persistent. This is a puzzle we must sort out.

INDIVIDUATING EVENTS

Abstract situations are all sets of one kind or another. Sets are individuated by their members, so there are no mysteries about the individuation of abstract situations. Real situations are a different matter. One might begin with an extreme position, that there is only one real situation, Reality. It has no real parts, just aspects, and these aspects are captured by various abstract factual courses of events. Our definitions of classification and correspondence are consistent with this conception. The notion of correspondence is a bit out of the spirit though, since courses of events of manageable size won't correspond to anything.

Why should we believe in more than one real situation? In general, we are led to believe in multiplicities of objects by applying the principle of the indiscernibility of the identical, or its contrapositive, the non-identity of the discernible. If we can find real situations with differing properties, then they must be different situations.

An interesting point emerges here. As long as we limit ourselves to events with individuals, properties, relations, and locations in their domains, and continue to assume that all actual events are compatible, we are not forced to discriminate among real events. It is only when we start dealing with events that ascribe properties to other events, or ascribe relations between events and other things, that we have to discriminate real events that are only parts of Reality.

This is one reason why the semantics of sentences like JOE SAW JACKIE BITE MOLLY assumes a special importance for us. We argue that what this sentence describes is a relation between Joe and a certain event, one in which Jackie was biting Molly. That is, in e: at l: seeing, Joe, e_0; yes,

where

in e_0: at l_0: biting, Jackie, Molly; yes.

We think that attitude reports quite generally describe relations between agents and situations.

The common sense view of the world, the view reflected in ordinary language, recognizes the existence of many real situations. It recognizes dangerous ones, embarrassing ones, unlucky ones, and so on. Besides describing such situations, we explicitly refer to them with nominals like

JACKIE'S BITING MOLLY,

which then appear as components of larger expressions like

JACKIE'S BITING MOLLY DISTRESSED JOE.

It is natural to interpret an utterance of this sentence as describing a state of affairs that involves a relation between Joe and a certain event e_1, the event referred to by the nominal:

in s: at l: distressing, e_1, Joe; yes

People act according to the types of situations they find themselves in and the types of situations they want to be in. Consequently various properties of situations and relations to situations are reflected in talk about human activity. Such talk would be uninterpretable if we did not countenance real situations of appropriate types, real situations distinguishable from one another.

We can emphasize this same point using various sorts of examples. For instance, suppose we say, "Sarah won because Jim helped her." It is natural to interpret this statement as describing a relation between events:

in e: at l: because, e', e''; yes,

where

in e': at l': wins, Sarah; yes

in e'': at l'': helps, Jim, Sarah; yes.

Here we have two abstract events appearing as constituents of another abstract event. Now suppose we also had, for some e''':

in e: at l: because, e', e'''; no.

Assuming that e classifies a real event $\mathbf{e}$, the indiscernibility of the identical requires that we distinguish the real event $\mathbf{e}''$ from $\mathbf{e}'''$; for e" stands, while e"' does not stand, in the "because" relationship to e'. So if e is actual, it seems we must countenance more than one real event.

It is important to insist on the difference between describing a situation and referring to a situation. Situations are described by indicative statements, as in (1), whereas they are referred to by nominals, as in (2), for the purpose of describing some other situation:

(1) JACKIE WAS BITING MOLLY.

(2) JACKIE'S BITING MOLLY DISTRESSED JOE.

Notice that if we want to refer to the state of affairs described in (2), we must again use some noun phrase, for example the nominal in (3).

(3) JOE'S BEING DISTRESSED BY JACKIE'S BITING MOLLY UPSET JONNY.

There is another related issue here. Given that we accept many real events or situations, it is natural to ask just how many there are, how finely they are individuated. For example, Jackie bit Molly on the ear at noon. Jackie's biting Molly distressed Joe. Jackie's biting Molly at noon caused me to miss lunch. And Jackie's biting Molly on the ear caused Molly's ear to be sore.

Let e be the actual event with parts e_1, e_2, e_3, where:

e_1: = at l: biting, Jackie, Molly; yes
e_2: = at l: biting, Jackie, Molly; yes
        noon; yes
e_3: = at l: biting, Jackie, b; yes
        ear-of, b, Molly; yes

Besides e, which of e_1, e_2, and e_3 are actual and which are just factual? The argument from the non-identity of the discernible might be thought to show that they are all actual, since it doesn't seem that Jackie's biting Molly on the ear caused me to miss lunch, or that Jackie's biting Molly at noon caused Molly's ear to be sore.

These are familiar issues in the philosophy of language.[8] For an interesting discussion of these issues surrounding the individuation of events, see Davidson (67a) and Vendler (67). One of the advantages of setting up the definition of situation structure the way we have is that we can avoid taking a definite stand on this issue and look at things either way. We can say that there is one actual event e, and that its factual parts e_1, e_2 and e_3 correspond to its being several different types of events at once. Then we would say that the cause/effect relation between events holds in virtue of their being of various types. This fits very well with our theory of event-types and meaning developed in the chapters that follow. But we could equally well say that all the events are actual and fit together in various ways into larger events. Depending on how we view the matter, we will see the situation structure that represents the world as having fewer or more *actual* events, but the same *factual* events.

CHAPTER FOUR

Event-Types

Let us briefly review the objects identified in our theory so far. First we have various primitives—individuals, locations, and relations. Then we have objects built out of these, including situation types, states of affairs, and courses of events. In getting from the former to the latter, we use "truth values" which we indicate with "yes" and "no," but which are really just the numbers 1 and 0. In this chapter we come to one of the central notions in our theory of situations, what we call "event-types."

The objects of our theory are singled out with four interlocking purposes in mind. We want to classify: (a) real situations, and (b) the relations between them that give rise to meaning and the flow of information. The objects singled out so far serve well for (a) but not for (b). But our interest in classifying situations and meaning grows out of the desire to give a semantic account of human languages. So we must also have objects that classify: (c) expressions in terms of how *they* are used to classify situations, and (d) mental states in terms of how *they* classify situations.

How many different ways do we have of characterizing similarities and differences among courses of events? Our primitives provide one way; the domain of one course of events can overlap that of another in various ways. Situation-types provide another, for one course of events may assign the same type to one location that another assigns to some other location. States of affairs provide another, for two courses of events may assign the same situation type to a single location, and thus share a state of affairs. This is just an instance of a more general way of getting at uniformities, for courses of events contain, as parts, other courses of events.

But one can easily think of many other kinds of uniformities, which we are not yet capable of singling out. Suppose, for example, that two courses of events have different philosophers, at different times, being both tired and hungry. Such situations have something important in common, but none of our concepts will yet pick it out. Similarly, it is clear that abstract situations in which everyone who is kissing something is also touching that thing differ in an important way from those in which someone is kissing something but not touching it. These latter situations violate a fundamental necessary constraint. But we do not yet have an entity in our theory capable of representing that constraint, capable of capturing the similarity shared by the former situations but lacking in the latter.

In this chapter we extend our theory of situations with an eye toward capturing these and other uniformities. We will abstract from courses of events to arrive at entities which we call *event-types*, entities that allow us to capture additional uniformities crucial to any scheme for classifying events, meaning, expressions and mental states. We build up event-types by using the same strategy we have used so far, combining our primitives and our set-theoretic resources to define further abstract objects, and to explain how these objects function in our classificatory scheme.

EVENT-TYPES

Let us begin with the simple case of the philosophers. We have two courses of events that characterize different individuals, at different locations, as being tired, hungry, and philosophers. Intuitively, there is a complex property that both *coe*'s ascribe to these different individuals—namely, the property of being a tired, hungry philosopher. How, using the abstract objects available so far, might we get at this complex property?

The first thing to notice is that it makes no difference whether we view this property as a similarity among individuals, or, dually, as a similarity among situations, those in which the property is had. Consequently, given the machinery developed thus far, it is natural to take the complex property of being a tired, hungry philosopher to be that which is common to all situations of a particular type. This is what we will do. We will identify the complex property with an event-type, the one shared by all situations in which some individual, at some location, is tired, hungry, and is a philosopher.

Now what sort of object should this event-type be? A straightforward approach, though not one we will adopt, is to take the event-type to be a collection of courses of events, those that have in common just what we described:

{e| for some *l* and *a*, in *e*, at *l*; tired, *a*; yes

hungry, *a*; yes

philosopher, *a*; yes}

The underlying strategy here is one often used in philosophy: new entities are introduced as equivalence classes of old ones, classes that are then identified with the feature the old ones have in common. Perhaps the most famous application of this strategy is Russell's definition of cardinal numbers. On this account, the number two, for example, is the collection of all two-membered sets.

There are a couple of problems with this strategy. One is that it misses the role of the individual in the event. Consider, for example, all those events that have, at some location, one individual kicking another:

{e| for some *l, a, b*, in *e*, at *l*: kicking, *a, b*; yes}

This class could not be used to represent the complex property of kicking something, since we would then be unable to distinguish this property from that of being kicked *by* something. This is one sort of problem to be solved.

The other and more serious problem can be illustrated by analogy with Russell's definition of the number two. The collection of all two-membered sets is not itself a set, at least on any current theory of sets. It is simply "too big." And thus it is not an element of any other sets. This makes talking about properties and relations between numbers difficult if not impossible. For this reason, Russell's definition isn't used as the definition of cardinal number. The alternative to Russell's strategy now used is to identify cardinal numbers with canonical representatives, say initial ordinal numbers.[1]

Rather than thinking of an event-type as an equivalence class of events or any other huge collection, we will introduce some purely abstract set-theoretic entities to stand proxy for individuals, locations, and relations. We will then take an event-type to be exactly like a course of events, save that one or more of the abstract proxies may appear in place of genuine individuals, genuine relations and genuine locations. To carry this out, we begin by adjoining to the sets A, $\mathcal{R}$ and L of individuals, relations, and locations, certain purely abstract objects that we call *basic indeterminates:*

$\dot{a}$, $\dot{b}$,...   individual indeterminates
$\dot{r}$, $\dot{s}$,...   relation indeterminates
$\dot{l}$, $\dot{l}'$...   location indeterminates

We will later allow ourselves even more flexibility by allowing certain complex indeterminates that we call *roles.* [2]

Before formally introducing event-types, we should say a few words about the status of these indeterminates. If it is kept in mind that we are simply using mathematical objects to classify reality, indeterminates will not seem ontologically objectionable. Individual indeterminates are not, for example, some strange new kind of individual that we have miraculously discovered. The role they play in the theory, like that of the "truth values" 0 and 1 used in constructing situations types and *coe's,* is entirely classificatory.

It makes little difference exactly which abstract objects we choose for our indeterminates, as long as they don't have a structure that will conflate them with other objects we use. Many objects are generated in the set-theoretic universe, like the pure sets and ordinals, that do not correspond to anything in our semantic theory. Any of these artifacts of the set-construction process could be used as the indeterminates. Alternatively, the indeterminates could be taken as abstract new primitives. Since it isn't important for the purposes of this book to say what we are using as indeterminates, we simply won't make this decision.

We now define *event-type* as we did *coe,* except that individual, location, and relation indeterminates are allowed in addition to the genuine individuals, locations, and relations. Thus, in a trivial sense, every *coe* is also an event-type, one with no indeterminates. We use E, E'... to range over event-types. [3] When we wish to indicate which indeterminates are constituents of E, we display them in a parenthetical suffix. Thus if $\dot{a}$, $\dot{r}$ and $\dot{l}$ are the indeterminates in E, we may indicate this by writing $E(\dot{a},\dot{r},\dot{l})$.

Anchors

Given an event-type E ($= E(\dot{a},...,\dot{r},...,\dot{l},...)$), a function f assigning individuals, relations, and locations to some of the indeterminates in E is called an *anchor* for E. Given an anchor f, we can construct a new event-type by replacing each indeterminate $\dot{x}$ in the domain of f by its value $f(\dot{x})$. We denote this event-type $E[f]$ or, less formally, by $E[a,...,r,...,l,...]$, where $f(\dot{a}) = a,...,f(\dot{r}) = r,...,f(\dot{l}) = l,...$. If f is defined on all the indeterminates in E, then $E[f]$ will have no indeterminates left as constituents, and so will be a course of events. An anchor defined on all the indeterminates in E is called a *total anchor* for E.

The Events of a Given Type

We are now prepared to say what it means for an event to be of a given type, say the type of having a tired hungry philosopher.

Example. Suppose a is a tired, hungry philosopher at l, b a tired, hungry philosopher at l'. If we abstract over a and l in his situation and b and l' in hers, we get the same type of situation, say $E(\dot{a}, \dot{l})$.

in E: at $\dot{l}$: philosopher, $\dot{a}$; yes

tired, $\dot{a}$; yes

hungry, $\dot{a}$; yes

Intuitively, the two separate situations are of this common type because the *coe*, $E[a, l]$ is part of the first, $E[b, l']$ part of the second.

To make this precise, we define what it means for e to be of type E. A *coe* e is said to be *of type* E if $E[f]$ is part of e, for some anchor f. (Such an anchor is necessarily total for E, since otherwise $E[f]$ could not be part of the *coe* e.)

Example. Suppose that in e John is sleeping at l but is awake and eating at $l' \succ l$:

In e: at l: sleeping, John; yes

at l': sleeping, John; no

eating, John; yes

$l \prec l'$

Suppose we want to view e as a special case of those events in which some individual is asleep at l and awake at l'. To abstract away from John we form the event type $E(\dot{a})$

E: = at l: sleeping, $\dot{a}$; yes

at l': sleeping, $\dot{a}$; no

$l \prec l'$

Then e is of type E because $E[\text{John}]$ is part of (though not all of) e. Similarly the *coe* e' that has Frenchie sleeping at l, awake at l', and not eating at l' is of type E. For $E[\text{Frenchie}]$ is the *coe* that has Frenchie sleeping at l and awake at l', and this is part of e'. We might also want to abstract away from the particular locations l and l'. The resulting event-type $E'(\dot{a}, \dot{l}, \dot{l}')$ is given by:

E': at $\dot{l}$: sleeping, $\dot{a}$; yes
   at $\dot{l}'$: sleeping, $\dot{a}$; no
   $\dot{l} \prec \dot{l}'$

The event-type E'[Mary Ellen] $(\dot{l}, \dot{l}')$ is the type of those events that have Mary Ellen sleeping at some l but not sleeping at some $l' \succ l$.

It makes perfectly good sense to ask of a given event e whether or not it is of a particular type E. Consequently, with a given set or collection S of event types, it makes sense to ask which type or types $E \in S$ the event e is of. Every event e is itself an event-type, the type of those events of which e is a part. Consequently, two different events can't be of exactly the same types, for then each would be a part of the other, and hence identical.

SOME PRELIMINARY USES OF EVENT-TYPES

Event-types prove to be extremely useful devices. For one thing, they give us many ways to impose conditions of similarity upon situations and their constituents—individuals, locations, relations. We illustrate a few in this section, as warm-up exercises.

Ambiguity

Certain kinds of ambiguity can be viewed as an ambiguity as to what type of event is being described. Suppose that someone says, "Jim found his raincoat." If the pronoun HIS has JIM as antecedent, then the described event is of the following type:

E: = at $\dot{l}$: finds, $\dot{a}, \dot{b}$; yes
      belongs to, $\dot{b}, \dot{a}$; yes
      raincoat, $\dot{b}$; yes

On the other hand, if HIS is used to refer to someone the speaker is pointing to, then the event need only be of this type:

E': = at $\dot{l}$: finds, $\dot{a}, \dot{b}$; yes
       belongs to, $\dot{b}, \dot{c}$; yes
       raincoat, $\dot{b}$; yes

If someone were to say, "Jim found his raincoat," pointing at Jim without realizing that the person he was referring to was the same Jim he was referring to (the reader can make up a story to make this plausible), then the best way of describing his utterance would be to say that it describes a situation of type E' with both $\dot{a}$ and $\dot{c}$ anchored to Jim. Note that any event of type E is also of type E', but not vice versa. That is, $E[a,b]$ is $E'[a,b,a]$, but $E'[a,b,c]$ is not $E[a,b]$ unless $a = c$.

Incoherent Situations of Coherent Type

The definitions of coherent and compatible courses of events are extended directly to event-types. For example, the event-types E_1 and E_2 below are both coherent, but they are not compatible because their union is incoherent.

$E_1 =$ at l: sleeping, $\dot{a}$; yes
  sleeping, $\dot{b}$; no

$E_2 =$ at l: sleeping, $\dot{a}$; no
   at l': sleeping, $\dot{a}$; yes
   $(l \prec l')$

Certain kinds of incoherence turn on the question of what kinds of anchors anchor the indeterminates in a given event-type. For example, suppose Jim is confused and fails to recognize the sleeping Molly as his brother's dog Molly. When Jim says, "She is sleeping but Molly isn't sleeping," the situation he takes himself to be describing is of type E_1 above, but the situation he is actually describing is:

at l: sleeping, Molly; yes
   sleeping, Molly; no

That is, since he is, in fact, referring to Molly with both SHE and MOLLY, the indeterminates are both anchored to Molly. So the situation is $e = E_1[\text{Molly,Molly}]$.

One of the main advantages of admitting incoherent courses of events is that it allows us to represent the way incoherence may arise from coherent-sounding statements or coherent-seeming beliefs, simply in virtue of the way we are anchored to the world.

Object Types

As another example of the use of event-types, we consider those that classify individuals. An *object-type* is an event-type $O(\dot{a})$ with exactly one individual indeterminate. The example in the last section, obtained by abstracting over John in a certain situation, is one. An object-type $O(\dot{a})$ is *realized by an individual a* if the *coe* $O[a]$ is factual; that is, if a actually has all the properties and stands in the relations to various individuals that it does in $O[a]$. If $O(\dot{a})$ is realized by some individual, then it is said to be *realized.* Otherwise O is called *unrealized.*

Notice that an object-type $O(\dot{a})$ is realized in case some actual event e is of type $O(\dot{a})$. Once we introduce roles in the next section, we will have a mechanism for taking an object-type $O(\dot{a})$ and forming a new indeterminate $\dot{o}$ that can be anchored only to individuals of type O.

Complex Properties and Relations

We have introduced properties and relations as primitives, corresponding to uniformities across real situations. Thus we assume, for example, that there is a property of being a chair and a relation of sitting on, and that these arise out of uniformities across situations encountered in the world. But what about the property of sitting on a particular chair? Intuitively, it doesn't seem right to think of this as a basic uniformity. After all, it might well be a brand new chair, one that no one has ever sat in.

Similarly, while there are basic properties of being tired, hungry, and a philosopher, there seems no reason to suppose that there is a basic property of being a tired hungry philosopher. It seems that just as we are able to construct non-actual situations out of actual individuals, properties, and relations, we are able to construct complex properties out of basic individuals, properties, and relations. We can mirror this ability in our theory by using event-types.

Consider an event e in which a particular individual a is sitting on a particular chair b at l:

in e: at l: chair, b; yes
　　　　　sitting-on, a,b; yes

We can abstract over five different things here, or any subset of them: the location l, either of the individuals, the property, or the binary relation. The characteristic of sitting on chair b at space and time l is adequately captured by the object-type obtained by abstracting over a:

E: = at l: chair, b; yes
　　　　sitting-on, $\dot{a},b$; yes.

The property of sitting on b, however, is independent of location, so we also need to abstract over l:

E': = at $\dot{l}$: chair, b; yes
　　　　 sitting-on, $\dot{a},b$; yes.

We define a *complex property* to be an event-type $E(\dot{a},\dot{l})$ in exactly one individual indeterminate and exactly one location indeterminate. We now have, of course, the solution to the problem with which we began our discussion of event-types. Our tired, hungry philosophers both share the complex propety $E''(\dot{a},\dot{l})$:

E'': = at $\dot{l}$: tired, $\dot{a}$; yes
         hungry, $\dot{a}$; yes
         philosopher, $\dot{a}$; yes

This complex property is also precisely what is common to all situations in which some individual is tired, hungry, and a philosopher; any such situation will be of type E''. Again, once we introduce roles, we will have a mechanism for having an indeterminate; say $\dot{ihp}$, that can be anchored only to tired, hungry philosophers.

A complex n-ary relation is an event-type $E(\dot{a}_1,..., \dot{a}_n, \dot{l})$ in exactly n individual indeterminates and one location indeterminate. As an exercise we leave it to the reader to construct the complex relation of a tired, hungry philosopher yelling at another one.

Referring to Events and to Types of Events

We typically refer to events with nominal expressions like the following:

(1) CAT HAIR BEING IN THE BUTTER
    JACKIE'S BITING MOLLY

(2) THAT HAIR IN THE BUTTER
    THE SITUATION WHEN JACKIE BIT MOLLY

The nominals in (1) are called *gerundive nominals,* those in (2) *derived nominals* (Chomsky, 72). There is an interesting semantic difference between gerundive and derived nominals that refer to events. Gerundive nominals are used to refer not only to events, but also to general types of events. By contrast, derived nominals refer to specific situations or events. Consider, for example, the following sentences. (We use the linguist's "#" notation to indicate that the sentence is semantically odd.)

(3) CAT HAIR BEING IN THE BUTTER ALWAYS MEANS A CAT IS IN THE HOUSE.
    JACKIE'S BITING MOLLY ALWAYS UPSETS THE PERRYS.

(4) #THAT HAIR IN THE BUTTER ALWAYS MEANS A CAT IS IN THE HOUSE.
    #THE SITUATION WHEN JACKIE BIT MOLLY ALWAYS UPSETS THE PERRYS.

The sentences in (4) seem odd because the particular events referred to with derived nominals are not the sort of things that can "always mean" something or "always upset" someone. Notice that if (4b) is read as making sense, it still refers to one event. On this reading, the meaning of (4b) is something like that of:

> (5) THE SITUATION WHEN JACKIE BIT MOLLY ALWAYS
>   UPSETS THE PERRYS (WHEN THEY REMEMBER IT).

We don't want to overstate the case. It's not that gerundive nominals never refer to specific events. In fact, it seems that if ALWAYS is removed from the sentences in (3), the nominal can refer either to a type of event or to a specific event. Another way to see that gerundive nominals can sometimes refer to specific events is to use them with CAUSED:

> (6) SCRUFFY'S BEING ON THE TABLE CAUSED THE HAIR'S BEING IN
>   THE BUTTER.
>   JACKIE'S BITING MOLLY CAUSED JOE TO YELL.

The point we want to make, though, is that the semantics of gerundive nominals in general must deal not just with specific events, but with types of events. Thus the study of something more or less equivalent to event-types is an inevitable part of semantics.

The difference between events and types of events is especially important to understanding the meaning of MEANS. In Chapter 1 we pointed out the different ways the word is used, both for efficient meaning (which we called "event-type meaning"), and for the results of event-type meaning in a particular situation (which we called "event meaning"). Thus the sentence

> (7) CAT HAIR BEING IN THE BUTTER MEANS A CAT IS IN THE HOUSE

can be used to make a general statement about types of situations and what they mean, or about a particular situation where there is cat hair in the butter and what it means. We will delve into the structure of meaning in the next chapter, and into the interpretation of utterances involving sentences like (6), which involve the interaction of MEANS with singular *NP*'s (noun phrases), in Chapter 7.

ROLES

Recall that one problem with taking event-types to be collections of events was that it offered no way to isolate the different roles played by the constituents of events. It seemed we would be unable to distinguish the property of kicking from the property of being kicked, the property of hitting from the property of being hit, and so forth. Yet, these are, in an important sense, different properties, a point obvious to even the most insensitive of us. Roles are not simple uniformities across events, nor simple uniformities across individuals and locations. Rather, they are uniformities across individuals (or locations) together with events in which they occur. So we might think of roles as classes of pairs of events and individuals. The role of the hitter would be the class of pairs of hittings and hitters in them. A role would then be a relation between events and occupants of the roles in those events. But as with event-types, this presents us with foundational difficulties, since such a relation could be a proper class and so not suitable to play the role it was designed for in our theory. With roles, as with event-types, we can circumvent these difficulties by using indeterminates.

Imagine a situation e in which one or more persons are hitting one or more persons. Let us see if we can work out a formal way to identify the hitter in e, the victim in e, and the location of the hitting in e, at least in those circumstances where this makes sense.

Any event that fits the description we have given will be of type $E(\dot{l}, \dot{a}, \dot{b})$:

> E: = at $\dot{l}$: person, $\dot{a}$; yes
> person, $\dot{b}$; yes
> hitting, $\dot{a}$, $\dot{b}$; yes.

The fact that e is of type E seems to suggest an immediate solution to our problem. For we know that there must be some total anchor f such that $E[f]$ is part of e. And so, given this anchor, the hitter is $f(\dot{a})$, the victim is $f(\dot{b})$, and the location of the attack $f(\dot{l})$.

There is only one problem with this solution. For all we know, there may be many ways of anchoring E to e, none of which agrees on the value assigned to the indeterminates $\dot{a}$, $\dot{b}$, and $\dot{l}$. Suppose, for example, that e is actually given by:

> e: = at l: person, a; yes
> person, a'; yes
> person, a''; yes
> hitting, a, a''; yes
> hitting, a', a''; yes
> hitting, a'', a; yes

Here e has each of $E[l, a, a'']$, $E[l, a', a'']$ and $E[l, a'', a]$ as parts. Thus our definition of role will have to recognize that more than one individual can fill a given role, and that a given individual can fill more than one role.

For certain purposes it is convenient to have indeterminates that can be anchored only to certain types of things. For example, given the complex property $E(\dot{a},\dot{l})$ of being a tired, hungry philosopher, and given an inordinate interest in tired, hungry philosophers, you might want to develop a theory of how tired, hungry philosophers behave. And so you might find it convenient to have a special indeterminate, say $\dot{t}h\dot{p}$ so that given a *coe* *e*, $\dot{t}h\dot{p}$ could only be anchored to individuals *a* such that for some *l*, *a* is a tired, hungry philosopher at *l* in *e*. And if your theory of tired, hungry philosophers is to be any help in locating them, you may also want a location indeterminate, say $\dot{l}_{thp}$, to range over locations where there are tired, hungry philosophers. Rather than introduce such indeterminates in an *ad hoc* manner whenever we happen to need them, we introduce a systematic way of forming new indeterminates from old.

Definition of Roles

To give ourselves this flexibility, we extend the definition of "indeterminate" recursively by the clauses:

- Every basic indeterminate is an indeterminate;
- If $\dot{x}$ is an indeterminate and $E(\dot{x},...)$ is an event type, then $\langle \dot{x}, E \rangle$ is an indeterminate.

The latter indeterminate is called a *role* and sometimes denoted $\dot{x}_E$. The event type E is called the *kind of event where the role is defined.*[4]
    Example. If E is given by

$E_{thp}:$ = at $\dot{l}$: tired, $\dot{a}$; yes
                  hungry, $\dot{a}$; yes
                  philosopher, $\dot{a}$; yes

then our special roles are the indeterminates $\dot{t}h\dot{p} = \langle \dot{a}, E_{thp} \rangle$ and $\dot{l}_{thp} = \langle \dot{l}, E_{thp} \rangle$.

Anchors for Roles

Anchoring the complex indeterminates that we call roles is a bit trickier than anchoring basic indeterminates. Consider our example just above, the roles of $\dot{t}h\dot{p}$ and $\dot{l}_{thp}$, and some event-type, say $E(\dot{t}h\dot{p}, \dot{l}_{thp}, \dot{l}')$ given by:

E = at $\dot{l}'$: eating, $\dot{t}h\dot{p}$; yes
         $\dot{l}_{thp} \prec \dot{l}'$

Intuitively, this event-type is supposed to be that in which someone who was a tired, hungry philosopher at one time is eating at a later

time. This means that the anchors for $\overset{\cdot\cdot}{thp}$ and $\overset{\cdot}{l}_{thp}$ are not independent. Suppose, for example, we have an event e in which there is one
tired, hungry philosopher A at a location l_A and another tired, hungry
philosopher B at a location l_B. We must not allow an anchor simulta-
neously to assign A to $\overset{\cdot\cdot}{thp}$ and l_B to $\overset{\cdot}{l}_{thp}$, because the assignment of A
to $\overset{\cdot\cdot}{thp}$ should carry with it the assignment of l_A to $\overset{\cdot}{l}_{thp}$. Similarly, the
assignment of l_B to $\overset{\cdot}{l}_{thp}$ should carry with it the assignment of B to $\overset{\cdot\cdot}{thp}$.

With this example in mind, we extend our definition of anchor
given earlier to roles. A partial function f from indeterminates (both
basic and complex indeterminates) to individuals, locations, and relations is an *anchor* provided that:

- for every basic individual, location or relation indeterminate $\dot{x}$
  in the domain of f, $f(\dot{x})$ is an individual, location, or relation,
  respectively.
- for every role $\dot{r} = \langle \dot{y}, E \rangle$ in the domain of f, f is an anchor for
  each indeterminate in E and $f(\dot{r}) = f(\dot{y})$.[5]

An anchor f for a role $\dot{r} = \langle \dot{y}, E \rangle$ is said to *anchor $\dot{r}$ in e* if $E[f]$ is part
of e.

Exercise. Let the roles of hitter, victim and location of a hitting be
defined by:

$$hitter = \langle a, E \rangle$$
$$victim = \langle b, E \rangle$$
$$\overset{\cdot}{l}_{hit} = \langle \dot{l}, E \rangle$$

where E is

at $\dot{l}$: hitting, $\dot{a}, \dot{b}$; yes.

Let f be an anchor for these three roles which anchors them in the
event e described at the beginning of this section. Verify that $f(hit-
ter)$ is hitting $f(victim)$ at $f(\overset{\cdot}{l}_{hit})$ in e.

Unique Roles

In a given situation, it may not make sense to ask who played *the*
role of hitter, speaker, or whatever, for there may be more than
one individual who plays that role. To get a unique individual or
location, we may have to look at some part of the given situation, a
smaller situation. Consider, for example, a situation s where two
people are speaking simultaneously, each of them saying (1) to the
other.

(1) I AM RIGHT, YOU ARE WRONG

s: = at l: speaking, a; yes
           speaking, b; yes

      addressing, a,b; yes
      addressing, b,a; yes
      asserting, $a,(1)$; yes
      asserting, $b,(1)$; yes

If we are going to give an analysis of this actual event, we must look at its part, for just what is being said here depends crucially on who has the role of the speaker and who that of addressee. It is natural to identify these roles with $\langle \dot{a},D \rangle$ and $\langle \dot{b},D \rangle$ where the kind of event D, where these roles are defined, is:

    D: = at $\dot{l}$: speaking, $\dot{a}$;   yes.
          addressing, $\dot{a},\dot{b}$; yes

In our example, though, there are two speakers and two addressees, two different ways that these roles can be anchored in s' but if we look at just the part s_0 of this situation, that leaves out the fact:

    at l: speaking, a; yes

then we get a factual coe that has a unique speaker, b. Moreover, even though there are still two addressees, there is only one anchor f, so that $E[f]$ is part of s_0:

$$f(\dot{a}) = b, \; f(\dot{b}) = a, \; f(\dot{l}) = l.$$

Given a role $\dot{r} = \langle \dot{x},E \rangle$, what does it mean for some x to have *the* role $\dot{r}$ in some situation e? The examples above should motivate the following definition. If e is a *coe* of type E, then an object x *has the role* $\dot{r}$ in e provided the only ways in which e is of type E have $\dot{x}$ anchored to x. That is, the following two conditions are met:

- e is of type E;
- for every total anchor f for E such that $E[f]$ is part of e, $f(\dot{x}) = x$.

Note that there may be more than one anchor, as in the case of a single victim being hit by three hitters, given below; it is only required that the anchors all agree on the indeterminate $\dot{r}$. In this case we write this uniquely determined value of $\dot{r}$ in e as $\dot{r}_e$.

Example. Let e be an event where three people, a, b, and c, are all hitting a fourth, d, at a location l, but no one else is hitting anyone. Then $victim_e = d$ but $hitter_e$ is undefined, because there is more than one hitter in e.

Contexts

If we are given an event-type $E(\dot{r}_1,...,\dot{r}_n,...)$ defined on some roles $\dot{r}_1,...,\dot{r}_n$ (and perhaps some basic indeterminates), we define a *context for E* to be any situation e where all the roles in E are uniquely defined.[6] In this case, e uniquely determines each of $\dot{r}_{1_e},...,\dot{r}_{n_e}$. We let E_e be the result of replacing the roles in E by the unique things filling the roles. Notice that E_e is an event-type, but only if e is a context for E. Otherwise "E_e" doesn't refer to anything. As a function of e, E_e is essentially partial.

Example. If $E(victim, hitter, \dot{l}_{hit}, \dot{l})$ is the type of event where the victim sues the hitter at some time l later than the time of the hitting, then a context for E will be an event e where there is a unique way of assigning a hitter, victim, and location of hitting. The event e in the previous example is not a context for E, but there are situations that are parts of e and *are* contexts for E. Given such a part e', say one where b is the only one hitting d, then E_e is the event-type in a single location indeterminate $\dot{l}'$, the location of the suing. Note that the hitting need not be part of $E_{e'}$.

Roles play a classificatory role in our theory, not a causal role in the world, so we have a great deal of freedom, at the outset, when we establish that some role $\dot{r} = \langle \dot{x}, E \rangle$, as to which event-type and indeterminate we use. But once we get started, we have to be systematic. In the next section we begin a systematic list of some roles we are going to be using later. Our heaviest use of the notion of a role will be in representing the mental in Chapter 10. We will not go into that in detail here, but we will develop a little more of the machinery we will need when we do.

INDEXED EVENT-TYPES

As we explained at the beginning of this chapter, we need objects in our theory capable of classifying mental states. Like sentences and other meaningful uniformities, mental states are efficient, they enable different people at different locations to perceive, know, and believe different things. Clearly, courses of events themselves don't fill the bill. They correspond to what is seen, known, or believed, independent of how it is seen, how it is known, or how it is believed. They provide objective ways of classifying cognitive agents, not efficient ways, and so do not correspond to efficient mental states.

But event-types are a different matter. As we shall see, event-types don't answer all our needs, but they certainly are a step in the right direction. Consider a Putnam-like example. Harry and Harry$_1$ are in exactly the same mental states. In particular, they are both saying to themselves the sentence GEORGE IS A FOOL. But Harry's use of GEORGE is connected to one person, George, and Harry$_1$'s use of GEORGE is connected to another person, George$_1$. So what they believe is different. Harry believes that e is factual, Harry$_1$ that e' is factual; where

> in e: = at l, fool, George; yes
>
> in e': = at l', fool, George$_1$; yes

Perhaps Harry's belief is right, while Harry$_1$'s belief is wrong. So obviously we can't use what they believe, the states of affairs e and e', to represent what they have in common.

These states of affairs are both of type $E(\dot{a},\dot{l})$, though:

> E: = at $\dot{l}$, foolish, $\dot{a}$; yes

Harry's e is $E[\text{George}, l]$ while Harry$_1$'s e' is $E[\text{George}_1, l]$. So with event types we can begin to bring out what Harry and Harry$_1$ have in common as well as how they differ. They believe in states of affairs which share a type but which are differently anchored. Even here, it should begin to look a bit more plausible that the uniformities across efficient mental states can be captured by a theory based on the structure of external events. A simple theory of belief based on this idea might classify belief states with event-types, and hold that belief involves being in such a state anchored to the world in some way or another.

But it is clear that this sort of theory is still far too simple. Suppose that Alice hits Tom. Both Alice and Tom see this happen, and believe that it happens. So, in a sense, they see and believe the same thing, the event

> in e: = at l, hitting, Alice, Tom; yes.

But clearly the different perspective Alice and Tom have on this event, in virtue of the different roles they play in it, must be reflected in a difference in their mental states. We cannot get at this difference in terms of sameness of type with difference of anchors. We need some way to bring the perspective into the theory. We need some way to classify Alice with other attackers and Tom with other victims, Alice with those who believe they have hit someone and Tom with those who believe they've been hit.

We solve this problem with a systematic use of event-types with distinguished indeterminates. These allow us to capture the differences in perspective, held by, say, someone who is the agent in an event and someone who is merely an outside observer. We set up a special system of roles for this purpose. We will specify certain special roles as fixing the meaning of certain indeterminates. Once these are fixed, any other event-types in these indeterminates will be called *indexed event-types.* We use the term "indexed" because any indexed event-type E gives us a family of event-types indexed by contexts for E, situations that are of the kind where all the constituent roles are uniquely filled:

$\{ E_e : e$ is a context for $E \}$.

The notation E_e indicates, as the reader will recall, that e is a *coe* where all the roles in E are uniquely filled, and denotes the result of replacing the roles in E by the things that fill them.

Located Individuals

The first two of our special roles will employ the event-type LI (for "located individual").

LI: = at $\dot{l}$: present, $\dot{a}$; yes.

We let $\dot{i}$ be the role $\langle\dot{a},LI\rangle$ and $\dot{b}$ be the role $\langle\dot{l},LI\rangle$. We call the role $\dot{i}$ *the agent* and the role $\dot{b}$, *the agent's location.* We use $\dot{i}$ and $\dot{b}$ because of their connection with "I" and "here." A *located individual* is a situation m where these roles are uniquely filled—that is, a course of events m with only one individual present at some location.

As an example of an indexed event-type employing these two indeterminates, we might consider:

E: at $\dot{b}$, hitting, $\dot{i}$, $\dot{a}'$; yes

The special roles we have just set up allow us to use E only to classify events from the perspective of the agent and the agent's location in the world. A context for E is just a located individual m. Thus the type E gives us an operation from located individuals m to the object type $E[\dot{i}_m, \dot{b}_m]$ $(\dot{a}')$, which we also write $E_m(\dot{a}')$. $E_m(\dot{a}')$ is realized by an object, say Tom, just in case the agent $\dot{i}_m$ is hitting Tom at location $\dot{b}_m$.

For another example of the use of LI, consider the indexed event-type E' given by:

E': = at $\dot{b}$, belongs to, $\dot{a}'$, $\dot{i}$; yes

This gives us a function from located individuals m to the object type E'_m ($\overset{.}{a}'$), the type characteristic of those objects that belong to the agent i_m at his or her location $\overset{.}{b}_m$. This in turn gives rise to a function from anchors f for $\overset{.}{a}$ to the state of affairs $e' = E[m,f]$, so that e' is:

at $\overset{.}{b}_m$: belongs to, $f(\overset{.}{a}')$, i_m; yes

We could also use E' to determine a role $\langle \overset{.}{b}, E' \rangle$, the role of belonging to the agent.

Next, let *lft-of* be the three-place relation that holds between x, y and z if x is to the left of y from the perspective of z. Then consider,

E'': = at $\overset{.}{b}$: *lft-of, $\overset{.}{a}$, $\overset{.}{b}$, $\overset{.}{i}$*; yes

Given our located individual m, E'' gives us an event-type E_m ($\overset{.}{a},\overset{.}{b}$) in two indeterminates. Note that if I say, "Alice is to the left of Tom," what I am reporting is that such a relation, determined by taking me as the agent, obtains between Alice and Tom. What is really a three-place relation between Alice, Tom and me appears from my perspective to be a two-place relation between Alice and Tom.

These indexed event-types are crucial in the theory of mental states, because mental states are efficient. This simply reflects, as does my use of "Alice is left of Tom," the fact that we perceive and act on reality from a position within it. We can emphasize this point first with an example not directly related to the attitudes we study.

Consider your ability to tell whether you are sitting or standing. It's easy; you can do it with your eyes closed. But notice that it is not so easy to tell if you were sitting or standing an hour ago. You might have to try hard to remember, or consult your diary. At each time during the day it is easy for you to determine whether you satisfy a certain condition. At twelve o'clock, for example, you have no trouble determining whether you satisfy the condition,

(1) in E: = at 12 o'clock: sits, $\overset{.}{a}$; yes

But it is not easy for you to determine at 12 o'clock whether you satisfy the condition,

(2) in E: = at 11 o'clock: sits, $\overset{.}{a}$; yes

It was easy for you to determine this at 11, though.

There are two ways to look at this phenomenon. An unusual way would be to say that you are constantly gaining and losing abilities as time passes: at 11 you have the ability to tell what position you are in at 11, while at 12 you have the ability to tell what position you are in at 12 but not at 11. In other words you have an ability to recognize (2) at 11 but (1) at 12.

It seems more natural to say that you had the same ability all along, the ability to tell what position you are in. But then the ability conforms not to conditions like (1) and (2), but to the indexed condition:

(3) E: at $\dot{b}$, sitting, $\dot{i}$; yes.

Relative to a context which supplies an agent and a location, this gives us a condition that the agent at the location can easily verify. So now we have a uniformity across agents and locations, one that can be used to represent a simple ability they share.

Notice that we could also have adopted an intermediate position. We might have said that you have one ability, the ability to determine whether *you* are sitting, and that I have another, the ability to determine whether *I* am sitting. That is, for each individual b we could have identified the ability by

(4) in E_b: = at $\dot{b}$, sits, b; yes.

This captures the ability to tell what position b is in at any given time, an ability only b has. But there is certainly a sense in which we all have the same ability. That shared ability is classified by the indexed event-type (3), not by (4). And it is this notion that we need if we are to explain why members of a species, or of a particular linguistic community, have a given ability.

Of course, we can't *identify* the ability with the indexed condition. Abilities are properties of organisms, not event-types or the resulting functions from contexts to events. We simply use the indexed conditions to classify abilities, and they give us a more discriminating way of classifying abilities than either events or event-types by themselves. Note that the discrimination comes not from being a finer grained sort of entity than an event, but an entity that allows us to classify across the grain of events.

The Object of Attention

Before leaving abilities, let's look at a somewhat more complicated example. Consider the ability to identify the object before one in some relatively gross fashion, say to recognize whether or not it is a telephone. Here we introduce a new role $\dot{t}$ (for "this") by augmenting the kind, located individual, with an additional role, the object the agent attends to. Thus we let $\dot{t} = \langle \dot{b}, ALI \rangle$ where:

ALI: = at $\dot{b}$: attending to, $\dot{i}, \dot{b}$; yes

Thus the role $\dot{t}$ determines the role of being the object attended to by the agent in a situation. A situation in which the roles $\dot{i}, \dot{b}, \dot{t}$ are uniquely filled is called an attending located individual. Note that you could have an attending located individual who was not a located individual if there were two individuals present but only one of them attending to something. That is, there is one and only one way to anchor all three of the roles simultaneously to have an attending located individual.

Using this role we could classify the ability to recognize telephones by the indexed event-type E':

E': = at $\overset{\centerdot}{b}$, telephone, $\overset{\centerdot}{t}$; yes

E' gives us a function from attending located individuals to states of affairs in which the object the agent is attending to is a telephone. This entity could be used to classify an ability most of us have, the ability to tell whether the object we are attending to is a telephone.

Finally, let us return to Alice and Tom. Recall that Alice is hitting Tom, so both Alice and Tom see and believe in:

e: = at l, hits, Alice, Tom; yes.

The following indexed event-type can be used to classify the perceptual and belief states that Tom is in, but not those Alice is in:

E: = at $\overset{\centerdot}{b}$, hitting $\overset{\centerdot}{i}, i$; yes
$\qquad$ person, $\overset{\centerdot}{t}$; yes

On the other hand, E' can be used to classify the perceptual and belief states that Alice is in, but that Tom is not:

E': = at $\overset{\centerdot}{b}$, hitting $i, \overset{\centerdot}{i}$; yes
$\qquad$ person, $\overset{\centerdot}{t}$; yes.

The kinds of events we shall use to classify psychological states are all further augmentations of those we have defined here. The indeterminates reserved for these roles are $\overset{\centerdot}{b}$, $\overset{\centerdot}{i}$, $\overset{\centerdot}{t}$, and $\overset{\centerdot}{u}$. We shall call an event type defined on any or all of these four indeterminates a *diagram*.

Two Linguistic Roles

Many roles are played in even the most basic of utterances. We will examine a couple of the simplest here, the roles of speaker and addressee.

Let's look at an example we have used before. Two philosophers, call them A and B, are arguing, each saying "I am right, you are wrong." Obviously there is a way in which A and B are different, for they are making different claims. But there is also a way in which they are similar. This similarity is reflected in the fact that they both sincerely utter exactly the same sentence. How can we characterize the relevant similarities and differences?

Two differences are easy to spot. There are different people speaking, and they claim different things. To get at both the similarities and the differences we isolate a special role, that of the speaker in a discourse situation. Thus we let *speaker* = $\langle \dot{a}, D \rangle$ and *discloc* = $\langle \dot{l}, D \rangle$, where:

$$D: = \text{at } \dot{l}: \text{speaking, } \dot{a}; \text{yes}$$
$$\text{saying, } \dot{a}, \dot{\alpha}; \text{yes}$$

A situation where these roles are uniquely filled consists of a situation where there is only one person present who is speaking, together with the expression uttered. We call these *discourse situations*. We use $d, d'_{...}$ to range over discourse situations, a_d for the agent of the discourse situation, l_d for the spacetime location of the discourse situation, and α_d for the expression.

The first similarity we find is that our philosophers share a *type* of discourse situation, with the same expression

I AM RIGHT, YOU ARE WRONG

playing the role of the expression uttered, at the same time and, for all intents, at the same location. But even if they are speaking at the same time, A and B are in different discourse situations, for the two situations have different agents.

Our two philosophers also believe different states of affairs: s and s':

$$s: = \text{at } l, \text{wrong, } A; \text{yes}$$
$$\text{right, } B; \text{yes}$$

$$s': = \text{at } l, \text{wrong, } B; \text{yes}$$
$$\text{right, } A; \text{yes}$$

There is more similarity than we have captured so far, though, for there is nothing in the similarity described above to show that they each think the other is wrong. They could each be addressing some common third party for all that's been said so far.

We get a beginning on what else they have in common when we notice that the states of affairs believed in share the type:

$$E: = \text{at } l, \text{wrong, } \dot{a}; \text{yes}$$
$$\text{right, } \dot{b}; \text{yes};$$

since,

$$E[f] = s, \text{ where } f(\dot{a}) = A, f(\dot{b}) = B;$$

and,

$E[g] = s'$, where $g(\dot{a}) = B$, $g(\dot{b}) = A$.

But this won't quite do. Imagine a bemused onlooker, who agrees with A. He believes in the same state of affairs as A, and so too a state of affairs of type E. But he isn't in the same mental state as A and B, the one that leads them to say I AM RIGHT AND HE IS WRONG. To get at what A and B have in common with each other, but not with the bemused onlooker, we need to move to an indexed event-type. The kind of event we need is just another augmentation of the located individual, $\dot{u} = \langle \dot{b}, U \rangle$ where:

U: = at $\dot{l}$, addressing, $\dot{a}$, $\dot{b}$; yes

A discourse situation that is of type U is one with an addressee.

The indexed event-type E' needed to classify what is common to the states of mind of A and B is:

E': = at $\dot{l}$, wrong, $\dot{b}$; yes
right, $\dot{a}$; yes;

Just as this indexed event-type yields different events, relative to different contexts, being in the state it identifies results in different beliefs when different people are in it.

SCHEMATA

Event-types classify events as being one certain way. They are adequate as far as they go, but for some purposes we need to classify events as being one of several ways. If I draw a card out of a deck I know that there are 52 possibilities. I know the event is of one of the following 52 types:

E_1: = at $\dot{l}$: Ace-of-spades, $\dot{a}$; yes
E_2: = at $\dot{l}$: King-of-spades, $\dot{a}$; yes
...
E_{52}: = at $\dot{l}$: 2-of-clubs, $\dot{a}$; yes

To classify this sort of situation we need not a single event-type, but a set of them.

Or consider those sorts of situations in which one of two individuals is hitting another, Joe:

E_1: = at $\dot{l}$: hitting, $\dot{a}$,Joe; yes
E_2: = at $\dot{l}$: hitting, $\dot{b}$,Joe; yes.

Then we must represent this type of situation by means not of an event-type but in terms of a set $S = \{E_1, E_2\}$ of event-types.

A *schema* S is a set (!) of event-types. An anchor for a schema S

is an anchor for the event-types in S. If f is an anchor, then $S[f]$ is
the set of all event-types $E[f]$ for $E \in S$. An anchor is a total anchor
for S if it is a total anchor for each $E \in S$. An event e is of *type S*
if it is of type $E[f]$ for some $E \in S$, and some f.

For example, if we let

$$S: = \{E_1, E_2, ..., E_{52}\}$$

then any event of drawing a card from a standard bridge deck will be
of type S. If we take some proper subset, say

$$S': = \{E_1, ..., E_{13}\}$$

then an event of drawing a card will be of type S' just in case the
card is a spade.

All of our remarks about indexed event types extend naturally to
indexed schemata, schemata defined on roles.

The remainder of this chapter can be skipped on first reading without serious problems. It is somewhat technical.

Addition

There are some relatively straightforward ways of combining event-
types and schemata. Given event-types E_1 and E_2 we can form their
sum, $E_1 + E_2$, just taking their union:

$$E_1 + E_2 = E_1 \cup E_2$$

The presence of indeterminates in event-types makes this operation
a bit trickier than one might think. For example, an event e might
be of type E_1 and be of type E_2 without being of type $E_1 + E_2$ (if the
anchors f_1 and f_2 such that $E_i[f_i]$ is part of e disagree as to the value
of some indeterminate). Otherwise, there is nothing unexpected and
the following lemma follows immediately from the definition. Recall
that for a *coe e'*, e' is part of e just in case e is of type e'.

Lemma 1: If f is a total anchor for $E_1 + E_2$, then e is of type
$(E_1 + E_2)[f]$ just in case e is of type both $E_1[f]$ and $E_2[f]$.

Since we can add two event-types, we can add any finite set of them.
But we can also add infinite sets of event-types together, if there are
any. Given any set $F = \{E_i : i \in I\}$ of event-types (not thought of as a
schema, but just a set we want to add together) we can define their
sum by:

$$\Sigma_{i \in I} E_i : = \text{the union of all the } E_i.$$

Of course if F is finite, say $\{E_1, ..., E_n\}$, then this summation is just the
same as $E_1 + ... + E_n$.

Lemma 2. If f is a total anchor for each E_i in F, then an event e is of type $\Sigma_{i \in I} E_i [f]$ if and only if e is of type $E_i[f]$ for each $i \in I$.

Given schemata S_1 and S_2 form their sum by adding together all the pairs E_1 in S_1 and E_2 in S_2. That is:

$$S_1 + S_2 = \{ E_1 + E_2 : E_1 \in S_1, E_2 \in S_2 \}.$$

Lemma 3. If f is a total anchor for $S_1 + S_2$, then e is of type $(S_1 + S_2)[f]$ just in case it is of types both $S_1[f]$ and $S_2[f]$.

We often identify an event-type E with the schema $\{ E \}$ since they classify the same events. Thus we can write $S + E$ for $S + \{ E \}$, which is the set

$$\{ E_1 + E : E_1 \in S \}.$$

Adding more than two schemata is not quite so straightforward. Since we can add two together, we can add any finite number. But we cannot in general add together a set $F = \{ S_i : i \in I \}$ without making some additional set-theoretic assumption, something like the assumption that for any two sets A and B there is a set of all functions from A into B. We won't worry about this here, and assume, whenever we take the sum of a family of schemata, that the family is finite, or that the additional assumptions have been made that allow its formation. We use the construction only rarely.

The Complements of Event-Types and Schemata

Closely related to the notion of two event-types being incompatible is that of two event-types conflicting. Event-types E_1 and E_2 *conflict* if there is a "fact" in E_1 that is assigned the opposite truth value in E_2. Otherwise, they don't conflict. Note that if E_1 and E_2 are compatible, then they don't conflict. The converse does not hold for a couple of reasons. One of the event-types might, for example, claim that two different objects were the same. Then it is not compatible with anything, even itself, though it may not conflict with various other event types.

One reason we need schemata arises out of event-types. Suppose we have an event-type like:

$E := $ at l: hitting, a, b; yes

hitting, b, a; yes

and that f is a total anchor for E. If we know that the situation $E[f]$ is incompatible with some actual situation e, then we know that e is either of type E_1 or of type E_2, where:

E_1: = at l: hitting, a, b; no
E_2: = at l: hitting, b, a; no

But we don't know which. Consequently, to characterize those events that are in conflict with $E[f]$ we need not an event-type, but a schema, a set of event-types. We conclude this section by working out how to complement event-types and schemata to capture this notion of conflicting event-types.

Given a simple event-type E (one with no proper parts), we use $-E$ for the result of replacing 1 by 0 and 0 by 1. Thus, if E is

E: = at $\dot{l}$: r, $\dot{a},\dot{b}$; yes

then

$-E$ = at $\dot{l}$: r, $\dot{a},\dot{b}$; no,

and vice-versa as far as "yes" and "no" are concerned.

Lemma 4. If E is a simple event type and f is a total anchor for E then an event e is of type $-E[f]$ iff e is in conflict with $E[f]$.

If E is an arbitrary event-type, then we define $-E$ to be the schema

$\{-E_0 : E_0$ is a simple part of $E\}$.

Lemma 5: Let E be an event type and f a total anchor for E. Then e is of type $-E[f]$ iff e conflicts with $E[f]$.

Proof. If e is of type $-E[f]$, then e is of type $-E_0[f]$ for some simple part E_0 of E. By the previous lemma, e conflicts with $E_0[f]$ and so with $E[f]$. Conversely, suppose that e conflicts with $E[f]$. Then it must conflict with some simple part $E_0[f]$ and so by the previous lemma be of type $-E_0[f]$ and so of type $-E[f]$.$\Box$

If $S = \{E_i : i \in I\}$ is a schema, we define $-S$ to be the sum

$\Sigma_{i \in I} -E_i$,

if this is defined, which it will be if S and all the members of S are finite.

Lemma 6: Let S be a schema, let f be a total anchor for S and let e be a *coe*. Then e is of type $-S[f]$ iff e is in conflict with every *coe* e' of type $S[f]$.

Proof. A *coe* e is of type $-S[f]$ iff for each E in S, e is of type $-E[f]$. On the other hand, e' is of type $S[f]$ iff there is an E in S such that e' is of type $E[f]$. So suppose e is of type $-S[f]$, e' of type $E[f]$ for E in S. Then by the previous lemma, e and e' must conflict. Conversely, suppose that e is not of type $-S[f]$. Then there is an E in S such that e not of type $-E[f]$. But then e does not conflict with $E[f]$, by the previous lemma, and so with some *coe* e' of type $S[f]$, namely $e' = E[f]$.$\Box$

CHAPTER FIVE

Constraints

A central claim of this book is that meaning resides in the world, in systematic relations of a special sort between different types of situations, and that linguistic meaning is meaning of just this sort. These systematic constraints are what allow one situation to contain information about another. Attunement to these constraints is what allows an agent to pick up information from one situation about another. The aim of this chapter is to make this notion of constraint more precise by giving it a place in our theory of situations.

CLASSIFYING CONSTRAINTS: THE PROBLEM

For all our theory of situations reflects so far, reality is a very loose affair. Though things happen here and there, there is no real connection between them. But according to the theory of meaning outlined earlier, for reality to support intelligent life it must be highly structured. What happens at one place and time must contain information about what has happened or will happen, elsewhere and elsewhen. So we need to provide an apparatus in the theory of situations to characterize this structure.

At the core of our theory is the notion of a *constraint.* Constraints give rise to meaning; attunement to constraints makes life possible. Some constraints are *unconditional* or *ubiquitous,* holding at every location or, equivalently, at the universal location l_u. Other constraints are *conditional,* holding only under certain special circumstances or conditions. Attunement to conditional constraints is as important to an organism's interaction with the environment as is attunement to ubiquitous constraints. But conditional constraints also make error possible, since an organism may rely on these constraints even in the absence of the requisite conditions.

The problem we face in this chapter is to incorporate the notion of constraint into our theory in a way compatible with the various sorts of constraints that we encounter in the world, and in particular those which are important for semantics. In this section we distinguish several categories of constraints that are crucial to our specific project. In distinguishing these categories of constraints, we do not claim to have provided a complete account of this central philosophical notion, but only to have made a first step in developing a realist theory of meaning and information.

Constraints From Our Metatheory

First, we note the constraints that arise out of our definitions and the basic set-theoretic apparatus they presuppose. Our theory requires all situations to meet these constraints, simply because otherwise they would not qualify as situations. Such constraints are worth mentioning because they reflect decisions we have made about how much to incorporate directly into the apparatus of the metatheory.

The set theory we use, Kripke-Platek with urelements, builds in various constraints. In this set theory one starts with the sets of urelements and then, using certain predicative principles, adds any set that can be constructed from those elements already countenanced. As a consequence, a set cannot be a member of itself; by the time it becomes eligible for membership in any set, it is too late to be included in itself. As a consequence of this, courses of events cannot be defined upon themselves, and this is a matter of some importance when we get to the attitudes. So here we have a constraint built right into our set theory. We think it is a good one, reflecting a common sense view of situations, but it is a decision that could have gone the other way. We could have used a set theory without the axiom of foundation, a theory that embodied a different conception of set.

Many similar consequences follow from our metatheory. However, our metatheory is weaker than most, and so builds in fewer assumptions than a standard model-theoretic semantics.

A Basic Metaphysical Constraint

We defined situation types and courses of events as relations rather than functions. This decision allows incoherent situations, in which something both is and is not the case.[1] We decided to allow such situations because they enable us to distinguish between different kinds of inconsistent statements and incoherent beliefs. Consider the following sentences:

> DAD IS FAT AND HE IS NOT FAT.
>
> DAD IS STUPID AND HE IS NOT STUPID.

These statements both describe situations that cannot be factual. If we did not allow incoherent situation types, we would be forced to say that their interpretations were both empty, and consequently that the two statements have the same interpretation. This would itself be unsatisfactory. But once one introduces event types and their anchorings, it becomes increasingly important to admit incoherent events. For, as we saw in the previous chapter, an incoherent event can arise from a perfectly coherent event type by way of an anchor that assigns one object to two distinct indeterminates. This feature will be central to our characterization of a particular sort of incoherent belief.

Once we recognize the possibility of utterances with interpretations that are not in fact the case, which surely we must, there is no obvious reason to discriminate against utterances with incoherent interpretations. It is just important to keep two distinctions in mind. The first is the distinction between real and abstract situations. Incoherence can appear only among the latter. The second distinction is between two relations that an abstract situation can have to reality. It may classify a real situation, and naturally no incoherent course of events can have *that* relation to a real situation. But there is also the relation of interpretation. An abstract course of events can serve to interpret a *real utterance.* This is why we want to allow incoherent courses of events, nevertheless recognizing the constraint that they are never factual.

A very basic constraint, one that underlies the *Principle of Non-Contradiction,* is that *any two actual coe's are compatible.* We have built this into our theory in a roundabout way, by assuming that actual *coe*'s are always coherent, and that any two factual *coe*'s are part of some common actual *coe.* These constraints have been incorporated into our definition of a situation structure.

Constraints on the Structure of Reality

The constraints discussed above are not specific to various properties or relations recognized in natural language, but pertain instead to any system of abstract situations. However, the most important constraints we must deal with are considerably more specific. These constraints are what provide reality with a structure that supports the flow of information in general and linguistic communication in particular. The ones that we focus on are:

- necessary constraints;
- nomic constraints;
- conventional constraints; and
- conditional constraints.

1. Necessary constraints. Constraints that arise from necessary relations holding among the properties and relations that we recognize are called *necessary constraints*. Every woman is a human, every kiss is a touch, and every dog is a mammal. In each case, the first property or relation is a refinement of the second, a finer-grained way of isolating uniformities across situations. There are also relations that hold between properties, on the one hand, and relations, on the other. For example, if someone is eating, that individual is eating something. Similarly, if something is empty, nothing is in it, and conversely. In both cases we have a necessary relation between a property and a binary relation.

Necessary constraints may also arise from the individuation of individuals. Hans is not Robin, even if they look alike and the cooks confuse them. Just so, Highway 101 is not Highway 1, even though there is a stretch of road where the two coincide. Here we can easily imagine reality being carved up differently, in such a way that what we now consider to be two highways with a common part is actually one highway with coastal and inland extremities. Or we might have counted three highways or four where now we count one. But given the way things are carved up, the one highway is not the other, and could not be.

One way to think about mathematics is as the study of a particular class of necessary constraints. Having two individuals present is a property certain situations possess, as is having four. The fact that 2 + 2 is the same as 4 can be viewed as a necessary relation between these properties of situations, no more confusing than the other necessary relations that hold between various properties. Just how much of mathematics can be looked at in this way is not a matter we have given much thought to, but it seems a promising line.

2. Nomic constraints. There are inviolable patterns in nature beyond those which arise out of the individuative process, patterns that are usually called natural laws. We call these patterns *nomic structural constraints.*

In order to be successful, in order to perceive and act in the course of events in which it finds itself, an organism must be attuned to the most important nomic constraints, either implicitly or explicitly. When Sarah throws a basketball, she knows it will come down. This much is explicit knowledge. But what makes Sarah a good basketball player is her extensive *implicit* knowledge of the constraints that affect her, the ball, and the other things around her on the court. When we speak of attunement to constraints, we only assume this sort of implicit attunement.

Nomic constraints are essential to an account of information, since natural meaning depends on them. The usual models for natural laws or nomic constraints are the very general laws of science, the laws we study in physics or chemistry. But it is also important to recognize local nomic constraints, laws that don't hold in all locations, but only in a limited part of reality. Here again the example of Sarah's skill at basketball is helpful. It would be wrong to say that Sarah's behavior manifests an attunement to the law of universal gravitation. For if Sarah were suddenly placed on a basketball court located (say) on the moon, the nomic constraints she is presently attuned to would no longer serve her.

3. Conventional constraints. Another type of pattern that is important in this study is what we call *conventional structural constraints.* These are constraints that arise out of explicit or, more often, implicit conventions that hold within a community of living beings. Examples of this sort of constraint are the relation between the ringing of the bell and the end of class, and the relation between those situations in which someone says "Here's a cookie" and those in which one person gives a cookie to another.

Such constraints are neither necessary nor nomic; conventions can be violated. It is obviously not necessary that the ringing of the bell should mean the end of class, and a sister can tease her brother by saying, "Here's a cookie" when there is no cookie to be had. In spite of this, being attuned to these patterns is crucial to our coping with the situations in which we find ourselves.

Our knowledge of language consists primarily of *implicit* knowledge about *implicit* conventional constraints. That is, to know

English we must know the meanings of the basic lexical items, know how to form sentences and other expressions, and how to use these expressions to convey information, ask questions, give orders, and so forth. This is all knowledge about various conventional constraints that hold within our linguistic community. And it is this implicit knowledge that those of us who study language attempt to make explicit.

4. Conditional constraints. Conditional constraints are not a fourth kind of constraint, as our numbering might suggest. Rather, this classification cuts across the grain of the other constraints. Conditional constraints are those which hold only in certain conditions, whether the constraints themselves be necessary, nomic, conventional, or of some other kind entirely. We have already mentioned one example of a conditional nomic constraint: the constraint to which Sarah is attuned but which would fail her if she tried to play basketball on the moon. Most of the constraints we are attuned to actually take this conditional form. As a species we evolved in a particular setting, one in which certain conditions were, by and large, fulfilled. As long as we stay in a setting where these conditions are satisfied, the constraints to which we are attuned can be exploited to get information about one situation from another. However as we stray from that setting, or if the setting is radically changed, we may mistakenly rely on these constraints in situations where the requisite conditions are not met, thus in situations where the constraints may no longer hold.[2] Let us take a simple example. Consider how a bird determines whether there is an unobstructed path between itself and an observed object. It relies on a simple constraint which, unfortunately, no longer holds with complete universality. In the setting in which birds evolved, seeing something meant that there was an unobstructed path from the observer to the thing being observed. But of course in that setting there were no panes of glass. The bird is attuned to a conditional constraint, one that holds only in situations containing no large pieces of glass. The bird's continued reliance on this constraint will still, for the most part, provide it with accurate information about its surroundings. But the constraint will also, in certain situations, lead it astray.

Similarly, we grow up in a particular linguistic community, one in which a certain language is spoken, with a certain dialect, and with certain local usages and customs. As we move further and further from that community, we will be led astray if we continue to rely on the same conventional constraints to interpret others and to plan what we say. Again, the constraints to which we are attuned are conditional.

An important point to notice here is that as long as we stay within the appropriate environment, we needn't be aware of the conditions at all. Birds don't need any attunement to glass as long as they stay in an environment where there is no glass. And the child doesn't have to be aware of the conditions under which her language is spoken, as long as she stays put and only communicates with those who speak it the way she does. It is only when one wanders out of one's setting that it becomes important to be attuned to the conditions under which the old constraint remains applicable.

In our normal daily activities we constantly exploit what we know of necessary, nomic, and conventional constraints. Consider, for example, the simple act of answering the telephone. The phone rings, and you answer "Hello," expecting someone to respond. First there are the necessary constraints, the properties a thing must have in order to be the kind of uniformity we call a phone. A giant chocolate bar that looks like a telephone is not a telephone—it's a chocolate bar. Then there are the many nomic constraints that allow sound to be encoded by electric impulses and then decoded to give a reasonable facsimile of the original sound. And there are the conventions that govern the use of the phone. People are assigned telephone numbers by convention; we only dial a number when we want to speak to one of the people who have that number; people usually answer the phone when it rings. Naturally the conventions can be violated. Children sometimes dial a number just to pester whoever happens to answer. And of course the conditions under which all this works may break down. For example, the phone may break. No necessary, nomic, or conventional constraints are broken when a phone is out of order. It's just the phone that is broken, and so the usual constraints simply don't apply.

In the following sections we will incorporate structural constraints into our theory of situations, and say just how they give rise to meaning and the flow of information.

CLASSIFYING UNCONDITIONAL CONSTRAINTS

Our first task is to provide a technique that will allow us to classify ubiquitous constraints, those which hold at all locations. We will turn to the question of conditional constraints in the next section.

Involving

Unconditional constraints are facts like other facts, somewhat more abstract, perhaps, but facts nonetheless. That phones work the way they do is a state of affairs. The question is how to get at states of affairs of this sort. We do this by introducing a primitive relation between types of events, the relation of *involving*. We doubt that all structural constraints can be classified using just this one relation, but it will suffice for our purposes here.

Intuitively, one type of event S_1 involves another type of event S_2 if every actual event e_1 of type S_1 is part of an actual event e_2 of type S_2. For example, every event of type E below involves one of type E', because kissing involves touching.

$$E: = \text{at } \dot{l}: \text{kisses}, \dot{a}, \dot{b}; \text{yes}$$
$$E': = \text{at } \dot{l}: \text{touches}, \dot{a}, \dot{b}; \text{yes}.$$

To represent this constraint that kissing involves touching, we use the state of affairs $C0$ given by:

$$C0: = \text{at } l_u: \text{involves}, E, E'; \text{yes}$$

Here the state of affairs $C0$ is the constraint, a course of events with only event-types and the relation of involving in its domain. (Formally, $C0$ is $\{\langle l_u, \langle \text{involves}, E, E' \rangle, [1] l \rangle\}$.)

We define a *simple constraint* to be any state of affairs of the following form:

$$\text{at } l_u: \text{involves}, E, S; \text{yes}$$

where E is an event-type and S is a schema. We will take a *constraint* to be any course of events that has a simple constraint as a part. (We do not need to allow schemata in the antecedent on a simple constraint, since the same effect can be achieved by a set of simple constraints.[3])

Most of our examples will be of the form

$$\text{at } l_u: \text{involves}, E, E'; \text{yes}$$

where E and E' are both event-types.

The idea of a constraint is that it manifests itself in what happens. If constraint $C0$ holds, then every kissing is a touching. Clause (4) in the definition of situation structure (repeated below) builds this connectedness into our theory.

If C is any factual constraint in $\mathfrak{M}$ then $\mathfrak{M}$ respects C.

Without this condition there would be structures of situations in which the constraint $C0$ was actual, but in which there were actual kissings that weren't part of actual touchings.

We will define what it means for a structure of situations to respect a constraint. Before giving this definition, we must explain how an arbitrary constraint C gives rise to the following property of situations and two relations that hold among situations:

- $e_0 \in MF_C$: e_0 is meaningful with respect to C;
- e_0 precludes$_C e_1$: e_1 is precluded by e_0 with respect to C; and
- $e_0 MO_C e_1$: e_1 is a meaningful option from e_0 with respect to C.

We will give definitions of these notions after motivating them with a series of examples.

Example 1. A necessary constraint is that *if one is eating, one is eating something.* Any event in which someone has the property of eating is part of one in which that individual is eating something. Let us use eating$_p$ for the property things have when they are eating, and eating$_r$ for the relation between the eater and the eaten. Then this constraint, which we call $C1$, can be formulated as follows:

$$C1: = \text{at } l_u: \text{involves}, E, E'; \text{yes},$$

where

$$E: = \text{at } \dot{l}; \text{eating}_p, \dot{a}; \text{yes}$$

and

$$E': = \text{at } \dot{l}: \text{eating}_r, \dot{a}, \dot{b}; \text{yes}.$$

An event e_0 is meaningful with respect to $C1$ if someone is eating in e_0; that is, if e_0 is of type $E[l, a]$ for some individual a and location l. The meaningful event e_0 precludes an event e_1 if e_1 is incompatible with e_0; for example, if in e_1, a is not eating at l. Notice that if e_0 is factual, then no other factual event can be precluded by e_0. An event e_1 is a meaningful option from e_0 if in e_1 there is something that a is eating at l. In other words, e_1 is a meaningful option from e_0 if there is a b such that e_1 is of type $E'[l, a, b]$. There will be many different meaningful options from a given event e_0, options in which a is eating different things. Intuitively, if this constraint is actual, and if e_0 is factual, then one of these options must also be factual. That's what it means for a structure of situations to respect this constraint.

Example 2. *Anyone who has a wife is a married man.* We can state this as a constraint $C2$:

$C2$: = at l_u: involves, E, E'; yes,

where $E(\overset{.}{a},\overset{.}{b},\overset{.}{l})$ is

E: = at $\overset{.}{l}$: wife-of, $\overset{.}{a}$, $\overset{.}{b}$; yes

and $E'(\overset{.}{b},\overset{.}{l})$ is

E': = at $\overset{.}{l}$: man, $\overset{.}{b}$; yes
married, $\overset{.}{b}$; yes.

The meaningful situations e_0 are those in which there is an individual a who is the wife of an individual b at some space-time region l. An event e_1 is a meaningful option from e_0 (with respect to $C2$) if b is a married man at l in e_1. Given such a meaningful e_0, it precludes a lot of events e_1 from being factual, namely, any e_1 that is incompatible with e_0 or in which b is definitely not a man or not married at l. That is, it precludes those e_1 of type $-E'[b,l]$. If $C2$ is an actual constraint, and if e_0 is factual, then there must be a factual e_1 that is a meaningful option from e_0. In other words, if it is a fact that individual a is the wife of b at l, then it is also a fact that b is married at l and is a man at l.

Example 3. *There is at most one president of the United States.* Here the border between necessary and conventional constraints is fuzzy. This is clearly a constraint, nonetheless. We can state this as a constraint $C3$:

$C3$: = at l_u: involves, E_0, E_1, yes,

where $E_0(\overset{.}{l},\overset{.}{a},\overset{.}{b})$ is

E_0: = at $\overset{.}{l}$: President-of-U.S., $\overset{.}{a}$; yes
President-of-U.S., $\overset{.}{b}$; yes,

and $E_1(\overset{.}{l},\overset{.}{a},\overset{.}{b})$ is

E_1: = at $\overset{.}{l}$: same, $\overset{.}{a}$, $\overset{.}{b}$; yes.

In connection with E_1, recall that no coherent event can classify two different objects as being the same. Thus if $E_1[l,a,b]$ is factual (and hence coherent), then $a = b$. A situation e_0 is meaningful with respect to this constraint if it has a state of affairs with at least one individual a having the property of being president at some location l (since then $E[l, a, a]$ is part of e_0). Such a situation e_0 precludes any situation incompatible with e_0, and any situation in which some U.S. presidents are classified as not being the same at l. If e_0 is meaningful with respect to C, then e_1 is a meaningful option from e_0 if for any individuals a, b that are president at l in e_0, a and b are classified as the same at l in e_1:

In e_1: at l: same, a, b; yes.

But then, since e_1 is coherent (in virtue of its being compatible with e_0), $a = b$. If the constraint $C3$ is actual, and if e_0 is factual, then so is one of the meaningful options from e_0. Consequently, $a = b$.

Example 4. Let us consider a constraint that employs a schema. *If you toss a coin, it must land either heads or tails, not both.* We will oversimplify things a bit and state the constraint as:

$C4$: = at l_u; involves, E, S; yes,

where

E: = at $\dot{l}$: tossing, $\dot{a}$, $\dot{b}$; yes
   coin, $\dot{b}$; yes,

and $S = \{E_H, E_T\}$, where these event types are given by:

E_T: = at $\dot{l}$: heads, $\dot{b}$; yes
   tails, $\dot{b}$; no,

and

E_H: = at $\dot{l}$: tails, $\dot{b}$; yes
   heads, $\dot{b}$; no

respectively. Any coin toss is meaningful with respect to $C4$. A given coin toss e_0 precludes any state of affairs in which the coin lands with both heads and tails showing, or neither. And an event e_1 is a meaningful option from the coin toss if it is one where the coin has either the heads, not tails, showing, or if it has the tails, not heads, showing.

With these examples in mind, we turn to the formal definitions.

Definitions

Let C be a simple constraint, say

C: = at l_u: involves, E, S; yes.

1. A *coe* e_0 is *meaningful* with respect to C (written $e_0 \in MF_C$) if e_0 is of type E.

2. If e_0 is meaningful (wrt C) then e_1 is a *meaningful option from* e_0 with respect to C (written $e_0 MO_C e_1$) if for every total anchor f for exactly the indeterminates in E, if e_0 is of type $E[f]$, then e_1 is of type $S[f]$.

3. Let e_0 be meaningful with respect to C. We say that e_0 *precludes* an event e_1 with respect to C (written e_0 precludes$_C$ e_1) if e_1 is incompatible with e_0 or if there is an anchor f for the indeterminates in E such that e_0 is of type $E[f]$ but for every extension of f to an anchor g for the indeterminates in S, e_1 is of type $-S[g]$.

To treat the general case where the consequent is a schema, not just an event-type, makes the definitions a little hard to digest. We urge the reader to go back and examine the above examples to see that these definitions give us the desired events as precluded$_C$ and the right ones as meaningful options, MO_C.

If e is any course of events, we write

in e at l_u: MO, e_0, e_1; yes

just in case there is a simple constraint C which is part of e such that $e_0 MO_C e_1$. On the other hand, if C is a part of e and we do not have $e_0 MO_C e_1$, we write

in e at l_u: MO, e_0, e_1; no.

Notice that the presence in e of a simple constraint, say that kissing involves touching, generates a proper class of facts of the above forms. If we tried to identify the constraint that kissing involves touching with a relation between situations—rather than as a relation between types of situations, as we have done—the constraint would be too big to be an object that can enter into relations with other objects. Only by taking constraints to be relations between types of situations which in turn generate relations between situations do we obtain a mathematically coherent notion of constraint. And only then are we able to represent constraints as part of the causal order.

Definition. A structure of situations 𝔐 *respects a simple constraint* C provided for every actual e_0 in 𝔐, if e_0 is meaningful with respect to C then some factual situation e_1 of 𝔐 is a meaningful option from e_0 (wrt C). 𝔐 respects an arbitrary constraint C if 𝔐 respects each simple part of C.

The fourth condition [(4) above] on situation structures is that a structure 𝔐 must respect every factual constraint C. A consequence of this is that if C is a factual constraint then, in the terminology of Chapter 3, the relation MO_C must be informational.

There are a number of consequences of this condition in the presence of the other three. For example, while we have assumed a condition only on actual e_0's (that is, on e_0 in M_0), it follows for arbitrary factual e_0's (that is, for all e_0 in M). Similarly, in the condition that some meaningful option e_1 be factual, we could have required that e_1 be actual and have e_0 as a part. We state this in the form of a proposition, just to review how some of these ideas fit together. It also follows that no factual event can preclude any other factual event with respect to a factual constraint.

Proposition. Let $\mathfrak{M}$ be a situational structure, let C be a factual constraint, and let e_0 be any factual situation that is meaningful with respect to C. Then:

(1) there is an actual e_1 with e_0 as a part that is a meaningful option from e_0 (wrt C).

(2) there is no factual e_2 that is precluded by e_0 (wrt C)

Proof. (1) Since e_0 is factual, there is an actual e'_0 of which e_0 is a part so e'_0 is also meaningful with respect to C. Then there is a meaningful option e'' from e'_0 which is actual. But then there is an actual e_1 that has both e'_0 and e'' as parts, and so is a meaningful option from e_0. (2) Suppose that e_2 is factual but precluded by e_0. Use (1) to find an actual e_1 that has e_0 as part and is a meaningful option from e_0. Since e_1 and e_2 are both factual, they must be compatible, but that contradicts the definition of precluding.□

Humean Structures of Situations

While our fourth condition on situation structures requires that any factual constraint be reflected in what happens, it does not require the converse. That is, there may be nonfactual constraints C that are nonetheless respected by a structure $\mathfrak{M}$. This corresponds to the intuition that not all patterns that happen to hold correspond to real constraints. Some patterns might just be accidental, and accidental patterns do not give rise to meaning.

Humeans might well not agree with this; they might insist that constraints are not additional facts, over and above what happens. To capture this point of view, we define a structure of situations $\mathfrak{M}$ to be *Humean* provided every constraint C that $\mathfrak{M}$ respects is in $\mathfrak{M}$. Restricting attention to Humean structures would be equivalent to taking "involves" as *defined* rather than primitive.

Humean structures satisfy a condition that situation structures in general won't satisfy. In a Humean structure, anything that is not precluded happens. More precisely, if $\mathfrak{M}$ does not contain C, where

$C := $ at l: involves, E, S; yes

(for example, if it contains $-C$), then there is an e in M that is of type $E[f]$ for some anchor f for E, but such that e is not part of any e' in

M of type $S[f]$. The reason this holds is straightforward. If constraint C is not in M, then there must be a counter-instance of C, by the definition of Humean structure.

We think that it would be a serious mistake to restrict our attention to Humean structures. The world is full of meaning but not *that* full. In Humean structures, we would lose the very flexibility that situations have purchased us. Even if there is some deep sense in which the Humean view is correct—and we are not sure it isn't—it is certainly not a view reflected in ordinary language.

We have stated the constraints in this section as though they were universal, as though they held equally at all regions of space and time. But as we saw in the discussion of conditional constraints, this need not be true. To treat conditional constraints, we must bring in the conditions which classify the situations in which they hold. In particular, we will have to bring in the regions where local constraints hold. For an important part of our picture of information is that there are local constraints, which obtain in some locations and provide information there but which don't obtain in other locations and so give rise to error in these.

Some More Sample Constraints

Let's use the notions we have developed to state some further constraints. We continue to beg the reader's indulgence if, for the sake of illustration, we pretend that certain conditional constraints are, in fact, unconditional.

Example 5. *The Law of the Excluded Middle.* This is not a constraint we assume, but we state it as an example of one that some readers will want to assume. For simplicity we will state the law as it applies to a binary relation r. Let E be given by:

$$E: = \text{at } \dot{l}: \text{present}, \dot{x}_1; \text{yes}$$
$$\text{present}, \dot{x}_2; \text{yes},$$

and let $S = \{E_1, E_2\}$ where:

$$E_1: = \text{at } \dot{l}: r, \dot{x}_1, \dot{x}_2; \text{yes}$$
$$E_2: = \text{at } \dot{l}: r, \dot{x}_1, \dot{x}_2; \text{no}$$

Then the constraint is:

$$C5: = \text{at } l_u: \text{involves}, E, S; \text{yes}.$$

Example 6. *Everything is the same as itself.* We can formalize this by requiring that anything present in a situation is the same as itself in some (possibly expanded) situation:

$C6$: = at l_u: involves, E, E'; yes,

where

E: = at $\overset{.}{l}$: present, $\overset{.}{a}$; yes,

and

E': = at $\overset{.}{l}$: same as, $\overset{.}{a},\overset{.}{a}$; yes.

Example 7. *Domains of Relations.* Certain types of relations come with domains. For example, people are the sort of things that have husbands and wives. Women are the sort of people that have husbands, men the sort that have wives. There is obviously a difference between being an unmarried man, one that does not happen to have a wife, and being an unmarried football. Footballs are not in the domain of the relation of being married.

Thus, for example, there is a constraint $C7$ given by:

$C7$: = at l_u: involves, E_1, E; yes

where

E_1: = at $\overset{.}{l}$: married-to, $\overset{.}{a}$, $\overset{.}{b}$; yes

and

E: = at $\overset{.}{l}$: human, $\overset{.}{a}$; yes

Example 8. If someone says, "Here's a cookie," then there is a cookie present. This is a conventional constraint.

$C8$: = at l_u: involves, E, E'; yes

where

E: = at $\overset{.}{l}$: asserts, $\overset{.}{a}$, HERE'S A COOKIE; yes

and

E': = at $\overset{.}{l}$: present, $\overset{.}{b}$; yes
$\qquad\qquad\qquad$ cookie, $\overset{.}{b}$; yes.

An event is meaningful wrt $C8$ if the event is an assertion of HERE'S A COOKIE. The meaningful options are those where there is a cookie present at the spatiotemporal location of the discourse.

Constraints, Meaning, and Persistence of Information

The notions of event-type and constraint allow us to give some content to what we called the relation theory of meaning in Chapter 1.

Consider an actual event e_0 and a factual constraint C. C places requirements on what the larger actuality of which e_0 is a part can be like. An organism that is attuned to C and perceives or otherwise learns of e_0 has the information that this is what the wider world is like. This idea is captured by the relation MO_C between e_0 and the various options e_1 that are left open by C, i.e., those for which

$e_0 \, MO_C \, e_1$ and not e_0 precludes$_C$ e_1.

As in Chapter 3, we denote the collection of all such e_1 by $[\![e_0]\!]_C$. This collection is called the *interpretation of e_0* with respect to the constraint C.

Consider $C0$, our sample constraint involving kissing and touching. If e_0 is an event in which Jonny kisses Melanie at some space-time location l, then any e_1 in $[\![e_0]\!]_{C0}$ will have Jonny touching Melanie at that location. Notice that there will be many such e_1, and that if e_0 is actual *at least one* of the e_1 must be.

Let's return to an example we used repeatedly in Chapter 1: that smoke means fire. We'll need something a bit more specific to start with, say that a smoking building means that there is something inside it on fire. So the constraint is just:

$C: = $ at l_u, involves, E, E'; yes,

where

$E: = $ at $\overset{.}{l}$: smoking, $\overset{.}{a}$; yes
              building, $\overset{.}{a}$; yes

and

$E': = $ at $\overset{.}{l}$: burning, $\overset{.}{b}$; yes
               in, $\overset{.}{b}, \overset{.}{a}$; yes.

Suppose that smoke is pouring from my uncle's lumber yard at l. This event is meaningful with respect to C. Thus according to C, something inside of it must be burning. Any event that has something inside my uncle's lumber yard at l and burning at l will be in the interpretation of this event with respect to C. The burning item might be his tractor, or his truck, or perhaps one of his barrels of paint thinner. But notice that we wouldn't say, "That smoke pouring from my uncle's lumber yard means that his tractor is on fire," at least not if we only had constraint C to go on. We would just say, "That smoke pouring from my uncle's lumber yard means that something in it is on fire." The embedded statement, "something in it is on fire," describes all of the events that stand in the interpretation (with respect to C) of the smoke pouring from the lumber yard. In a later chapter we will use this idea to interpret statements like the above, statements in which one situation is said to mean that φ, or to contain the information that φ.

In Chapter 3 we defined a simple notion of persistence and expressed the conviction that it came close to capturing an important property of information, but showed that it missed in some important way. Notice that for any C and e_0, the collection

$$\{e_1 : e_0 MO_C e_1\}$$

is persistent. However, as we saw in Chapter 3, it does not fully capture the information present in e_0. What is missing is that e_0 can preclude certain events with respect to C. That is why we have defined $[\![e_0]\!]$ as the intersection of this collection with the collection

$$X = \{e_1 : \text{not } (e_0 \text{ precludes}_C e_1)\}$$

This intersection $[\![e_0]\!]_C$ is not in general persistent. For example, the interpretation of a situation e_0 in which Reagan is president, relative to the constraint $C3$, is not persistent, because e_0 is part of some situation in which there are two presidents, such situations being ones that are precluded by $C3$.

Let P and X be collections of coe's. P is *persistent on X* if for any pair e and e' in X, if e is part of e' and $e \in P$, then $e' \in P$. It follows immediately that for any e_0 and constraint C, $[\![e_0]\!]_C$ is persistent on the collection of situations that are not precluded$_C$ by e_0. This is the sense in which information is persistent, available to any creature who perceives e_0 and is attuned to C.

The Flow of Information and Dretske's Xerox Principle

We have concentrated so far on understanding how one situation can carry information about another. However, as the example of Jackie's broken leg shows, many different constraints and intermediate situations may come into play. There we saw that an informational chain began with Jackie's physical situation and concluded in Jonny's cognitive situation. Along the way there was the X-ray, the vet's cognitive situation, and the vet's utterance.

In examining the flow of information, Dretske isolates an important regulative principle, the one he recognizes as "inherent in and essential to the ordinary idea of information, something that any *theory* of information should preserve" (81, p. 57). He calls this principle the "Xerox Principle," after its most obvious illustration, and states it as:

Xerox principle: If A carries the information that B, and B carries the information that C, then A carries the information that C.

[81, p. 57]

On our account, information is relative to constraints. One constraint may be involved in extracting the information that B from the situation in which A, and an entirely different constraint may be required to extract the information that C from the situation in which B. To extract the information that C from the situation in which A requires both constraints, or perhaps a new constraint which short-cuts the two steps. The Xerox Principle amounts to the claim that the relation of involving is transitive. In other words, if the following constraints are factual:

$C1$: = at l_u: involves, E, E'; yes
$C2$: = at l_u: involves, E', E''; yes,

then so is:

$C3$: = at l_u: involves, E, E''; yes.

To incorporate Dretske's insight into our theory, we could either add this as a fifth condition on situation structures or state it as a higher-order constraint by introducing event-type indeterminates, E, E', E''. The latter approach appeals to us, but we won't go into that here, and so won't build it in.

As we have already observed, organisms don't really have to be attuned to ubiquitous or unconditional constraints to learn from their environment. Conditional constraints are good enough, as long as the conditions are met in the vicinity of the organism. Of course, strictly speaking, these constraints will not be factual. But nonfactual constraints and the meaning relations to which they give rise are still extremely important. This is because attunement is often, perhaps always, to such nonfactual constraints. And when it is, the interpretation of an event may not be information contained in the event, but misinformation contained in it. We return to this point in the last two chapters of the book. For now, let us turn to the formalization of conditional constraints.

CLASSIFYING CONDITIONAL CONSTRAINTS

We will not try to spell out a full-blown theory of conditional constraints here, but simply sketch the way we think the theory should go.

We begin by moving from ubiquitous constraints to local constraints, ones that hold only through some limited region l of spacetime. Suppose we have a simple ubiquitous constraint $C(\dot{l},\dot{a},\dot{b})$ of the form:

C: = at l_u: involves, E, E'; yes

where E and E' are given by:

E: = at $\dot{l}$: $p,\dot{a}$; yes
E': = at $\dot{l}$: $r,\dot{a},\dot{b}$; yes
$q,\dot{b}$; yes

If C is factual and an organism is attuned to C, then the organism can learn from the fact that some object has property p, that the object stands in relation r to some b with property q. A vulture can learn from the fact that a lion is eating in the distance that it is eating something that will provide nourishment for the vulture. A person can learn from the fact that someone is a father that he is married to a woman.

A typical problem, one that arises in both of these examples, is that the constraints are not factual, though they do hold under certain conditions that obtain widely. Some misguided scientist might discover a vulture poison that didn't bother lions. And though the second constraint worked quite well in the environments where the authors grew up, it doesn't work any more.

Let's consider the case where the constraint $C(\dot{l},\dot{a},\dot{b})$ is not factual but holds at locations l_0 within some limited region of spacetime—say, all those that temporally precede some location l. Then the factual constraint is not C but C':

C': = at l: involves, $E + E_1$, E'; yes,

where E_1 is:

$\dot{l} \prec l$.

Notice that if an organism lives entirely before l, it can learn just as much from its environment using the nonfactual constraint C as it could using the factual constraint C'. Only if it survives into l will it be led to make mistakes, to get misinformation by exploiting C. As long as the situations the organism finds itself in meet the condition of preceding l, then things will be fine.

For a different type of condition, suppose the above constraint $C(\dot{l}, \dot{a}, \dot{b})$ is not factual but C'' is:

C'': at l_u: involves, $E + E_2, E'$; yes,

where

E_2: = at $\dot{l}$: p', $\dot{a}$; yes.

In other words, as long as a has both properties p and p', it must be related by r to some b with property q. Again, as long as the organism remains in an environment where everything has property p', or everything with property p has property p', then constraint C will do just as well as C''.

With these examples in mind, we offer the following definitions. Given a simple constraint C

at l_u: involves, E, S_1; yes

and an event-type E', we define $C + E'$ to be the constraint

at l_u: involves, $E + E', S_1$; yes.

Given an arbitrary constraint C and schema S we define $C + S$ the set of all $C_0 + E'$, for C_0 in C and E' in S. We define a *conditional constraint* $C|S$ to consist of a pair $\langle C, S \rangle$ where C is a constraint and S is a schema, called the *condition* of the conditional constraint. The conditional constraint $C|S$ is factual if $C + S$ is factual. Thus, in the above examples, the conditional constraint

$C|(l \prec l)$

is factual if C' is factual, and the conditional constraint

$C|(\text{at } \dot{l}: p', \dot{a}; \text{yes})$.

is factual if C'' is factual.

An event e is meaningful with respect to $C|S$ provided it is meaningful with respect to $C + S$, and e' is a meaningful option from e with respect to $C|S$, written,

$e\, MO_{C|S}\, e'$

provided it is a meaningful option from e with respect to $C + S$. Similarly for "precludes."

There are some interesting issues involving conditional constraints and the flow of information. Imagine two actual conditional constraints $C_1|S_1$ and $C_2|S_2$. The first constrains situations of type S_1, the second those of type S_2. Suppose that C_1 is used to get the information that φ from an event e_0, and suppose that C_2 is used to get from there to the information that ψ. The Xerox Principle says that e_0 should contain the information that ψ. But if we combine C_1 and C_2, we obtain a constraint $C_3|(S_1 + S_2)$, one that constrains situations of type $S_1 + S_2$. What's interesting is that there is nothing to ensure that there are many, or even any, situations of type $S_1 + S_2$. And even if there are, there is nothing to ensure that anyone could be attuned to $C_3|(S_1 + S_2)$. Imagine a constraint that only applies up to and including the stroke of midnight, December 31, 1999, and another that holds from that instant on. Individually these may be perfectly reasonable conditional constraints, of the kind individuals actually exploit to pick up information. But there is a real question about the combination.

CONSTRAINT-TYPES AND INDEXED CONSTRAINTS

Getting hit by a rock involves getting hurt. Let us see what tools we have at hand to represent this constraint in useful ways. First, there is the simple ubiquitous constraint C given by:

$$C := \text{at } l_u: \text{involves}, E, E'; \text{yes},$$

where $E(\dot{a}, \dot{b})$ and $E'(\dot{a})$ are given by

$$E := \text{at } \dot{l}: \text{hitting}, \dot{b}, \dot{a}; \text{yes}$$
$$\text{rock}, \dot{b}; \text{yes}$$
$$E' := \text{at } \dot{l}: \text{hurting}, \dot{a}; \text{yes}$$

This is a good example of a conditional constraint, since the actual constraint is conditional on the thing being hit being alive, among other things. But since only living things are attuned to constraints (one supposes), we can let this condition take care of itself.

Notice, however, that this is not really the constraint that a given individual a needs to be attuned to just to avoid getting hurt by rocks. For that end, individual a need only be attuned to the constraint C/a given by:

$$C/a := \text{at } l_u: \text{involves}, E[a](\dot{b}), E'[a]; \text{yes}$$

where the indeterminate a in the event-types are anchored to a. However, this is not quite what we want either, if we want to capture what a knows that makes him avoid getting hit by rocks. After all, a and a' react differently if they are both attuned to C/a and see a rock coming at a. Individual a ducks, whereas a' might yell "Look out!" or chuckle, depending on her relation to a. Again we need a technique for representing an *efficient* mental state, one that leads each of us to duck when we see a rock coming our way.

What is required is some way to capture types of constraints, uniformities across constraints. Specifically, we need a way to capture the uniformity across all the various C/a, for different a's. Or, returning to the original constraint C, we need to represent the *type* of constraint one gets by anchoring the indeterminate $\dot{a}$ to some individual. To represent this type of constraint we will write $C/\dot{a}$. Given C as above, $C/\dot{a}$ is an event-type, the type of all constraints C/a for some a. In specifying a constraint-type $C/\dot{a}$ we use the notation

$$C/\dot{a} := \text{at } l : \text{involves}/\dot{a}; E, S; \text{yes}$$

to indicate that the indeterminate a must be anchored to some individual a before we get the schemata $E[a]$ and $S[a]$ such that $E[a]$ involves $S[a]$. The resulting constraints might be actual for some individual, but not for others.

To characterize what people know who know that getting hit by a rock always hurts, then and there, we really need an event-type that employs the roles $\dot{i}$ and $\dot{h}$:

$$C/\dot{i},\dot{h} := \text{at } l_u : \text{involves}/\dot{i},\dot{h}, E(\dot{i},\dot{h},\dot{b}), E'(\dot{i},\dot{h}); \text{yes},$$

where

$$E(\dot{i},\dot{h},\dot{b}) := \text{at } \dot{h} : \text{hitting}, \dot{b},\dot{i}; \text{yes}$$
$$E'(\dot{i},\dot{h}) := \text{at } \dot{h} : \text{hurting}, \dot{i}; \text{yes}.$$

In general, an *indexed constraint* is a constraint-type $C/\dot{x}$ where $\dot{x}$ is an indeterminate or set of indeterminates that have been assigned special roles. These indexed constraints will be used to represent what agents know when they know how to maneuver in the world.

We can also use constraint-types to give us interesting object-types. For example, some individuals are happy when they are eating chocolate, some aren't. We can characterize those who are by the following constraint-type $C/\dot{a}$, a particular object-type.

$$C/\dot{a} := \text{at } l_u : \text{involves}/\dot{a}, E, E'; \text{yes}$$

where

E: = at $\overset{\bullet}{l}$: eating$_r$, $\overset{\bullet}{a}$, $\overset{\bullet}{c}$; yes

chocolate, $\overset{\bullet}{c}$; yes

and

E': = at $\overset{\bullet}{l}$: happy, $\overset{\bullet}{a}$; yes.

PART C

Situation Semantics

CHAPTER SIX

Sentence Meanings

In Part A we sketched a view according to which the structure of reality arises out of the interaction of perceiving, acting organisms with limited parts of their environment, i.e., real situations and events. The invariants differentiated by an organism provide the internal structure of situations the organism encounters, at least that part of the structure displayed to the organism. Information can only be information *about* this structured reality. Information is relative to constraints, whether conditional or unconditional, that hold between types of situations, and they provide information for an organism only if the organism is attuned to the constraints. Information conveyed by linguistic means was seen within this general picture.

In Part B we developed a theory of situations that allowed us to give some mathematical precision to this view of reality. Having put all the machinery of our theory of situations in place, it is time to return to the problems of natural language discussed in Chapter 2.

The linguistic meanings of expressions in a language are conventional constraints on utterances. To study semantics is to attempt to spell out these constraints, to spell out what it is the native speaker knows in knowing what utterances of his language mean. There are many ways one might try to do this. Our strategy is to adopt the thesis discussed in Chapter 2, that the primary function of language is to convey information. Thus we focus on a relatively straightforward type of information-conveying utterance: one in which a speaker uses an indicative sentence assertively and thereby conveys information to a single listener.

Neither the thesis nor the strategy is new. What is new is the mathematical theory of situations now at our disposal to classify the meaning of such assertions. Thus, given an indicative sentence φ, we think of the meaning of φ as a relation $u \, [\![\varphi]\!] \, e$ between situations u in which φ is uttered and situations e described by such utterances. This relation constrains both u and e.

The constraints $[\![\varphi]\!]$ puts on the described situation e are what is traditionally studied in model-theoretic semantics. The constraints it puts on the utterance u are harder to get at but are at least as important. For instance, we don't convey information simply by uttering the words:

HE IS WRONG.

Among many other things, we must be talking *about* someone and we must be referring to that person with HE. In the past the various constraints language puts on the domain of its meaning relation were usually seen not as part of semantics proper, but as part of the study of speech acts, speaker intentions, knowledge and beliefs. Our perspective on meaning forces us to take to heart the criticisms leveled against traditional semantics by speech act theory. We must pay systematic attention to both sides of the meaning relation, u as well as e.

Some of the constraints placed on the utterance u are not very problematic. For example, indexical and deictic reference—who the speaker is referring to with a particular use of I, YOU, or HE—can be incorporated without too much difficulty. These are the kinds of constraints we take up in this chapter and the next. Others are more problematic. For example, a speaker cannot communicate information she doesn't have, so one constraint on u is that the speaker have certain information. But the notion of having information is no simple matter; it is much like knowing or believing, and so is what we call an attitude. Indeed, having certain information turns out to be a most important attitude. So, in focusing on assertive utterances that convey information, we must take out advances on several topics to be discussed in Part D, where we discuss the attitudes.

DISCOURSE SITUATIONS AND SPEAKER CONNECTIONS

In this chapter we are going to work out the semantics of some simple sorts of English utterances, those in which the sentence φ consists of a name or pronoun followed by a verb phrase, along with conjunctions and disjunctions of such. We consider verb phrases that are in the present or past progressive, and that consist of either an intransitive verb or a transitive verb followed by another name or pronoun. Our main example in this section will be the sentence

(1) JACKIE IS BITING MOLLY.

The discussion will be informal, though we include an appendix that describes an artificial language which illustrates the points we make here.

As we have emphasized, an expression like (1) is efficient. It can be used over and over by different speakers, at different times, about different Jackies and Mollys. Imagine a specific utterance u of (1). Suppose that in u Joe says to Jonny, "Jackie is biting Molly," thereby accurately describing an actual situation s that he wants Jonny to do something about, Jackie being Jonny's dog. Here we have two distinct situations, an utterance u involving Joe and Jonny, and another situation s involving a couple of dogs. These situations are somehow related by virtue of the meaning of (1). We must uncover the crucial features of u, and the meaning of (1) that enables u to describe s. Or, to put it in our own terms, we must describe the uniformities across utterances like u, the uniformities across situations, like s, and the constraints that hold between them, and make u mean s. It is these uniformities and constraints that we begin to uncover by extracting from utterances their *discourse situations* and *speaker connections*.

Discourse Situations

A "discourse situation" consists of the more or less public aspects of an utterance; it involves who is speaking, when and where, what words are being uttered, and to whom. To make this intuition precise, we will employ the notion of a role developed in Chapter 4. We already have several linguistic roles at our disposal, and can put them together using the event-type DU, the sum of types D and U introduced earlier:

$$DU: = \text{at } \dot{l}: \text{ speaking, } \dot{a}; \text{ yes}$$
$$\text{addressing, } \dot{a}, \dot{b}; \text{ yes}$$
$$\text{saying, } \dot{a}, \dot{\alpha}; \text{ yes}$$

We can now take our linguistic roles to be the following:

$$\textit{speaker} = \langle \dot{a}, DU \rangle$$
$$\textit{addressee} = \langle \dot{b}, DU \rangle$$

Jackie is biting Molly.

Joe's utterance.

$disc\text{-}loc = \langle \mathring{l}, DU \rangle$
$expression = \langle \mathring{\alpha}, DU \rangle$

A situation d in which there is a unique way to anchor these roles is called a *discourse situation*. Thus every discourse situation is of type DU and, further, has a unique speaker, a unique addressee, and so forth. For simplicity, we will abbreviate *speaker$_d$* (that is, the unique individual speaking in discourse situation d) as a_d, addressee$_d$ as b_d, disc-loc$_d$ as l_d, and expression$_d$ as α_d. In our example, these roles are filled by Joe, Jonny, the location of the utterance, and sentence (1), respectively.

There is something involved in saying (1) that is so obvious as to go almost unnoticed, but which actually assumes some importance as the theory develops. Saying (1) involves saying the words that constitute it in the right order. More generally, there is a necessary structural constraint on saying: a_d saying a compound expression ($\alpha\beta$) at l_d involves a_d saying α and β at sublocations $\mathring{l}'$ and $\mathring{l}''$ of l_d with $\mathring{l}' \prec \mathring{l}''$. (We leave it to the reader to write out the constraint more formally.) This constraint requires that any utterance u of a compound expression ($\alpha\beta$) have parts u' and u'' that are utterances of α and β respectively, all the way down to basic expressions.

In our example, then, part of what is involved in Joe's saying (1) at l_d is his saying the words that constitute (1) in the right order at appropriate sublocations of l_d.

In u: at l_1: saying, Joe, JACKIE; yes
    at l_2: saying, Joe, IS BITING MOLLY; yes
    $l_1 \prec l_2, l_i \subseteq l_d$

Combining this with other obvious constraints shows that if d is to be factual, then there must be factual discourse situations d_1 and d_2, that are also parts of u:

d_1: = at l_1: speaking, Joe; yes
             addressing, Joe, Jonny; yes
             saying, Joe, JACKIE; yes

d_2: = at l_2: speaking, Joe; yes
             addressing, Joe, Jonny; yes
             saying, Joe, IS BITING MOLLY; yes

Note that these really are discourse situations, ones in which the speaker and addressee are the same as those of d though the location and expression are different.

This is all quite general. An utterance u of a sentence φ gives us not just one discourse situation d for φ that is part of u, but also discourse situations d_α for every constituent expression α of φ, discourse situations that are also parts of u. Notice, too, that if a word like JACKIE or SHE is used twice (possibly to refer to different individuals), the two uses will be in different discourse situations since they occur at different times. Thus, part of what the utterance gives us is the set

$\{d_\alpha : \alpha \text{ is } \varphi \text{ or a constituent of } \varphi\}$

of discourse situations. Whenever we pair d with some expression α, we will assume that d is a discourse situation in which α is uttered.

The Role of Referent and Speaker Connections

So far we have nothing to connect the utterance u with the situation s it describes; the dogs Jackie and Molly have yet to enter the picture. Here is where the meaning of English and the speaker's connections to the world begin to make a contribution. We are assuming that Joe is speaking English and that his utterance is about his dog Molly and Jonny's dog Jackie. It is a structural constraint on utterances of English that if the name JACKIE is used appropriately, it must refer to

an individual, named Jackie. (We will not consider cases in which
JACKIE is used as a common noun in this section.)

Generally, to use a name or pronoun properly, a speaker must
refer to someone. With pronouns there are two ways this can happen:
a pronoun may either have some other noun phrase as an antecedent, and so pick up its referent indirectly, or else it may be used
deictically, and so refer directly. Names are simpler in this respect,
since they can only refer directly. The first step in getting at the
situation described by the utterance as a whole is to find the individuals referred to by the uses of names and the deictic uses of pronouns. What we need is an individual with the role of referent.

We can construct the role of the referent by employing a simple
augmentation of DU. We let $\dot{ref} = \langle \dot{a}_1, REF \rangle$, where REF is the event-
type:

REF: = at $\dot{l}$: speaking, $\dot{a}$; yes
       addressing, $\dot{a}$, $\dot{b}$; yes
       saying, $\dot{a}$, α; yes
       referring-to, $\dot{a}$, α, $\dot{a}_1$; yes

We will call a situation c in which the role $\dot{ref}$ is uniquely filled a
referring situation. Clearly, any referring situation will also be a discourse situation, or else contain a discourse situation as a part. If in
c the speaker uses a noun-phrase α to refer to a unique individual,
$\dot{ref}_c$, this individual is called the *referent* of α in c. We write $c(\alpha)$ for
the referent of α in c.[1] In our example, we see that it is not d_1 that
gets Jackie, Jonny's dog, into the picture, but something a bit bigger:

c: = at l_1: speaking, Joe; yes
      addressing, Joe, Jonny; yes
      saying, Joe, JACKIE; yes
      referring-to, Joe, JACKIE, Jackie; yes

It is due to the fact that $c(\text{JACKIE})$ = Jackie that Joe's utterance is
about Jonny's dog. Similarly, there will be a referring situation in
virtue of which Joe's use of MOLLY refers to his own dog Molly, a
situation c such that $c(\text{MOLLY})$ = Molly.

Both of these referring situations are part of what makes utterance u the utterance it is, one that describes the situation it does.
Similarly, though more simply, since the verb BITE is unambiguous,
Joe is using BITING to refer to the relational activity of biting. And
finally, he is using the present tense marker IS to refer to some location l' temporally overlapping l_d.

In u: at l_2: referring-to, Joe, IS, l'; yes
     (where $l_d \circ l'$)

In this particular example each word can be seen as having a referring function, as providing a referring situation c that is part of the
utterance. This is rather unusual. Many words (like prepositions and
determiners) do not refer so much as tell us how to combine other
things referred to in an utterance to get at the described situation.
And often words that do refer do so indirectly, as in the case of pronouns with antecedents. But for those words α that *are* assigned referents by u we use $c(\alpha)$ for the referent.

Thus we see that an utterance gives rise to a partial function from
referring words α to their referents $c(\alpha)$. This function is called the
speaker's connections in the utterance. It is this function that links
the utterance u to the described situation s:

in s: at l': biting, Jackie, Molly; yes

where $l'(= c(\text{IS})) \circ l_d$, Jackie = $c(\text{JACKIE})$ and Molly = $c(\text{MOLLY})$.

If a speaker uses a name more than once, the uses will be at different locations, and so the connections depend on which location is
under consideration. In this case, our notation will not serve us very
well. If the word is used twice, say at locations l_1 and l_2, we use subscripts $c(\alpha_1)$ and $c(\alpha_2)$ for the referent in the referring situations c_1
and c_2 at l_1 and l_2 respectively. For the most part, we will just avoid
this issue by assuming that names are only used once in a given utterance.

It is instructive to see what happens when the role of referent is
not filled properly. Let us fill all of the roles above except that of the
referent of JACKIE, getting the event-type:

E: = at l_1: speaking, Joe; yes
          addressing, Joe, Jonny; yes
          saying, Joe, JACKIE; yes
          referring-to, Joe, JACKIE, *ref*; yes

There are two ways the role *ref* might fail to be filled in our utterance. First, Joe might not be referring to anything at all, the event
might not be of type E. For example, Joe might simply be making
up the name. Then his utterance would not describe any situation at
all. The sentence would still be meaningful since it can be used to
describe real situations. But in the case we are imagining, Joe's utterance carries no information about a described situation.

A different problem would arise if the utterance provided no unique referent for JACKIE, say if there were two Jackies that Joe was referring to at once. Perhaps the two Jackies look a lot alike and Joe has always assumed they were the same dog. Suppose one is Jonny's dog (Jackie$_1$) while the other is presently biting Molly (Jackie$_2$). Now which Jackie should we take Joe to be talking about? Jackie$_2$, the dog he has just seen biting Molly? Then why bother to tell Jonny? Or is he talking about Jackie$_1$? If so, he is clearly mistaken, since Jonny's dog is sleeping peacefully at home.

The most sensible thing to say here seems to be that the utterance has two interpretations, depending on which of its parts we are considering, the part where Jackie$_1$ plays the role of referent, or that in which Jackie$_2$ plays this role. Yet it also seems that a proper utterance of (1) would not involve this sort of thing, but would require that the expression JACKIE be used to refer to a unique Jackie.

We are going to consider only utterances where names are used properly. This will allow us to use a partial function c to represent the speakers connections arising from the various referring situations that are part of the utterance.

We have been looking at our example from the speaker's perspective. When we switch to that of the addressee, there is an obvious problem. Let us imagine two different situations. In the first Jonny knows just who and what Joe is talking about, and comes to believe as a result of Joe's statement that Jackie is biting Molly. In the second, though, we suppose that Jonny believes Joe, but that he has never seen or heard of Molly before, that this utterance is Jonny's first "encounter" with Joe's dog. Then what Jonny knows is that the situation being described by Joe is of the following type E, where we replace Molly by an individual indeterminate $\dot{b}$:

$E := $ at l': biting, Jackie, $\dot{b}$; yes.

There are many events of this type besides the actual one that Joe is describing, say one where Jackie is biting the little girl next door. This event is not one described by Joe's utterance, but since it is of the type E, it could be for all Jonny knows.

A more pervasive case is where the exact location of the described event is unclear. Then we could say that as a result of the utterance, Jonny knows the event to be of type $E'(l)$:

In E': at l: biting, Jackie, Molly; yes.
$$l_d \circ l$$

Again, there are many such possible situations, at different places around the world, and only some of them are described by Joe's statement. While the interpretation of Joe's utterance consists of just those situations actually described by him, these examples should convince the reader that this omniscient perspective does not automatically preclude us from accounting for the gap between what Joe says and the information Jonny is able to pick up.

In general there are many factors in an utterance that affect its interpretation, including things like stress, intonation, dress of the speaker, season of year, weather, and so on. However, it seems that the three most influential factors have been isolated: the expression, the discourse situation d and the speaker connections c. We begin our study with these first three parameters of linguistic meaning. Rather than write $u[\![\varphi]\!]e$, we write $d,c[\![\varphi]\!]e$.

COMPOSITIONALITY AND THE MEANING OF PHRASES

Part of the task of semantics is to account for the productivity of language, the relation between the meanings of expressions and the meanings of their parts. We have skipped right over this problem in our discussion of (1), moving directly from the connections to the described situation.

The constituent expressions that go into making up a sentence are not usually sentences but noun phrases (*NP*'s), verb phrases (*VP*'s), determiners (*Det*'s) and the like. Uttering such expressions in isolation does not describe a situation, so we must decide how these meanings fit into our general account of meaning. Let's look at some examples and then return to the general issue.

Tensed VP *Meaning*

Consider the meaning of the tensed verb phrase IS BITING MOLLY, a uniformity across the meaning of such diverse sentences as

> JACKIE IS BITING MOLLY
>
> SHE IS BITING MOLLY
>
> THE DOG WITH THE BROKEN LEG IS BITING MOLLY
>
> THE DOG WHO IS BITING MOLLY IS ANGRY

What is common to a meaningful utterance of any of these sentences is that the speaker is describing or exploiting a situation in which some individual is biting Molly. Thus we can view the meaning of the tensed *VP* as a relation between discourse situations, connections, individuals, and courses of events:

$d, c \llbracket \text{IS BITING MOLLY} \rrbracket a, e$
    iff
in e: at l: biting, a, Molly; yes

where Molly $= c(\text{MOLLY})$ and $l(= c(\text{IS})) \circ l_d$.

The meanings of the related VP's

    WAS BITING MOLLY

    ISN'T BITING MOLLY

    WASN'T BITING MOLLY

are similar. For example,

$d, c \llbracket \text{WASN'T BITING MOLLY} \rrbracket a, e$
    iff
in e: at l: biting, a, Molly; no

where Molly $= c(\text{MOLLY})$ and $l(= c(\text{WAS})) \prec l_d$.

The Setting for an Expression Provided by an Utterance

With these examples in mind, let us consider the general issue of the meaning of expressions that are not sentences but only constituents of sentences. While it is true that uttering a tensed VP in isolation does not describe a situation, uttering one as a suitable part of an assertive utterance u does provide situation elements that contribute in a systematic way to the description of e. The other parts of the utterance will provide an individual that fits together with the VP interpretation.

If we think of the utterance of an expression α as taking place in the context of an assertive utterance u, then u provides not just a discourse situation and connections, but other situational elements σ that the utterance of α helps combine into the described situation e. In the case of a tensed VP, this setting σ is just an individual, but for other types of expressions, the settings will be more elaborate. Thus, we can think of the meaning of α as a relation $d, c \llbracket \alpha \rrbracket \sigma, e$ between discourse situations, connections, a *setting* σ provided by other parts of the utterance, and a described situation.[2] This is the format in which we present our discussion of the meaning of subsentential expressions.

To get a better feel for the notion of a setting, let us examine what the various tensed VP's we discussed above have in common.

The Meaning of Tenseless VP's

Consider first the meaning of the tenseless *VP* BITING MOLLY, a uniformity across all of the above meanings. We see that the setting σ in which this expression is used provides not only an individual (which we now write a_σ) but also a location l_σ and a truth-value tv_σ of either 1 (yes) or 0 (no):

$d, c \, [\![\text{BITING MOLLY}]\!] \, \sigma, e$

iff

in e: at l_σ: biting, a_σ, Molly; tv_σ

where Molly = $c(\text{MOLLY})$. The reader might want to see how the meanings of such *VP*'s can be conjoined and disjoined so that they capture the correct uniformity across the meanings of sentences like those of

JACKIE WASN'T BITING MOLLY OR BARKING.

Here it is important to note that this sentence means roughly the same as,

JACKIE WASN'T BITING MOLLY AND SHE WASN'T BARKING.

Meanings of Tenseless Sentences

Expressions like

JACKIE BITING MOLLY

JACKIE BITE MOLLY

act like sentences syntactically, but they are semantically incomplete since they have no tense marker. They are well-formed constituents of sentences like:

I SAW JACKIE BITING MOLLY,

I SAW JACKIE BITE MOLLY,

and so must have meanings that are systematically related to those of their parts. We propose to identify the meanings of these expressions with relations on discourse situations d, connections c, a location l_σ provided by their setting in some larger utterance, and described situations.

$d, c \, [\![\text{JACKIE BITING MOLLY}]\!] \, l_\sigma, e$

iff

in e: at l_σ: biting, Jackie, Molly; yes,

where Jackie and Molly are the individuals determined by the speaker's connections c.

A Remark on Compositionality

In determining the linguistic meaning of a subsentential expression, we are guided by a version of the principle of compositionality. The intuition behind this principle is that an expression α makes a systematic contribution to the meanings of expressions that contain it and so, in particular, to the meanings of sentences φ in which it occurs. The meaning of φ is a conventional constraint $C(\varphi)$ on utterances and described situations. In describing the meaning of φ as a relation $u[\![\varphi]\!]e$ we are really describing the meaningful option relation $MO_{C(\varphi)}$ that this constraint gives rise to.[3] But if we step back and think abstractly of the meaning of φ as a constraint, and hence as an abstract state of affairs, then it becomes clear that the meanings of expressions other than sentences are just uniformities across these constraints. Just as changing the discourse situation or connections brings about a systematic change in the interpretation of an utterance, so too changing an expression α in φ to some other expression α' brings about a systematic change in the meaning of φ. And just as keeping d and c fixed but changing the sentence uttered effects a systematic change in the interpretation, so, too, keeping α fixed but changing the sentence in which it occurs effects a systematic change in meaning. This is what gives rise to the uniformity that we capture in the linguistic meanings of subsentential expressions.

Notice that not every expression α is sensitive to each of the four coordinates d, c, σ and e of the relation $d, c[\![\alpha]\!]\sigma, e$. An expression that constrains d in a nontrivial way is called *discourse situation sensitive,* or *dss* for short. These are expressions like I, YOU, tensed verb phrases and the like. Others we call *discourse situation insensitive,* or *dsi.* Expressions that depend on the connections in a nontrivial way are called *connection sensitive,* others are *connection insensitive.*

THE MEANING OF NAMES AND PRONOUNS

The examples of the last section show the basic structure our rules for linguistic meaning will take. The comments at the end of the section show that the account we gave was still incomplete, even for expressions as simple as those we considered there. Let us now turn to the meanings of pronouns and proper names, building on our discussion of *VP* meanings.

The Meaning of I

A representational account of linguistic meaning tries to find, for the meaning of I, some mental representation of the self, or some rule that assigns to each speaker such a representation. This strikes us as unnecessarily mysterious. Indeed, from our perspective, I has a particularly straightforward meaning. Whenever I is used by an English speaker a_d in some discourse situation d, it stands for that speaker:

$$d, c [\![I]\!] a_\sigma, e \text{ if and only if } a_\sigma = a_d$$

This is just what a person must know to use the word correctly, and to understand other people's use of the word. What more could we ask? I is *dss* but connection insensitive.

The Meaning of YOU

The meaning of the singular pronoun YOU is similar to that of I except that it designates b_d the addressee in d, instead of the speaker.

$$d, c [\![\text{YOU}]\!] a_\sigma, e \text{ iff } a_\sigma = b_d.$$

We are only considering the singular pronouns and so the singular use of YOU. YOU, like I, is *dss* and connection insensitive.

Though the speaker and location of an utterance are usually easily determined, the addressee may not be obvious—especially if there is more than one person present besides the speaker. There are cues that listeners use in determining the addressee, such as noticing who the speaker is looking at, but there don't seem to be any hard and fast rules. Basically, it's just up to the speaker. This suggests that a more refined analysis might want to make the meaning of YOU both *dss* and connection sensitive.

Names

We want the meaning of a name β to be a relation between utterances of β and individuals it is used to refer to. The simplest account would simply be:

$$d, c [\![\beta]\!] a_\sigma, e$$

iff

$$c(\beta) = a_\sigma$$

This account is in the spirit of the accounts of proper names advanced recently by Donnellan and Kripke. They emphasize (in our terminology) that the properties that the speaker or others may associate with the referent of a name are not part of the interpretation. Names are not hidden descriptions (Donnellan 70, Kripke 72). We think this is basically the right spirit to be in, but that the above account of $[\![\beta]\!]$ won't quite do. We will simply mention the problem here, and then give a modified account at the end of the next chapter.

First, a preliminary point. Meiland (Meiland 70) has emphasized the importance of the often ignored fact that many people have the same name, and Burge (Burge 73) has noted that names are often used as common nouns:

> HE IS THE DAVID KAPLAN OF THE MEDICAL SCHOOL, NOT THE DAVID KAPLAN WHO WROTE "DTHAT".

Used in this way, DAVID KAPLAN designates a property which all David Kaplans have, being a David Kaplan. The problem is that possession of such a property is part of the information about the referent that we can pick up from the utterance of a name, and there is nothing in our account that explains this. Suppose I introduce you to Joe by saying, "This is Joe." Then you will have the information that Joe is a Joe. It would have been inappropriate for me to introduce him in this way, if he were a Fred or a Nigel. But our account has not required that $c(\beta)$ be a β. For now, we shall set this problem aside, but at the end of the next chapter we show how to resolve it, without abandoning the basic insights of Donnellan and Kripke.

As we remarked earlier, if the name β is used twice in a given utterance, say at l' and l'', then the speaker connections will be determined not just by the use of the name, but by the name as used at the given location, and such uses may well disagree. It will only be at the restricted locations l' and l'' that it will make sense to talk about "the" referent of β. We will simplify things by assuming that this doesn't happen, though realizing that it actually does is important for understanding some puzzles about belief and names. The same sort of problem comes up with tense.

The Meaning of Third-Person Pronouns

The third person pronouns (IT, HE, HIM, SHE and HER) are used to refer to things with which the speaker is connected. They can either pick up their referents by going directly through the speaker or by having some other noun phrase as an antecedent. The two uses can be illustrated with:

(1) THE CAT SCRATCHED THE DOG THAT BIT HER.

In one case, the speaker uses the pronoun HER to refer to some female not mentioned elsewhere in (1). Perhaps the speaker is using HER to refer to another dog, say Molly, who has been bitten by Jackie, the dog the cat scratched. In this case the utterance u has connections c with

$c(\text{HER}) = $ Molly.

In another case the speaker may use HER to refer to the individual described by THE CAT. Imagine that Jim utters (2) in the course of re-telling a story about a cat he has never seen. Jim doesn't connect HER directly to the cat; instead, his use of HER picks up its referent by having the noun phrase THE CAT as antecedent. To represent these uses of the pronoun we will employ the expressions (1.0) and (1.1) respectively:[4]

(1.0) THE CAT$_1$ SCRATCHED THE DOG THAT BIT HER$_0$.
(1.1) THE CAT$_1$ SCRATCHED THE DOG THAT BIT HER$_1$.

These subscripts do not mean that we have different pronouns, HER$_0$ and HER$_1$, or that HER has two meanings. They only serve to indicate different uses of the pronoun in different types of utterances. This will be discussed at greater length in the next section.

The meaning of the third person pronouns is given by the following rules:

$d, c [\![\text{IT}_1]\!] a_\sigma, e$ if and only if $c(\text{IT}_1) = a_\sigma$
$d, c [\![\text{HE}_1]\!] a_\sigma, e$ if and only if $c(\text{HE}_1) = a_\sigma$
$d, c [\![\text{SHE}_1]\!] a_\sigma, e$ if and only if $c(\text{SHE}_1) = a_\sigma$

The account of pronouns, like our account of names, will be supplemented at the end of the next chapter. There we will explain how a use of SHE, for example, can convey the information that the individual referred to is a female. This feature is similar to the way a use of JOE conveys the information that the person referred to is named Joe. (The meanings of HIM and HER are the same as those of HE and SHE, respectively.)

LOGICAL FORM AND THE WAYS OF USING AN EXPRESSION

Sentence (1) of the last section was ambiguous, and so we replaced it with sentences (1.0) and (1.1). Or should we say "sentences"? What sorts of expressions are (1.0) and (1.1)? They certainly don't look like ordinary English sentences. Let us consider a somewhat more interesting example that involves attitudes:

(2)   JON THINKS THAT JOHN SAID THAT HE WAS WRONG

(2.0) JON_1 THINKS THAT $JOHN_2$ SAID THAT HE_0 WAS WRONG

(2.1) JON_1 THINKS THAT $JOHN_2$ SAID THAT HE_1 WAS WRONG

(2.2) JON_1 THINKS THAT $JOHN_2$ SAID THAT HE_2 WAS WRONG

Expression (2.0) indicates a use of sentence (2) in which HE acquires its referent, independently of the referent for JON or JOHN. In contrast (2.1) indicates a use in which HE has JON as an antecedent, and so automatically picks up its referent from the speaker's referent of JON. Similarly for (2.2) and JOHN. Our introduction of expressions like (2.0)–(2.2) forces us to broach, once again, the issue of logical form and its role in a semantic theory.

To a student of a typical logic course, the logical form of an English sentence φ is an expression φ^* of some artificial language $\mathcal{L}$ (usually first order logic), an expression whose truth conditions, as given by the semantics of $\mathcal{L}$, capture the teacher's intuitions about the truth conditions of the original English sentence φ. A sentence that speakers classify as semantically ambiguous will have two nonequivalent logical forms. The traditional goal of studying the "logical forms" of expressions is to lay bare the logical properties of an English sentence, properties thought to be hidden by the syntax of English and by the meanings of the so-called nonlogical words.

Many linguists have a quite different idea about logical form. They see logical form as part of the grammar of a language, as input to the semantic interpretation component of the language (see Chomsky, 81, for a view similar to this). In this sense (2.0)–(2.2) can be seen as approximations to the various logical forms of (2).

Our perspective on meaning suggests that the traditional emphasis on the possible ambiguity of *sentences* puts the cart before the horse. What should be primary is the interpretation of utterances; sentences exist only as uniformities across utterances. The simple fact of the matter is that the sentence

(3) JOHN SAID THAT HE WAS WRONG

can be used in two quite different ways. The sentence is a uniformity across different types of utterances, one where HE picks up its referent automatically along with the preceding use of JOHN, the other where it doesn't. As a result, sentence (2), in which (3) is embedded, can be used in three distinct ways. Any particular utterance of (2) must use (2) in one of these three ways. To know which situations are described by a particular utterance of (2) we must know in which of these ways it is being used. This in turn requires that we know in which way sentence (3) is being used, that is how (3) is embedded in (2).

If we are to think of the meaning of an expression as a relation between utterances of the expression and situations described by those utterances, we must admit that there is more that goes into an utterance than we have recognized so far. Our interpretations of sentences like (2) and (3) just aren't fine grained enough as invariants across utterances. These considerations show that our theory must adopt one of two tactics. We call these the fine-grained expression approach, and the added parameter approach.

Fine-grained expressions: Assign meanings to invariants across situations that are more fine grained than the sentences of the language. In our example this would correspond to assigning meanings to something like (2.0)–(2.2) rather than to (2). One might want to call these refinements of an expression its logical form.

Added parameter: Assign meanings to sentences of the language (like (2)) but find other uniformities across utterances to act as ways of uttering the expression. These additional uniformities would then be an additional parameter of meaning, getting us from the meaning of the sentence to its interpretation.

It would be nice if there were *explicit* ways of uttering otherwise ambiguous expressions, explicit techniques, say, for disambiguating sentences like (2). For example, you could imagine that the speaker had to point to the referent of a pronoun, or had to hold up a certain number of fingers, indicating which of the earlier names was the antecedent. Language, however, is just extremely flexible. There don't seem to be any fixed rules for indicating whether an utterance uses (2) one way rather than another. Consequently, if we are to adopt the added parameter approach, the parameter must in general be a rather abstract feature of the utterance.

It is easy to see that there is no *essential* difference between the two approaches. A theory employing either tactic can be converted into a theory employing the other. Given a theory of the first type, we can turn it into a theory of the second type by simply using the fine-grained expression of the first theory as the added parameter of the second. And given an added parameter theory, we obtain a theory with fine-grained expressions by taking the expressions of the new theory to be ordered pairs $\langle \alpha, w \rangle$ where α is an expression of the old theory and w varies over the added parameter.

Whichever approach one chooses, part of what a semantic theory should make explicit are the various ways a single expression can be used. For example, a semantic theory of English should make explicit the fact that although (3) can be used in two different ways, one of these alternatives is not available with (4):

(4) HE SAID THAT JOHN IS WRONG.

In (4) the pronoun HE cannot automatically secure its referent along with the subsequent use of JOHN. This is not to say, however, that no utterance of (4) will have HE and JOHN referring to a single individual. Imagine that Michael is going around the room pointing to people who have said that John is wrong. He might point at John and say "He said that John is wrong," perhaps not realizing that the man he is pointing at is John. Thus it's not that the noun phrases in (4) can't co-refer, it is just that (4) can't be used in such a way that they *automatically* co-refer, the way (3) can." In this respect (4) differs from (3). And this is the sort of fact that a semantic theory needs to make explicit.

Since the fine-grained expression and the added parameter approaches are formally equivalent, we are free to choose between the two according to the overall simplicity of the resulting theory. In the body of this book we follow the fine-grained expression approach, but only as an expedient. We feel that the added parameter approach is probably more satisfactory in the end, and develop a version of such a theory in our treatment of Aliass in the appendices.

We should mention in passing that there is also a view of logical form that combines the two mentioned above: it is treated both as input to semantic interpretation and as something like an expression in first-order logic. We see no reason to suppose that this approach is natural or even feasible. Indeed, we reject the assumption that the right way to find the proper invariants across utterances has anything to do with the syntax of first-order logic, as well as the assumption that linguistic meaning has much if anything to do with the traditional model-theory of first-order logic. To suppose it does is simply to be over-awed by the fact that first-order logic is a fairly-well developed part of mathematics and that it is called "logic."

SENTENCE CONNECTIVES

Let us now turn to the traditional sentence connectives AND and OR. Basically, these expressions work in the traditional manner, a conjunctive statement describing those situations described by both conjuncts, a disjunctive statement describing those described by either disjunct. But there are a few subtleties, usually ignored, that become important when one takes natural language seriously.

Consider, for example, a statement made with the sentence

(1) JOE ADMIRES SARAH AND SHE ADMIRES HIM.

Let us confine our attention to the utterances in which (1) has the antecedent relations indicated by:

(1') JOE$_1$ ADMIRES SARAH$_2$ AND SHE$_2$ ADMIRES HIM$_1$.

While sentence (1) is a conjunction of two sentences, a statement made with (1) in the way indicated by (1') is not a conjunction of independent statements. There is an important interaction between the two halves. And once we break the sentence apart, the second half displays different semantic properties. In particular, it has free pronouns and so a different domain of meaning than the whole. For an isolated utterance of SHE ADMIRES HIM must provide connections defined on the free pronouns SHE and HIM. Thus to get the antecedent relations right in the conjunctive statement, we will begin by augmenting the rule for the meaning of names to square with the fact that they may serve as antecedents for co-indexed pronouns.

$$d, c \llbracket \beta_i \rrbracket a_\sigma, e$$
$$\text{iff}$$
$$c(\beta_i) = a_\sigma, a_\sigma \text{ is named } \beta,$$
$$\text{and if } c(\text{HE}_i) = b, \text{ then } b = a_\sigma.$$

The strategy here may be the opposite of what the reader expected. Rather than forcing the pronoun to agree with its antecedent as to reference, we require the antecedent to agree with any pronouns for which it serves as antecedent. Thus the function c cannot be defined on both an indexed name and a co-indexed pronoun unless it agrees on these values, that is, unless it assigns the same individual to both the name and the pronoun. Note, however, that our rule still allows c to be defined on an indexed name while undefined on a co-indexed pronoun.

With this out of the way, we can define

$$d, c \llbracket \varphi \text{ AND } \psi \rrbracket e$$
iff
there is an extension c' of c such that
$$d, c' \llbracket \varphi \rrbracket e \text{ and } d, c' \llbracket \psi \rrbracket e.$$

Notice that this condition automatically guarantees that d, c' is in the domain of each relation $[\![\varphi]\!]$ and $[\![\psi]\!]$. But it does not guarantee that d, c is. That is, the conjunction may be true relative to a c that is *undefined* on pronouns with antecedents that appear in the first half of the conjunction. (But c will have to be defined on any names or pronouns without antecedents *in the conjunction,* to be in the domain of $[\![\varphi \text{ AND } \psi]\!]$.) Consider the utterance of (1) with the antecedent relations displayed in (1'). According to our rule, such an utterance may be true even though c provides no direct referents for SHE$_2$ and HIM$_1$. But this is only natural, since these pronouns are not used deictically, but pick up their referents through the antecedent relations and values c assigns to JOE$_1$ and SARAH$_2$. This flexibility is not only natural, but necessary, when complex noun phrases are used as antecedents, for reasons that will be apparent in the next chapter.

The same considerations apply to disjunctions, though the domains must be dealt with explicitly. That is

$$d, c [\![\varphi \text{ OR } \psi]\!] e$$

iff

there is a c' extending c so that d, c' is in the domain of each relation $[\![\varphi]\!]$ and $[\![\psi]\!]$, and either $d, c'[\![\varphi]\!] e$ or $d, c'[\![\psi]\!] e$.

The simplest form of negation in English is verb phrase negation, rather than sentence negation. Compare:

(2) A DOG WASN'T BARKING

with

(3) IT IS NOT TRUE THAT A DOG WAS BARKING.

In (3) there is an embedded sentence, while in (2) there is none. The type of negation in (2) can easily be handled in *VP* rules, as has already been indicated in an earlier section. But sentence negation is a complicated matter, not one we take up in any detail here. If I say "A dog is not barking," this can describe any factual situation in which some dog is not barking at the location referred to. However, if I say "It's not true that a dog is barking," my new utterance doesn't mean that. Indeed, to ask what situation I am describing seems to miss the mark. Rather it seems that my utterance, if informative, serves primarily to preclude certain types of situations, namely, those with barking dogs.[5]

SOME LOGICAL ISSUES

By *statement* we mean the utterance of an indicative sentence. The *interpretation of a statement u* is determined by decomposing *u* into its constituent expression φ, a discourse situation *d* and connections *c*; the interpretation itself is the collection of *e* such that $d, c \, [\![\varphi]\!] \, e$.

A statement is *persistent* if its interpretation is persistent in the sense of Chapter 3: whenever it describes a *coe e,* it also describes any *e'* of which *e* is a part. The basic sentences we have discussed in this chapter all give rise to persistent statements, largely because we have restricted ourselves to very simple noun phrases, names and pronouns.

For example, Joe's utterance of JACKIE IS BITING MOLLY is interpreted by those *coe*'s *e* in which the Jackie that Joe was referring to was biting, at the space time location that he was referring to, the Molly that he was referring to:

in *e* at *l*: biting, Jackie, Molly; yes.

This is a persistent statement because if Jackie is biting Molly at *l* in a particular *coe,* then she is also biting Molly at *l* in any *e'* of which *e* is a part. Conjunction and disjunction keep us within the class of persistent statements, since the intersection and union of persistent collections is persistent.

For persistent statements there is nothing problematic about the notion of truth. For example, when Joe says that Jackie is biting Molly, what he says is true if there is an actual *coe* in which Jackie is biting Molly at *l*. In general a persistent statement is *(absolutely) true* if there is an actual situation *e* in its interpretation. Otherwise it is false.

Two points are worth making. The first is that absolute truth is a property of statements, not of sentences. This is a consequence of the efficiency of sentences. But in the next chapter we will see that persistence is also not a property of sentences. That is, certain sentences can be used to make some statements that are persistent and others that are not. The second is that on this account, persistent statements are either true or false. We do not have some kind of three valued logic here, as it might appear at first sight. We will discuss truth for nonpersistent statements in the next chapter, where such statements arise naturally.

With this much of the theory under our belts, we can return to the question of whether logically equivalent sentences must describe the same thing, as has often been assumed.

It already should be clear that it is statements, not sentences, that should be compared to see whether one entails the other, or whether they are equivalent in some sense. For the purposes of this discussion we can identify a statement Φ with a sentence φ together with a discourse situation d and connections c such that d, c is in the domain of $[\![\varphi]\!]$:

$$\Phi = \langle d, c, \varphi \rangle.$$

If we are given statements $\Phi = \langle d, c, \varphi \rangle$ and $\Psi = \langle d, c, \psi \rangle$ *with the same d and c,* we can form new statements $(\Phi \& \Psi)$ and $(\Phi \vee \Psi)$ by conjoining the sentences involved:

$(\Phi \& \Psi)$ is $\langle d, c, (\varphi \text{ AND } \psi) \rangle$

$(\Phi \vee \Psi)$ is $\langle d, c, (\varphi \text{ OR } \psi) \rangle$

However, we cannot conjoin arbitrary statements.

More to the point, and more startling from a traditional perspective, we cannot always break apart a statement composed of conjoined or disjoined statements and make two separate statements out of it. This is apparent from our discussion in the preceeding section. If there are pronouns in the second constituent that have antecedents in the first, as in the examples below, the connections won't be in the domain of the constituent meanings.

JOE ADMIRES SARAH AND SHE ADMIRES HIM

JONNY OWNS A DOG AND HE LOVES IT

The second example is somewhat inappropriate in this chapter, since it contains the singular *NP* A DOG. But such *NP*'s show how hopeless it would be to try in general to divide a statement involving conjoined sentences apart into two separate statements involving the individual conjuncts. For any utterance of the sentence HE LOVES IT must have the speaker referring to some particular individual with IT. That is, $c(\text{IT})$ will have to be defined.

We have also seen that there are complicated issues surrounding negation. Let us use $\sim\Phi$ for the statement which results by replacing the sentence φ by its verb-phrase negation $\sim\varphi$.

While we set these qualifications to one side, let us examine the propositional logic of statements. For any statement $\Phi = \langle d, c, \varphi \rangle$, we have its interpretation $[\![\Phi]\!]$ defined by:

$$[\![\Phi]\!] = \{e : d, c [\![\varphi]\!] e\}.$$

We say that one statement Ψ *is a strong consequence of* another statement Φ, and write $\Phi \vdash \Psi$, provided $[\![\Phi]\!]$ is a subcollection of $[\![\Psi]\!]$; that is, provided every situation described by Φ is also described by Ψ. And let us define Φ and Ψ to be *strongly equivalent* if they have exactly the same interpretation.

By contrast, let us say that Ψ is a *weak consequence* of Φ if Ψ is true in any situation structure in which Φ is true. Ψ and Φ are *weakly equivalent* if they are true in exactly the same situation structures. Notice that if Ψ is a strong consequence of Φ, then it is also a weak consequence, but not conversely. For a trivial example, everything is a weak consequence of a statement involving the sentence

(1) DAD₁ IS FAT AND HE₁ IS NOT FAT

simply because such a statement is not true in any situation structure. There are, however, abstract states of affairs of the form:

$$s: = \text{ at } l: \text{ fat}, a; \text{yes}$$
$$\text{fat}, a; \text{no}.$$

Notice, however, that this state of affairs is not described by either of the following, so s will not be in either of their interpretations:

(2) DAD₁ IS AWAKE

(3) DAD₁ IS AWAKE OR HE₁ IS NOT AWAKE

Thus, a statement made with (1) will not strongly imply any statement made with (2) or even with (3). Thus, in general,

$$(\Psi \ \& \sim \Phi) \nvdash \Psi \text{ and } \Phi \nvdash (\Psi \vee \sim \Psi),$$

where $\nvdash$ means "is not a strong consequence".

MEANS THAT

Before turning to the semantics of singular noun phrases and the attitudes, we want to look briefly at the semantics of simple sentences involving the phrase MEANS THAT, sentences like:

(1) JACKIE'S BITING MOLLY (ALWAYS) MEANS THAT JACKIE IS SCARED

(2) JACKIE'S BITING MOLLY MEANT THAT SHE WAS SCARED

(3) THE CAT HAIR IN THE BUTTER DIDN'T MEAN THAT SCRUFFY WAS IN THE HOUSE

(4) THAT SITUATION MEANT THAT JACKIE WAS IN THE HOUSE

(5) WORLD WAR I MEANT THAT THE WORLD WAS SAFE FOR DEMOC-
RACY

Event-Type Meaning

A statement made with a sentence like (1) describes a constraint. If the described constraint is factual then the statement is true; if not the statement is false. The constraint described by (1) is

$C := $ at u: involves, $E(l)$, $E'(l)$; yes
where
$E := $ at l: biting, Jackie, Molly; yes
$E' := $ at l: scared, Jackie; yes

We won't go into the semantics of gerundive nominals in this book any more than the short remark above. We leave the detailed treatment to our next book, where we show how gerundive nominals can be taken as refering to event-types as in our example above.

Event Meaning

English has names for some specific events, such as World War I, but in general events are referred to by nominals of various kinds, a subject outside the scope of this book. However, as (4) shows, we can also refer to events directly with the demonstrative THAT. Consider the meaning of

(6) THAT MEANS THAT JACKIE IS IN THE HOUSE

Let u be an assertive utterance of (6). The connections will assign some specific situation e_0, the one referred to by the speaker, to the demonstrative THAT, $e_0 = c(\text{THAT})$. What the speaker claims is that there are patterns or constraints in virtue of which e_0 requires that some situation be actual, some situation in which Jackie is present in the house. In other words, if $C(e)$ is the set of constraints that are part of an event e, then the speaker claims that the actual situation e is one such that Jackie is in the house in all coe's e_1 that are meaningful options, with respect to the constraints $C(e)$, of e_0.

In general, we can define the meaning of sentences of the form

(7) THAT MEANS THAT φ

by

$d, c \llbracket \text{THAT}_1 \text{ MEANS THAT } \varphi \rrbracket e$

if and only if the event $e_0 = c(\text{THAT}_1)$ is part of e and for every e_1 such that

    in e: at l: MO, e_0, e_1; yes,

we have

    $d, c \llbracket \varphi \rrbracket e_1.$

CHAPTER SEVEN

The Meaning of Singular Noun Phrases

The problems about attitudes that drove Frege and Russell to such heroic lengths dealt with the interaction of attitude reports with singular noun phrases, *NP*'s like:

NANCY REAGAN'S HUSBAND,

THE PRESIDENT,

THE DOG THAT BIT HER,

A CAT THAT SCRATCHED ME.

For this reason we will restrict attention to singular *NP*'s and their interaction with attitude reports in this book.

SOME BACKGROUND ON DEFINITE DESCRIPTIONS

Expressions like THE MAN and THE DOG THAT BIT HER are *definite descriptions;* expressions like A MAN and A DOG THAT BIT HER are *indefinite descriptions.* We shall concentrate largely on definite descriptions, but we will show that our approach is easily extended to indefinite descriptions and to other kinds of singular noun phrases, including the above and also possessives like MY DOG.

In order to explain the basic ideas of our theory of descriptions, three semitechnical notions will be useful: *the object described* by a (definite) description; *the describing condition;* and the *constituents of an interpretation.* It will also be helpful to be rather casual about issues of tense and location while the discussion remains informal. One reason for this is that the familiar theories of descriptions, with which we will be comparing our own, were not developed with systematic attention to questions of tense.

Let us say that the definite description THE PRESIDENT OF THE U.S.

(currently) describes Ronald Reagan. That is, he is the unique person who fits the description. The definite description THE KING OF ENGLAND does not currently describe anyone; no person fits this description. We will say the same thing of THE SENATOR FROM CALIFORNIA since there is not just one senator from California, though we will see later that there are special (resource) situations in which it describes one of the two. The describing conditions in these examples are simply being president of the United States, being king of England, and being the senator from California, the conditions that the objects described are supposed to fit uniquely.

Any object, property, relation, or location that appears in a course of events is called a constituent of the *coe*. If something is a constituent of every *coe e* such that

$$d, c \llbracket \varphi \rrbracket e$$

then it is called a constituent of the interpretation of φ in d, c.[1]

Consider an utterance u of the sentence

(1) RONALD REAGAN IS SNEEZING

by one of the authors of this book at a given time. The interpretation of this statement is the set of courses of events that have Ronald Reagan sneezing at that time; Reagan will be a constituent of it. On the other hand, Reagan will not be a constituent of the interpretation of an utterance of

A NAIVE MAN WITH GREY HAIR IS SNEEZING.

Perhaps Reagan will be a constituent of some *coe*'s in the interpretation of this utterance, but not all of them.

Now consider an utterance u' by one of the authors of this book at this very moment in 1982 of

(2) THE PRESIDENT OF THE U.S. IS SNEEZING.

Will Ronald Reagan be a constituent of the interpretation of this statement? To ask the question more generally: When a definite description is used in an utterance u of a simple indicative sentence, one with no embedded sentences, will the object the definite description describes be a constituent of the interpretation?

On Russell's theory of descriptions, the answer is no. Russell would say that the statement in question is true if there is one and only one president of the United States, and that person is sneezing. There are various ways this idea might be built into situation semantics, but one can see that the result would always interpret the

statement with courses of events in which various individuals satisfied the condition of being president. Some of these would not have
Reagan in them at all, and so he would not be a constituent of the
interpretation. On the other hand, being president would be a constituent. Each of the courses of events would be defined at the
present time, and each would consider the property of being president at that time. Russell's theory puts the describing condition into
the interpretation, but not the described individual.

Strawson made just the opposite decisions (Strawson, 50). The described individual, but not the describing condition, is a constituent
of the interpretation. Both of these views have considerations in their
favor. That is why Strawson's criticisms of Russell's theory led to
such an interesting debate.

Donnellan distinguishes two uses of definite descriptions, the
referential and attributive (Donnellan, 66). We would put the distinction in the following way: when descriptions are used attributively, the describing condition is a constituent of the interpretation.
When they are used referentially, the described individual is a constituent of the interpretation (Wettstein, 76, Wettstein, 81). We
think Donnellan is right, as far as he goes, but that the distinction is actually between two cases of a more general phenomenon.

OUR THEORY OF DEFINITE DESCRIPTIONS

Our basic picture of definite descriptions is very simple. Definite
descriptions can be used to identify an object by the properties
he, she, or it has in some situation. That is, they exploit what is
going on in one situation to identify an object. One situation, what
we call a *resource situation,* is exploited. In order to serve as a resource situation for a definite description, a situation must have
an object satisfying the definite condition. This object can then be
used in describing another situation.

Similarities with Indexicals

Definite descriptions are similar to indexical expressions in that both
exploit a situation to identify an individual. But there are also important differences. First we will dwell on the similarities, and then look
at the differences.

Consider

(3) THE DOG GROWLED AT THE RABBIT THAT SNEEZED.

Suppose Jim has been telling us about a situation. He has mentioned only one dog, Clarissa, and two rabbits: Hugh, who sneezed while eating Clarissa's food, and Fang. We would naturally take Jim's utterance of (3) to describe the event e:

in e: at l: growling at, Clarissa, Hugh; yes

where l is the location to which Jim was referring, a location temporally preceding that of the utterance. The definite descriptions THE DOG and THE RABBIT THAT SNEEZED contribute Clarissa and Hugh to the event described. Two factors enable them to do this:

1. the properties various parts of the expression designate;
2. the unique possession of those properties by Clarissa and Hugh in the situation built up by Jim's discourse.

Thus it is very natural to take the descriptions to identify functions from situations to the unique objects in them that "fit" the descriptions. And it is very natural to take the objects that are the values of the functions, not the functions themselves, to be the constituents of the propositions expressed.

There is much here that is similar to the use of indexical expressions. When Jim says, "I rushed to help Clarissa," we associate with I a relation between discourse situations and individuals, in fact a function from discourse situations to individuals. And it is the individual that is the value of the function at the discourse situation that is a constituent of the utterance's interpretation.

Just as we say that different uses of I are associated with the same function but designate different individuals in different (discourse) situations, so too different uses of the same definite description, with a single meaning, can designate different individuals in different (resource) situations. Consider (3) again. Suppose Jim is interrupted in the midst of his story by a sneeze and a growl. "What happened?" we ask. Jim utters (3), looking at a dog and two rabbits behind us, hidden from our view until we turn. Then we would naturally take the descriptions to stand for that dog and one of those rabbits, not Clarissa and Hugh. We wouldn't think the meaning had changed from use to use.

Differences with Indexicals

There are important differences between definite descriptions and indexical expressions, however. First notice that in our two imagined uses of (3), we had the same speaker, in the same location. The difference in the designation of the descriptions did not turn on these relatively objective features of the discourse situation. In the second case, the perceptual accessibility of the dog and rabbits was important in Jim's ability to designate them with definite descriptions—their use seems similar to a use of THIS DOG or THAT RABBIT. In the first case, however, the rabbits and dog were not perceptually accessible. They were not present in the discourse situation, although discourse about them was. Definite descriptions seem to give us a "further reach" than indexical expressions, a reach that allows us to pluck objects from all manner of resource situations.

Another difference is the freedom one has in the exploitation of resource situations. One cannot simply choose which discourse situation to exploit. I cannot exploit a discourse situation with Napoleon as speaker; even if I am fully convinced that I am Napoleon, my use of I designates me, not him. Similarly, I may be fully convinced that it is 1789, but it does not make my use of NOW about a time in 1789. However, one has considerable freedom in the choice of resource situations to exploit.

Thus in order to handle descriptions we need to introduce the resource situation as a new parameter of meaning. To see how this works, it will be helpful to look at a description that also has an indexical element:

(4) THE DOG THAT BIT ME

When I use this description, which dog it designates depends on which situation I exploit. I have been bitten by a goodly number of dogs over the years, at many different locations, but always on the ankle. The definite description, once I am fixed as the speaker, gives us various dogs, depending on which resource situation I refer to. Once the discourse location is fixed, we get a certain function from situations to dogs. If we consider a different discourse situation, however, we will get a different function, a different relation between resource situations and dogs. Suppose Phil and I use this description, both referring to the time that we broke up a dog fight between Bear and Dimples:

Phil: The dog that bit me was black, ugly, mean, and big.
Me: The dog that bit me was puce, cute, scared, and small.

The same expression designates different dogs, not because the resource situations are different, but because the discourse situations are.

The Meaning of Definite Descriptions

These examples, and similar ones with regular pronouns, show that the *meaning of a definite description* THE π is a relation between discourse situations, connections, situations, and objects. (When we take into account our theory of compositionality and sentence meaning, this becomes a relation between discourse situations, connections, situations, and settings; we will occasionally ignore this complication below.) It is given by[2]

$$d, c \, [\![\, \text{THE} \, \pi \,]\!] \, a_\sigma, e$$
iff
$$d, c \, [\![\, \pi \,]\!] \, a_\sigma, e;$$
and there is at most one b such that $d, c \, [\![\, \pi \,]\!] \, b_\sigma, e$.

We can also think of $d, c \, [\![\, \text{THE} \, \pi \,]\!]$ as giving a partial function from situations e to individuals a:

$_{d,c}[\![\text{THE } \pi]\!](e)$ is defined and $= a_\sigma$
iff

$d,c[\![\text{THE } \pi]\!]\, a_\sigma, e.$

For example, if e corresponds to the event where Dimples bit me, then

$_{d,c}[\![\text{THE DOG THAT BIT ME}]\!](e) = $ Dimples.

There is a useful analogy to be drawn between third-person pronouns and definite descriptions. A third-person pronoun can pick up a referent in two distinct ways, directly through speaker connections or indirectly by having some other referring expression as an antecedent. Our subscript notation introduced in the previous chapter is supposed to be an informal reflection of these two ways of using pronouns. Similarly, a definite description α can apply in two sorts of situations. As we have seen, it can exploit a situation e_1 given by the speaker's connections—that is simply the one the speaker is refering to, $e_1 = c(\alpha)$. This is what happens with referential uses of definite descriptions. But the definite description α can also constrain a situation e described by some previous part of the utterance, some part of the utterance of which α is a part, or the situation e described by the utterance as a whole. The latter is the attributive use. We will survey these various uses below.

We have identified the meaning of a definite description α. When we ask what the "interpretation" of α is, we must make a terminological decision. Up until now, the interpretation of an *NP* has met two conditions:

1. the interpretation is what we have when we fix the discourse and connections.
2. the interpretation (of a noun phrase) is an object, a constituent of the interpretation of the smallest sentence containing it.

In the case of a referential use of a definite description, fixing the discourse situation and connections, *including* the connection to the resource situation, gives an individual. In the other cases, however, fixing the discourse situation and the connections only, gives us a relation between situations and individuals. But this relation or function is not in general what gets into the interpretation. (Sometimes it does, as we will see below.) That honor is reserved for the value of the relation (considered as a function) at some particular situation.

From now on, we shall distinguish between the *value-free* and *value-loaded* interpretations of an expression. Often these will be the same, say for proper names and pronouns. But in the case of descriptions, they will not be the same. The value-free interpretation of a description is a relation, a partial function from courses of events to individuals. The value-loaded interpretation is the value of the function when applied to some particular resource situation.

THE MEANING OF OTHER SINGULAR NP'S

We have seen that we can identify the meaning of a definite description with a four-place relation between discourse situations d, connections c, resource situations, and individuals. Fixing d and c gives us a value-free interpretation, a relation between resource situations and individuals. Fixing an appropriate resource situation gives us the value-loaded interpretation, an individual. Exactly the same works for any singular *NP*, the only difference being that, in general, the value-free interpretation will be only a relation, not a function.

A couple of examples should suffice to make the general point. Consider the phrases:

A DOG THAT BIT HIM

MY DOG

The value-free interpretation of the first phrase (given d and c) is just the relation that obtains between an individual a and an event e if:

in e: at l: dog, a; yes

biting, a, c(HIM) yes.

That is,

d, c ⟦ A DOG THAT BIT HIM ⟧ a, e

just in case the above holds, where l is the location assigned to the past tense marker in the phrase by c. Note that for a given d, c, e, there may be more or less than one such a. That is, there may be more than one dog that bit him.

Similarly, the value-free interpretation of MY DOG, given d and c, will be the relation that holds between a and e just in case

in e: at l: dog, a; yes

possess, a_d, a; yes,

where l is a location in space-time assigned to MY DOG by c.

USES OF SINGULAR *NP*'S

Referential Use

As we have seen, a singular *NP* is often used to designate an individual in the described situation. One common way for this to occur is for the resource situation to be a perceptually accessible situation.

THE MAN IN A RED VEST IS A FOOL.

Let the situation we are looking at be s_0. Then suppose

$_{d,c}$⟦ THE MAN IN A RED VEST ⟧(s_0) = Lee

Then it is natural to take me as describing a situation s satisfying:

In s: at l: fool, Lee; yes

You might report my utterance by saying,

HE SAID THAT LEE IS A FOOL

or

HE SAID THAT THAT GUY IS A FOOL

or, if Lee is also the only man in the scene wearing a blue coat,

HE SAID THAT THE MAN IN A BLUE COAT IS A FOOL.

Such uses of definite descriptions motivate the treatments of definite descriptions by Frege and Strawson, and exhibit what Donnellan calls a referential use of a definite description.[3] Situations can become resource situations in a variety of ways. We call situations that can be used as resource situations *accessible.* In addition to scenes and situations perceivable in other ways, a situation may be accessible by having been built up in conversation. Every situation is potentially accessible, in that a given description can be evaluated or loaded in any situation the interpreter is in a position to consider. But the situations that can be actually used by a speaker to communicate with a given audience are more restricted. Nevertheless, any situation on which the speaker can focus attention is fair game.

Suppose a speaker a_d utters some sentence containing the phrase THE DOG at some sublocation l_0 of the location l_d of the utterance u, and suppose that he or she is using it with some accessible resource situation s_0. There is no alternative to admitting that these are simply facts of the utterance, just as the speaker connections are. We might represent them as follows:

in u: at l_0: says, a_d, THE DOG; yes

resource for, s_0, THE DOG; yes

We count this as part of the connecting situation of the utterance and so write $c(\text{THE DOG}) = s_0$. In general there is no reason to suppose that there is at most one resource situation per utterance any more than that there should be only one thing around referred to by IT in a given utterance.

Traditional theories are often explained as though the whole world were accessible and, indeed, as if this were the only accessible situation. To make this plausible they choose for their paradigms those rare definite descriptions that are defined for this large situation, such as THE FIRST CHILD BORN IN THE 21ST CENTURY or THE AUTHOR OF WAVERLY. It is an advantage of our approach that we can naturally explain the fact that most definite descriptions manage to pick out individuals without finding describing conditions that are uniquely satisfied in the whole world.

Attributive Use

We now turn to another use of singular noun phrases that fits neatly within our theory, the attributive. Suppose that in telling you my plans for the soccer season I say:

THE PLAYER THAT WINS THE RACE WILL BE THE RIGHT WING.

Now it may be that Fred will win the race, and I might mean to describe a situation with Fred as a constituent, but that is certainly not the natural interpretation of what I say. Rather, I seem to be describing a situation with no particular individual in it, but with the describing condition, winning the race, as a constituent. Roughly speaking, the situation e that I describe must satisfy:

In e: plays right wing, $_{d,c} [\![\text{THE WINNER OF THE RACE}]\!](e)$; yes

What I have said will be true if the winner of the race, whoever it turns out to be, plays right wing, be it Fred, Derek, or even Jacob. Each of these players is a constituent of one of the situations described by my utterance, but none of them is a constituent of all, so none of them is a constituent of its interpretation. But the condition of winning the race is a constituent; it is a constituent of each situation described. It must be for the definite description to be defined there. This corresponds more to the way that Russell looked at definite descriptions (though not exactly to his theory, of course), and to what Donnellan calls the attributive use of definite descriptions.

One of the most transparent attributive uses occurs when the singular *NP* is used predicatively, as in

FRED IS THE WINNER OF THE RACE.

If I say this, I am not saying that Fred is the same as Fred, but rather describing those e such that

$$_{d,c} \llbracket \text{THE WINNER OF THE RACE} \rrbracket (e) = \text{Fred}.$$

Note how this effect was achieved in both cases. *The situation being described is also serving as the resource situation.* That is, in order to get the attributive use of the definite description, we do not directly put the describing condition into the proposition. It is forced to be a constituent because each situation described must be defined on it, in order to provide a person to be the winner of the race and play right wing.

We find the term *constraining-donating expression* useful in thinking about how singular *NP*'s work. The value-free interpretation constrains one situation, picking up an individual to donate to another (possibly distinct) situation. The definite description will not get us to an individual unless the resource situation is defined on the describing condition. The resource situation is constrained to have this condition in its domain, or no individual will be available to be a constituent of the described situation. When we are looking at a group down the road and I say,

THE MAN IN THE RED VEST IS THE GOVERNOR

I have not said that there is a man down the road with a red vest on. The condition of wearing a red vest is not part of the described situation. The definite description is taken referentially, so only the man himself and the property of being governor make it into the described situation. The situation down the road is constrained by my utterance to have such a man in it, however; only if it does, can my utterance turn out to be true. The interpretation of my utterance has a man in it, one who gets donated from the resource situation. Hence, definite descriptions are constraining-donating expressions. The attributive use is simply the special case where the situations provided by the interpretation must themselves serve as the resource situations. In the example about the soccer team, the situations are constrained to consider the property of winning the race.

We have concentrated on attributive uses of definite descriptions, but the interpretation of all singular *NP*'s are relations between situations and individuals and so can be used to constrain and to donate, that is, attributively. Some of the uses of MY WIFE in Chapter 2 are attributive.

We want to introduce a notation to differentiate different ways of using singular *NP*'s: referentially, attributively, and other ways. We exploit the analogy with pronouns and our notation there. Consider, for example, the sentence

(1) THE α IS β-ING.

To indicate an attributive use of (1), where the situation described by the whole is constrained by THE α, we use a common superscript j on the sentence and the *NP*, as in:

$[(\text{THE } \alpha)^j \text{ IS } \beta\text{-ING}]^j$.

Here the sentence is describing an event e_j, an event that is also constrained to have a unique α in it. By contrast, a purely referential use will be indicated by having a superscript on the *NP* that is not common to any earlier or containing sentence, as in:

$[(\text{THE } \alpha)^0 \text{ IS } \beta\text{-ING}]^1$

This indicates that the statement is describing an event e_1, whereas the *NP* is used in a value-loaded manner, at a resource situation e_0.

Inner Attributive Use

Suppose I point to a Persian cat hair in the butter dish and say

THAT MEANS THAT A PERSIAN CAT IS IN THE HOUSE.

Which situation has a Persian cat in it, the one described, some external resource situation, or all the situations that are meaningful options from the situation of the cat hair in the butter? One can cook up examples where the first two are possible, but the most likely case is the latter. There are many possible situations that are meaningful options, with different Persian cats in the house. Thus,

$_{d,\,c} [\![\text{A PERSIAN CAT}]\!]$

is being evaluated not at the external resource situation e_0 ($= c$ (THAT)) or at the described situation e_1 but at the various meaningful alternatives e_2 from e_0. We call such uses of singular *NP*'s the *inner attributive*. This use would be indicated in our notational convention by:

$[\text{THAT MEANS THAT } ((\text{A PERSIAN CAT})^2 \text{ IS IN THE HOUSE})^2]^1$

Notice that the most likely reading of this would be one in which the house we are in is the house in question, so that $[\![\text{THE HOUSE}]\!]$ is evaluated at a resource situation.

Many of the traditional puzzles of Frege and Russell about the interaction of definite descriptions and attitude reports center on inner attributive uses of singular *NP*'s, so it will be discussed at length in the next chapter. The notation introduced above will come in particularly handy with attitude reports, as in

[SARAH SAID THAT [(THE COACH)^j WAS TALL]^2]^1

If $j = 0$, this indicates a use where the coach is determined at some external resource situation e_0. If $j = 1$, this indicates a use of the sentence where the situation described by the statement as a whole is constrained to have a coach in it, and Sarah said of her that she was tall. With $j = 2$, it indicates an inner attributive use, one where the property of being coach is part of the interpretation of Sarah's reported utterance.

We reserve the superscript "0" for external resource situations and "1" for the situation described by the utterance as a whole.

Appositive Use

Suppose I say

JIM WAS CHASING MOLLY, THE DOG THAT BIT ME.

Here we have the same old definite description that we have seen before, but it is functioning rather differently. It is not being used to pick out an individual, the use of MOLLY having already done that. But it is not exactly the attributive use either, at least if one thinks of the attributive use as one where you can always add a parenthetical WHOEVER IT IS. That clearly makes no sense in this example.

The noun phrase here is functioning as an appositive relative clause, to tell us something additional about Molly. This fits very neatly in our theory, for it simply amounts to another way of using the value-free interpretation of the phrase, the opposite to the referential use. Instead of fixing a situation and thereby picking up an individual, we fix an individual and thereby constrain the described situation to be one where that fixed individual fits the defining condition. Thus the interpretation of our sentence is those situations e such that:

in e at l: chasing, c(JIM), c(MOLLY); yes

and $_{d,c}$ [[THE DOG THAT BIT ME]] $(e) = c$(MOLLY)

where $l = c$(WAS).

Appositive relative clauses are very interesting from our perspective. By and large, they always seem to put constraints on the situations e_1 described by the whole utterance, as opposed to the situations

$$d, c [\![\text{The number of sleeping students}]\!] (e_{l_1}) = 3$$
$$d, c [\![\text{The number of sleeping students}]\!] (e_{l_2}) = 5$$
$$d, c [\![\text{The number of sleeping students}]\!] (e_{l_3}) = 9$$
$$d, c [\![\text{The number of sleeping students}]\!] (e_{l_4}) = 19$$

described by some part of it that contains the appositive. Consider, for example, an utterance of this on a Sunday morning:

FRENCHIE, JOHN'S WIFE, IS SLEEPING OR SHE IS READING THE PAPER IN BED.

This utterance describes only situations e_1 where Frenchie is John's wife, even though it is a disjunction of two sentences, one of which does not entail that Frenchie is John's wife. The second sentence doesn't mention John or the wife relation. This is one of the standard puzzles for truth-conditional accounts. From our perspective, focusing on the relation between utterances and described situations, it is quite natural. In terms of our notational conventions, it means that appositive relative clauses constrain the described situation, and so should be superscripted with "1". The setting σ provided by the utterance contains a described situation e_1 that will be constrained to have Frenchie being John's wife. To be in the domain of a disjunction, a d, c and setting σ must be in the domain of both disjuncts, so will have Frenchie being John's wife in the situation described by the whole.

Functional Use

In our theory the (value-free) interpretation of a definite description is a partial function from situations to individuals. We have seen ways that this function can be used, various combinations of constraining its arguments and donating its values. But if our account is correct, there should also be uses of definite descriptions where properties of the function itself are described by the containing sentence. The famous Partee puzzle[4] is one such case:

> THE TEMPERATURE IS NINETY,
> THE TEMPERATURE IS INCREASING,
> THEREFORE, NINETY IS INCREASING,

or, to anticipate an example from the next chapter:

> THE NUMBER OF SLEEPING STUDENTS WAS 9,
> THE NUMBER OF SLEEPING STUDENTS WAS INCREASING,
> THEREFORE, 9 WAS INCREASING.

When we say that the temperature is increasing, we are commenting on the function, on the value-free interpretation of THE TEMPERATURE, not on its value at a particular location. Similarly for the number of sleeping students. Numbers don't increase, functions do. A similar case of this is something like:

> THE NUMBER OF PEOPLE VOTING FOR PRESIDENT PEAKED IN 1956.

Again, it is functions that peak (reach a local maximum), not numbers. It is no more difficult to interpret these sentences, given our treatment of definite descriptions, than it is to define what it means for a function to increase or peak. For example, a function f from locations to numbers is increasing on l if for every two sublocations l_0 and l_1 of l, if $l_0 \prec l_1$, then $f(l_0) < f(l_1)$. Thus the number of sleeping students was increasing at the space-time location l in the *coe e* if the function

$$d, c \, [\![\text{THE NUMBER OF SLEEPING STUDENTS}]\!] \, (e_{l'})$$

as a function of l', is increasing on l. We did not have these sorts of puzzles in mind when we worked out our theory of definite descriptions, and so feel it is an additional confirmation of our theory that they work out so smoothly.

To indicate a functional use of a definite description we use a superscript F, as in:

    ((THE NUMBER OF PEOPLE VOTING FOR PRESIDENT)^F PEAKED IN 1956)

Relative Persistence and Relative Truth

The interpretation of statements involving attributive, appositive, and functional uses of definite descriptions are not absolutely but only relatively persistent. This requires a complication in our account of truth.

Consider the interpretation P of my utterance of I AM THE COOK.

$$P = \{e : d, c \, [\![\text{I AM THE COOK}]\!] \, e \}$$

If $e \in P$, then e will have just one person (me) doing the cooking at the relevant location $l = c(\text{COOK})$. But any such e will be a part of other e' which have more than one person cooking there. Such e' will not belong to P because there will be no person who is *the* cook. So P is not persistent. This raises a problem for our account of truth in the following way. Suppose my wife and I collaborate on cooking for a party. And suppose that at a certain point in the party I say, "I am the cook," referring to l. Is what I have said true or not?

The answer is, "It depends on which situation I am describing." First, suppose someone comes up to me and says, "The food at this party is delicious! Who is the cook?" If I say, "I am the cook," I have clearly not described things accurately. I have claimed to be *the* person who did the cooking for the party. But suppose instead someone comes up to me eating a piece of my famous cheesecake pastry and says, "Who made this?" Then I may truly say that I am the cook.

The first case shows that the account we gave of truth for persistent statements does not work for nonpersistent statements. For in that case there is a factual situation, *part* of the situation referred to by the guest, where I am the unique cook. So there will be a factual (maybe even an actual) *coe* in *P,* and on our earlier account of truth, my statement would be true, whereas in fact it isn't. But surely nonpersistent statements can be true, for in the second case, what I said was true. A theory that did not allow for this would be unfair to me. So we need an account of truth that can be applied to nonpersistent statements.

The same sorts of problems come up with a vengeance when we turn to general *NP*'s, which are outside the scope of this book. Suppose I am in a room full of people, some of whom are sleeping, some of whom are wide awake. If I say, "No one is sleeping," have I told the truth, or not? Again, it depends on which situation I am referring to. If I am referring to the whole situation including all the people in the room, then what I have said is false. However, one can well imagine situations where I am clearly referring only to a part of that situation. Imagine, for example, that I am conducting an experiment which requires an assistant to monitor sleeping people, and I look around the sleep lab to see if all of my assistants are awake and ready to go. Surely, then I may truly and informatively say, "No one is asleep. Let's begin."

Notice that in both examples, the interpretation of my statement is not absolutely persistent, and it is this lack of persistence that causes the difficulty for the definition of truth given in Chapter 6. Notice also that the problem does not, as one might think, disappear for one who rejects our theory of situations for one big situation, Reality. For then almost none of our ordinary uses of definite descriptions and general *NP*'s are accounted for. For example, if we required that the world were in the interpretation of an utterance, then neither of the true examples given above would count as true.

The crucial insight needed goes back to Austin (61). As Austin put it, a statement is true when the actual situation to which it refers is of the type described by the statement.[5] That is, just as there are conventions about what situations can be used as resource situations, there are also conventions about what situation a person is describing. One can make a false statement by violating these conventions just as surely as one can by using a different statement.

Let u be some statement with interpretation P. We define a relative notion of truth by saying that u is *true relative to* an actual situation e if e is in P. If we are to define an absolute notion of truth for non-persistent statements, we must make a decision. One option is to follow Austin and require of an assertive utterance u that it comes with an actual situation e_u referred to. In that case we could define u as being (*absolutely* true) if e_u is in P. The only other option is to assume the existence of a world, a largest situation w in $\mathfrak{M}$ (our structure of situations), and define an utterance u to be absolutely true if w is in P.

Our general skepticism about the existence of a largest actual situation w leads us to favor the former approach, but some readers will feel differently. Notice, though, that the second approach would count as false all those examples which require the speaker to refer to a proper part of reality, like the true versions of "I am the cook" and "No one is sleeping" above.

Language is a big juggling act. Speaking truly puts constraints on the expression, connections, and resource situations, as well as on the situation referred to. For example, it must not only be described by my utterance, but also not be precluded by my utterance. In the examples above, the situation in which there are two cooks is precluded by my statement that I am the cook, so what I said precludes me from referring to that situation. Similarly, the situation in which there are people sleeping is precluded by my saying that no one was sleeping, so it is not one to which I can truly refer. The interpretation of an utterance is not in general absolutely persistent, but it is persistent relative to the situations not precluded by my utterance, the situations to which I may legitimately refer.

MY WIFE: AN EXAMPLE

In Chapter 2 we used the phrase MY WIFE to illustrate the complicated ways that information could be conveyed with language. In this section we want to see if our interpretation of singular *NP*'s is adequate to account for these facts. Before doing this, though, let's look at a simple three-place relation to examine various ways it can be used to convey information.

Recall from Euclidean geometry that the sides of a right triangle must stand in the relationship $x^2 + y^2 = z^2$. Recall further that one often got problems that were greatly simplified if you remembered that $(3,4,5)$ and $(5,12,13)$ were triples (x,y,z) that satisfy this relation. Those triples (x,y,z) of numbers such that $x^2 + y^2 = z^2$ are called Pythagorean Triples. The student of geometry quickly becomes attuned to the simplest cases of this relation, since it is certainly relevant to his well-being. If he has a Pythagorean Triple $(3,4,z)$, he knows that z is either 5 or -5. If he has $(5,y,13)$ he knows that y is 12 or -12. And so on. By fixing two parameters of this relation, he gets information about the third. If you fix only one, say $z = 5$, the result is a two-place relation of x and y:

$$x^2 + y^2 = 25,$$

that constrains both x and y but does not narrow things nearly as much, since there are so many possibilities.

According to our theory of singular NP's, the meaning of MY WIFE is a four-place relation $R(d, c, b, e)$, that we write as:

(1) $d, c \llbracket$ MY WIFE $\rrbracket b, e$.

(We'll ignore settings for the time being.)

We've been sloppy about locations in this chapter, but they are essential to interpretation. Any use of a common noun like WIFE has to be connected to some space-time location l, given by the speaker connections;

c (WIFE) $= l$.

Relation (1) holds just in case the speaker a_d has b as wife during the period of time covered by l, according to the *coe e*:

In e: at l: wife-of, b, a_d; yes,

where c (WIFE) $= l$. Usually when one uses the phrase MY WIFE, one is referring to the present time, the time of the discourse situation l_d. This fixes one of the four parameters, l. To see how the other factors balance each other, let us imagine two distinct discourse situations

d_1 and d_2; d_1 with Jon as speaker, d_2 with John as speaker. Let us further assume that e satisfies the following:

> in e: at l: wife-of, Mary Ellen, Jon; yes
> wife-of, Frenchie, John; yes.

If d_1 is the discourse situation, then the only b such that

$$d_1, c \llbracket \text{MY WIFE} \rrbracket b, e$$

is Mary Ellen, so anyone who knows that d_1 and e are actual (and that the speaker is referring to l) will take the utterance to be about Mary Ellen. The listener will interpret the phrase referentially.

Suppose instead that the phrase is clearly used with reference to Frenchie, that the listener knows e to be factual, and that the speaker is referring to l. Then the listener will conclude that it is d_2, not d_1 that is the discourse situation, and that John is speaking.

Next suppose that it is clear that d_1 is the actual situation, that the speaker is clearly referring to l, and that the phrase is obviously used as a description of Mary Ellen. Then the listener will have available the information that Mary Ellen is the present wife of the speaker Jon.

Now suppose, contrary to fact, that Jon had been married to Janet in the distant past, say at $l' \prec l$, so that in addition to the above,

> in e: at l': wife-of, Janet, Jon; yes
> wife-of, Mary Ellen, Jon; no.

If d_1 is the actual discourse situation, e is known by the listener, and the phrase MY WIFE is clearly used with reference to Janet (see case 5 in Chapter 2), then the listener will conclude that the speaker Jon is referring to the period of time covered by l', not that of the discourse situation.

Finally, what about the case where the actual discourse situation is d_2, but the listener doesn't know John—indeed, because he is dressed as a rabbit, is not even sure of his gender? Let us suppose it to be clear that he is referring to the time of the discourse l, but that Frenchie is not present or known in any way to the listener. What information can the listener pick up from John's use of the phrase MY WIFE, as in "My wife will be late"?

If the phrase is being used appropriately, then whatever the actual state of affairs e vis-à-vis John's marital state, there has to be some b so that

$d, c \llbracket \text{MY WIFE} \rrbracket b, e$;

and in order for this to hold, e must satisfy

  in e: at l: wife-of, b, John; yes.

So the listener can pick up the information that John has a wife.

How about the fact that John is male? Remember that John is in costume and unrecognized by his listener. He's even speaking in a very rabbity voice, to further disguise himself. This is where structural constraints come in. Having a wife means that you are male; that is just the way the relation and property interact. Thus the listener attuned to this structural constraint will also have available the information that John is a male.

There are more combinations that could be rung, but this should give some idea of the incredible flexibility of the simple phrase MY WIFE to convey information. There are, in fact, 16 ($= 2^4$) ways to convey information with the phrase, corresponding to the fact that we can fix any set of the four parameters of the relation. (Two of them are trivial: one where we fix no parameters, one where we fix all.) It is an interesting exercise to come up with stories where each of these is plausible as the information conveyed by a single sentence, say:

  (2) MY WIFE IS DRINKING PEPSI.

There are just two interpretations of an utterance of (2), one where the *NP* interpretation is value loaded, one where it is value free.

  (2.0) $[(\text{MY WIFE})^0 \text{ is drinking Pepsi}]^1$
  (2.1) $[(\text{MY WIFE})^1 \text{ is drinking Pepsi}]^1$

The different kinds of information come from understanding the balancing act of language, that the meaning of (2) requires that (2) be used as in (2.0) or as in (2.1). And there is nothing to prevent the speaker from using it one way, as in (2.0), and the listener interpreting it another, as in (2.1). Indeed, such things are an important aspect of the flow of information.

The temptation to think that all the information available from an utterance must be part of its interpretation we call the *fallacy of misplaced information*. We think that what is called the performative analysis (where a sentence like JACKIE IS BARKING is assumed to have some sort of "deep structure" of the form I TELL YOU THAT JACKIE IS BARKING) is a typical case of the fallacy of misplaced information, an attempt to put part of the information about the discourse situation into the described situation. Similarly, to assume that definite descriptions invariably constrain the described situation to meet the defining condition is an attempt to put part of the information about resource situations into the described situation, and is another instance of the fallacy of misplaced information.

NAMES

We can use our discussion of descriptions to clarify certain issues surrounding the use of names and then complete our account in a way that handles the problem we left in Chapter 6. Broadly speaking, we can distinguish two approaches to names in the literature, represesented by Russell,[6] Frege, and Searle (58) on the one hand, and Donnellan and Kripke on the other. In our terms, the first type of theory finds some describing conditions to be constitutents of the interpretation of the statement in which a name occurs, while the second kind of theory takes the individual named to be the constituent. We think the considerations Donnellan and Kripke have raised make the second kind of theory much more plausible, especially once one has a semantical theory that can accommodate it.

The arguments Donnellan and Kripke use show that any of the properties one might naturally look for to be constituents of the interpretation simply don't belong there. For example, if the only thing I believe about Aristotle is that he was Alexander's teacher, one might suppose that my use of ARISTOTLE contributes the property of being Alexander's teacher to the interpretations of my statements about Aristotle. But things just don't seem to work this way. My statement that Aristotle was Alexander's teacher isn't a triviality, as it seems it would be. It doesn't fail to be about Aristotle, even if it turns out that Aristotle didn't teach Alexander, or he was only one of a number of teachers of Alexander. The theory of descriptions in situation semantics probably provides ways of improving theories of the Frege–Russell–Searle variety, by taking names to be referential uses of the associated descriptions. But this is not the approach we take. Names are names, not hidden descriptions.

But we think there is an aspect of names that has not been emphasized by our theory so far, and not properly emphasized by Kripke and Donnellan. Names are not unique (Meiland, 70), and this is reflected in their semantical properties; they serve not only as noun phrases, but also as common nouns (Burge, 73). Although my use of

ARISTOTLE has no intimate semantic connection with most of the properties I believe Aristotle had, it does have an intimate semantic connection with one he had, being an Aristotle.

Names and Properties

When Joe says "Jackie is biting Molly," the situations in the interpretation of his utterance all have Jackie biting Molly, but they don't all have Jackie being a Jackie, and Molly being a Molly. Some of them may have Jackie named MOLLY and Molly named JACKIE. If they were actual, what Joe said would be true, but to say it he would have had to say, "Molly is biting Jackie."

The fact that Jackie's being a Jackie isn't part of what Joe asserts can lead to the overreaction of denying that this property has anything to do with the working of the name "Jackie." Indeed, if a "Proper Name" is a name that refers to its bearer all by itself, then we don't think there are many Proper Names, as opposed to proper uses of names. Belief in Proper Names is just an instance of the fallacy of misplaced information, in this case going from the absence of information in the interpretation to denying that it exists. When Lee introduced himself by saying, "I'm Lee," I learn what his name is, even though he hasn't mentioned his name, and being a Lee isn't a constituent of what he asserts, as it would be if he'd actually said, "I'm a Lee." If I assume that what he says is true, then I know that his name is Lee. It is not part of the interpretation of his utterance, but part of the information I get from it, and I get it because I know how names work, and know that the property associated with the name LEE is being named Lee.

Preoccupation with names of individuals can obscure the important role that the properties associated with names have. For most names β, being a β isn't important, because there are many generalizations across situations where different individuals have the same name. What do all Lees have in common except being Lees? It is probably true that most Nixons are defensive about their names and that most Jons are proud of the way their name is spelled, but these are more the exception than the rule. Often, however, such properties are quite important. The names of many entities are determined by systematic naming conventions, and the resultant property can play quite an important role. Each Wednesday is to be kept open for department meetings, but such meetings should not be scheduled on a Christmas or a Yom Kippur.

So each name β has an associated property, which we express with the phrase "being a β." For simple names of individuals, this property will just amount to having that name, which sounds simple enough, although it probably isn't.

Inverse Information and Names

We saw above that not all the information we can get from an utterance comes from the interpretation. We think that the information I get from Lee about his name belongs in this category of *inverse information,* and we want our theory of names to reflect this.

A simple way to achieve this is to add the following condition (2) to our account of the meaning of names:

$$d, c \, [\![\beta]\!] \, a_\sigma, e$$
iff
  1. $c(\beta) = a_\sigma$
  2. a_σ is a β.

But there is a problem with this, which appears as soon as we try to spell out the second condition explicitly within the theory of situations. Where must a_σ be a β? It does not seem correct to require that this be part of the discourse situation. It seems to us that the right requirement is a bit more subtle. What is part of the discourse situation is that the speaker has the information that the individual to whom he refers has the name the speaker uses. For example the reader of this book by now has picked up information about various members of the authors' families, including their names. He or she has the information that a certain person is named Frenchie for example. This information is part of the inverse information in a statement like "Frenchie is the wife of John." It is not part of the interpretation that Frenchie is a Frenchie but it is part of the inverse information available. And so the hearer of such a statement, and the reader of this book, has this information and can use it to refer to Frenchie with the name FRENCHIE. Notice that having the information that Frenchie is named Frenchie does not mean that one could necessarily identify Frenchie in any way. The connection can be tenuous indeed. If you hear me using the name you might have no idea whom I am talking about and ask, "Who is Frenchie?" In this case just about all the information about Frenchie that you have is that she is a Frenchie and that I am talking about her.

If such a reader says, "Frenchie must have endured a lot while

John was working on that book," the reader would have satisfied our condition on names. Such a reader may not *know* or even *believe* that Frenchie is a Frenchie, for he may strongly suspect that the individuals and names used in this book are made up. But since in this case they are not, there has been a real flow of information from the authors through the book to the reader, and he has the information, whether he believes it or not. It is in this sense that the reader has the information the Frenchie is a Frenchie.

To express this condition properly, we need to borrow from our theory of attitudes. Later we will explain how to represent the attitudes as relations to schemata, sets of event-types. We will use *inf* for the relation of having information that. We represent our second condition not with (2) above but as follows:

3. in d: at l_d: *inf*, a_d, E; yes
   of, $\dot{b}$, a_σ; yes

where

E: = at l, being-a-β, $\dot{b}$; yes

The relation *of* in the second line indicates that $\dot{b}$ is anchored to a_σ. A similar condition takes care of the gender implications of pronouns like SHE. When I say, "She has been very patient," referring to Frenchie, I have not said that Frenchie is female, but this is certainly inverse information that can be picked up from my utterance.

PART D

The Attitudes

CHAPTER EIGHT

Seeing

We use the term *attitude* both for a group of verbs and for the kinds of situations described by statements using them. The verbs may be roughly characterized as those which embed sentences and are used to report perception and cognition. Here are examples of *attitude reports* employing attitude verbs we study:

(1) MELANIE SAW JIM EAT AN ANCHOVY.

(2) SARAH HEARD JIM EATING AN ANCHOVY.

(3) MELANIE SAW THAT JIM WAS EATING AN ANCHOVY.

(4) MELANIE KNEW THAT A RED HAIRED BOY WAS EATING AN ANCHOVY.

(5) MELANIE BELIEVED THAT JIM WAS EATING AN ANCHOVY.

(6) MELANIE SAID THAT JIM WAS EATING AN ANCHOVY.

(7) JONNY BELIEVED THAT JIM ATE THE ANCHOVY OR JOE HID IT FOR HIM.

(8) SARAH HAD THE INFORMATION THAT JIM ATE THE ANCHOVY.

(9) SARAH BELIEVED THAT JOE HID IT FOR HIM.

With perception verbs we distinguish between constructions in which the embedded sentence is tensed, as in (3), and those in which it is tenseless, as in (1) and (2). We use SEE$_n$ to indicate uses of SEE which embed untensed sentences, as in (1), and SEE$_t$ to indicate uses of SEE which take a THAT-complement followed by a tensed sentence, as in (3).

The attitude verbs we study are related to two wider classes of verbs. First, there are those like INTENDS, WANTS, and DESIRES, which embed infinitive verb phrases, rather than sentences or sentence-like elements: JIM WANTS TO AVOID NUCLEAR WAR; MELANIE INTENDED TO REFER TO JOE. These verbs are also attitude verbs, and we believe that the analysis we give can be extended to them in a natural way. This is a major virtue of the theory of situations, but we do not treat them in this book. Second, there are sentence-embedding constructions like IT IS TRUE THAT, IT IS PROBABLE THAT, IT IS NECESSARY THAT, and IT IS POSSIBLE THAT, which are not used to report perceptual or cognitive activity. We have already discussed one such construction: MEANS THAT. Beyond this and the highly tentative remarks on sentence negation in Chapter 6, we do not discuss these other sentence-embedding constructions.

Like MEANS THAT, we place the attitudes in the category of *verbs of indirect classification,* and our analysis of these latter verbs is parallel to our two-step analysis of the former. First we examine relations between individuals and situations, like the unexplained relations *MO* of Chapter 3. Then we look for the underlying uniformities that give rise to these relations in the way that the constraints of Chapter 5 give rise to the *MO* relations.

EVIDENCE FOR A THEORY OF THE ATTITUDES

The attitude verbs play an enormously important role in daily life. Their use can be viewed, with some simplification, as falling into two main categories. We often use attitude verbs in explanations of what people think and do: because Melanie saw Jim eat an anchovy, she believed that he ate anchovies and that he wouldn't mind having anchovies on the pizza; because Sarah believed that Joe hid the anchovy, she looked for it. This suggests that attitude reports describe psychological states of individuals that are connected in a lawlike way to other psychological and behavioral states. This idea has gained widespread acceptance in recent theories of the mind, theories we build upon without taking a stand on many of their subtle differences. A central idea we use is that natural language embodies a common-sense psychological theory, *folk psychology* in David Lewis' apt phrase, a theory which postulates psychological or mental states that different people at different times are in (Lewis, 66). Our ordinary psychological concepts, like belief and desire, get at such states indirectly through their causal or functional roles. The main differences among these theories have to do with the relation of such states to states of the central nervous system. We shall not worry about this connection, though what we say is relevant to some of the arguments that have appeared.

The second use of the attitudes is as evidence about the external world, the world outside of the agent's mind. When Melanie told Jon that Jim ate an anchovy, Jon believed her; he took her claim as evidence that he had eaten an anchovy. Some of the attitudes provide stronger evidence than others. Melanie might have said that Jim was eating an anchovy, even though he wasn't. But if she knew that he was eating an anchovy, or saw that he was eating an anchovy, he must have been eating one. Melanie cannot know that φ or see that φ unless it is true that φ.

These two uses are clearly related. We think that the psychological states people are in are systematically related to the types of situations they are in, so that learning about one can often give us information about the other. Any theory of the attitudes should account for these two uses of attitude reports and the connection between them.

The evidence that has always played the greatest role in the semantics of the attitudes is their "logical behavior." Since the writings of Frege and Russell, the beginning wisdom in the philosophy of attitudes has been the failure of the principle of substitutivity. We may state this principle using ATTS as a dummy attitude verb and t_1, t_2 as either names, pronouns, or definite descriptions, as follows:[1]

If a atts that $\varphi(t_1)$ and t_1 is t_2, then a atts that $\varphi(t_2)$.

Two sorts of apparent failure need to be distinguished: those involving names and pronouns, and those involving definite descriptions. Here are examples of each type:

THALES BELIEVES THAT HESPERUS IS VISIBLE.

HESPERUS IS PHOSPHORUS.

SO, THALES BELIEVES THAT PHOSPHORUS IS VISIBLE.

GEORGE IV BELIEVED THAT SCOTT WROTE *WAVERLY*.

SCOTT WAS THE AUTHOR OF *IVANHOE*.

SO, GEORGE IV BELIEVED THAT THE AUTHOR OF *IVANHOE* WROTE *WAVERLY*.

In certain circumstances we would be reluctant to accept the substitutions involved in these little arguments, a reluctance which is taken to show that the principle is false.

Frege and Russell took different positions toward the apparent breakdown of the principle of substitutivity. Frege thought the principle was really not valid for the attitudes and gave a semantic explanation for its failure: the expressions in the embedded sentence

do not have their usual reference.[2] In fact, Frege thought that in attitude reports the expressions refer to their usual sense. We call this move "abandonment of semantic innocence," after a remark of Davidson's:

If we could but recover our pre-Fregean semantic innocence, I think it would be plainly incredible that the words "the earth moves," uttered after the words "Galileo said that," mean anything different, or refer to anything else, than is their wont when they come in other environments. (Davidson, 69)

Russell thought that the principle of substitutivity was correct, but didn't apply in examples like those above. Once we apply Russell's theory of descriptions to the second inference, we get a reading to which the principle of substitutivity simply doesn't apply:

GEORGE IV BELIEVED THAT SCOTT WROTE *WAVERLY*.

THERE WAS ONE AND ONLY ONE AUTHOR OF *IVANHOE*, AND HE WAS SCOTT.

SO, GEORVE IV BELIEVED THAT THERE WAS ONE AND ONLY ONE AUTHOR OF *IVANHOE*, AND HE WROTE *WAVERLY*.

On Russell's theory both inferences, the original and the translation of it immediately above, are invalid; the original merely looks as though it is an application of the principle of substitutivity, because of the misleading surface structure of the sentences. Russell then used the same sort of explanation for the cases with names. Using his doctrine that ordinary names are hidden definite descriptions, Russell gave the same explanation for the first sort of case.

Russell's account is innocent in a way that Frege's is not, for Russell treats expressions in embedded sentences just as they are treated elsewhere. But Russell gives up a bit of common sense that Frege does not: that descriptions are syntactic units whose semantic values are (at least in some cases) individuals. Also, by taking ordinary names to be hidden descriptions, Russell really gives up another bit of common sense: that the semantic value of an ordinary name is an individual. We want to build these pieces of common sense into our notion of semantic innocence.

There is one more element we want to build in too, the common-sense idea that statements are *about* things. To make this more concrete, we are committed to the falsity of the principle that logical equivalents are substitutable:

If a atts φ and φ is logically equivalent to ψ, then a atts ψ.

We think the falsity of this principle is another bit of common sense. For example, from

MELANIE SAW JIM EAT AN ANCHOVY

it does not follow that

MELANIE SAW JIM EAT AN ANCHOVY AND SARAH EAT A PICKLE OR SARAH NOT EAT A PICKLE.

From an utterance of the first we do not learn that Melanie saw Sarah, although this would follow from a truthful utterance of the second. It is obvious from this that the inference is no good.

Such a knock-down argument against the principle for the other attitudes is harder to find, but the arguments seem strong enough. Why should we suppose that just because Melanie knows that Jim ate an anchovy, she knows that Fred Lynn does or does not play center field for the Red Sox? Melanie has never seen nor heard of Fred Lynn, and knows nothing about him.[3] We propose, then, that an innocent semantics for the attitudes must meet the following conditions:

- Embedded sentences in attitude reports are syntactic units, parts of the embedding report,[4] and expressions in them work just as they do elsewhere.

- Names, pronouns, and referential and (outer) attributive uses of definite descriptions have individuals, not senses or meanings or functions, as their semantic values.

- The principle of substitution of logical equivalents fails.

Our commitment to semantic innocence means that we are committed to the principle of substitutivity when t_1 and t_2 are restricted to names, pronouns, referential and (outer) attributive uses of descriptions. For example, we are committed to the first but not the second of the following arguments, the first being an outer attributive use of THE COOK, the second an inner attributive use.

HELEN KNEW THAT HENRY WAS ALWAYS LATE.

HENRY WAS THE COOK.

(HELEN KNEW THAT (THE COOK)^1 WAS ALWAYS LATE.)^1

HELEN KNEW THAT HENRY WAS ALWAYS LATE.

HENRY WAS THE COOK.

HELEN KNEW THAT ((THE COOK)^2 WAS ALWAYS LATE)^2

The pattern of inferences and non-inferences comes out correctly in our semantics, and this is what we think the evidence demands.

As we indicated in Chapter 2, however, we see intuitions about valid patterns of inference as only a small part of the evidence for a semantical theory. Agreement in intuitions often depends on an artificially restricted set of examples. Where there is agreement, what is agreed upon often leaves open many questions that must be settled before one has a real semantic theory of the attitudes.

Our theory will be presented in two steps, parallel to our theory of MEANS THAT. First, in Chapters 8 and 9 we present an innocent account of the semantics of attitude reports. In Chapter 8 we take SEE$_n$ as our first attitude verb. We interpret seeing$_n$ as a relation between individuals and certain sorts of situations, *scenes.* In Chapter 9 this theory is extended to SEES$_t$, the first of the truly epistemic constructions. All the problems that have plagued the semantics of the attitude verbs come between SEE$_n$ and SEE$_t$. Once we have worked out our theory of SEE$_t$, it is easy to extend it to KNOW, BELIEVE, ASSERT, and DOUBT. Basically, the difference between SEE$_n$ and SEE$_t$ will be explained by whether the agent stands in a relation to a single situation, the one she sees, or a collection of alternative situations, the ones that are compatible with what she sees and with what she knows about how the world is and works. We call the latter situations the agent's *visual alternatives.* Similarly, in our account of knowledge we will invoke an *epistemic alternative* relation, and for belief a *doxastic alternative* relation. These various relations are reminiscent of Hintikka's treatment of the attitudes in (62), and we owe a great debt to his work. The ways in which our treatment differs from his will be explained below.

The theory of these two chapters deals with the facts traditionally explained by semantic theories, and it resolves a number of puzzles that the other accounts leave unresolved, especially those which revolve around the assumptions of the slingshot, the principle of substitutivity, and the traditional semantic indiscernibility of logically equivalent sentences. We have come to feel, however, that the theory which rests the attitudes on relations to situations is incomplete in several ways. So, in the final two chapters we dig deeper into the theory of situations in an attempt to ground these relations in the agent's cognitive activity.

The parallel with MEANS THAT is worth mentioning. In Chapter 3 we assumed that there were meaningful relations MO between situations and saw how to use them to define interpretation. The relations were, by and large, proper collections of pairs of situations. In Chapter 5 we saw how the relations are grounded in structural constraints, actual situations of a certain sort. With the attitudes we can explain many of the semantic properties of attitude reports by assuming the existence of relations SO, KO, BO between agents and the agent's visual, epistemic or doxastic option situations, respectively. However, the same sorts of problems that arise with the relations MO also come up here and point to missing uniformities across cognitive situations. In Chapter 10 we look for the cognitive analogue of these missing uniformities.

SHAKEN ATTITUDES

The attitudes are traditionally called "propositional." The verbs embed a sentence, and the semantic contribution of the embedded sentence to the whole is traditionally taken to be a "proposition." Here tradition splits, since there is no semblance of a consensus as to what in the world a proposition is, or even what sort of thing it might be: a state-of-affairs, sentence, sentence meaning, Fregean sense, mental representation, or set of possible worlds.

In an earlier paper (Barwise and Perry, 81a) we defined "realistic propositions" as certain classes P of coe's, the kind that serve as the interpretation of utterances. There we sketched a semantics that took attitudes to be relations to realistic propositions, the one "designated" by the embedded sentence. We pointed out certain problems with this account and proposed a solution.

In this book we have deliberately avoided the terms "proposition," and "propositional attitude." We think that propositions are an artifact of the semantic endeavor and not the sorts of things that people usually talk about, even when reporting someone's attitudes. To explain why we think this is important, we must digress a bit.

The primitives of our theory are all real things: individuals, properties, relations, and space-time locations. Out of these and objects available from the set theory we construct a universe of abstract objects, situation types, coe's, event-types, and so on. Our aim is to have every component of the semantic theory be one of these abstract objects. Of course, there will also be objects that are artifacts of the set-theory and not used in the semantic theory, but that is neither here nor there.

A mathematical theory of meaning must inevitably be constrained by the abstract objects one has available for classifying aspects of reality. These constraints do not disappear by ignoring them. We are working in set theory, with a conception of sets based on Zermelo's cumulative hierarchy. We start with certain primitives and allow sets of these, sets of these sets, and so on. On this conception certain collections of sets are inherently too "big" to be sets. These collections are called Proper Classes, and are construed as ways of speaking of objects, not as objects per se. Sets can stand in relations to other sets, but these proper classes can't. Proper classes can be used to classify objects in various ways, but they do not correspond to objects. Now it turns out that the interpretation of an utterance, the realistic proposition it designates, is a proper class.[5] These propositions are not the sorts of things that can enter into relations in situations! This is not just a mathematical nuisance, but a reflection of the fact that these propositions do not correspond to any part of the causal order of things.

If attitudes are attitudes toward propositions that are proper classes of events, it must be in a way that is supported by things in the causal order, and attitude reports must give us information about these things. Our contention is that (a) attitude reports give us information about relations between the agent and situations, but that (b) these relations must be supported by cognitive states of the agent. Chapters 8 and 9 are devoted to (a), Chapters 10 and 11 to (b).

We start our account with SEE$_n$, where the claim that the idea that seeing reports a relation to a situation (scene, event) is certainly more plausible on the face of it than the claim that it reports a relation to a proposition.

SEEING$_n$: THE FORGOTTEN PARADIGM

If you, as special prosecutor, had to convince a jury that Nixon saw Rosemary Woods erase the crucial part of the Watergate tape, you would have a pretty good idea of the sort of evidence you would need. You would need to prove that Rosemary Woods did indeed erase the crucial part of the tape and that Nixon saw it. For example, a film of Nixon watching Miss Woods erase that part of the tape would be pretty good evidence. But what if you had to prove that Nixon saw *that* Rosemary Woods erased the crucial part of the Watergate tape? Your old evidence will no longer suffice, since Nixon could claim that he didn't know it was the Watergate tape, or that he didn't know that she was erasing it, or that he knew she was erasing part but didn't know it was the crucial part. To prove the first (and weaker) claim, one has to show that Nixon had his eyes open and functioning, and that an event of a certain sort was taking place before him. To prove the stronger claim, one needs to prove something about what he recognized and what thoughts were going through his mind.

These remarks illustrate the difference between two ways in which language allows us to report perceptual attitudes: *epistemically neutral* and *epistemically positive perceptual reports.* (1), (3), (5), and (7) are epistemically neutral, (2), (4), (6), and (8) are epistemically positive:

(1) AUSTIN SAW A MAN GET SHAVED IN OXFORD.

(2) AUSTIN SAW THAT A MAN GOT SHAVED IN OXFORD.

(3) DICK SAW MARY REMOVE THE CRUCIAL PART OF THE WATERGATE TAPE.

(4) DICK SAW THAT MARY REMOVED THE CRUCIAL PART OF THE WATER-GATE TAPE.

(5) RALPH SAW A SPY HIDING A LETTER UNDER A ROCK.

(6) RALPH SAW THAT A SPY WAS HIDING A LETTER UNDER A ROCK.

(7) THE MOTHER HEARD HER BABY CRYING.

(8) THE MOTHER HEARD THAT HER BABY WAS CRYING.

Epistemically neutral perception reports are an extremely interesting class of reports for our purposes. Received theories do not fit them well, if at all, while our theory seems made to order for them.[6]

Epistemically neutral perception reports embed sentences, just as other attitude reports do. The embedded sentences are in a naked infinitive, (*NI*) form ((1) and (3) are examples), or in a gerundive (*G*) form ((5) and (7)). In these forms the embedded sentences do not have their verbs conjugated normally. There is a simple semantic explanation for this, roughly that what is perceived occurs, or is taken to occur, at the same time as the perceiving. The important point is that like attitudes generally, these neutral perception reports embed sentences.[7]

The *NI* and *G* forms of perceptual reports behave slightly differently. For example, if you saw me close the door (an *NI* report), I closed the door. On the other hand, if you saw me closing the door, then it only follows that I was closing the door, not that I closed the door. I may have been interrupted, or perhaps stopped when I noticed you were watching. In this book we want to avoid aspectual matters and so restrict ourselves to the simpler case, that of *NI* reports.

One reason for treating *NI* reports is that the *NI*-complement construction is part of a simple characterization of perception verbs, observed by James Gee (77). Of all the verbs that take sentence complements, only the perception verbs both take *NI* complements and allow anaphora with respect to these complements, as in:

RALPH SAW ORTCUTT HIDE SOMETHING. VAN SAW IT TOO.

Notice that the anaphoric IT in the second sentence is not just a syntactic replacement for the *NI* complement, for the above implies that Ralph and Van both saw Ortcutt hide a particular thing. But that does not follow from:

RALPH SAW ORTCUTT HIDE SOMETHING. VAN SAW ORTCUTT HIDE SOMETHING TOO.

The point here, though, is that no other transitive verbs allow both the *NI* complement and anaphora with respect to these complements.

The Logic of NI-Perceptual Reports

Yet another reason for treating *NI*-perceptual reports first is that among the attitude reports, the *NI*-perceptual reports seem to have the clearest semantic properties. That is, there are a number of fairly clear semantic intuitions involving these reports, intuitions that fall right out of the semantics we give but which are quite difficult or even impossible to capture on more traditional accounts. We now list a number of apparently correct informal principles about one kind of *NI*-perception reports, those in which the verb SEE is followed by an *NI* sentence. The verb SEE is the most flexible and interesting of our perception verbs. But the points we make apply by and large to any epistemically neutral perception report.

A word of caution is in order concerning the principles listed below. They are not hard and fast rules that apply to sentences radically different from the simple indicative sentences we use to motivate them. There are a number of obvious exceptions, which we point out below. These exceptions are no problem for our account, as long as our treatment of the different types of embedded sentences predicts their behavior.

A. *The Principle of Veridicality:* If b sees φ, then φ.

This principle lies behind the use of epistemically neutral perception reports as evidence about the world. Suppose, for example, that we sent a scout up to the top of a nearby hill to watch out for hostile pioneers. If the scout saw hostile pioneers come this way, then such pioneers came this way, and we would have been well advised to get ready for them.

B. *Principle of Substitutivity:* If b sees $\varphi(t_1)$, and t_1 is t_2, then b sees $\varphi(t_2)$.

Thus we are claiming that the beginning wisdom about the attitudes, that Substitutivity fails, is just plain false for SEE$_n$. In other words, in these *NI*-perceptual reports, different ways of describing the same individual in the embedded sentences do not affect the truth value of the whole. Note, for example, the validity of the following sort of inference:

RUSSELL SAW G. E. MOORE GET SHAVED IN CAMBRIDGE.

G. E. MOORE WAS (ALREADY) THE AUTHOR OF *PRINCIPIA ETHICA*.

SO, RUSSELL SAW THE AUTHOR OF *PRINCIPIA ETHICA* GET SHAVED IN
CAMBRIDGE.

The principle of substitutivity, like the principle of veridicality, supports the idea that we use SEE$_n$ when we are interested in the subject matter, what is seen, not the state of the observer's mind. This is also supported by our next principle.

> C. *Existential Generalization:* If b sees φ(the π), then there is something$_1$ such that b sees φ(it$_1$).

For example, if Helen saw the chairman of the department answer the phone, then there is someone whom Helen saw answer the phone.

> D. *Negation:* If b sees $\neg\varphi$, then b doesn't see φ.

Here we are $\neg\varphi$ for the verb phrase negation of φ. Some instances of principle (*D*):

RALPH SAW MARY NOT SERVE BILL.

SO, RALPH DIDN'T SEE MARY SERVE BILL.

JAMES SAW SOMEONE NOT LEAVE THE ROOM.

SO, JAMES DIDN'T SEE EVERYONE LEAVE THE ROOM.

Two obvious but important principles:

> E. *Conjunction distribution:* If b sees φ and ψ, then b sees φ and b sees ψ.

> F. *Disjunction distribution:* If b sees φ or ψ, then b sees φ or b sees ψ.

An instance of the latter is:

RALPH SAW ORTCUTT OR HORTCUTT HIDE THE LETTER.

SO, RALPH SAW ORTCUTT HIDE THE LETTER OR HE SAW HORTCUTT HIDE
IT.

Of course there is no reason to suppose that Ralph knew which person hid the letter.

A principle that is closely related to (*C*) and (*F*) involves distribution of indefinite descriptions over SEE$_n$.

> G. *Distribution of Indefinite Descriptions:* If b sees φ(a π), then there is a π_1 such that b sees φ(it$_1$).

For example, if Hans saw a tall, thin man climb in the window of 333 Miramonte, then there was a tall, thin man whom Hans saw climb in the window. Again there is no implication to be drawn that Hans recognized who it was. If he had, he probably wouldn't have dropped the sandbag on him.

A point that we have mentioned, but want to re-emphasize, is that the principles (A)–(G) are informal summaries of certain semantic judgments about *NI* perceptual reports. They serve us as a convenient shorthand for facts to be explained *by* a semantic theory, not as part *of* the theory. In particular, they are not "axioms in the logic of perception." They also give us a convenient way to contrast SEE$_n$ with SEE$_t$ and the other epistemic attitudes.

As we mentioned above, there are rather obvious exceptions to some of these loosely formulated principles. For example, an "application" of (A) might suggest that the following was valid:

> ALICE SAW NO ONE WALK ON THE ROAD.
>
> SO, NO ONE WALKED ON THE ROAD.

Similarly, an "application" of (B) might suggest that we thought that the following was valid:

> JOHN SAW THE NUMBER OF SLEEPING STUDENTS INCREASE.
>
> THE NUMBER OF SLEEPING STUDENTS WAS NINE.
>
> SO, JOHN SAW NINE INCREASE.

And similarly, (D) might suggest the following inference:

> JONNY SAW JACKIE NOT CATCH ONE RABBIT.
>
> SO, JONNY DIDN'T SEE JACKIE CATCH ONE RABBIT.

None of these inferences fall out of the semantics we assign to *NI*-perception sentences, as of course they should not. This is one of the advantages of giving a genuine semantic analysis, as opposed to taking the old fashioned "logical form" approach to inference. With the right semantics, the inferences take care of themselves.

THE SEMANTICS OF *NI*-PERCEPTION STATEMENTS

We have discussed the syntactic structure of a certain class of sentences, and listed some inferences that seem to be part of the logic of the expressions in question. At the beginning of the chapter we said what we thought was involved in the truth of these statements—that a person has to see a situation of the sort described by the embedded sentence in the report. Now we must try to put these pieces together to form a coherent picture.

Sentences act like indefinite descriptions of situations, the ones they describe. Similarly, *NI* sentences act like indefinite descriptions of situations, the difference being (as we saw in Chapter 6) that since they are tenseless, the spatiotemporal location of the situation is left open. Embedded in perception reports, they assert that the agent saw such a situation. A statement using MELANIE SAW JACKIE RUN asserts that Melanie saw an event in which Jackie was running. Since Jackie has done a lot of running at different times and places over the years, there are many such actual situations. As long as Melanie was seeing one of them, the statement will be true.

The meaning of JACKIE RUN is really a relation between connections, locations, and situations, since there are many Jackies that might get referred to with JACKIE. And other *NI* sentences, like JACKIE BITE ME, have discourse sensitive expressions in them as well. In general, the meaning of an *NI* sentence is a relation between discourse situations, connections, locations, and situations.[8]

$$d, c \, [\![\text{JACKIE BITE ME}]\!] \, l, e$$

will obtain, just in case there are individuals x and y such that

i) $d, c \, [\![\text{JACKIE}]\!] \, x$
ii) $d, c \, [\![\text{ME}]\!] \, y$
iii) in e: at l: biting, x, y; yes.

No constraint is put on the relation between the time of the discourse and the location l, since there is no tense in the *NI* sentence. If Jackie bites people all the time, there will be many discourse situations, connections, and actual situations that stand in this relation. If Jackie is well behaved and never bites anyone, there won't be any. (Actually, she is pretty well behaved, despite our examples.)

Seeing is clearly a causal relation, but also, and importantly, an information-preserving one. When one sees, one picks up information about a situation at some distance, in virtue of the information-preserving causal chain that leads from that situation to the detected arrays of ambient light at the surfaces of one's eyes. The other attitudes we study, including SEEING$_t$, are sensitive to how the information (or misinformation) actually influences the agent's thought and action. By contrast, epistemically neutral perceptual reports, those using SEES$_n$, are concerned only with the nature of the situation about which information is detected by the agent.

As was emphasized in Chapter 3, at any location there are a number of situations. Among these are scenes, situations whose types deal with visually observable properties and objects. It is these situations that are seen, and serve as the designations of the naked infinitive sentences that we embed with SEE. There will be a great many such scenes at any given location *l*. If you and I are watching Jackie run from different positions, you may be able to see things I cannot, and vice versa. Perhaps her left front paw will be visible from where you are, but not from where I am. Even though we both see Jackie run, we see different scenes. But there are also scenes we both see. For example, you might see the first of these scenes, I the second, and both of us the third:

in *e*: at *l*: present, Jackie; yes
      running, Jackie; yes
      moving, Jackie's left paw; yes

in *e'*: at *l*: present, Jackie; yes
      running, Jackie; yes
      moving, Jackie's right paw; yes

in *e"*: at *l*: present, Jackie; yes
      running, Jackie; yes

In this case, it would be correct to say that we saw the same thing, and also correct to say we saw different things, although each claim could be misleading in certain circumstances.

We can now see that the meaning of a verb phrase like SEES JACKIE RUN or SEES JACKIE BITE ME has to be a relation between the following factors:

- a discourse situation, to provide a designation for ME in the second example;
- connections, to provide the reference for names, and the location for the verb SEE;
- a course of events, to classify which individuals are seeing which scenes in various locations; and
- an individual, the potential see-er.

There is an issue left over, though, namely where the location for the embedded tenseless sentence is to come from. There seem to be two choices open to us. (1) We can have the location of the embedded sentence be the same as that assigned to the main verb SEE. Alternatively, (2), we could quantify over arbitrary locations.

These different strategies, applied to the verb phrase SEES JACKIE BITE ME, are illustrated below:

(1) d, c ⟦ SEES JACKIE BITE ME ⟧ a, e

if and only if there is a *coe e'* and a location $l = c$ (SEES) temporally overlapping that of the discourse situation such that

d, c ⟦ JACKIE BITE ME ⟧ l, e'

in e: at l: seeing, a, e'; yes.

The second strategy would be to define

(2) d, c ⟦ SEES JACKIE BITE ME ⟧ a, e

if and only if there is a *coe e'*, a location $l = c$ (SEES) temporally overlapping that of the discourse situation and a location l' such that

d, c ⟦ JACKIE BITE ME ⟧ l', e'

in e: at l: seeing, a, e'; yes.

Whichever strategy we choose, the sentence, MELANIE SEES JACKIE BITE ME, will have one less parameter. We will have

d, c ⟦ MELANIE SEES JACKIE BITE ME ⟧ e

just in case there is an individual a such that

d, c ⟦ MELANIE ⟧ a

d, c ⟦ SEES JACKIE BITE ME ⟧ $a, e.$

The two strategies make somewhat different predictions, and lead to different complications for complex complements. All things considered, we prefer the first, and so adopt it here. However, the points we wish to make regarding the attitudes are independent of this decision.

There is a very important element missing in the account so far. We have failed to ensure the veridicality of *NI*-perceptual reports. In earlier treatments we built this into the semantics of the reports by adding a clause to the interpretation of them. However, it seems more accurate to reflect this not as a fact about language, but as a fact about seeing, that whatever is seen is actual (or perhaps factual):

at l_u: involves, E, E'; yes

where E and E' are given by:

E: = at $\overset{.}{l}$: seeing, a, e; yes
E': = at $\overset{.}{l}$: actual, e; yes.

The general treatment of *NI*-seeing reports is not much more complicated than that of the special case we have treated. *NI* sentences are taken as describing *coe*'s, and a sentence of the form *A* SEES φ asserts that *a* sees an event of the type described by φ. There are some complications concerning where the singular *NP*'s in φ are evaluated; that we'll return to.

Before showing how this simple semantics explains the facts we have observed, we turn to a brief discussion of the relationship between seeing scenes and seeing individuals. From a semantic point of view, the relationship is nowhere as straightforward as one might think. In general it seems to follow that if Melanie saw Jackie bite me she also saw Jackie. And in normal circumstances she would also see me, or at least part of me. You might, however, see your spouse write me a letter without seeing me. And you might see Joan shoot a bear without seeing Joan. In one case the individual serving as the object of the verb is missing from the scene, while in the other case the individual described by the subject of the verb is missing from the scene.

Our account of this is as follows. The verb phrase SEES JACKIE is interpreted as the relation

$$d, c \, [\![\text{SEES JACKIE}]\!] \, a, e$$

just in case there is a *coe e'*, an individual *b*, a location $l = c\,(\text{SEES})$ overlapping that of *d* which satisfies:

$$d, c \, [\![\text{JACKIE}]\!] \, b$$
in *e'*: at *l*: present, *b*; yes
in *e*: at *l*: seeing, *a*, *e'*; yes.

Different properties and relations have different constraints in terms of what has to be present in a situation in order for the relation to hold. For example, there is a structural constraint that any visible situation in which *b* is running is one where *b* is present. But most visual situations in which *a* is writing to *b* are ones where *b* is absent.

EXPLANATION OF THE LOGICAL PRINCIPLES

The semantics we have given for SEE$_n$ enables us to understand the informal logical judgments listed above. We will consider them in order.

A. Veridicality: If *b* sees φ, then φ^*.

Here φ is an *NI* sentence, and φ^* is a corresponding tensed sentence. Thus instances of (A) are

(1) IF MELANIE SAW JACKIE RUN, THEN JACKIE RAN.

(2) IF MELANIE IS SEEING JACKIE RUN, THEN JACKIE IS RUNNING.

This principle follows from our treatment of the embedded *NI* sentence, certain considerations about locations and tense, and the constraint that if in e a sees a scene e', then e' is factual. The extra considerations involving tense are best explained by example.

Consider (2). If (2) is true, then it describes some actual course of events, a set of situations. Parts of some of these are seen by Melanie, and in at least one of them Jackie runs. It follows that there is an actual situation where Jackie runs. But is it at the right point in time? The tense of SEE in (2) tells us that Melanie is seeing e at a time that overlaps that of the utterance. Standard intuitions assume that the location of a visually apprehended situation temporally overlaps that of the seeing, so the present tense is appropriate. Thus (2) will be judged valid under normal circumstances.

But do things work out right in odd cases, say those involving observations over extraordinary distances? It seems to us that they do, although there is no particular reason to suppose they should, since language developed when such long-distance observations were not understood as they are now. Suppose, for example, that Melanie is watching Jackie through an extraordinarily powerful telescope, while she alternately runs and rests on a distant planet. Then the location of the seeing will be a space-time cylinder, stretching from the location of the scene through time to Melanie's observation. There is a very real sense in which this complex cylinder l is the one where the seeing takes place.

Our basic justification for (A) is that if e' is part of e and e is factual, then so is e', by the structural constraint reflecting the basic veridical nature of seeing. As long as the sentence φ can only be used to make absolutely persistent statements, so that if it describes e' it also describes any e of which e' is a part, then a version of (A) will hold for φ. For sentences that do not give rise to absolutely persistent statements, (A) will in general fail. Consider, for example, NO ONE IS WALKING ON THE ROAD. This gives rise to statements which are not absolutely persistent, since part of a road on which there are people walking may be one where no one is walking. And so it does not follow that if Alice saw no one walking on the road, then no one was walking on the road.

B. Substitutivity: If b sees $\beta(t_1)$, and t_1 is t_2, then b sees $\beta(t_2)$.

We will split this principle into two cases. The first is where t_1 and t_2 are names, pronouns, or descriptions used referentially or attributively. We assume, of course, that if a referential description is used, the resource situation is the same throughout. This restricted principle we shall sometimes call the *principle of innocence*. The second case is where either t_1 or t_2 is a description used functionally or inner attributively.

In the first case, our semantics predicts that (B) will hold, and it does. We gave an example earlier, involving Russell and Moore. Here are some more:

> MELANIE IS SEEING JOE RUN.
>
> JOE IS THE PITCHER.
>
> SO, MELANIE IS SEEING THE PITCHER RUN.

> MELANIE SAW THE BROTHER OF JOE AND SARAH EAT AN ANCHOVY.
>
> I AM THE BROTHER OF JOE AND SARAH.
>
> SO, MELANIE SAW ME EAT AN ANCHOVY.

If t_1 or t_2 is a description used functionally, (B) does not hold. For example,

> JOHN SAW THE NUMBER OF SLEEPING STUDENTS INCREASE.
>
> THE NUMBER OF SLEEPING STUDENTS WAS NINE.
>
> SO, JOHN SAW NINE INCREASE.

But this is no problem for our account, since it does not predict that this inference will hold. We would use the major premise in a case where the scene was a course of events, in which students were falling asleep as John lectures. No particular number will be a constituent of this scene, and in particular nine won't be, even if the minor premise is true, with reference to a particular point in the lecture. So our account simply doesn't have this inference coming out valid.

With the other attitudes another use of the definite description—in Chapter 6 we called it the *inner attributive*—is found. This corresponds to what is often called the "de dicto" reading of an attitude report. For example, if you say to me, "Your wife is drinking a pepsi," I might report this as, "He said that my wife was drinking a Pepsi." As we will explain when we come to SEE$_t$, the semantics for this provides a range of variation, just as with the functional use of a description. It is not a range of locations, but a range of alternative courses of events that is compatible with what you said. My wife is drinking a pepsi in some of these, but in others someone else is my wife and is drinking a pepsi. So, just as in the functional case, there is no one individual picked out by the definite description (Saarinen et al., 79). The inner attributive use is not a threat to an innocent account.

We claim that (B) holds for all of the attitudes we study, with the exception of cases involving functional and inner attributive uses of definite descriptions. This is just what our semantics predicts, so substitutivity does not present a problem. We expect some skepticism on this point from our readers, even if their intuitions agree on SEE$_n$, as most people's do. For this reason we want to make one further point.

Let's return to Melanie and Jim and the anchovy. Suppose Melanie meets Jim the next day. Jim would surely be correct in saying, "You saw me eat an anchovy," even if Melanie did not recognize Jim as the anchovy eater of the day before and adamantly refused to admit that such a nice boy could have done such a thing. Once she is convinced of her error, however, Melanie will have to say, "I was wrong, I did see you eat an anchovy." She won't be able to say something like, "Since I didn't know it was you, I didn't see you eat an anchovy."

But notice something about this example. In certain imaginable cases, it would be misleading and inappropriate for Jim to say, "You saw me eat an anchovy." Suppose, as above, Melanie clearly didn't recognize him. And suppose she orders the pizza without anchovies, saying, "I'm sure that no one here would think of eating an anchovy." Jim can certainly correct her by noting that he has eaten anchovies, and he may even observe that she has seen him do it. But he can't say, "But you have seen me eat an anchovy," as a complaint about her behavior. This would suggest that she is acting inappropriately given what she knows about those in her group. We might think that there is a rule of etiquette that goes roughly, "If you have seen someone in your group eat an anchovy, don't deny that anyone in your group would think of eating an anchovy." It would be inappropriate for Jim to invoke this rule. It obviously wasn't intended to apply to people in Melanie's position.

Now what *is* Melanie's position? Common sense suggests that she has two different concepts of the same person. There is the boy she saw yesterday eating an anchovy, and there is the fellow across the table. These concepts haven't "merged" in her mind, a point that might be put misleadingly by saying she doesn't realize they are concepts of the same person. So she is not in a position to follow the rule of etiquette, even though her intentions are pure. When Melanie is in this position, it is inappropriate for Jim to complain, by saying, for example, "How rude of her; she saw me eating an anchovy just yesterday."

Our thesis is that not only rules of etiquette but also a great many explanatory principles using the attitudes work only when one assumes the agent has only one concept of the subject of the attitude; or if there are several, then the relevant one is operative and characterized by the report (in our example, Melanie is the agent, Jim the subject). It is the inappropriateness of invoking these explanatory principles when these conditions are not met, not invalidity, that is at the heart of much of our reluctance to substitute. The intuitions that pass as logical intuitions are really intuitions about loss of explanatory potential. To make good this account, we need to develop the notion of a concept and to explain how different concepts can be relevant to different embedded statements, even when the course of events they describe are the same. This we will do in Chapter 10. For now we want merely to correlate the reluctance to substitute, even if the case of SEES$_n$ substitutivity holds, with the inappropriateness of such substitutions given various laws of folk psychology and other rules of behavior. We hope thereby to suggest that for the attitudes in general our reluctance to substitute in certain cases is not because of invalidity.

   C. *Existential Generalization:* If a sees φ(the π), then there is something$_1$ such that a sees φ(it$_1$).

The explanation of this principle involves nothing new above and beyond (A) and (B) and so is left for the reader.

   D. *Negation:* If a sees $\neg\varphi$, then a doesn't see φ.

Basically, this is guaranteed by our most primary structural constraint, the law of noncontradiction. Any two actual *coe*'s must be compatible. If a sees a scene where $\neg\varphi$ holds, that scene is an actual *coe* incompatible with φ holds, so there can't be an actual *coe* where φ holds, so there can't be one that a sees where φ holds.

There are some qualifications that need to be made. First it should be observed that (D) is only correct if the two uses of SEES are connected to the same location. We might use the present tense in a different way, as in a running commentary on what someone is seeing:

SHE SEES HIM RUN; HE STOPS; SHE SEES HIM NOT RUN TILL THE OTHERS
GO BY...

Next, there is the fact that our argument only works for sentences
φ with the property that if e and e' are compatible, then it can't be
the case that φ holds in e and $\neg\varphi$ holds in e'. This is fine for simple
sentences, but it is not right for sentences that involve complex *NP*'s.
For example, just because no one is walking on the road in e, and e
is compatible with e', it doesn't follow that no one is walking on the
road in e'. And that Jackie is not catching one rabbit in e doesn't
mean she isn't catching one rabbit (a different one) in some compatible e'—maybe even the same e.

We conclude this discussion with F:

F. *Disjunction distribution:* If b sees φ or ψ, then b sees φ or b sees
ψ.

If b is seeing a scene e' where (φ or ψ) is the case, then one of the two
must be the case in that scene.

INNOCENCE AND THE SLINGSHOT

Before moving to SEES$_t$, we want to emphasize one point. It might be
assumed that the abandonment of innocence in other theories of the
attitudes is motivated *solely* by a need to explain exceptions to
principles (B) and (C). This is not correct. Because of the influence
of the slingshot, it has seemed that an innocent account was impossible. If the notion of logical equivalence is built into the very way
we think about language, we will be predisposed to assume that principle (B) *must* fail, and we think this has been one reason people
have been too easily led to think that it *does* fail. (B), together with
the premise that logically equivalent statements have the same semantic value, leads, by a version of the slingshot, to the unacceptable
conclusion that the attitudes are truth-functional, and leads Quine,
for example, to despair of a semantics for the attitudes (Quine, 66a,
66b). A semantics of the sort we have just given for SEES$_n$ has long
been deemed impossible. It is in this sense that SEES$_n$ serves as our
paradigm for the attitudes, even though it is in many ways a very
special case.

CHAPTER NINE

Attitudes as Relations to Situations

We now turn to the semantics of SEE$_t$ and other epistemic attitudes, KNOW, BELIEVE, DOUBT, ASSERT—attitudes that tell us not just what the situations the agent has an attitude toward are like, but also about the agent's states of mind. This difference is reflected in the logical principles that describe inference patterns involving statements made with these verbs, facts that must be accounted for by the semantics we assign these verbs.

In the last chapter we discovered that the logic of b SEES φ is accounted for by assuming that it is used to report a relation between b and a scene s described by φ. In this chapter we try out the idea that the epistemic attitude b SEES THAT φ is used to report on a relation between b and situations s described by φ. We use the different inference patterns that seem to hold for SEES THAT to explore the nature of this relation. We then extend the account to other epistemic attitudes. We have a rather ambivalent attitude toward the resulting theory. We think it ranks high among available theories of the attitudes in the way it handles the semantic evidence, and working it out has clarified a lot of our thinking. But in the last section we find reasons for not being satisfied with it.

LOGICAL PRINCIPLES INVOLVING SEES THAT

We are going to examine the analogues of the principles $(A)-(G)$ that guided us in our search for a semantics for NI-seeing statements, to compare the logical properties of the NI-reports with those involving SEE THAT. Just as the logic of SEE$_n$ dictated the semantics we assigned to these statements, so, too, the logic of SEE$_t$, and our basic perspective of viewing statements as giving us information about objective situations in the world, dictates the semantics we assign to SEE$_t$ statements.

Primary vs *Secondary* SEES$_t$

For shorthand, we call utterances made with SEE$_t$ sentences SEE$_t$-*reports*. In sorting out our intuitions about SEE$_t$-reports, it is useful to follow Dretske (1969) and make a pragmatic distinction between what he calls *primary* SEE$_t$-reports and *secondary* SEE$_t$-reports.

In general, SEE$_t$-reports describe acquisition of knowledge through perception. A primary SEE$_t$-report is one that reports a direct acquisition of knowledge via perception. A secondary report is one that reports an acquisition of knowledge based on perception augmented by what one knows must be the case based on what one sees. The most natural reading of (1) is with (a) taken as primary, (b) as secondary. Similarly with (2). We use a version of Dretske's notation to mark this distinction.

(1) (a) I SAW$_p$ THAT THE TREE WAS WHIPPING AROUND, (b) SO I SAW$_s$ THAT THE WIND WAS BLOWING.

(2) (a) SUE SAW$_p$ THAT TANNER LIBRARY WAS EMPTY, (b) SO SHE SAW$_s$ THAT HELEN WAS NOT IN THE LIBRARY.

Our aim is to develop a plausible account of the semantics of SEE$_t$ sentences that covers both kinds of reports. While it is often natural to take a SEE$_t$-report as primary, it is largely a matter of suggestion. The implicature that it is a primary report can always be canceled in one of several ways. Consider for example:

(3) JONNY SAW THAT A CAT WAS CHASING A RAT.

Taken in isolation, it is tempting to take this as a primary report, a report of Jonny seeing a cat chasing a rat and being aware of what he is seeing. But if we follow (3) by either (4a) or (4b), the temptation vanishes.

(4) (a) . . . BUT HE DIDN'T SEE A CAT CHASE A RAT.

(4) (b) . . . BUT HE DIDN'T SEE THE RAT.

The trick used in (4a) is to note that since it focuses on just what is correctly seen rather than on what is inferred, a primary SEE$_t$-report must entail the corresponding *NI*-report—at least in those cases in which the *NI*-report is grammatical. We summarize this observation as follows:

(5) If (a) is used as a primary SEE$_t$-report, then infer (b),
where φ^* is the *NI* form of φ:
    (a) *a* sees that φ
    (b) *a* sees φ^*.

This gives us a general way of canceling the implicature that a sentence is being used as a primary report. We need only say

    a saw that φ but he didn't see φ^*.

This is a rather crude way of canceling the implicature. Another was given in (4b) and others will be seen below. The point, though, is that since the primary/secondary distinction is pragmatic, it is not reflected in our semantics for SEE$_t$ sentences. The semantic account has to fit both uses. We will see, however, that the semantics also provides a natural explanation of the distinction.

With this distinction in mind, we can turn to an examination of the SEE$_t$ analogues of (A)–(G). We take the opportunity to make a few comments on the logic of the other attitudes as well. We begin with the following summary table and then discuss the entries that are most germane to the semantics of the attitudes we develop.

	see	see that	know that	believe that	assert that	doubt that
A. Veridicality	+	+	+	−	−	−
B. Substitution (i)	(+)	(+)	(+)	(+)	(+)	(+)
(ii)	−	−	−	−	−	−
C. Exist Gen (i)	+	+	+	+	+	+
(ii)	−	−	−	−	−	−
D. Negation	+	+	+	(−)	(−)	(−)
E. Conj Dist	+	+	+	+	+	−
F. Disj Dist	+	+(p)	−	−	−	+
G. Dist of Indef Desc	+	+(p)	−	−	−	−
H. Weak Subst	+	+	+	+	+	−

The +(p) entries under SEE THAT indicate that the principle usually holds for primary SEE$_t$ reports but often fails for secondary SEE$_t$ reports. The symbol (+) means the inference is valid, but we are reluctant to use it in certain cases. The symbol (−) means the inference is invalid, but we are willing to use it in certain cases. The split of (B)

and (*C*) corresponds to (i) names, pronouns, referential, and outer attributive uses, and (ii) inner attributive uses, respectively. Weak substitution, (*H*), will be introduced in the discussion of (*B*). We use ATTS THAT as our dummy attitude verb.

   A. Veridicality. If *b* atts that φ, then φ.

Among the attitudes we study, SEE, SEE THAT, and KNOW THAT are veridical, and the others aren't. If Helen sees that I am in Palo Alto, then I am in Palo Alto. And if Jonny saw that Scruffy was chasing a rat, then she was chasing a rat. But just because Sue believes that (or doubts that) I am in Palo Alto, that is no proof that I am in Palo Alto, no matter how reliable Sue happens to be. And just because Joe believes that Jackie is biting Molly, that is no proof that she is.

   Substitution and Existential Generalization.
   B. If *a* atts that $\varphi(t_1)$ and t_1 is t_2, then *a* atts that $\varphi(t_2)$.
   C. If *a* atts that φ(the π), then there is something$_1$ such that $\varphi(\text{it}_1)$.

Frege worried about the morning star and the evening star; Russell worried about the author of *Waverley,* the author of *Ivanhoe,* Scott, and the present king of France. Their worries concerned these principles, which appear not to hold for the doxastic attitudes (BELIEVES, DOUBTS, SAYS), or the epistemic attitudes (KNOWS and SEES). This drove Frege to his realm of sense and Russell to his theory of logical form, and has been thus seen as a crucial stumbling block to the development of a straightforward innocent semantics. If, for example, it is the object described and not the description or its meaning that is relevant in the attitude report, why should such substitutions make a difference?

   The dominant view of the attitudes among philosophers today is an amalgam of the views of Frege and Russell.[1] On this view, normal attitude reports are thought to be roughly as Frege took them to be: the embedded statement provides a "thought" or proposition, some sort of conceptual entity, toward which the agent has the attitude. Substitution and existential generalization do not work for these normal or "*de dicto*" attitude reports, for it is the concepts and senses and thoughts that are taken as described. But different senses can refer to the same individual, and there can be senses that do not refer to anything.

   The pure Fregean theory has a number of shortcomings, which have emerged with progress in the philosophy of language. Iterated

attitudes present problems that have never been satisfactorily re-
solved. But there are even more basic problems. For the theory to
work, expressions that appear in the embedded sentences in meaningful attitude reports must have a sense or "conceptual content" which
the agent's mind grasps. But many expressions in such reports seem
to have no such content to provide, and others seem to provide the
wrong content.

Suppose I say, "Melanie saw Jim, and she believed that he was eating an anchovy." The pronoun HE does not seem to provide any sense
that, together with the senses provided by the rest of the words in
the embedded sentence, would give us a thought. The only conceptual content of HE seems to be maleness, but the statement really
doesn't even imply that Melanie could tell from where she was
whether it was a boy or a girl eating the anchovy. Definite descriptions seem to be paradigm providers of conceptual content, but they
don't always give us the proper content. If I say, "Melanie believes
the red-haired boy was eating an anchovy," I needn't imply that Melanie has any thought that the person she believes to have been eating
an anchovy was red-haired. If I am using THE RED-HAIRED BOY referentially, he might have been wearing a cap when she saw him. Russell
thought that ordinary names were disguised descriptions, and Frege
seems sympathetic to this idea in places. But it has been laid to rest,
at least in the form the Fregean theory would require, by the work
of Donnellan (70) and Kripke (72). If I say, "Melanie believes that
Jim was eating an anchovy," I really haven't provided any sense or
conceptual content at all for Melanie to grasp—just an individual.
And finally, suppose Jim says, "Melanie believes that I was eating an
anchovy." The word I certainly has rich psychological implications—
but they are irrelevant to getting at how Melanie thinks of Jim. Jim
hasn't disclosed how Melanie was thinking of him at all (Castaneda,
68).

For each sort of problem, Russell's theory of logical form can be
appealed to, together with the notion of a sense variable. Thus we
can suppose that what Jim really meant was:

There is a sense *s*, such that I am the reference of *s*,
and Melanie believes that *s* was eating an anchovy.

Attitude reports that require such removal of an offending expression
from the embedded sentence in favor of a sense variable are called *de
re*.

From our perspective there are two problems with this strategy, apart from whatever skepticism one might share with us about Fregean senses and logical form in the first place. The move isn't sufficient to handle names and pronouns, and it isn't necessary to handle definite descriptions. Our theory shows the latter, and the following example shows the former.

Suppose that Melanie saw Jim from a distance yesterday, dangling an anchovy over his open mouth. She thus believes that Jim was eating an anchovy. Today she meets Jim for the first time, not recognizing him. She tells him what she saw someone doing the day before. Jim can say, "So you believe that he was eating an anchovy." It seems that the answer must be "Yes." Can Jim then substitute, and say, "So, you believe that I was eating an anchovy"?

Suppose one says that he cannot validly make this substitution. Then here is a counterinstance to (B) for which neither the Fregean theory nor the theory of de re belief provides any explanation. The Fregean theory cannot provide an explanation, for neither the word HE in Jim's original report, nor the word I in his conclusion, provides Melanie's sense for Jim. The augmentation of the theory with logical form and sense variables certainly cannot provide such an explanation, for the whole point of such a theory is that the real logical form of Jim's remarks has HE and I outside the embedded statement, hence in a context where there is no explanation of why the one cannot be substituted for the other.

Suppose one says (as we shall) that Jim can validly (though misleadingly) make this substitution—that something other than invalidity explains his reluctance to do so. Then we are explaining the case as only an apparent exception to principle (B), and undermining the sort of "logical intuition" that suggested the Fregean theory in the first place.[2] Again, consider the various cases where we are reluctant to substitute proper names in attitude reports. Jonny and Joe are going to take an exam on Roman History. We know that one of the questions is

TRUE OR FALSE: TULLY WAS A FAMOUS ROMAN ORATOR.

Mary Ellen says, "Jonny knows that Cicero was a famous Roman orator." We might be very reluctant to restate this as, "Jonny knows that Tully was a famous Roman orator," feeling that this would lead his parents to overconfidence about his performance on the exam. Or, again, consider Kripke's famous Pierre (Kripke, 79). We are very reluctant to say that Pierre believes that London is beautiful, as he looks about it saying, "Boy, is this city ugly," even though he avows, "I believe Londres is quite a beautiful city."

In all of these cases, there is a reluctance to apply principle (B). And in all of them, Frege's theory provides no solution to our problem at all. We conclude that it was wrong to see a solution to problems about principle (B) in his theory, or any theory along similar lines.

A more promising line emerges if we notice that we are quite willing to apply (B) in very different circumstances. Suppose I talked to Melanie after she saw Jim dangling the anchovy. I have no reason not to say, "Melanie believes that you were eating an anchovy." After missing the question on the exam and rereading the chapter, Jonny might say, "I knew that Tully was a Roman orator, but I forgot his name." If you say to me, "I believe that you are wrong," I quite confidently reply, "So you believe that I am wrong." Further, Jim might even say to Melanie, on first meeting her, "You saw that I was eating an anchovy." He wouldn't be saying something false, he would be telling her where she has seen him before.

In general, it seems to us that reluctance to substitute does not have a simple semantic explanation. It isn't simply a matter of the *type* of expression involved, but also of the sort of *use* that is being made of the attitude report and particular circumstances.

On our account, principle (B) is valid for pronouns and nouns, but applications of it are extremely misleading when the following three conditions are all met:

- the resulting attitude report is being used to explain or predict behavior;

- the agent of the attitude has two different concepts of the subject of the attitude (as Melanie has two concepts of Jim, one formed when she saw him from a distance, and one formed when she met him); and

- the difference in concepts is relevant to the behavior to be predicted or explained.

To support this claim, we need a notion of a concept, and we need to explain how, on an innocent theory of the attitudes, different expressions designating the same individual in an attitude report can make different concepts of the same individual relevant. This part of our theory is spelled out in Chapter 10.

Principle (C) also seems to have some exceptions involving names and pronouns. Can't it be true that a child believes that Santa Claus is coming, even though in such a case there is no one he believes to be coming? When a frightened person shouts, "I believe you are trying to break in," and there is really no one there, didn't that person really believe something? These cases require more reflection than we give them in this book; but we are confident that they can be handled using the ideas of Chapter 10. They provide no support for the Fregean theory, for the reasons mentioned above in the discussion of examples involving substitution of names and indexicals.

It is not a non-innocent theory of the attitudes that is needed, but an appreciation of the flexibility of language. Suppose that Jim introduces himself to Melanie, saying, "Hi, I am Jim." He couldn't achieve the same effect with, "Hi, Jim is Jim." This doesn't mean that we need to deny that both statements have the same interpretation. It's just that we are free to exploit the fact that the information conveyed by our utterance goes way beyond the interpretation. The information that Melanie gets, and that Jim intends to convey, is not that Jim is Jim, but that the person speaking to Melanie is Jim; he is just exploiting what we called one of the inverse interpretations of his utterance in Chapter 7. The same sort of thing explains why he is reluctant to say, "So you believe that I was eating an anchovy," although the precise explanation of what is going on can't be developed until Chapter 10.

Now let's turn to definite descriptions. As we saw, the Fregean theory cannot account for the case where the definite description is used referentially, to identify the individual the agent has a belief about, but not to identify the way in which that agent thinks of the individual. Our theory of descriptions enables us to explain that sort of case without resorting to a logical form that takes the description out of the embedded sentence, and it also allows us to explain the sort of case that motivated Frege's theory, where the description *does* tell us how the agent thinks of the individual about whom she believes something. Let's see how this works.

Unrestricted substitutivity fails already with SEE THAT, whether primary or secondary. Let's examine the following argument to see just where the problem comes from.

(6) MELANIE SAW THAT THE YELLOW CAT WAS PLAYING WITH JACKIE.

THE YELLOW CAT WAS THE CAT NAMED SCRUFFY.

SO, MELANIE SAW THAT THE CAT NAMED SCRUFFY WAS PLAYING WITH JACKIE.

Taken one way, the inference seems valid. Taken another, it seems invalid. How do we sort things out?

Given the understanding of definite descriptions and other singular noun phrases developed in Chapter 7, we can pinpoint the problem precisely. Even with unembedded sentences we needed to distinguish among different types of uses—in this example between the referential, the outer attributive, and the inner attributive. When a description in an attitude report is used to describe how the agent thinks of the object in question, it gets an inner attributive reading. If this is the reading in the conclusion of our argument, it is invalid. If the descriptions are consistently referential or outer attributive, the argument is valid.

The possibility of an inner attributive reading arises naturally whenever we are dealing with information, as is the case with the epistemic and doxastic attitudes. To see why, let's first see what sense can be made of inner attributive reading where there is no mental activity involved. Consider:

THE PERSIAN CAT BROKE THE GLASS.

This has referential and attributive readings that are clear enough. But now consider our analysis of

(7) THAT MEANS THAT THE PERSIAN CAT BROKE THE GLASS.

On our theory of definite descriptions, this has three possible readings, (7.0), (7.1), and (7.2). With (7.0) we have the referential reading:

(7.0) THAT MEANS THAT (THE PERSIAN CAT)^0 BROKE THE GLASS.

A typical use of this is where the Persian cat is there in the visible scene e_0 licking up the milk around the broken glass.

With (7.1) we have the outer attributive:

(7.1) (THAT MEANS THAT (THE PERSIAN CAT)^1 BROKE THE GLASS)^1.

Suppose I know that someone has delivered a Persian cat to our formerly catless house. I have not yet seen it, but I see in the scene e_0 broken glass and cat tracks through the milk. In such a case I might well use (7) as in (7.1).

The inner attributive reading of (7) is indicated by (7.2). This is the use for which substitution fails:

(7.2) THAT MEANS THAT ((THE PERSIAN CAT)^2 BROKE THE GLASS)^2

Suppose that in the scene e_0 we find characteristically Persian cat hair and know from past experience that no two of our Persian cats are ever in the room at the same time. In such a case (7.1) would be inappropriate, but (7.2) would be fine.

It is characteristic of verbs involving information that they supply us with such a range of events. Given our analysis of MEANS THAT, we have

$d, c \llbracket$ THAT MEANS THAT THE PERSIAN CAT BROKE THE GLASS $\rrbracket\, e_1$

if and only if: e_0 is part of e_1 and for every e_2, if

in e_2: $MO,\ e_0,\ e_2$; yes

then

$d, c \llbracket$ THE PERSIAN CAT BROKE THE GLASS $\rrbracket\, e_2$.

When we further analyze the embedded statement, we have a choice (7.0), (7.1), and (7.2), which corresponds to the following, respectively:

in e_2: at c (BROKE): breaks, a, the glass; yes

where

$(7.0)\ _{d,c}\llbracket$ THE PERSIAN CAT $\rrbracket\,(e_0) = a$;

$(7.1)\ _{d,c}\llbracket$ THE PERSIAN CAT $\rrbracket\,(e_1) = a$;

$(7.2)\ _{d,c}\llbracket$ THE PERSIAN CAT $\rrbracket\,(e_2) = a$.

So with the inner attributive reading, there is a range of situations e_2 with different values a of the Persian cat in them. It does not make sense to try to substitute for one of the values. Notice, for example, that the following argument makes sense only under the first two readings of (7):

THAT MEANS THAT THE PERSIAN CAT BROKE THE GLASS.

THE PERSIAN CAT IS YOUR CAT.

SO THAT MEANS THAT YOUR CAT BROKE THE GLASS.

Now let us return to (6), which we repeat:

(6) MELANIE SAW THAT THE YELLOW CAT WAS PLAYING WITH JACKIE.

THE YELLOW CAT WAS THE CAT NAMED SCRUFFY.

SO, MELANIE SAW THAT THE CAT NAMED SCRUFFY WAS PLAYING WITH JACKIE.

If the two definite descriptions are read uniformly as referential or as outer attributive uses, then the inference is fine. The inference fails only when they are given the inner attributive readings. The exact cause of the failure depends on whether the sentences are given their primary or secondary readings. But even if the first premise is given the strongest (primary) reading and the conclusion the weakest (secondary) reading, the inference fails:

> MELANIE SAW$_p$ THAT ((THE YELLOW CAT)^2 WAS PLAYING WITH JACKIE)^2
> THE YELLOW CAT WAS THE CAT NAMED SCRUFFY.
> SO MELANIE SAW$_s$ THAT ((THE CAT NAMED SCRUFFY)^2 WAS PLAYING WITH JACKIE)^2.

The hypothesis tells us, intuitively, that in the scene of which Melanie was perceptually aware, there was a single yellow cat playing with Jackie. The conclusion asserts, intuitively, that in every situation consistent with what Melanie sees and knows to be the case, the cat she saw has the property of being named Scruffy. But of course this only follows if Melanie *knows* that the cat is named Scruffy.

Melanie has certain information on the basis of what she sees, information that will be captured by a range of alternative situations compatible with what she is visually aware of and what she knows based on what she sees. This makes an inner attributive reading possible. The inner attributive reading captures the case where Melanie has the information that it is a yellow cat. It doesn't follow that she has the information that it is a cat named Scruffy.

We see that just as in the case of MEANS THAT, a realist account is in no way committed to the Principle of Substitutivity for the inner attributive use of definite descriptions. In the semantics, the problem is that the hypothesis that the yellow cat is the cat named Scruffy only ensures that there is an actual situation where two functions have the same value; what we need for the conclusion of (6), however, is that they have the same value in all of the situations that agree with what Melanie sees and knows to be the case. If we make this explicit, the inference is fine:

(8) MELANIE SAW THAT THE YELLOW CAT WAS PLAYING WITH JACKIE.
MELANIE SAW THAT THE YELLOW CAT WAS THE CAT NAMED SCRUFFY.
MELANIE SAW THAT THE CAT NAMED SCRUFFY WAS PLAYING WITH JACKIE.

We can state this more generally:

H. *Weak substitution.* If t_1 and t_2 are each given the same interpretation (referential, outer attributive, or inner attributive throughout), then: If b sees that $\varphi(t_1)$ and b sees that t_1 is t_2, then b sees that $\varphi(t_2)$.

In the veridical attitudes the object described by the embedded sentence will have the requisite property in an actual situation. However, there is no reason to suppose in the case of a belief report that the donated object will satisfy the description in the situation described by the attitude report as a whole, in some particular resource situation, or indeed in any actual situation.

Whether or not there are mental representations or something like them involved in seeing (and we think the term is a confused one), there is no reason here to give up an innocent account of the semantics of SEE$_t$ reports by supposing that the definite description above refers not to the cat named Scruffy but to some mental representation. It is a completely implausible idea, as is the idea that it refers to some Fregean sense.[3] Our conclusion is that substitution is valid when restricted to names and referential and outer attributive uses of descriptions, just as our innocent approach predicts. When an inner attributive use is involved, however, substitution fails, and our semantics can account for it by assuming that there is a range of alternative situations involved.

D. Negation. If a atts that not -φ, then not a atts that φ.

This principle is valid for the veridical attitudes. If Sue sees that Helen is not in Tanner Library, then Sue certainly doesn't see that Helen is in the library. But with the nonveridical attitudes something interesting happens—something like the mirror image of substitutivity. The principle is invalid, but in certain situations we confidently apply it.

Consider Melanie and Jim again. Melanie is looking at Jim. She believed he was not eating an anchovy yesterday. But she remembers a certain boy, the one she saw eat the anchovy, and she still believes that *he* was eating an anchovy. And that boy is Jim. She believes Jim wasn't eating an anchovy, and yet she believes he was. So, for BE-LIEVES, the principle is invalid. This violation of (D) is possible because Melanie again has two concepts of Jim. As long as only one of her concepts is relevant, we will naturally apply (D). If we are worried about how she will treat Jim, the boy in front of her, then her memory of him is irrelevant. If we are concerned with Melanie's beliefs about the day before, then her memory is relevant.

Principles (B) and (D) both suggest that attribution of attitudes is sometimes relative to the concepts that are relevant to the behavior to which the attitude is relevant. We shall develop this idea in the next chapter.

E. Conjunction. If *a* atts that φ and ψ, *a* atts that φ and *a* atts that ψ.

This analogue of the principle distributing SEE over a conjunction is true of all the "positive" attitudes, but fails for the negative attitude *doubt.* Just because you doubt that Barwise and Perry wrote this sentence does not imply that you doubt that Barwise did it and that you doubt that Perry did it.

F. Disjunction. If *a* atts that φ or ψ, then *a* atts that φ or *a* atts that ψ.

The principle does not hold in general, of course. From the fact that

Sarah saw$_s$ that Joe or Jim ate her egg

we cannot infer that

Sarah saw that Joe ate her egg or Sarah saw that Jim ate her egg.

The inference seems all right in the case of a primary SEE$_t$ report, but not in the case of secondary reports. Indeed, one way of forcing a secondary reading is by explicitly denying this inference.

Sarah saw that Jim or Joe ate her egg but she didn't see that Jim ate it or that Joe ate it.

What Sarah actually saw was her plate, empty and dirty, and Jim and Joe sitting there innocently looking at the comics, but with no other way for her egg to have disappeared. There are various alternative situations compatible with what she sees to be the case and with what she knows about the world and the way it works. In each of these alternatives, either Jim or Joe ate the egg. But it was Jim in some, Joe in others.

The inference also fails with BELIEVE THAT and SAY THAT. However, with DOUBT THAT it does work. In fact we get something much stronger than we had even with *NI*-perception reports. From

Sarah doubts that Joe or Jim is sitting on her egg

we can infer each of

Sarah doubts that Joe is sitting on her egg.
Sarah doubts that Jim is sitting on her egg.

Abstractly, we get:

(F') If a doubts that φ or ψ, a doubts that φ and a doubts that ψ.

G. *Distribution of Indefinite Descriptions.* If b atts that φ (a π) then there is a π_1 such that a atts that φ (it$_1$).

As with (F) this works with primary reports but not secondary. A secondary reading can be forced by denying the inference:

JONNY SAW THAT A CAT HAD BEEN IN THE BUTTER BUT HE DIDN'T SEE THAT ANY PARTICULAR CAT HAD BEEN IN THE BUTTER.

The validity of (F) for DOUBT THAT suggests that (G) might also hold for DOUBT THAT, but it doesn't. For example, it does not follow from the fact that Melanie doubts that a centaur stole her pizza that Melanie has doubts about any particular centaur, since she in fact doubts that there are centaurs.

These facts all need to be accounted for by the semantics we assign to attitude reports. They all suggest that we take attitudes to be relations between agents and a range of alternative situations. This is the approach we develop in the remainder of this chapter. Once the details of this approach are spelled out, we will examine the problems with it, which force us to confront age-old problems about ideas, images, and the like, head on.

A slight digression concerning DOESN'T SEE and DOESN'T KNOW is in order. It is sometimes thought that a statement like

SARAH DIDN'T SEE THAT JOE ATE HER EGG

entails that Joe ate her egg, just as much as the statement

SARAH SAW THAT JOE ATE HER EGG.

This is just a confusion between what is genuinely entailed by the statement and what is conversationally implicated by it. We can cancel the implicature of the first, as in

Sarah didn't see that Joe ate her egg, since Jim ate it.

But there is no similar way to cancel the inference with the positive attitude report. It is interesting to try to isolate something in the semantics that explains why these implicatures exist, but they are not part of the logic in the same sense that the earlier principles were.

SEES$_t$ AS A SITUATIONAL ATTITUDE

Attitude reports involving the phrase SEE THAT give one information about what an agent has come to know by way of seeing an actual situation or event and combining this with what he knows about how the world is and works. In this section we investigate how this information can be viewed as information about how the agent is related to various situations and courses of events. This allows us to define the semantics of SEE$_t$ sentences and in so doing discover the structure that extends naturally to the other attitudes.

A familiar theory of perception, due to Bruner, characterizes perception in terms of the categorization of objects, properties, and relations in the agent's field of vision. This suggests that we simply modify our account of SEE by having SEE THAT express a relation between an agent^a and an event^e, which the agent has correctly categorized perceptually. So consider the relation ST that holds between a and e in this case:

a ST e iff a is perceptually aware that e is the case.

If we simply modify our treatment of NI-perception statements by replacing the relation of seeing with the ST relation, it would be partially successful. It would get the logic of the primary reports right, but it would not give us a general account of SEE$_t$ reports. For example, we could not explain the failure of (F), the distribution of OR. From

SARAH SEES THAT JOE OR JIM ATE HER EGG

the argument that worked for SEE would show that

SARAH SEES THAT JOE ATE HER EGG OR SHE SEES THAT JIM ATE IT

is also true. But we saw above that this is not right. The first statement is consistent with:

SARAH DOESN'T SEE THAT JOE ATE HER EGG AND SHE DOESN'T SEE THAT JIM ATE IT.

Seeing is an activity, performed by agents with visual abilities, agents in the world, with various needs and desires, and with knowledge about how the world is and works. Based on what they see$_p$ to be the case, what they know, and what their concerns are, they learn that some things are the case, some aren't, and some are left as open alternatives. And when we are told that they have seen that φ, we

learn that φ fits the alternatives that are open to them as a result of this cognitive classification of situations.

Suppose that there is a certain event e_0 to which Sarah is an eye-witness. She approached this event knowing a fair amount about how things work—that is, about the constraints that are actual, and with certain concerns and desires. As a result of Sarah's seeing e_0, she is in a state that contains information about her surroundings. She knows that certain types of events are precluded, but that there is a range of options e_1 compatible with what she sees and knows.

Let us perform a thought experiment. Imagine a situation s in which Sarah classifies some events as compatible with what she sees and knows, others as incompatible:

in s: at l: SO, a, e_1; yes   if e_1 is compatible with what a sees and knows;

in s: at l: SO, a, e_2; no   if e_2 is incompatible with what a sees and knows.

It is reasonable to assume that if

In s: at l: SO, Sarah, e_1; yes

then (1) the scene e_0 of which Sarah was aware is part of e_1, (2) it is not the case that e_0 precludes$_C$ e_1, and (3) $e_0 MO_C e_1$, where C is the set of constraints to which Sarah is attuned and which are activated by her desires and concerns. In keeping with our emphasis on partial information, we must not suppose that every event e_1 is classified one way or the other. The question is, given this classification, under what circumstances would we be justified in saying of Sarah that she saw that φ. And when would we be justified in saying that Sarah didn't see that φ?

In a given situation s, we say that a *coe* is a *visual option for a* if

in s: SO, a, e; yes.

On the other hand, we say that e is a *visual alternative for a* if it is *not* the case that

in s: SO, a, e; no.

If s is coherent, then every visual option for a is also an alternative for a, but there may be many alternatives for a that are not options for a. If s is coherent and total, then the two notions coincide. It seems clear that if there is a visual option e for a in which φ fails (that is, not d, $\ulcorner \llbracket \varphi \rrbracket e$), then a doesn't see that φ, for a clearly recognizes a possibility where φ does not hold.

When should we feel confident that a does see that φ? It clearly does not suffice to know that φ holds in all of a's visual options. In the example, Sarah might have not bothered to classify a lot of her options as such. She might have classified only those in which φ holds in spite of the fact that there are others in which φ fails, but which, were she to classify them one way or the other, she would classify as options. The only way we can tell for sure that she sees that φ is to make sure that φ holds in all her alternatives: that she has explicitly ruled out those in which φ fails.

Some examples suggested by the last section may help clarify this.

(1) Sue sees$_p$ that Tanner is empty and so she sees$_s$ that Helen is not in Tanner.

Sue, it is presumed, is looking for Helen. If she didn't even know Helen, it would be inappropriate to say that she sees that Helen is not in Tanner. The scene e that Sue actually sees and is aware of (Sue ST e) is one in which the library is empty.

This is not one of Sue's visual alternatives, however, because it does not include everything that she knows to be the case. All of her alternatives e' have Helen not in Tanner, since all the rest are ruled out by what she sees, from the fact that she is looking for Helen, and from the fact that she knows Helen can't be in an empty library.

(2)   Jonny sees that Scruffy has been in the butter but he doesn't see Scruffy in the butter.

What Jonny actually saw$_p$ was the butter dish with Scruffy's hair on it and buttery pawprints on the linen table cloth. But he is responsible for all of Scruffy's mischief. He has to clean up after her. The scene e that he sees (Jonny ST e) is one thing, while what he knows is something more. His alternatives all have Scruffy in the butter. The others are simply excluded by what he sees and knows.

(3)   Sarah sees that Joe or Jim ate her egg but not which.

What happened was this. John cooked Sarah's egg, put it at her place, and went back to cook his own breakfast. Sarah saw$_p$ all this before going off to wash. When she comes back, there are Joe and Jim looking very innocent, her plate dirty and empty. Molly is outside. John is still in the kitchen. Sarah is hungry. She knows eggs don't disappear on their own. One of these two jokers ate it. On the basis of what Sarah sees and knows, there are certain visual options e', Sarah SO e', and in each of them, one of the two boys ate her egg while she was away:

in e': at l: eating, a, b; yes

at an appropriate l and with a either Joe or Jim and with b the egg. The other coe's are excluded (Sarah not-SO e') by what she saw and knew and by what she was concerned about—the egg and what happened to it.

ST and SO are relations between an agent and events, not between the agent and any sort of mental representation of how things might be. They are determined by the agent's cognitive activity in ways to be discussed in the next chapter. For now, though, we just take them to be interdependent relations between an agent and coe's, relations about which statements of the forms

a SEES THAT φ

a DOESN'T SEE THAT φ

give us partial information.

To define the semantics for attitude reports of these kinds we need to do two things: (i) define what it means for $d, c \llbracket$ SEES THAT $\varphi \rrbracket$ a, e, and (ii) spell out the structural constraints on the relations ST

and *SO* that are reflected in the basic semantic properties of such reports. Actually, the relation *ST* comes in only in capturing the primary/secondary distinction. If we ignore that, only the relation *SO* is needed for the semantics.

Our idea is to use the above thought experiment to define the meanings of SEE THAT reports. If a sentence like

> *a* SEES THAT φ

is to give us information about a relation between an agent and situations, it must be about the relation *SO* used above. The information must be what we saw would warrant our asserting either that *a* sees that φ or that *a* doesn't see that φ. Using this idea, we can define the meaning of SEES THAT φ,

> $d, c \llbracket$ SEES THAT $\varphi \rrbracket a, e$,

the one that works in general, for both primary and secondary SEE$_t$ reports and generalizes to KNOW THAT and BELIEVE THAT in a straightforward way. A situation *e* is one where *a* sees that φ if φ holds in each of *a*'s visual alternatives at the appropriate location *l*. That is:

> $d, c \llbracket$ SEES THAT $\varphi \rrbracket a, e$

holds just in case for every *e'*, either $d, c \llbracket \varphi \rrbracket e'$ or

> in *e*: at $l = c$ (SEES): *SO, a, e'*; no.

A situation *e* is one where *a* doesn't see that φ just in case there is a visual option *e'* for *a* which φ fails to fit. Formally:

> $d, c \llbracket$ DOESN'T SEE THAT $\varphi \rrbracket a, e$

holds just in case there is an *e'* such that

> not $d, c \llbracket \varphi \rrbracket e'$

and

> in *e*: at $l := c$ (SEES): *SO, a, e'*; yes.

We now turn to the second of the two tasks mentioned above, spelling out the structural constraints behind the semantic principles for see$_t$. In the next chapter these constraints will be seen to follow from the basic structure of the visual and epistemic situations. For now, we will just state them in English. One of the most important constraints is reflected in the veridicality of SEE THAT reports. It is based on the fact that what one sees and knows to be the case cannot be incompatible with every actual course of events. Or, to put it differently, some actual *coe* must be a visual alternative for *a*:

it is not the case that for every actual e',
in e: at l: SO, a, e'; no.

This is actually the only constraint that is needed for the semantics of SEE$_t$ sentences, but we can't resist the temptation to attempt to relate the semantics to the primary/secondary distinction and to *NI*-perceptual reports. Let us write a SEES$_p$ THAT φ to mean that a sees that φ in the primary sense and a SEES$_s$ THAT φ to mean that a sees that φ, in the secondary sense.

The semantics we assign to these expressions is determined by the following rule:[4]

$d, c \llbracket$ SEES$_p$ THAT $\varphi \rrbracket a$, e

if there is an event e_1 such that $d, c \llbracket \varphi \rrbracket e_1$ and

in e: at $l = c$ (SEES): ST, a, e_1; yes

With this definition one also wants a couple of rather obvious constraints:

If in e: at l: ST, a, e'; yes,
then
in e: at l: SO, a, e''; yes

for some e'' with e' as a part. This guarantees that all that is seen to be the case is part of some option, so that if one sees$_p$ that φ, one also sees that φ, for persistent φ.

To capture the intuition that there is a unique scene of which one is aware, we impose the following constraint:

If a is present in e at l, then there is a unique e' such that
in e: at l: ST, a, e'; yes.

The case where e' is the empty *coe* corresponds to the case where a is not visually aware of anything at all. In this case a doesn't see$_p$ that φ, no matter what "φ" is. No sentence describes the empty *coe*.

We saw in the last section that, at least for simple φ, if a sees that φ, then a sees φ^*, where φ^* is the *NI* form of φ. To capture this in the semantics, we need to ensure that the scene e' that a is visually aware of is part of the scene a sees in the epistemically neutral sense. This requires another constraint:

If in e: at l: ST, a, e'; yes,
then e' is part of some e'' such that
in e: at l: seeing, a, e''; yes.

KNOWING, BELIEVING, AND DOUBTING

Knowing

Seeing is a way of knowing. But there are other ways of knowing. We can learn by means of the other senses. And there is nothing in the structure of language that precludes our knowing things by nonperceptual means. But we cannot know what is not the case. That much is part of the meaning of KNOW. Similarly, we cannot know that φ and ψ without knowing that φ and knowing that ψ. But we can know that φ or ψ without knowing which. These facts, too, fall out of the meaning of KNOW.

Similarly, knowing is a way of believing, a way that is somehow grounded in the actuality of what is known. We will present our own theory of the relation between knowing and believing in the next chapter. At a semantic level, however, all we need to account for is differences. If a knows that φ, then a believes that φ, but one can believe that φ even though φ is not the case.

By now it should be pretty clear what line we want to take. Attitude reports involving the phrases KNOWS THAT and BELIEVES THAT report on an agent's relations to various courses of events, relations determined by her state of mind at the time. They do not refer directly to these states of mind. What we learn about a's cognitive situations when we learn that she knows that φ is that φ is the case in all of her "epistemic alternatives"—that is, all of the coe's not precluded by what she knows to be the case. And if we learn that a doesn't know that φ, then we learn that φ fails in some active, epistemic alternative coe.

Formally, then, we introduce a relation KO, parallel to the relation SO, with exactly the same structural constraints, and with parallel definitions of:

$d, c [\![\text{KNOWS THAT } \varphi]\!] a, e,$

$d, c [\![\text{DOESN'T KNOW THAT } \varphi]\!] a, e.$

To reflect the facts that seeing that is a way of knowing that, we also require the following necessary structural constraints: any situation that is precluded by what you see, on the basis of what you know, is precluded by what you know.

If in e: at l: SO, a, e'; no,

then in e: at l: KO, a, e'; no.

It follows that if a sees that φ, then a knows that φ.

We impose the same veridicality constraint on *KO* that we imposed on *SO*. One can't know that what is the case isn't.

Believes That

We want to pursue the same approach to believing that we took toward seeing and knowing. But first we need to make a distinction that will enable us to have a realistic hope of saying something helpful about the vast topic of belief. There are two ways of conceiving of the relation between knowledge and belief, each of which fits some of the facts.

Belief as failed knowledge. Knowledge reflects cognitive states that are tied closely to the information contained in the situations an organism is in, to the constraints to which the organism is attuned, through evolution, Divine providence or learning, and to the activities of the organism in adjusting to its environmental situation. It is this view that leads ecological psychologists to think of knowledge in general and perception in particular as basic and relatively intelligible, but to be skeptical about the whole category of belief.

Constraints are often conditional, however, and an organism can find itself in a situation where the conditions do not hold. The bird flies into the glass patio door because nothing in the evolution of birds has prepared it for such things. The bird had the visual properties it would have had if there had been nothing in its way, but the world didn't cooperate.

This is the first kind of belief, belief as failed knowledge. Here belief takes up the slack when we recognize that the agent has done his bit for knowledge, but something in the environment has let him down. For example, if the vet tells Jonny that his dog has a broken leg and Jonny accepts what he says, Jonny knows that his dog has a broken leg if the vet knew. But if the vet was wrong or joking, Jonny is classified as believing that his dog has a broken leg. The difference is not in Jonny but in the world.

Knowledge as successful belief. Alternately, we can look at belief as a probabilistic strategy, a capacity for going into cognitive states less closely tied to information available in the agent's environmental situation and to patterns in the environment. We think that humans clearly have this capacity to form beliefs that are not just failed knowledge but also the result of weighing the possibilities and judging some of them to be unlikely, and to suit their degree of conviction in the resulting belief to their weighing of the possibilities.

This is a rather high order of adaptive strategy that exploits probabilistic patterns in the environment. And knowledge can result from successful belief of this kind.

To account for the first type of believing, believing that is just like knowing except that the world doesn't fully cooperate, we can introduce a third alternative relation BO to classify coe's into "doxastic alternatives." We give completely parallel definitions of

$d, c \llbracket$ BELIEVES THAT $\varphi \rrbracket a, e$

$d, c \llbracket$ DOESN'T BELIEVE THAT $\varphi \rrbracket a, e$

in terms of φ holding or not holding in the appropriate doxastic alternative.

To give an account of believing as a probabilistic strategy would be more complicated, but could proceed along similar lines. We would, however, have to assign weights to doxastic alternatives and require not that φ hold in all alternatives, but that the combined weight exceeded some threshold, one that would depend on the gullibility of the agent.[5]

Our discussion of belief in this book is aimed at belief as failed knowledge. This type of belief fits our perspective and strategy best, of course, so we avoid a lot of problems with this limitation. We hope we are thereby only deferring complex problems, not begging crucial questions.

Every doxastic alternative is an epistemic alternative, so we introduce a structural constraint:

If in e at l: KO, a, e'; no

then in e at l: BO, a, e'; no

so that if a knows that φ then a also believes that φ. Of course we do not impose the veridicality constraint on believing.

Doubting That

We give a very brief and overly simplified account, one in which doubt is related to belief, primarily to show that our theory of the attitudes doesn't automatically commit us to the claim that weak substitutivity holds of all the attitudes. Actually, there are two different uses of DOUBT THAT: one that expresses lack of belief and one that expresses actual disbelief. We restrict our attention to the former.

We will say that

$d, c \llbracket$ DOUBTS THAT $\varphi \rrbracket a, e$

if φ fails in one of a's doxastic options, that is, if there is a doxastic option e' in e such that not $d, c [\![\varphi]\!] e'$. And a doesn't doubt that φ if φ holds in all of a's doxastic alternatives. In other words, the roles of the alternatives are switched, owing to the negative nature of doubt. That is why even weak substitutivity fails for doubt. To say that a doubts that t_1 is t_2 is to say that there is one of a's doxastic alternatives where it is not the case that t_1 is t_2.

Note that if a doubts that φ or ψ then (φ or ψ) fails in one of a's doxastic options. But then both φ and ψ fail in that option, so a doubts that φ and a doubts that ψ, in accord with the observations given earlier. On the other hand, if a doubts that φ and ψ, then all we know is that (φ and ψ) fails in some doxastic option, so either φ or ψ fails in that option. There is no guarantee that both fail in any one option. That is why conjunction distribution fails with DOUBT THAT.

EXPLANATION OF THE LOGICAL PRINCIPLES

Since we have used the logical principle to motivate our treatment, we will be content with a few remarks on some of the more notable issues. In discussing the justifications of the various logical principles in the case of SEES THAT, it is useful to break things up into the primary and secondary cases, keeping in mind that it is the justification of the secondary case that generalizes to KNOW and BELIEVE. In moving from SEE, through SEE_p THAT, SEE_s THAT, KNOW THAT, and on to BELIEVE THAT, the greatest shift in the logic is the one between the two kinds of SEE THAT reports.

Veridicality. We treat two examples, one primary and one secondary. First, suppose that Joe saw that Jackie bit Molly. He saw the actual terrible event and was aware that that was what he saw. That is, Joe saw_p that Jackie bit Molly. It follows from what we said above that Joe saw Jackie bite Molly, and so by the veridicality of *NI* reports, Jackie bit Molly. (One can also verify this without the steps through *NI* reports, thus avoiding those constraints, in a manner similar to that of the next example.)

Now let's consider a more interesting case. Consider the course of events where Sue was looking for Helen. She went to the door of Tanner Library and saw_p that it was empty. So:

Sue saw_s that Helen was not in Tanner Library.

This is not a primary report because Helen is not part of what Sue saw. We must see how the semantics ensures that Helen was not in the library.

Let l be the location where Sue's seeing took place, and l' the location in the library at the same time. The semantics assigned to SEE$_t$ ensures that in each of Sue's visual alternative coe's, Helen is not in the library. That is:

for any e', either in e' at l': in, Helen, t, no
or in e at l: SO, Sue, e'; no

How did this come to pass? Well, presumably because Sue saw a scene s such that

in s: at l': empty, t; yes,

from which by some sort of cognitive activity Sue precludes any possibility of Helen being in t. We give our own model of such activity in the next chapter. If we apply the veridicality constraint, we get an actual e', that is, one of Sue's visual alternatives, and so,

in e': at l': in, Helen, t; no.

Notice that our semantics reflects the common sense ideas involved in the rejection of the principle of logical equivalence. It does not follow from the fact that Sue saw that the library was empty that she saw that Yiannis was not in the library. Sue has never met or even heard of Yiannis. She knows nothing about him whatsoever. He plays no role in her mental life, and there are visual alternative coe's for Sue in which he does not appear.

Substitutivity. The result we want is that substitutivity holds when restricted to names, pronouns, and referential and outer attributive uses of definite descriptions, but that it fails for the inner attributive uses. Let's look at a famous example in some detail to see how this all works out. Consider

GEORGE IV BELIEVES THE AUTHOR OF *WAVERLEY* WROTE *WAVERLEY*.

SCOTT IS THE AUTHOR OF *WAVERLEY*.

SO, GEORGE IV BELIEVES THAT SCOTT WROTE *WAVERLEY*.

Intuitively, the first premise might be used in a way that credited George IV with a significant belief, and then the conclusion follows. But it might also be used to credit George IV with a trivial belief, one he might hold without having any idea who wrote *Waverley.*

In the referential use, we "load" the description in a resource situation. Thus,

d, c ⟦GEORGE IV BELIEVES (THE AUTHOR OF *WAVERLEY*)^0 WROTE *WAVERLEY*⟧ e

describes *coe*'s only relative to a resource situation e_0 used to load the description, say with the individual

$$a = {}_{d,c} ⟦ \text{THE AUTHOR OF } WAVERLEY⟧ (e_0).$$

That given, it describes those *coe*'s e such that every e' satisfies one of:

in e: at l: *BO*, George IV, e'; no,

or

in e': at l': write, a, *Waverley*; yes

where $l = c$ (BELIEVES), and $l' = c$ (WROTE). This ascribes to George IV a belief about the particular individual a, one that is in each of his doxastic alternative *coe*'s. If e_0 is part of the actual *coe*, then a is Scott. With this use of the description, the argument is valid without even using the premise (2)!

Contrast this now with the second use of the definite description.

d, c ⟦(GEORGE IV BELIEVES THAT (THE AUTHOR OF *WAVERLEY*)^1 WROTE *WAVERLEY*)^1⟧ e.

This does not need a resource situation, for each e under consideration loads the definite description itself. Thus this statement describes those events e such that every e' satisfies one of:

in e: at l: *BO*, George IV, e'; no

or

in e': at l': write, a, *Waverley*; yes

where

$${}_{d,c} ⟦ \text{THE AUTHOR OF } WAVERLEY⟧ (e) = a$$

and $l = c$ (BELIEVES), $l' = c$ (WROTE). This statement too asserts that George IV has a belief about some individual. But whereas there is an individual that is a constituent of the interpretation of the first attitude report, there is none in this case. In particular, Scott isn't a constituent of the interpretation of this use of (1). The report describes many courses of events, with different people writing *Waverley*. But in each of them George IV believes that this person wrote *Waverley*. However, if we combine (1) with (2), then we eliminate all those *coe*'s in which Scott is not the author, so the conclusion again follows.

Now let us look at the third reading of (1), the inner attributive.

d, c ⟦GEORGE IV BELIEVED THAT ((THE AUTHOR OF $WAVERLEY)^2$ WROTE $WAVERLEY)^2$ ⟧ e

It is the reading we would use to report a belief that George IV would express with an attributive use of "the author of *Waverley*." The definite description as it occurs in the report is not loaded at a resource situation, nor in the various events described by the report. Rather, it is used to establish a relation between courses of events that are George IV's doxastic alternatives and individuals in them. The statement describes those events e such that for each e', either

in e: at l: BO, George IV, e'; no

or

in e': at l': writes, *Waverley*, a; yes

where d, c ⟦THE AUTHOR OF $WAVERLEY$⟧ e', a and $l = c$ (BELIEVES), $l' = c$(WROTE). This would ordinarily be a rather trivial sort of belief for George IV to have, unless the issue were, say, whether the author of *Waverley* (whoever he or she might have been) wrote *Waverley* or dictated *Waverley* to a secretary, as in fact he did.

When we turn to iterated attitude reports, like Jonny's

I KNOW THAT MELANIE SAW THAT (MY CAT)^i WAS IN THE BUTTER,

things get a little more complicated, since there are now four possible sources to load the definite descriptions. Besides the cases where ⟦MY CAT⟧ is evaluated in a resource situation ($i = 0$), or the situation described by the whole ($i = 1$), there are two more possibilities. One ($i = 2$) is that in which ⟦MY CAT⟧ is evaluated in all of Jonny's epistemic alternatives. This would be roughly equivalent to the statement:

I KNOW THAT THERE IS A CERTAIN CAT THAT BELONGS TO ME AND THAT MELANIE SAW THAT IT WAS IN THE BUTTER.

Jonny is not claiming that Melanie saw that it was his cat. The other interpretation ($i = 3$) is that in which ⟦MY CAT⟧ is evaluated in the *coe*'s that are Melanie's visual alternatives—in Jonny's epistemic alternatives. This would be roughly equivalent to Jonny's saying:

I KNOW THAT MELANIE SAW THAT THERE WAS A CAT IN THE BUTTER AND THAT SHE SAW THAT IT WAS MY CAT.

Working out the formal details, for once, gives us for this interpretation:

d, c [[I KNOW THAT MELANIE SAW THAT ((MY CAT)^3 WAS IN THE BUTTER)^3]] e_1

just in case each of Johny's epistemic alternatives e_2 in e_1 (those for which it is not the case that in e_1 at $l = c$ (KNOW): KO, Jonny, e_2; no):

d, c [[MELANIE SAW THAT ((MY CAT)^3 WAS IN THE BUTTER)^3]] e_2.

And this latter requires that each of Melanie's visual alternatives e_3 in e_2 at $l' = c$(SAW) be one where

d, c [[MY CAT WAS IN THE BUTTER]] e_3.

And this in turn requires that

in e_3: at $l'' = c$ (WAS): in, a, b ; yes,

where

$_{d,c}$ [[MY CAT]] $(e_3) = a$
and $_{d,c}$ [[THE BUTTER]] $(e_3) = b$.

(We are assuming the inner attributive reading for THE BUTTER, as well.)

PROBLEMS WITH INTERPRETING ATTITUDES AS RELATIONS TO SITUATIONS

At one point in the writing of this book we thought the semantics could end here. We thought we would provide a theory of efficient mental states as a background to the semantics of the attitudes, but not as a part of it. There are, however, deficiencies and basic problems with this approach that we have gradually come to see as demanding an explanation that takes us beyond this account. We list here what seem to us the most serious of these problems.

Folk Psychology

There is an inadequacy in our preliminary account in that it does not account for the role of attitude reports in Folk Psychology. There is a big difference between your knowing that I am hungry and my knowing that I am hungry. Yet on our account, you and I stand in exactly the same relations to the same situations if you and I both know that I am hungry—namely, we both classify as not-KO all those situations in which I am not hungry here and now. Thus, it classifies both of us in the same way, even though I am the one to get up and go make a sandwich.

There is also a problem when we attempt to use the semantics to interpret not just simple attitude reports but more complex uses of the attitude verbs in the statements of Folk Psychology. For example, the statement "A mother who believes that her child is hungry will feed it" is a pretty reliable guide to understanding certain patterns of behavior. But the semantics we have assigned to BELIEVES is inadequate to deal with it, for the reason hinted in the last paragraph. Intuitively, a mother might believe that her child was hungry in the usual way, in which case she would usually feed it. But then she might be a nurse monitoring stomach growls in a nursery, believing that a certain child is hungry, not recognizing from the monitor that it is *her* child. The relations to situations are the same in both cases.

Missing the Mental

There are a host of notions that common sense and common language suggest are related to the attitudes, notions like images, thoughts, beliefs, ideas, perceptions, and the like. None of these has entered into our account. What, for example, is the relation between what is seen (a scene) and the images involved in seeing it? For that matter, what sort of thing is an image? And what is the relation between what is believed (say, that I am hungry) and the belief itself? Are they the same or different? And if different, what sort of thing is the belief? These mental states and activities have not been given any place or role in our account of the attitudes.

This deficiency is related to the one above. There is surely some intuitive sense in which you and I have different beliefs if we both believe that I am hungry. A mother who believes that her child is hungry in the usual way would seem to have a different belief from one who is unaware that it is her very own child.

Capturing the Constraints

Some of the constraints that we have stated in this chapter cannot be stated in the form we used to state the constraints in Chapter 5, where one event-type or schema is supposed to involve another. For example, the constraint:

It is not the case that for every actual e',
in e: at l: SO, a, e'; no

is not of this form. It seems that a case of veridical perception involves a proper anchoring of an image in reality, and that veridicality is a consequence of this proper anchoring. But we cannot state this constraint with the relation of involving unless we have the type of things images are as part of our theory. The deficiency mentioned above thus has rather serious consequences for a general theory. Similarly, as we have mentioned just above, the account here does not let us capture the constraints embodied in common sense psychology.

Foundational Problems

We were well aware of the first three problems when we began thinking about the semantics of the attitudes. Since, according to our theory, attitude reports describe mental states only indirectly, we thought a theory of mentality would not be a proper part of the semantics but simply have a place alongside it, explaining why we *use* attitude reports the way we do. But we have come to see that this won't work, because of a basic mathematical problem that has been obscured by the presentation so far. Consider an utterance:

JOE SAW THAT JACKIE WAS BITING MOLLY.

In order for this to describe a situation e, we must have at $l = c$ (SAW), for every e_1, either

$$d, c \, [\![\text{JACKIE WAS BITING MOLLY}]\!] e_1,$$

or

in e: at l: SO, Joe, e_1; no.

However, there is a proper class of events e_1 in which Jackie was not biting Molly, events that must thus be classified with SO-no. But then $coe\ e$ required to classify Joe's visual state must be a proper class.

This might not seem like such a serious problem until one recalls that proper classes are not constituents of other sets, hence cannot be constituents of other situations. In particular, the event e above could not be a constituent of any other situation. This means that an iterated attitude report like

Jonny knew that Joe saw that Jackie bit Molly

could never describe any situation at all! In other words, our discussion of iterated attitudes in the last section sluffed over the point that there could be no situations of the kind described by the iterated report.

Proper classes are not objects *per se,* but cumbersome ways of classifying uniformities that are objects. We have seen examples of this before. Event-types could be classified with proper classes, but such classes could not be used as constituents of constraints. Similarly, the relations MO_C between events are proper classes more efficiently classified by means of the constraints C. Similarly, the relations SO, KO, and BO give rise to cognitive situations that are proper classes because we are missing the underlying uniformities across mental events that give rise to them, the same uniformities that are needed to solve the first three problems mentioned above.

Jens-Eric Fenstad has pointed out a related foundational problem with the approach of this chapter. Suppose we ignore the problem just mentioned, about interesting cognitive situations being represented only by proper classes. There would still be a serious problem. Consider an actual doxastic situation e, for example, one where some false belief is held. Since e is actual but the belief is false, e cannot be a doxastic alternative, thus it must be classified with a "BO-no". This violates the axiom of foundation of set theory, for it makes e a constituent of itself. Or, to put it more strikingly, if we found a way around the proper class problem, we would then be stuck with the conclusion that all actual doxastic situations are situations where what is believed is true.

We conclude, somewhat reluctantly, that to have a coherent theory of the attitudes one must represent the mental. One must isolate those uniformities across mental states and activities that support the relations to situations that serve as the interpretation of attitude reports. It is to this task that we now turn.

CHAPTER TEN

Representing Mental States and Events

Sarah sits in her family room watching the Giants' game on TV. She sees that they are playing the Dodgers. She hopes that the Giants are winning, but she doubts that they are. She knows that Clark is playing but believes he is well when in fact he has a stiff neck.

According to the account developed in Chapter 9, these statements give us information about Sarah's attitudes toward various situations, actual and otherwise. In all of her epistemic alternatives, the Giants are playing the Dodgers. In some of her doxastic alternatives the Giants are winning, in some they are losing. In all of them Clark is well, when in fact he has a stiff neck. But what is it about Sarah, sitting there on the couch eating an apple, that supports these various contentions, that makes the difference between what she knows, believes, and doubts, and what she doesn't? It is not her future behavior. While her future behavior may lend support to our contentions about her attitudes, it is not this future behavior that makes what we now say true. It is something about Sarah herself, and how she fits into the world at large, that supports Sarah's attitudes toward these situations and so makes the statements true.

Common sense tells us that it is Sarah's frame of mind and how it is anchored to things in the world that determines what her attitudes are. In this chapter we develop a theory of frames of mind, or, as we call them, efficient cognitive properties, and we show how they support the innocent semantic theory of the last two chapters, and how this explains the role that attitude reports play in natural language and Folk Psychology.

The account we give is necessarily speculative and overly simple; it is at best a first step in such an account. Still, we think it is a step in the right direction. We hope its merits are sufficient to intrigue others to develop it further.

THE INDIRECT CLASSIFICATION
OF COGNITIVE STATES AND EVENTS

What in the world are we up to when we use attitude verbs to describe someone's mental state? On our innocent account, we somehow managed to describe Sarah's mental state by referring not to anything in Sarah's circuitry or inner world, but to people, places, properties, and relations miles away from Sarah, things that could not possibly be in Sarah's head. When we say either of

SARAH SAW THAT CLARK STRUCK OUT.

SARAH BELIEVES THAT CLARK IS WELL.

we use embedded statements referring to things far away from Sarah to get at something significant about Sarah herself.

What is usually called the problem of the "intentionality of mind" is really just this problem. How can we describe minds by referring to situations that aren't mental, situations external to minds and brains, and those that may not even be real—like the situation of Clark's being well?

A Lockean or Fregean will think we have posed the problem wrongly, for on a non-innocent account there *is* no reference to Clark in our report of Sarah's belief. The statement is embedded in the belief report, and is not about Clark at all. On such an account, it is about Sarah's idea of Clark, or a sense of Clark that Sarah's mind can somehow directly grasp. On our view, however, it is Clark himself who is somehow being used to classify Sarah's state of mind.

We do not want to ignore mental events, and the flow of consciousness, image, idea, perception, and thought. Just the contrary. We want to emphasize the importance of looking closely at how natural language and common sense conceive of the mind. The assumption we reject is that attitude reports give us a direct window into the mind by having the embedded statement *directly* describe states of mind, ideas, images, or thoughts. That is simply not how attitude reports work.

A central theme of this book has been *indirect classification*, by which we mean *the exploitation of patterns and constraints to classify one situation with another*. The constraints allow the latter to contain information about the former. An attitude report is yet

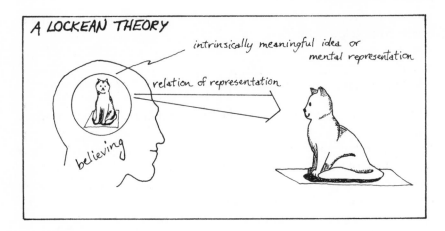

A LOCKEAN THEORY

intrinsically meaningful idea or
mental representation

relation of representation

believing

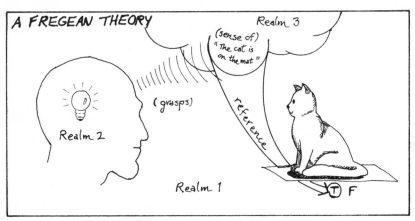

A FREGEAN THEORY

Realm 3

(sense of)
"The cat is
on the mat"

(grasps)

reference

Realm 2

Realm 1

T F

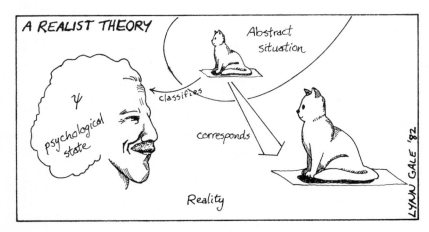

A REALIST THEORY

Abstract
situation

ψ

psychological
state

classifies

corresponds

Reality

LYNN GALE '82

another example of indirect classification. The situation described by the embedded sentence classifies the agent's cognitive situation by exploiting constraints of Folk Psychology. The attitude verb used (SEE, KNOW, BELIEVE, DOUBT, ASSERT, etc.) signals which constraints are relevant.

Different attitude verbs signal different kinds of information. In discussing the attitudes, it is useful to make a rough and ready three-way distinction. A given situation can carry information about earlier situations, temporally overlapping situations, and later situations. We call these *backward-looking, present-looking,* and *forward-looking information,* respectively. In general, a situation will contain all three kinds of information, relative to various constraints.

Imagine an expert chess game in progress. The current position is a situation in its own right, one that contains all three kinds of information. It contains backward-looking information about the play that resulted in the position. Only certain sequences of legal moves, and even fewer of expert moves, could have resulted in the position. Here the constraints are the rules of chess and the patterns present in expert play. The position contains forward-looking information about the possible outcomes. It may be possible to say, for example, that white has a mate in two moves. The position also contains present-looking information, at least for anyone who understands chess and Folk Psychology. If there is a mate for white in two moves, one can have a pretty good idea of the plans and mental states of the two players. The physical situation right there on the board can be used to get at various aspects of the cognitive situations of the two players—it can be used to represent their mental and emotional situations.

Indirect classification is a ubiquitous phenomenon. Once this fact is recognized, its role in attitude reports, hence in the intentionality of mind, becomes much less mysterious. To aid in this recognition, we present more examples.

Imagine two aerosol cans, one of bug spray, the other of hair spray. Why do we use the words BUG and HAIR in classifying these sprays? The cans don't contain bugs and hair. As in the case of attitude reports, we are using something not in the can to classify what is in the can. We are exploiting a nomic constraint between spraying bugs with certain chemicals and dying bugs to classify the chemical by referring to bugs. Similarly with the hair spray. For a chemist the descriptions might be hopelessly vague, but for most of us they are far more useful than a definite description of the chemical composition.[1]

Imagine a house full of insects. Mary Ellen asks Jon where all the mosquitoes are coming from, to which he replies "I just closed the door." At face value, his response is a non sequitur. She didn't ask him what he just did. In fact, though, his reply is perfectly reasonable. It exploits one constraint (that only open doors can be closed) to give some backward-looking information about the door, and another constraint (that mosquitoes can't fly through closed doors) to give some forward-looking information.

For an example that is full of this indirect classification, consider Jim's question, "Did you kiss me?" to Melanie. She answers, "I didn't touch you." And I report this by saying, "Melanie said that she didn't kiss Jim." Melanie is able to give some present-looking information about not kissing by describing a co-temporal not touching, exploiting the constraint that kissing involves touching, and the constraint that speakers of English are attuned to the constraint. We are able to describe Melanie's utterance, a complicated situation involving sounds issuing from Melanie, by referring not to the sounds but the activity of saying and to the situation of her not kissing Jim.

For a final example, one involving the epistemic attitudes, suppose that a mouse sees that there is a cat in front of it. The mouse's perceptual situation contains present-looking information, that there is a cat in front of the mouse. We exploit the connection between that situation and the cat's position relative to the mouse when we classify the former with the latter. The mouse's perceptual situation also contains forward-looking information about what the mouse will do. A mouse that sees a cat in front of it will run. At least there are things a normal mouse won't do, like walk aimlessly over to the cat and search its paws for cheese. We could also exploit these constraints to classify the mouse's perceptual situation by saying that the mouse saw something that would make any normal mouse run.

Indirect classification is also at the heart of the semantic endeavor, for we are using one sort of situation, abstract ones, to classify real situations, utterances, and meanings, by spelling out the constraints between the two. And so it is with the semantics of the attitudes. In the last chapter we attempted to do this with just situations and relations like *SO, KO,* and *BO* between agents and situations, but we found this classification to be inadequate. We need to represent the mental. In the present chapter we turn to this problem of representing the mental and connecting these representations with the indirect classification of cognitive situations by means of attitude reports. We then show how cognitive situations can have backward-, present-, and forward-looking information.

HOW TO REPRESENT THE MENTAL

The attitudes are only a small part of what natural language and common sense offer us in ways of talking about the mental. We have focused on them because misunderstandings of them shaped the history of logic and the philosophy of language, as well as formal approaches to mentality, to such an extent that approaches like ours have been systematically neglected.

Here we indicate how a common-sense theory of the mental can be developed within the theory of situations. We should emphasize—although it will probably be fairly obvious—that our theory is not the result of psychological research on our part. It is rather an attempt to formulate reflective common sense.

Common-sense folk psychology contains a good deal of knowledge about human perception, thought, and action. Indeed, when one considers the complexity of the nervous system, our ability to understand perception, thought, and action in the way that is necessary for the most commonplace human interactions is surely mankind's most extraordinary intellectual accomplishment to date, and is a precondition of most other such accomplishments, since it is a precondition of language.

Even at the level of common sense, our picture is very crude. We have not tried to incorporate all of the common-sense notions about mind and knowledge into our account. For example, in our simple model there are just two kinds of mental condition, perceptual and doxastic, and the only mode of perception we pay much attention to is vision. Our aim is to sketch how, even with a crude picture of the mind, one can handle the mental significance of language with the tools built up to handle its external significance. Nor have we attempted to incorporate all the insights about our concepts of mind and knowledge that are available from work in the philosophy of mind and related areas like artificial intelligence.

We should also emphasize the tentativeness of our view on these issues. We are convinced that the overall strategy is right, but less sure about how the details should be worked out. We don't want to take positions on issues that may look quite different when a full-fledged theory—one that takes account of intention and action, for example—is worked out. Also, we will need to state some constraints informally that we are not yet ready to state within our theory of constraints, since they would involve indeterminates for event-types and for constraints themselves. We trust that the reader who has borne with us this far will be intrigued enough by the possibilities to be not unduly put off by the shortcomings.

Perceptions and Images

We have expressions for many different kinds of mental conditions. There are dispositional states like belief and desire; activities like perceiving, thinking, evaluating, and deciding; intentions, actions, abilities, capacities, and so forth. We concentrate on perceiving, believing, and thinking, and we shall follow our strategy of starting with seeing.

J. J. C. Smart and others (Smart, 59; Lewis, 66) have emphasized that our ordinary concepts of the mental are topic neutral. It is not a part of common sense that these states and activities are physical, any more than it is part of common sense that they are not physical. But it is a part of common sense that they play causal roles in the physical world. We agree with this. We happen to think that mental events are in fact bodily events, uniformities across live individuals, representable, if one knew far more than we do, by *coe*'s involving complex relations among parts of human bodies. The skepticism about this in writers like Descartes was founded in part on beliefs about the limitations about what physical systems can do. But the capacity for complexity that has been uncovered in physical systems since Descartes' time severely undermines this form of skepticism.

Beliefs, thoughts, and perceptions are situations (including both states of affairs and events that include activities) involving an agent at a location being in bodily conditions. If the beliefs, thoughts, and perceptions are *of* anything, then these events will be anchored to the wider world in certain ways. When they are, such events are suited to be indirectly described with the attitude verbs. But to understand how attitude reports actually work to explain and predict behavior, and to see how they are rooted in the meaningfulness of cognitive situations, it is necessary to get to a more fine-grained, and also cross-grained, level of description. The language with which we ordinarily do this is already a part of natural language, for we are not by any means limited to attitude reports in our everyday descriptions of the mental.

Suppose I look out at the yard and see a football. For many purposes, this situation is described perfectly adequately by saying that I see a football lying in my front yard. In particular, if the purpose of the interest in my perceptual situation is to gain information about the front yard, or the location of the football, this level of description is ideal.

Now suppose I move my head from side to side or walk up and down the driveway while still looking at the football. It is quite obvious that something is changing. It is not the football or anything else about the front yard. We can get at part of the change by reference to the scene I see, for as I move, parts of the football and of the background may become visible that were not before. And we can note that the angle of my head or my position on the driveway changed. Commonsensically, however, it is not just the scene I am seeing that changes, and not just the angle of my head relative to the football, or my position on the driveway. Something about my own situation changes, the way I see the lawn and the football. At this point, we are inclined to talk not only of the football and the front yard, but of perceptions and images. The front yard does not change, but my perception of it does; the football does not move, but my image of it, in some sense, does "move" across my "field of vision."

Given a rudimentary understanding of vision, we suppose that the change in perception corresponds to a change in the pattern of stimulation of my retina with corresponding changes in the more interior parts of my central nervous sytem. And the "movement" of the image of the football is the change of the pattern of stimulation caused by the football relative to other aspects of the perception, a change that is also reflected in the more interior parts of the brain. And the change in perception results in a change in what I am disposed to do under various circumstances. As I move back and forth on the driveway, for example, I will move my arm differently if I wish to point at the football. And I will walk in a slightly different direction if I want to pick it up.

My perception of the football on the lawn is a certain event. This event means that there is a football on the lawn.[2] Nomic constraints involved in seeing allow one event, the perception, to carry information about the external scene that it is a perception *of*. Similarly, the moving image of the football is another event, a part of the larger perception. It carries information about the thing it is *of*—the football. A change in perception means a change in scene because of the systematic link between the two. We thus have a two-way flow of information. A change in my cognitive situation carries information about the change in scene. This is the direction I use in getting to the football. But a change in the scene can be used to classify a change in my cognitive situation too. This is the direction that you would use if you were to report on my change of cognitive state by talking of the change in scene.

Notice that I am directly aware of the change in the scene by virtue of the change in perception—that is, by virtue of the change in my perceptual condition. My awareness of the change in my perceptual condition is not so direct. I have to think about it, or look at a fixed object and move my head and think about what is happening. The traditional arguments about the relativity of perception establish one thing: that there are different ways of seeing the same thing—in this case, different ways of seeing that the football is on my front lawn. This fact has led some to the conclusion that there are immediate objects of perception, corresponding to these ways. This conclusion does not follow, nor is it embedded in common sense. All that follows is the much more modest conclusion that there are different conditions one can be in, by virtue of which one can see the same thing. Perceptual relativity should not lead us to posit immediate objects of perception. It should lead us to see the perceptual process in a certain light, as involving changes depending on one's orientation to what is seen, changes that shed light on the nomic constraints involved in seeing.

The relativity of information reflects the efficiency of information, and this, too, is part of the common-sense picture of the mental. Consider that football again. From where I stand, I can't tell which of the several footballs my family owns it might be. My perception is of a particular football on a particular lawn. But I could be in the same perceptual condition I am in, while looking at any of an indefinite number of footballs. And, for that matter, I could be looking at any of an indefinite number of lawns, although there are certainly not as many lawns that look just alike from this distance as there are footballs. Which football and which lawn the various perturbations of my perceptual apparatus are *of* depends not just on those conditions, but on how I am set in a wider world, on my connections to footballs and lawns. Furthermore, I believe that I could be in this condition at a different time and, moreover, that someone else could be in the condition I am in. All of this leads to a certain picture of efficient perceptual conditions that carry information about the scene before the agent at the time that agent is in the perceptual condition. This is, we think, the picture of perceptual conditions that is embedded in common sense, and we assume that it is basically correct even if perhaps not perfect.

Representing Perceptions and Images

It is at this point that the duality between an organism and its environment becomes important for the theory. While the organism's environment is real, independent of the organism, the organism/environment pair has a richer structure, for the needs and abilities of the organism are correlated with certain uniformities that the organism recognizes. That is, there are structural features of the organism that correspond to structural features of its environment. Presumably these structural features, or states, of an organism evolve as adaptations for dealing with the factors in the environment that matter to the organism. It is this duality between an organism and its environment that lets us develop the conception of perceptions and images discussed above within our theory of situations.

The basic idea is to use indexed event-types to classify both what is seen and how it is seen. The indeterminates in the indexed event-type will be anchored to an agent, a location, and objects and relations through facts about the perceptual event. The event-type and the indeterminates in it will *represent* a perception suited to carry information about the type of event that is seen. The event-types get at two different kinds of uniformities, across mental events and across scenes. The possibility of using event-types in this dual way is a result of the duality discussed above.

Consider the account of primary perception from the previous chapter. We have a relation ST between perceivers and courses of events:

in e_0: at l: ST, a, e; yes.

The event e is of various types. These event-types can be used by an observer to represent the perception e_0 of e. We can abstract over any or all of the individuals and locations with basic indeterminates, or with roles, provided there is a way to anchor the roles to get back to the event e.[3] That is, given any event-type E and a function f that anchors E in e_0 such that $E[f]$ is part of e, we can use E and f to represent aspects of the perception. The relation between agent a and event-type E induced by this abstraction process we call S_r ("r" for "represented") and write

in e_0: at l: S_r, a, E; yes   (1)
of, $\dot{x}$, $f(\dot{x})$; yes   (2) (for all indeterminates $\dot{x}$ in E)

provided the above conditions hold; that is f is a total anchor for E in e_0, $E[f]$ is part of e, and:

in e_0: at l: ST, a, e; yes.

Thus the relation S_r is one the observer brings to the situation when she characterizes the agent a as having a certain type of perception. An event of this kind we shall call a *(represented) perception* or *R-perception*. The first part (1) of the R-perception we refer to variously as the *frame of mind* or, more specifically, as the *perceptual condition* of the R-perception. The second part we refer to as the *setting* of the R-perception. Our formulation of the common-sense view of perception is that primary perception consists of being in a perceptual condition in a setting.

The roles i and $\dot{b}$ may well occur in E and are always anchored to the perceiver and his location. The other indeterminates in E represent images, and are anchored to suitable objects in the environment by the setting. The anchoring relation is then ultimately between two parts of reality, a perturbation in the mind and an object in the world, say a football or a front lawn. The event-types exploit the duality involved in perception; they classify a perceptual system as being in a condition suited for perception of a certain kind of environment, from a certain location in it, and an environment as suitable for a certain kind of perception. The role of the indeterminates is to coordinate these two complementary uniformities.

At the end of the previous chapter we discussed four related problems with our account of the attitudes. We will illustrate how R-perceptions allow us to solve one of these problems, namely how perceptual reports can fit into the general scheme of Folk Psychology to give the kind of information about people that they in fact do give.

We will illustrate the idea with a simple example, Joe's seeing that Jackie is biting his dog Molly, thought of as primary perception. If we use ST, we can represent this as:

in e_0: at l: ST, Joe, e; yes,

where

in e: at l: biting, Jackie, Molly; yes
    dog, Jackie; yes
    dog, Molly; yes.

As a way of classifying Joe's frame of mind, the event e has a definite limitation, one it shares with an eternal sentence or a Fregean thought. If we are told that Joe saw that Jackie was biting his dog Molly, we expect him to be upset, to act in ways that people act when they see their dog being attacked. It is part of Folk Psychology (let us suppose, to keep things simple at this point) that kids who see dogs being attacked get upset. The trouble with our representation of the event is that it is not efficient. It is absolutely unique and specific to the particular event. It doesn't exhibit any of the similarity between different kids who see different dogs bite each other at different locations. The principle of Folk Psychology, on the other hand, is a generalization over people who see different dogs bite each other at different locations, not just those who see Jackie bite Molly at l.

To get something more efficient, we shift to an indexed event-type, and an R-perception:

in e: at l: S_r, Joe, E; yes
    of, $\dot{t}'$, Jackie; yes
    of, $\dot{t}''$, Molly; yes,

where

E: = at h: biting, $\dot{t}'$, $\dot{t}''$; yes
    dog, $\dot{t}'$; yes
    dog, $\dot{t}''$; yes.

Perceptions different people have of different dogs biting other dogs at various locations can all be classified by E, so it brings out what it is they have in common that serves as the basis for the generalization.

Notice, however, that there are lots of situations that might fit this event-type. Any one dog biting any other dog would do. By abstracting away from Jackie and Molly, E has gotten at an important uniformity, but it has lost something too—Jackie and Molly. By itself, without the anchoring, E loses track of the fact that it was Jackie and Molly whom Joe saw fighting. Lots of different events might have caused Joe to be in the frame of mind we classify with E. He would have been in this frame of mind if he had seen Nancy's dog Bear biting Jackie, for example. Joe's entire frame of mind, let alone this particular aspect of it, does not by itself determine what Joe saw. One also needs the informational history of his frame of mind. To keep track of what he saw, we need to anchor his perceptual condition to the objects in the world which caused it. This is the reason we must factor the perceptual event into two parts that fit together, the *frame of mind* and the *setting*.[4] Our claim is that the use we make of attitude reports in Folk Psychology presupposes this bipartite classification of the perception. The uniformities across individuals captured by the constraints and patterns of Folk Psychology operate at the level of frame of mind. But the frame of mind alone loses track of the way the perceiver sits in his world, what has caused the perception and, hence, what the perception is of.

We have a fine-grained way of representing perceptual situations. Note, though, that an event-type need not abstract over everything, so there is a great deal of flexibility about just how fine-grained our representation is. We could use an event-type that contained Jackie and one indeterminate, for example, to get at a uniformity across people who see Jackie biting a dog.

A second problem that arose in the previous chapter was that the constraints we needed didn't fit into our theory of constraints. For example, the principle of veridicality could not be formulated. Now let us reconsider the issue of veridicality from the current perspective.

Veridicality might be regarded as a fact about language: we don't *say* that Joe saw Jackie bite Molly, unless she really did. As a remark about language, this is true enough, but it puts the explanation the wrong way around. The fact is that we trust perception. We think that *if* Joe is in the perceptual condition indicated, anchored in the way indicated, then Jackie must have been biting Molly. Imagine looking at a photograph, undoctored, unretouched, that shows one dog biting another. You point to the dogs in the picture and say, "If that is Molly and that is Jackie, then Jackie was biting Molly.

Cameras don't lie." But our perceptual apparatus is at least as trustworthy as a camera.

To say that our perceptual apparatus is *perfectly* trustworthy would be to say that the following constraint is factual:[5]

$$C: = \text{at } l_u: \text{Involves}, E, E'; \text{yes}$$

where

$$E: = \text{at } \dot{l}: S_r, \dot{a}, \dot{E}; \text{yes}$$
$$\text{anchors}, \dot{f}, \dot{E}; \text{yes}$$

and

$$E': = \text{the anchoring of } \dot{E} \text{ by } \dot{f}.$$

But we don't really think perception is perfectly trustworthy. One can imagine an experimental laboratory situation in which things look closer than they are. I might be in the frame of mind normally caused by dogs fighting five feet away, when in fact they are twenty feet away. My images are still anchored to the dogs I see and to the location where they are; I still see them fighting. What do we say in such a case? And does the psychologist conducting the experiment correctly say of me, "He sees that there are dogs fighting five feet from him"?

It seems that the psychologist might well speak this way, and according to our definition of S_r, and the semantics of SEES_p, he is perfectly entitled to. He is accurately representing my perceptual condition and the things it is anchored to. But if so, SEES_p is not veridical.

One way to think of this is that I am in a kind of environment in which the basic perceptual constraint C given above does not hold. The constraint is only conditionally factual. It holds in certain types of situations E_0, but the situation in the laboratory is not one of these situations. So we need to add the following clause to our definition:

There is an event-type E_0 such that $C|E_0$ is factual,
and e is of type E_0.

Given this analysis, perceptual events in a normal environment have what we called event-meaning; frames of mind have event-type meaning. Joe's frame of mind on seeing Jackie biting Molly means that there is an event of a certain type happening before him. His perceptual event, however, means that Jackie is biting Molly. To bring out the event-type meaning present in perceptual conditions, we can use the notation from Chapter 6. We let d be the located perceiver, which is analogous to the discourse situation, and c be the anchoring function provided by the setting, which is analogous to the connections. Then,

$$d, c \llbracket E \rrbracket \, e \text{ if and only if } E[d,c] \text{ is part of } e.$$

Here the double brackets don't stand for linguistic meaning, but meaning relative to our basic perceptual constraint C.

When we say that SEES$_p$ classifies agents by exploiting constraints, it is this basic perceptual constraint C we have in mind. When we say that Joe sees that Jackie is biting Molly, we are saying what Joe's perceptual situation means.

It is important to realize that perceptual conditions have forward-looking and backward-looking meaning, as well as present-looking meaning. That is, perceptions carry all three sorts of information. When Joe sees that Jackie is biting Molly, this carries the information that Jackie is biting Molly. It also carries information about the recent past, about the relation between Jackie and Molly. But it also carries forward-looking information. It means that Joe is going to get upset—at least it means that relative to our assumed principle of Folk Psychology.

We assumed a rather implausible principle of Folk Psychology to motivate our discussion of efficiency, namely, that every kid that sees one dog biting another gets upset. It would have been much more reasonable to assume that kids that see their own dog being bitten by another get upset. Suppose that this is in fact the constraint that applies to Joe. What more has to enter the account? A great deal. Joe has to be able to recognize Molly as his own dog. This takes us outside the sphere of primary perception, for being his dog is not a visual property. It also forces us to introduce ideas and concepts, so that we can discuss recognition. And before we do that, we have to discuss what it means for Joe to keep seeing the same thing throughout a whole event.

Seeing the Same Thing: Perceptual Constancies

Let us return to the less violent example of my walking down the driveway and seeing the football on the lawn. As I move down the driveway, not only do I continue to see a lawn with a football on it, but I continue to see the same lawn with the same football on it. But my images change constantly as I move about, and they change much more drastically than I am aware of, even when I am aware of the images themselves. The stability of the perceived world, in contrast with the instability of the corresponding images and perceptions, is what is known as perceptual constancy. As I move down the driveway, the images of the football have different "shapes" and "hues," but I don't for a moment suppose that the football is changing shape or hue.

For an idealist this must appear mysterious. If the image determines reality, in some sense, then why do these constantly changing images all determine the same thing? For a realist, though, one who sees the structure an organism finds in reality as dependent on the structure of the organism, and vice versa, this constancy will be a necessary precondition of perception, part of what it means to differentiate uniformities across various situations.

As I move down the driveway, each of my images of the football is in two senses of the same football. First, each succeeding one is of the same football as the last because the setting anchors each one to the same football as the one before. But there is another important sense in which they are of the same football. There is a relation between the succeeding images—a complex relation involving the perception of which they are a part—that obtains under normal circumstances just when one sees the same object, as one turns one's head or moves along a driveway. This relation obtains even if the flow of football images is interrupted—by my blinking, for example, or turning my head away for an instant.

This relation is not simply a relation between two images that are of the same thing. The latter may obtain without the former. I turn my head away, knowing that my children are playing on the front lawn. When I turn back, I see the same football. My new image is anchored to the very same ball as the preceding one. But I do not see$_p$ that it is the same ball. I may suspect that it is, or suspect that it is not. Most likely the issue never enters my head.

We shall say that images related in the way that images normally are when one continues to watch a single thing are *visually linked*. In normal circumstances, visually linked images are of the same thing. In abnormal circumstances, they may not be. Common sense does not assume that images that are of the same thing are visually linked, or parts of a sequence of linked images, for of course they often are not. When I go out to get the paper tomorrow morning and see the same football on the same lawn, I may or may not recognize the ball as being the same as the one I saw today. The very possibility of so recognizing requires that the images not be visually linked. We represent visually linked images quite naturally by using a single indeterminate in the various event-types representing the frames of mind. We use $\dot{\imath}, \dot{\imath}'$... for visual indeterminates that represent images and are anchored to objects in scenes the agent sees.[6] To see how this works in a very simple case, imagine that as I walk down the driveway, the relative position of the football and mailbox change. From my initial position at l, the football is to the left of the mailbox. From a later position l', the football is directly in front of the mailbox.

$$\text{In } e\colon \text{at } l\colon S_r, a, E\,; \text{yes}$$

of, $\dot{\imath}$, the football; yes
of, $\dot{\imath}'$, the lawn; yes
of, $\dot{\imath}''$, the mailbox; yes

$\quad$ at l': S_r, a, E'; yes

of, $\dot{\imath}$, the football; yes
of, $\dot{\imath}'$, the lawn; yes
of, $\dot{\imath}''$, the mailbox; yes

$\quad l \prec l'$

where

$\quad E\colon = \text{at } \dot{b}\colon \text{on}, \dot{\imath}, \dot{\imath}'; \text{yes}$

football, $\dot{\imath}$; yes
lawn, $\dot{\imath}'$; yes
mailbox, $\dot{\imath}''$; yes
lft-of, $\dot{\imath}, \dot{\imath}''$; yes

and E' is the same except that the last line is replaced by:

$\quad$ in E': at $\dot{b}$: lft-of, $\dot{\imath}, \dot{\imath}''$; no.

in front of, $\dot{\imath}, \dot{\imath}''$; yes

This event e is a complex perception. As I walk down the driveway, the images of the football and mailbox "move" so that the former is no longer to the left of the latter.

Notice that the use of a single indeterminate to represent these visually linked indeterminates does not force us to have them be of the same thing. We might be tricked. Someone might switch footballs on us in some way without our having the least idea of it. In that case, we have:

$\quad$ in e: at l': of, t, the substituted football; yes.

This brings us back to the problem of recognition with which we ended the previous subsection. There is no reason to suppose that two different images of the football, say on different days, are visually linked. Certainly if I don't recognize the football as being the one I saw earlier, they are not visually linked. In representing these images that are not visually linked, we could use two different indeterminates, anchored to the same football. But what happens when I suddenly recognize it as being the football I saw yesterday? Just what is involved in recognition? What happens when Joe recognizes the dog being bitten as his dog, Molly? To discuss this we need concepts and ideas, and that requires a discussion of beliefs.

Representing Beliefs and Ideas

I have been pacing up and down the driveway, thinking about the attitudes, seeing the football but not paying much attention to it. I turn from the lawn and head back into the house. As I do so, I don't think about the football at all. I sit down at my desk and resume working. Then I hear someone shout, "Where's the damn football?" I think that it is on the lawn—but say nothing. What does common sense tell us about my ability to have this thought about the football being on the lawn while sitting at my desk working on something quite different?

What we would ordinarily say about this seems to be more or less the following. When I saw that the football was on the lawn, I came to believe that it was there, more or less automatically. I retained this belief, even after I quit thinking about the ball. When I heard the shout, my attention was directed toward the ball and its whereabouts. I still believed that it had been on the lawn before, when I was outside. I assumed (or inferred or conjectured) that it was still there. This is what I thought. Throughout the episode I had a belief about the ball and where it was, and at the end had a thought about that very ball still being on that very lawn.

How do my intervening belief and final thought get connected to the football and the lawn? Commonsensically, one might say that I formed *ideas* of the lawn and the ball and a *belief* about the former being on the latter when I saw the former on the latter. Throughout the episode I had an idea of the ball and a belief about it and so was able to think about it later, when I heard the shout.

Beliefs are dispositional states; that is, real states known through their effects. As ordinary folk, the two of us have even less of an idea of what precisely goes on when we form and retain a belief than of what goes on when we perceive. But it seems to involve the head in an essential way, since people seem to be able to lose (or replace) virtually any other bodily part without losing their beliefs. We assume that belief states are efficient bodily conditions (about which virtually nothing is known) that have enough structure to account for the complex information-retaining and behavior-guiding capacities that we use them to explain.

We assume that *beliefs* are complex event-types, the constituents of which we call *ideas*. Ideas, like perceptual images, are ideally *of* things. But *what* they are of need not be perceived. And like images that are not of anything, we can sometimes have ideas that are not of anything, either. Just as we factored perceptions into efficient perceptual conditions and settings, so, too, we factor beliefs into efficient doxastic conditions and settings. The former is an additional component of the agent's frame of mind. We classify these efficient doxastic conditions with a relation B_r (for represented belief) and schemata, sets of indexed event-types. We need schemata, not just indexed event-types, to handle beliefs that would be reported using disjunctions, complex noun phrases, and the like. We will stick to event-types (singleton schemata) when dealing with simple examples, though.

When we dealt with perceptions, it was reasonable to suppose (as we implicitly did) that an agent had just one perception at a time. Common sense suggests that we have lots of beliefs at any one time. They are dispositional states, not activities. Thus we do not assume that an agent has only one big belief at any one time. This affects the definition of the relation between BO, the alternative relation of Chapter 9, and the relation B_r given in the next section.

We define a *(represented) belief*[7] to be a situation e_0 whose constituents at various locations l are of the form

(1)   in e_0: at l: B_r, a, S; yes
(2)   of, $\dot{x}, b$; yes,

where $\dot{x}$ ranges over indeterminates (not necessarily all) in the schema S, and b is the right sort of thing for $\dot{x}$ to be anchored to. We refer to the facts of the form (1) in e_0 as the *doxastic conditions* of the belief, the schema S as a *belief schema*, and the facts of the form (2) as the *setting* of the belief. The indeterminates in the belief schemata are called the *ideas* of e_0.[8]

As an example, take Joe's belief that Jackie is biting his dog Molly. We can represent this as follows:

in e_0: at l: B_r, Joe, E; yes
    of, $\dot{a}$, Jackie; yes
    of, $\dot{b}$, Molly; yes

where

E: = at $\dot{h}$: biting, $\dot{a}$, $\dot{b}$; yes
    belongs-to, $\dot{b}$, $\dot{i}$; yes
    dog, $\dot{a}$; yes
    dog, $\dot{b}$; yes.

Notice that the indeterminates $\dot{i}$ and $\dot{h}$ get anchored to Joe and l automatically by being the roles they are.

What is the meaning of a doxastic situation like this? Joe's believing that Jackie is biting his dog does not mean that Jackie is in fact biting Molly, of course. With the belief and the other doxastic attitudes things are not so simple. Common sense tells us that belief conditions have a causal role. Each belief condition has a certain effect on what a person thinks and does. A belief condition can thus be thought of as a strategy, one that will be suitable to some environments while unsuitable to others. If we assume that kids who believe that their dog is being bitten by another dog get upset and try to rescue their dogs, then Joe's belief will lead him to certain types of appropriate action.[9] The embedded statement in a belief report identifies something like the events in which Joe's belief would normally be an effective strategy. Thus, whereas there was forward-, present- and backward-looking meaning in perceptions, the meaning of a belief situation is largely forward-looking; that Joe believes that Jackie is biting his dog means something about what he will and won't do, relative, of course, to other factors, including what he wants, his other beliefs, and the like.

It is important to recall that perceptual conditions have forward-looking information, to the effect that the agent will form beliefs and perform actions appropriate to the kind of situation he sees himself to be in. That is, the agent will believe what his perceptual situation means. We might call this the loop of benevolence. Lots of individuals are in conditions that have backward-looking meaning and forward-looking meaning. Consider my shirt, for example. The dirt on my shirt means that I have been wearing it and that it will be washed. But the loop of benevolence is characteristic of adapted, intelligent organisms.

We assume that in the normal case, belief states are anchored, but

this is not necessary. If I think I see a football on the lawn but none
is there, I may later be in just the sort of state suitable for believing
that a football I actually saw before is still where I thought I saw it.
But in the former case my idea is not really of a football in that it
will not be anchored to anything, while in the latter it will. The connection between my idea and the image is the same in both cases; the
lack of an anchor for the image infects the idea by leaving it unanchored. We may thus concentrate on the representation of the
images, perception, ideas, and beliefs without worrying about how
the former are anchored.

Thus I look at a lawn, see a football there, and form ideas of
the football and of the lawn, and I have a belief involving those
ideas—namely, that the football is on the lawn. We shall use the
term *formative linking* for the relation between the image of the
football and the formed idea, as we did for the relation between
successive images in a normal case of seeing the same thing. Again
we use a common indeterminate to represent formative linking.
Thus the initial state can be represented by the following complex
condition:

$$\text{in } e \text{: at } l \text{: } S_r, a, E \text{; yes}$$
$$B_r, a, E_1 \text{; yes,}$$

where

$$E \text{: } = \text{at } \dot{h} \text{: on, } \dot{t}_1, \dot{t}_2 \text{; yes}$$
$$\text{football, } \dot{t}_1 \text{; yes}$$
$$\text{lawn, } \dot{t}_2 \text{; yes,}$$

and E_1 is E plus

$$\text{at } \dot{h} \text{: same, } \dot{l}, \dot{h} \text{; yes.}$$

The reason for the extra element of E_1 will emerge as we examine
what I must do to retain this belief that the football was where I saw
it, when I saw it.

Now as I go inside, I retain the belief that I had. Nothing happens
to cause me to doubt my senses. But what does this mean? Given the
nature of a belief, how can it be retained?

It would be implausible to suppose that retention of belief involves
staying in the same state. Indeed, it must require changing states, if
states have determinate causal roles, since a belief will cause different things as time goes by (Perry, 80a). For example, if my belief
continues to be represented by E_1 at some time $l' \succ l$, then I will
be confused, because I will believe that the football is there on the

lawn, rather than that it was on the lawn at l. To keep the same belief, I must change my frame of mind. At l' I need to be in the doxastic condition:

in e_1: at l': B_r, a, E_2; yes

where

E_2: = at $\dot{l}$: on, $\dot{t}_1, \dot{t}_2$; yes
football, $\dot{t}_1$; yes
lawn, $\dot{t}_2$; yes.

(We might even add $\dot{l} \prec \dot{b}$ to E_2 if we think that part of keeping the
same belief is to realize that time has passed.)

Here is our picture of what has happened. Perceptions give rise to
beliefs. A belief may be thought of as an information-preserving sequence of states. A computer analogy may be helpful. If I type my
midterm grades into a file in the department's computer, then the
computer is in a certain efficient state that contains information
about the grades I give my students. It also records the date at which
I create this file. A year later, with luck, it is still in a state that contains that information. But it is not in the same state in the most intuitive sense. At the level of electrical activity, there is a tremendous
flux, a continuous succession of states that the computer is in. Even
at higher levels of analysis, the states change. The information is first
stored on a disk, then shifted around on the disk for various reasons,
then perhaps put on tape. And it has a record of the date I created
the old file.[10]

So we assume that however the brain and central nervous system
work, there is an incredible flux of activity, in what we call retention
of a belief. We assume that there is a sequence of events—in our very
liberal notion of event, factual events which may be very complex
aspects of actual events—which are information-preserving. (They
may not contain information about the world in the first place, of
course). But if my being in state β early in the sequence contains the
information that φ, then my being in β' later in the sequence contains
the information that φ. We take *beliefs* to be such information-
preserving sequences of events. It is these beliefs that we indirectly
describe in natural language with embedded statements.

Recognition, Concepts, and Applied Beliefs

Consider the situation in which I return to the front of the house and
see a football on the roof. I *recognize* the football as the one I saw
yesterday on the lawn.

Our analysis of recognition involves concepts and modes of recognition. In common language the terms *concept* and *idea* are pretty much synonymous, at least when we speak of my idea of something and my concept of it. (There are other sorts of ideas that we are not discussing here.) We are regimenting things a bit, but not much. We have used the term *idea* only in the context of a belief:

in e_0: at l: B_r, a, S; yes
  of, $\dot{x}, b$; yes

.

.

.

and we use it for one of the indeterminates $\dot{o}$ in the schema S. We use the term *concept* for a pair $\langle \dot{o}, S(\dot{o},...) \rangle$. In a situation like e_0 we say that the agent a has a concept $S[a, l, f]$ of b, where f is the anchoring of all indeterminates given by e_0 except for the assignment to $\dot{o}$, if there is one. The concept may be more or less anchored, and e_0 may not even provide an anchor for $\dot{o}$, in which case the concept is not of anything.

We say that a concept $\langle \dot{o}, S \rangle$ is *applied* to an individual b in e if the agent has the belief

  E: = at $\dot{b}$, same, $\dot{o}, \dot{t}$; yes,

where t is a visual image in e that is anchored to b.

My concept of x may be full of misinformation about x. It may fall far short of providing an "identifying description," whether or not the information is included (Donnellan, 70). We often have concepts of individuals and locations that are rich and accurate enough to allow us to recognize them.

My recognition e of the football has the following structure: (A) a belief I have about the football I saw on the lawn yesterday, which gives me a concept of that football, (B) seeing the football again, this time on the roof, and (C) applying my old concept of the football to the football, and so coming to believe that it's the same football. That is:

  (A) in e: at l: B_r, a, E; yes
      of, $\dot{t}$, the football; yes
      of, $\dot{t}'$, the lawn; yes
      of, $\dot{l}, l$; yes
    at l': B_r, a, E'; yes
      of, $\dot{t}$, the football; yes

of, $\dot{t}$', the lawn; yes
of, $\dot{l}$, l; yes
(B) at l': S_r, a, E''; yes
of, $\dot{c}$, the football; yes
of, $\dot{c}$', the roof; yes
of, $\dot{l}$', l'; yes
(C) at l': B_r, a, E'''; yes
of, $\dot{t}$, the football; yes
of, $\dot{c}$', the roof; yes
$l \prec l'$

where

E: = at $\dot{b}$: on, $\dot{t}$, $\dot{t}$'; yes
football, $\dot{t}$; yes
lawn, $\dot{t}$'; yes
same, $\dot{l}$, $\dot{b}$; yes
E': = at $\dot{l}$: on, $\dot{t}$, $\dot{t}$'; yes
football, $\dot{t}$; yes
lawn, $\dot{t}$'; yes
E": = at $\dot{b}$: on, $\dot{c}$, $\dot{c}$'; yes
football, $\dot{c}$; yes
roof, $\dot{c}$'; yes
same, $\dot{l}$', $\dot{b}$; yes
E"': = at $\dot{b}$: same, $\dot{t}$, $\dot{c}$; yes.

This may just be a lucky guess, but in fact we are very good at recognizing things. And it seems that we should be able to represent these abilities by constraint types, so we present a tentative model of recognition. Consider Joe's concept $\langle \dot{o}, S \rangle$ of Molly. It is a very rich concept, which he couldn't come close to putting into words. That is, the most detailed description Joe could give would leave you far less able to recognize Molly under various circumstances than Joe is. These unverbalizable features of his concept are a very important part of it. This concept gives rise to a constraint-type. Any object Joe sees which fits this concept, or the perceptual part of it, is (let us suppose) Molly:

$C/\dot{i},\dot{b},\dot{t}$: = at l: involves, $S'(...\dot{t}...)$, E; yes,

where

E: = at $\dot{b}$: same, $\dot{t}$, $\dot{o}$; yes

and S' is part of S. (Here we are using notation introduced in footnote 3 of Chapter 5.)

The antecedent of such a constraint we call a *mode of recognition.* A concept may provide us with many modes of recognition, or none, and it may provide us with modes of misrecognition, too. The sort of mode of recognition just described we call *perceptual.* It allows Joe to recognize Molly when he sees her.

There are, however, many modes of recognition other than perceptual. An extremely important kind for understanding language is what we call *nominal modes of recognition,* the ability to tell who or what is being talked about. This is an important ability, which we all possess to a greater or lesser degree. A simple model of this ability is suggested by the picture of "proper names" that has often been assumed in philosophy and logic. If each name had just one bearer, then anyone who knew who the bearer of a name was would know who was being talked about in those situations where the name was used. But of course things are much more complicated than that.

Suppose, for example, that I enter a room in which people are using the name JULIUS. Are they talking about Julius Erving or Julius Moravcsik? They are extolling the virtues of this person's hook shot, and his finesse under the basket. That hardly settles matters. Then they mention his knowledge of Greek and transformational grammar, and I know it is Julius the philosopher that is being talked about.

The ability to figure out who is being talked about depends on various kinds of information: information about Julius, information about the people in the room and which Juliuses they are likely to know, and so forth. It may even depend on sharing some misconceptions about Julius. But I am able to do it. I hear the word JULIUS uttered, and recognize that it is being used to refer to Julius Moravcsik. In this case, the mode of recognition has the form

$$C / \dot{i}, \dot{b}, \dot{t} := \text{at } l : \text{involves}, S'(\dots \dot{t} \dots), E ; \text{yes}$$

where

$$E := \text{at } \dot{b} : \text{referring-to}, \dot{t}, \dot{o} ; \text{yes},$$

my concept of Julius is $\langle \dot{o}, S \rangle$, and S' is part of S.

One more topic needs to be discussed under the heading of concepts and recognition—our concepts of ourselves and our ability to recognize ourselves and references to us. This is a complex and subtle topic, from both the psychological and philosophical point of view, and while we think that the theory of situations has much to contribute to clear thinking on the matter, we don't want to attempt an extensive analysis here (Gibson, 79; Perry, to appear, b). But we can't resist the temptation to say a little.

We have emphasized that cognition takes place from a perspective in space and time, by representing cognitive conditions with indexed event-types. In a sense, all my perceptions and beliefs contain information (and misinformation) about me and my present location. Given any of my beliefs S, $\langle i, S \rangle$ will be a concept of me, and $\langle h, S \rangle$ a concept of my present location. The important point is that I may also have other, unmerged concepts of myself and my location. I may see myself in a mirror without knowing it, or read about myself on the post office wall without realizing the trouble I am in (Castaneda, 68; Perry, 79). I may see a spot on an up-to-date map that refers to my location without knowing that it does.

Suppose I have read a great deal about this character in the wanted poster, and indeed have a very rich concept of him. Yet I am strangely calm. I don't recognize that I am who is wanted. As soon as I do, I will start to tremble and probably head for a lawyer or have a nervous breakdown. But as long as I don't make the connection, all my knowledge of myself via the concept formed from reading the wanted poster does not play the role in explaining my thought and action that beliefs about myself are expected to. We expect people who know they are wanted by the FBI to act in a certain way, but I won't act in that way.

There is nothing particularly mysterious about this, from the point of view of how the mind works. I have two concepts of myself, a normal one $\langle i, S \rangle$ and another one, $\langle a, S' \rangle$. Only if I realize they are concepts of the same individual, me, and merge the schemata into $S + S'$, will I put two and two together and head for a lawyer. This is just part of a very general phenomenon. We call this the *application of beliefs.* First we will look at the general case, and then come back to the special case of having two concepts of oneself.

Let's return to Melanie and Jim. Melanie has two concepts of Jim, which are unmerged. She formed an idea of him when she saw him eat an anchovy, from a distance. She forms another idea of him when she meets him, just now. She behaves in a certain way toward him, and part of the explanation of this is her beliefs about him. But only her second concept is relevant here. The beliefs she gained when she saw him eat the anchovy, even though they provide her with a concept of Jim, have nothing to do with what she says to him. Her first concept is *of* Jim, but it is not applied to Jim in this situation.

The point is not that Melanie's first concept of Jim does not provide her with a mode of recognition. That is an inessential feature of this particular example. Perhaps Jim is a famous racing driver, and Melanie has read a lot about him. Perhaps she can even recognize him perceptually, under certain circumstances, when he is wearing his racing gear and sitting in his Porsche. But this third concept she has of Jim is not applied to him in this particular interaction with him, either. She doesn't ask him if he wants anchovies on his pizza, and she doesn't ask him what it was like to win the Daytona 500. She just treats him as a nice fellow she has never seen before and has never heard of.

Common-sense psychology contains many principles about how we deal with objects that we believe various things about. These are not iron-clad principles, but more like rules of thumb; they nevertheless embody an enormous amount of accumulated wisdom about how people work. One might be that a polite person ordering a pizza for two asks the other person if they want anchovies, if they have the slightest reason to suspect that the other person partakes of that vice. Another might be that a racing fan will talk to a racing star about racing if they ever meet. But these principles only apply if the believer recognizes the subject of these beliefs through some mode of recognition contained in the belief. Otherwise they are quite irrelevant. Melanie has three concepts of Jim, as the example now stands, and two of them are not applied to him in the current situation, and so are quite irrelevant to how she treats him.

The same basic idea has to be extended to cases in which information about *b*, and not *b* himself, is available to the believer, and to all sorts of cognitive states and activities, not just overt actions. If someone hears someone they trust say that *b* is an authority on Russian music, they will believe that *b* is an authority on Russian music. But this does not mean that every concept they have of *b* will be revised—only those will be which contain a mode of recognition that enables the believer to link the information to the concept.

Consider Jonny and the Roman History examination. As he looks at the exam sheet, he has two concepts of Cicero. One he has had for a long time, and it contains a lot about Cicero, including the fact that

Cicero was an orator. The other he has just gained, from reading the question TRUE OR FALSE. TULLY WAS A ROMAN ORATOR. It is a very slim concept, basically this,

$\langle \dot{c}, S \rangle$, where $S = \{E, E'\}$ and

> E: = Roman orator, $\dot{c}$; yes
>   refer to, "Tully", $\dot{c}$; yes
> E': = Roman orator, $\dot{c}$; no
>   refer to, "Tully", $\dot{c}$; yes.

This is a concept of Cicero, because the teacher's use of TULLY was anchored to Cicero. But it is not a rich enough concept of Cicero to be of much help to Jonny in answering the question. It is, however, the only concept of Cicero that he is applying to Cicero as he takes the exam. There is a principle of common-sense psychology that says that if a student wants a good grade on an exam and knows that someone was a Roman orator and is asked on the exam whether that person was a Roman orator, the student will say that he was. But this principle presupposes the student is in a position to apply this knowledge, which Jonny isn't.

When I stare at the poster in the post office, I have two concepts of myself. One I don't apply. One applies a concept $\langle \dot{c}, S \rangle$ to oneself, when one has the belief,

> E: = at $\dot{b}$: same, $\dot{c}$, $\dot{i}$; yes.

I don't have this belief, and that's why the bit of common sense that says that when normal, timid, completely law-abiding persons see that they are wanted by the FBI, they have a nervous breakdown— this bit of common sense does not apply to me.

The general moral we draw from all of this is that beliefs explain actions only when they are applied. And this should be pretty obvious, after all. We have taken great pains to state this bit of common sense because it points to a central puzzle in the philosophy of the attitudes, to which we now turn our attention.

Coherent Beliefs

We usually assume that a person is rational, that her beliefs are coherent in a certain sense. But just what does this assumption amount to? Or, to put it the other way around, what does it mean for an agent's actual beliefs to be incoherent? How can a person's beliefs seem coherent to her but be obviously incoherent to an observer?

First, we should note that incoherent beliefs are not necessarily incoherent doxastic situations as displayed below, for there are actual doxastic situations e_0 with incoherent beliefs, although no actual situation is incoherent. In representing what someone believes, we can never correctly attribute both:

in e_0: at l: B_r, a, E; yes, and
$\qquad\quad B_r$, a, E; no,

to an actual doxastic situation.

There are two forms of incoherence: cognitive incoherence and external incoherence. A doxastic situation e_0 is *cognitively coherent* if the sum of all belief schemata in e_0 is a coherent schema—that is, if it contains at least one coherent event-type. Otherwise e_0 is cognitively incoherent. By contrast, e_0 is *externally coherent* if the sum of all belief schemata anchored by their settings is coherent.[11] Otherwise it is externally incoherent. Any doxastic situation that is externally coherent is necessarily cognitively coherent, but the converse does not follow. In fact, we often have cognitively coherent beliefs that are externally incoherent.

Let's give a simple example. Recall Kripke's famous case of Pierre, the Parisian Pierre who grows up believing that Londres is not pretty, moves to London, not knowing that it is the same city as Londres, and believes that it is pretty. There seems to be nothing wrong with Pierre's logic, yet it seems that both his beliefs cannot possibly be right if they are both about London. This is often taken to be an insurmountable paradox for any innocent theory of the attitudes. We think the problem is simply not keeping track of the distinction between cognitive and external coherence.

Common sense says that Pierre has two different (and on our account unlinked) concepts of London:

in e_0: at l: B_r, Pierre, $E_0(\dot{a})$; yes
$\qquad\quad B_r$, Pierre, $E_1(\dot{b})$; yes
$\qquad\quad$ of, $\dot{a}$, London; yes
$\qquad\quad$ of, $\dot{b}$, London; yes,

where

in E_1: at l_u: pretty, $\dot{a}$; yes
in E_2: at l_u: pretty, $\dot{b}$; no.

This doxastic situation is cognitively coherent because $E_1 + E_2$ is a coherent event-type. However, with the setting f provided by this belief, with $f(\overset{.}{a}) = f(\overset{.}{b})$ = London, the situation is externally incoherent.

For another example, consider the cook at the Center who believes that Hans and Robin are the same person, a handsome Englishman with brown hair who comes through the lunch line twice every day. Intuitively, there is no trouble with the cook's understanding of the law of identity, that no two different things are the same. But yet, she does believe that two distinct individuals are one.

There are two slightly different ways to solve this puzzle, depending on the actual facts of the matter. If the cook has one concept which is of both Hans and Robin, we have one solution open to us. Or if, on a particular occasion, the cook has an image, say, of Robin, and does not make a conceptual link but just thinks that he is the same person she saw two minutes ago, then we have a different solution. In the first case the cook has a belief where the setting does not provide an anchor, that is:

in e_0: at l: B_r, the cook, $S(\overset{.}{o})$; yes
        of, $\overset{.}{o}$, Hans; yes
        of, $\overset{.}{o}$, Robin; yes.

In the second case we have two ideas which are believed to be ideas of the same person:

in e_0: at l: B_r, the cook, E; yes
        of, $\overset{.}{a}$, Hans; yes
        of, $\overset{.}{b}$, Robin; yes,

where

in E: at $\overset{.}{b}$: same, $\overset{.}{a}$, $\overset{.}{b}$; yes.

In both cases the belief is cognitively coherent (we may suppose) but externally incoherent. In the first case it is incoherent because we don't have an anchor. In the second case we have an anchor f, but $E[f]$ is incoherent, since Robin is not Hans.

REPORTING ATTITUDES

We now return to the linguistic meaning in general and the meaning of attitude reports in particular. At the end of the last chapter we saw various defects with treating attitude reports as giving information about primitive relations (*SO*, *KO*, *BO*, etc.) to situations.

Now we want to see how our method of representing the mental allows us to do better.

We will describe two approaches, concentrating on belief. The first simply uses represented beliefs to define BO. This resolves the foundational problems, but is not flexible enough to account for the use of the attitudes in explanations and their interactions with principles of Folk Psychology, particularly in cases involving externally incoherent beliefs. The second approach leaves BO to one side and gives a semantics for belief reports directly in terms of beliefs and their settings. The second is our official choice.

To remind ourselves of the efficient character of beliefs, we shall again borrow the notation we use for linguistic meaning. We write,

$$a, l, f [\![S]\!] e$$

iff

e is of type $S[a, l, f]$.

As in the case of the meaning of perception, mentioned earlier in this chapter, the double brackets indicate content relative to nonlinguistic constraints.

The idea behind both approaches is that attitude reports indirectly describe the agent's beliefs S by giving us information about their interpretation e.

The First Approach

A doxastic situation e_0 involving some agent a will have parts of the form:

in e_0: at l: B_r, a, S; yes (or no)
         of, $\dot{x}, f(\dot{x})$; yes (or no)

In this approach, we define the relation BO from the last chapter in terms of facts of this sort, and then apply the semantics as before.

In e_0: at l: BO, a, e; yes

just in case for every S, and f such that

in e_0: at l: B_r, a, S; yes
         of, $\dot{x}, f(\dot{x})$; yes,

there is a g extending f so that e is of type $S[a, l, g]$. Otherwise,

in e_0: at l: BO, a, e; no.

If we put these definitions together with those of Chapter 9, we obtain an account according to which

$d, c \llbracket$ BELIEVES THAT $\varphi \rrbracket a, e_0$

if, for each alternative e compatible with all of a's beliefs as anchored at c (BELIEVES) according to e_0, we have

$d, c \llbracket \varphi \rrbracket e.$

This definition resolves the foundational problems encountered at the end of the last chapter. Consider,

$d, c \llbracket$ JOE BELIEVES THAT JACKIE IS BITING MOLLY $\rrbracket e$

The problem was that there is a proper class X of events e_1 in which Jackie is not biting Molly at $l(=c(\text{IS}))$, and each of these will have to be classified with BO-no by e, so it too would have to be a proper class. Given this definition, e is only required to have Joe with a belief S anchored in a certain way f, so that none of the events in X is of type $S[\text{Joe}, l, g]$, where g is any extension of f.

One problem with this approach is that it does not give us the flexibility that BELIEVES seems to have in ordinary English, in dealing with externally incoherent beliefs. Consider Melanie's beliefs about Jim, from the last chapter. Given the semantics of the last chapter and the definitions just given, Melanie did not believe that Jim *had* eaten an anchovy and did not believe that Jim had *not* eaten an anchovy. She has BO-no to events in which he did eat one, as well as to events in which he didn't eat one. This is all we can say about Melanie, and it isn't enough. Because her beliefs don't agree, we have been left with nothing positive to say about them. But we think that in certain circumstances it would be appropriate and true for Jim to say, "She didn't believe that I had eaten an anchovy," and in other circumstances appropriate and true for him to say, "She believed that I had eaten an anchovy."

Furthermore, as we shall see below, this approach will not work when we consider principles of folk psychology that interact with attitude reports in explanations. We bring our method of representing the mental more directly into the semantics using our second method.

The Second Approach

On this approach we do not go through the relation BO, but simply require that the embedded statement in the attitude report capture the interpretation of some of the agent's beliefs.

Let us say that $\langle f, S \rangle$ is a *way of believing* $_{d,c} \llbracket \varphi \rrbracket$ *for a at l*, provided the interpretation of S given a, l and f strongly implies (i.e., is a sub-collection of) the interpretation $_{d,c}[\![\varphi]\!]$; that is, provided:

if $a, l, f[\![S]\!]\, e$, then $d, c[\![\varphi]\!]\, e$.

(The square brackets are used for doxastic meaning in the first part of this definition, but for linguistic meaning in the second part.) Then we define:

$d, c[\![$ BELIEVES THAT $\varphi]\!]\, a, e_0$

just in case there is an S and f such that

(i) $\langle S, f \rangle$ is a way of believing $_{d,c}[\![\varphi]\!]$
   for a at $l = c$ (BELIEVES),

(ii) in e_0: at l: B_r, a, S; yes
   of, $\dot{x}, f(\dot{x})$; yes

Notice that according to this definition, if a believes that φ, and if the statement that ψ is a strong consequence of the statement that φ, then a believes that ψ.

In defining what it means not to believe that φ, we must recall that there is a difference between not believing something and believing the contrary. Many people do not believe that Molly is Joe's dog simply because they have never heard of Joe or Molly. These people do not believe that Molly is not Joe's dog. We say that $\langle f, S \rangle$ is *a way of failing to believe* $_{d,c}[\![\varphi]\!]$, *for a at l* provided the latter is a subcollection of the interpretation of S given a, l and f; that is, provided for every e:

if $d, c[\![\varphi]\!]\, e$, then $a, l, f[\![S]\!]\, e$.

Then we define

$d, c[\![$ DOESN'T BELIEVE THAT $\varphi]\!]\, a, e_0$

provided there is an S and f such that

(i) $\langle S, f \rangle$ is a way of failing to believe $_{d,c}[\![\varphi]\!]$ for a at $l = c$ (BE-LIEVES),

(ii) in e_0: at l: B_r, a, S; no
   of, $\dot{x}, f(\dot{x})$; yes

Note that if a doesn't believe that φ and the statement that φ is a strong consequence of the statement that ψ then a doesn't believe that ψ either.

The account squares with the logic of belief, as described in the last chapter. But there are a number of principles one might expect which we do not have. Most importantly, we do not have

I. if *a* believes that not-φ then *a* doesn't believe that φ.

We do not even have the weaker

J. if *a* believes that not-φ and *a* doesn't believe that φ, then *a*'s beliefs are externally incoherent.

One might think, then, that we have developed an analysis of BELIEVES so flexible as to be utterly chaotic and useless. We don't think that this is so. In fact, we think that it is just what is required, and that can be seen by keeping several related things in mind:

- the difference between not believing something and believing the contrary;

- the possibility for, and the nature of, externally incoherent beliefs, and what people say about the thoughts and actions of people with such beliefs, in concrete uses of language, and

- certain Gricean principles about how attitude reports are used, which we discuss below.

We do have two weaker principles, which are more important than *I*, and in actual practice give us all the leverage we need to say useful things with our flexible concept of belief:

K. if *a*'s beliefs are externally coherent then *a* doesn't both believe that φ and believe that not-φ.

L. if *a* believes that φ *in a certain way*, then it is not the case that *a* doesn't believe that φ *in that same way*.

In actual practice, we describe an agent's beliefs with certain purposes in mind, which limit ways of believing, and in particular limit the settings in which we have any interest. So long as the agent's beliefs are externally coherent, relative to those limited ways of believing in which we are interested, we will not end up appearing to contradict ourselves in the way that the failure of principle *I* permits. These limitations are more or less automatic when we are interested in the beliefs a person has which constitute knowledge, and which we discuss below. Things are a bit more complex when we are trying to explain a person's thought and action by reference to her beliefs, for both parts of an incoherent set of beliefs may be relevant in explaining different things. We turn now to a discussion of the way such explanations work.[12]

It is important to be clear that we are still working at the level of external significance, so that our theory is innocent by the definition given earlier. We are describing the agent's beliefs by comparing the external significance of those beliefs with the external significance of the embedded sentence in our attitude report.

Some Constraints on the Use of Attitude Verbs

Grice (75) has emphasized the distinction between inferences we make from utterances based on what is said, and those based on the general purposes of language, using principles and maxims of conversational cooperation. The latter are cancelable, and a cooperative person will cancel them in circumstances in which inferences based on them might mislead. This distinction helps loosen the connection between "intuitions" about what one would and wouldn't say, and the semantic theory that accounts for this.[13] We do not try to develop a detailed interpretation of Grice's theory within situation semantics, but we do rely on his ideas in explaining how an innocent approach to the attitudes can handle the sort of evidence that has usually been thought to doom such an approach from the outset.

The general constraint on the speaker to be cooperative has a number of applications for the production of attitude reports and corollaries that allow the listener to draw conversational implicatures from them. We state two that are useful to keep in mind in the discussion to follow.

A. Speaker: When using an attitude report to explain a person's actions (as opposed to using it as evidence of what the world is like), do not use terms describing or suggesting the agent's unapplied concepts or irrelevant anchors or other modes of recognition not used by the listener. Listener: Assume that the speaker is referring to the agent's applied concepts, relevant anchors, and other modes of recognition used by the agent.

B. Speaker: Assume that people are cognitively coherent. Listener: In interpreting an attitude report that attributes an incoherent attitude to the agent, look for unapplied concepts and settings that make the attitudes cognitively coherent but externally incoherent.

There are also some guides to the use of attitude verbs in Folk Psychology that follow from the general nature of the way constraints are normally stated. The two that are relevant for our discussion are the following:

C. In the statement of principles of common-sense psychology, third-person pronouns usually have antecedents.

D. In the statement of principles of common-sense psychology, singular-noun phrases are usually used with the inner attributive reading.

We will exhibit the use of these four principles below. We do not claim that they are hard and fast rules; rather, they are sound guides to the uses of the attitudes.

Three Examples

Example 1. Consider Lynae and Barbara, both recent mothers. Lynae believes that her baby Erin is hungry; Barbara believes that her baby Beth is hungry. We expect each of them to feed her baby. There is clearly a significant uniformity here, one we might get at with,

(1) A MOTHER WHO BELIEVES HER BABY IS HUNGRY WILL FEED IT.

This uniformity does *not* show itself at the level of the relation *BO*. Lynae has *BO* to one event, in which Erin is hungry, Barbara has *BO* to another, in which Beth is hungry.

We can get at what Barbara and Lynae have in common at the level of B_r and indexed event-types. Both Lynae and Barbara have B_r to

$E:$ = at $\overset{*}{b}$: child of, $\overset{*}{a}$, $\overset{*}{i}$; yes

$\qquad$ hungry, $\overset{*}{a}$; yes.

They differ in how this belief condition is anchored to the world. At this level of analysis, we also get at what Lynae has in common with herself at different times when she thinks Erin is hungry, and Barbara at different times when she thinks Beth is hungry. And at this level we obtain a situation that interacts with the constraint described by (1).

When we take (1) in the natural way, as a fairly accurate principle or rule of thumb of common sense, we are taking HER BABY to be used inner attributively, and taking the HER to be anaphorically connected to A MOTHER. That is, we give it this "reading":

(A MOTHER)$_1$ WHO BELIEVES THAT [((HER)$_1$ BABY)$_2^2$ IS HUNGRY]^2 WILL FEED IT$_2$.

If we didn't take it this way, it wouldn't be the least bit plausible. If the noun phrase HER BABY were not taken as an inner attributive use, the principle would just say that a mother who believes that a baby, who happens to be her own, is hungry will feed it, and this isn't so.

The inner attributive use of the noun phrase, and the fact that A MOTHER is the antecedent of HER in this principle requires instances of it to be cases where the mother believes that *her own* baby is hungry.

If I am asked why Barbara left the room and went toward the nursery, and I say, "She believed her baby was hungry," I exploit in my explanation common knowledge of (1) as well as the inner attributive use and the pattern of coreference. If I just say, "She believes that Beth is hungry," I exploit knowledge of (1) and the knowledge of my audience that Beth is Barbara's child.

Now consider all the agents who fit the antecedent of (1), read in this way. They will *all* believe that their babies are hungry. *Most* of them will believe this in virtue of a belief of the type defined above:

$$E: = \text{at } \dot{b}: \text{hungry, } \dot{a}; \text{yes}$$
$$\text{child of, } \dot{a}, \, \dot{i}; \text{yes.}$$

But some may *not* believe that their babies are hungry, in *this* way. They may believe it by virtue of some other idea they have of themselves. The belief of the majority will be contextually anchored to themselves. For the minority there will be some other sort of anchor. We have in mind, of course, a Castaneda example (Castaneda, 66; Perry, 79). One might construct a story about someone who does research at her child's nursery school on files, coded for anonymity, of children at the nursery school and their families. The point, though, is that the constraint applies only to those who have the normal sort of belief. The interpretation of (1) will be to describe those constraints C for which:

$$\text{in } C: \text{at } l_u: \text{involves, } E_1, E_2; \text{yes}$$

where

$$E_1: = \text{at } \dot{i}: \text{mother, } \dot{b}; \text{yes}$$
$$B_r, \, \dot{b}, \, E; \text{yes } (E \text{ as just above})$$

and

$$E_2: = \text{at } \dot{i}': \text{feeding, } \dot{b}, \dot{a}; \text{yes}$$
$$\dot{i} \preceq \dot{i}'.$$

If we had used the first approach of connecting our method of representing beliefs with attitude reports, we would have been restricted, in stating this constraint, to the relation BO and events. It is at this point that the second approach is more flexible in allowing us to bring into the semantics the uniformity across believers represented by the event-type E, which both mothers have B_r to.[14]

Example 2. A golfer, Sarah, is looking intently at a ball in the grass before her. She decides it is not her ball, and starts to walk away. In fact it *is* her ball, and there is a sense in which she believes it is her ball. (At this point we have violated our first maxim. According to the second maxim, the reader should give both us and Sarah the benefit of the doubt and start wondering how Sarah can be anchored to the world so that she can believe that it is her ball but also believe it isn't.) She bought a ball this morning, has a vivid concept of it, believes it is hers, and the ball she is walking away from is that very ball. She has mistaken a little mud on the ball for a cut, and she believes that the ball on the grass is not a new one.

There is no mystery here, at the level of B_r and event-types. She has two concepts ($\langle \dot{t}, E' \rangle$ and $\langle \dot{o}, E'' \rangle$ as displayed below) of the same ball. She doesn't recognize it, and so the second concept, relative to which she believes it is hers, is not applied.

In e_0: at l: S_r, Sarah, $E(\dot{t})$; yes
$\qquad\qquad B_r$, Sarah, $E'(\dot{t})$; yes
$\qquad\qquad B_r$, Sarah, $E''(\dot{o})$; yes
$\qquad\qquad B_r$, Sarah, $E'''(\dot{t})$; no
$\qquad\qquad$ of, $\dot{t}$, Sarah's golfball; yes (2)
$\qquad\qquad$ of, $\dot{o}$, Sarah's golfball; yes (3)

where

$\quad E$: $=$ at $\dot{b}$: golfball, $\dot{t}$; yes
$\qquad\qquad\quad$ belongs-to, $\dot{t}$, $\dot{i}$; no,

where E' is E plus

$\quad$ at $\dot{b}$: new, $\dot{t}$; no,

where

$\quad E''$: $= \dot{l}$: golfball, $\dot{o}$; yes
$\qquad\qquad$ belongs-to, $\dot{o}$; yes
$\qquad\qquad$ new, $\dot{o}$; yes

and where

$\quad E'''$: $=$ at $\dot{b}$: belongs-to, $\dot{t}$, $\dot{i}$; yes.

Sarah's beliefs are cognitively coherent ($E' + E''$ is coherent), but her beliefs are externally incoherent (E'[the golfball] $+ E''$[the golfball] is incoherent). There is no reason why a person should not have such contradictory beliefs; it happens all the time. This doxastic situation has a common anchor for two indeterminates, $\dot{t}$ and $\dot{o}$. One (2) anchors Sarah's image of the ball before her to her own ball; the other (3) anchors her idea of her own ball to her ball. But the second anchor is irrelevant to what Sarah does, because she does not recognize it as her ball. That is what made our report based on (3) seem odd and misleading, and those which ignored (3) seem natural.

Looking at Sarah as she turns and walks away from the ball, or looking at the situation e_0 above and its one negative constituent, we would not simply say, "She believes it isn't hers," which is true, but would doubtless be willing to say, "She doesn't believe that it is hers." That is, we are able to say both that Sarah doesn't believe it is hers and (misleadingly) that she believes it is hers, and both reports are supported by the cognitively coherent situation e_0.

When we describe a person's doxastic situation, we are under no obligation to describe every aspect of all of her beliefs. To do so would usually be pointless and confusing. We describe only the relevant parts of the situation. This means that we ignore irrelevant anchoring facts, those which relate an individual to a concept of it that is not applied to it. This is the reason we ignore (3) and say that Sarah doesn't believe that that is her ball.

Example 3. Finally, consider Jonny as he ponders the question on his exam discussed in the previous section. How can we explain his difficulty with the question? We might say, "He doesn't believe that Tully was a Roman orator." But according to our innocent theory we seem committed to the claim that he does believe that Tully was a Roman orator, since he believes Cicero was one and Cicero is Tully. First we want to get clear about what is happening at the level of beliefs, and then see how this can be handled at the level of BELIEVES.

Jonny has one fairly rich concept of Cicero. When he sees the exam question,

TRUE OR FALSE: TULLY WAS A ROMAN ORATOR

he will acquire another rather meager concept of Cicero, unmerged with his first one. We can represent his new concept with the pair $\langle \dot{c}, S \rangle$, where $S = \{E, E'\}$ and

$E:$ = Roman orator, $\dot{c}$; yes
  refer to, "Tully", $\dot{c}$; yes

$E':$ = Roman orator, $\dot{c}$; no
  refer to, "Tully", $\dot{c}$; yes.

His belief can be represented by:

in e_0: at l: B_r, Jonny, S; yes
  B_r, Jonny, E; no

B_r, Jonny, E'; no
B_r, Jonny, E''; yes
of, $\check{c}$, Cicero; yes
of, $\check{c}'$, Cicero; yes

where

    in E'': at l: Roman orator, $\check{c}'$; yes
           named Cicero, $\check{c}'$; yes

Of course, we get exactly the same situation if we "replace" Cicero with Tully in e_0 because Cicero *is* Tully. Jonny's concept is of this person because the teacher's use of the term TULLY (which we have referred to with "Tully"), referred to him. The acquisition of the belief we represent with S is a significant fact about Jonny, one that might explain subsequent behavior, like his asking Devin who Tully was.

On our innocent account, we can describe this situation e_0 with any of the following sentences:

(2) JONNY DOESN'T BELIEVE THAT TULLY WAS A ROMAN ORATOR.

(3) JONNY DOES BELIEVE THAT CICERO WAS A ROMAN ORATOR.

(4) JONNY DOESN'T BELIEVE THAT CICERO WAS A ROMAN ORATOR.

(5) JONNY DOES BELIEVE THAT TULLY WAS A ROMAN ORATOR.

We can obviously use (2) or (3), but then we can also use (4) or (5) because we can refer to the individual Cicero in e_0 by either of his names. But, we argue, Maxim A above constrains us from using either (4) or (5) in these circumstances if we are to be cooperative. This is our explanation of the reluctance to substitute.

Jonny's first concept of Cicero contains a nominal mode of recognition that enables him to recognize tokens of CICERO as referring to Cicero, and apply the concept. *That* concept does not contain a nominal mode of recognition that enables him to recognize tokens of TULLY as referring to Cicero, and apply it. We shall say that the concept does not *comprehend* other names of Cicero, TULLY in particular. The fact is that when we use attitudes to explain or predict a person's interaction with linguistic information about an individual we identify with a name α, we are describing the beliefs they have about the individual which comprehend α and will be applied to linguistic information expressed with α. We ignore the agent's concepts of the individual that do not comprehend α and will not be applied to such information. Thus the anchoring facts that anchor the individual to such concepts are irrelevant.

But, a Lockean or Fregean might ask, "Does an innocent theory have any right to even *notice* what name is used in an attitude report? It is not the name but the individual referred to which gets into the interpretation of the report, so how can the name be in *any* way relevant, even to the appropriateness of the report?"

This objection contains an instance of the fallacy of misplaced information. The change in the report from TULLY to CICERO makes an enormous difference to the information made available by the report, and an innocent theory need not overlook this if it is combined with a relational theory of meaning. Part of the information you can get is the information that someone is called "Cicero," and of course you do not get this information if "Tully" is used instead. This is so even though the interpretation of the report stays the same.

The name used is often crucial to the information that is intended to be conveyed. Suppose Jim walks up to Melanie and says, "I'm Jim," intending to "tell her his name." The interpretation of this will be trivially actual, the courses of events in which Jim is Jim. What Melanie will learn is that the person speaking to her is called "Jim." This is part of the truth condition of the utterance and the information made available to Melanie, although it is not part of the interpretation of the utterance. The problems in the philosophy of language raised by identity statements almost always have to do with the fact that it is seldom the interpretation that we focus on when we pick up information from them.

When I report on Jonny's beliefs using TULLY, you learn that I have the information that the person I am referring to is named TULLY. You assume, if I am explaining or predicting how Jonny will deal with linguistic information about the person I am referring to with TULLY, that the relevant anchoring facts are those which anchor a concept of Jonny's that comprehends TULLY. This is an implicature, or suggestion, not something that is part of the truth conditions of my report. But, if the suggestion is right, then anchoring the fact to Jonny's first concept is not relevant; it is not part of what I am describing. The effect of the substitution, then, is to change the suggestion about which beliefs are being described, hence which anchoring relations are relevant.

KNOWLEDGE

Now we want to use our method of representing cognitive conditions, and our account of information, to give a sketchy account of knowledge, and the semantics of SEES THAT and KNOWS THAT using mental conditions.

The Relation between Knowing, Believing, and Having Information

Dretske has developed our favorite account of knowledge in his original and important book *Knowledge and the Flow of Information* (Dretske, 81). According to his account, one knows that φ if having the information that φ causes one to believe (or continue believing) that φ. Aside from some terminological differences, our account will differ from his in two ways. First, there are many subtleties of doctrine, example, and argumentation that we will not try to repeat or build into our account in detail—not because we disagree, but because our semantical task limits us to pursuit of a narrow line; our theory is too rudimentary to capture everything, and we don't want to explain poorly what he has already explained well. Second, we think the concept of information we have developed in this book is more suitable for this kind of theory of knowledge than the one Dretske actually uses, based on Shannon's theory of information (Shannon, 49). It seems to us to provide a clearer picture of how one situation can contain information about another. Dretske shows that Shannon's theory is really about *amounts* of information, but then argues that it is good enough to get at the notion of informational content. To us, this seems at best a detour.[15]

Before giving our version of Dretske's theory, we want to say a word about what we think one is up to in such a theory. Common sense says that knowledge is one thing, belief is another. There is no particular reason to think that one is in any sense more fundamental than the other, or that one can be defined in terms of the other. On the other hand, there are obvious relations between knowledge and beliefs. These relations amount to necessary structural constraints, and an account like Dretske's, or our minor modification of it, is an attempt to spell out some of these structural constraints. Thus we do not define a relation K_r in terms of B_r and the relation of having information. Rather, we take K_r as basic and examine the relations which hold between cognitive situations that one would call knowledge, those which are beliefs, and those which contain information for the agent.

Some beliefs contain information for the agent, some don't. The former constitute knowledge, the latter don't. That is, rather than speak of belief that is caused by having information, we shall speak of beliefs that themselves contain information. So our version of Dretske's idea is that a knowing that φ involves a having a belief that φ, one that carries the information that φ. It is important to remember that the information contained in a belief—a person's being in a belief condition at a location—will depend not just on the condition but also on the wider circumstances in which the event is embedded: its setting, including facts about how the belief was acquired and sustained.

Consider my knowledge that the coffee in my cup is black. I can't see into the cup from where I am. But it was black when I poured it. I saw it then, and formed the belief that it was black then. That perception and the belief to which it gave rise both constituted knowledge, because they both contained the information that the coffee was black. Here we assume that the process of going from perception to belief is information-preserving. The belief I have now is not just the one I had then. I still believe that the coffee was black then, but I also believe that it is black now. I haven't seen anyone pour anything into the coffee, nor have I noticed any cataclysmic events that might produce unexpected changes of color in the liquids in my environment. From our perspective, this is seeing that the conditions relative to which a certain constraint is actual have obtained. The constraint is that if the coffee in a cup is black, it will stay black for awhile. The process that took me from my old beliefs about the coffee's color, my observations, and my knowledge about when coffee changes color, is information-preserving. So my belief contains the information that the coffee is black, and constitutes knowledge.

My cognitive situation might contain the information that the coffee was black, even if I don't believe it. Perhaps I have been reading Descartes and have become extremely timid about believing anything. Perhaps I am so unconcerned with the coffee in the cup that I haven't formed a belief about it, though I would do so instantly if the question arose. One's situation contains much information that one does not believe or that one even disbelieves. The condition of my stomach may contain information about what I ate last night even though I have forgotten. I may see$_n$ a lot of things that I do not become perceptually aware of, and don't see$_p$. Yet my visual situation contains information about them. But if God or evolution is benevolent, some of my beliefs will not only reflect information contained by my situation, but will themselves be the aspect of my condition which carries that information.

For another example that illustrates some important points, let's return to Joe's seeing Jackie bite Molly. Let us suppose that Joe believes that his dog Molly is a border collie when, in fact, she is a mutt. When Joe sees Jackie biting Molly, he believes that Jackie is biting a border collie. Joe knows that Jackie is biting a dog, that Jackie is biting Molly, that a dog is biting Molly, and that Jackie is biting his dog. But he does not know that Jackie is biting his border collie. The problem is not just that Molly isn't a border collie. She might be a border collie, and Joe might believe it, but still not know it. The problem is that he doesn't have the information that she is a border collie. This part of his belief does not contain information about Molly, even if it turns out to be true.

In this case, Joe is applying his concept of Molly to the dog he sees. Suppose he is wrong, and it's not Molly. He still knows that Jackie is biting a dog, but of course he doesn't know that Jackie is biting Molly.

Suppose the dog Jackie is biting is covered with mud and not recognizable as Molly. Joe believes that it is Molly not because he recognizes Molly but just on a hunch. Here again Joe doesn't know that Jackie is biting Molly. We have to be careful, though, because such a hunch may actually be recognition based on a part of Joe's concept of Molly that he couldn't articulate, that usually doesn't come into play when he recognizes her.

As in Chapter 7, we use *inf* for representing mental conditions that contain information for the agent. Thus an informational mental state will be one of the form

> in e_0: at l: *inf*, a, S; yes
> of, $\dot{x}, f(\dot{x})$; yes,

where x ranges over various indeterminates in S. A constraint on this relation is that if such an e_0 is actual, then there is an actual situation of type $S[f]$.

Analogously, we represent knowledge by means of K_r, as in:

in e_0: at l: K_r, a, S; yes

of, $\dot{x}, f(\dot{x})$; yes.

The remarks made above suggest that there are several structural constraints relating K_r, B_r, and *inf*. Namely, they suggest that any knowing involves having beliefs that have the information, and vice versa.

  Let's take a more complicated example. I believe that eating the piece of cake in front of me will give me heartburn. In fact, not all cake will give me heartburn, only carrot cake and rutabaga cake. I have never had rutabaga cake. My belief about cake in general and heartburn was acquired from a steady diet of carrot cake. We want to say that if this piece of cake is a piece of carrot cake, then I know that it will give me heartburn, but if it is some other kind of cake, even rutabaga cake, I don't know this. To handle this example, we will have to discuss belief and knowledge in constraints.

Attunement to Constraints

We distinguish *being attuned* to a constraint C from *belief in C*. Belief in C is like belief in any other state of affairs. By contrast, an organism is attuned to C if, under certain circumstances, its cognitive conditions "follow" C. Consider the constraint that a certain kind of plant is edible for a certain kind of organism. An organism of this kind is attuned to the constraint provided it eats the plant if it sees it, under certain circumstances—say when it is hungry, and not busy escaping from predators or in the presence of more appetizing plants. Here we take eating a plant, an intentional activity, as a cognitive condition.

  A theory of attunement is beyond the scope of this book, for among other things it would require a theory of action, something we do not offer here. However, we can indicate something useful about it in a rough and ready way, with a simple diagram. To facilitate our drawing this diagram of attunement, let us temporarily write:

$S \Rightarrow S'$

to denote the (not necessarily actual) constraint

at l_u: involves, S, S'; yes.

On our theory of meaning, a situation s has the event meaning that there is a situation of type S' if there is an actual constraint $S \Rightarrow S'$ such that s is of type S.

  Let us use #S, #S', etc., to vary over efficient cognitive conditions, i.e., frames of mind of the kind we have been considering in this chapter. Fix a given agent a. In order that a be able to discriminate situations of type S there must be a type $\#S$ of cognitive condition that, under normal conditions, means that there is a situation of type S. That is, if a is in a frame of mind of type $\#S$ then, under normal circumstances, there is a situation of type S. In symbols, what is required for discrimination of situations of type S is that there be an actual (though probably conditional) constraint of the form $\#S \Rightarrow S$. Under more stringent conditions, one would also have $S \Rightarrow \#S$.

We can now say roughly what it is for our agent a to be attuned to a constraint C, say $S \Rightarrow S'$. What we need is for the agent to be able to discriminate these types of situations, and for the types of mental situations involved in the discrimination to be suitably linked:

$$S \Rightarrow S' \quad \text{("External")}$$
$$\Uparrow \quad \Uparrow$$
$$\#S \Rightarrow \#S' \quad \text{("Internal")}$$

For example, a's being in a visual condition of type $\#S$ involves there being an actual scene s of type S, and such a scene s involves there being a situation s' of type S'. Going around the other way, a's being in a visual condition of type $\#S$ causes a to go into a belief state of type $\#S'$, say, and that is systematically linked to states of type S'. The agent a being attuned to the constraint C amounts to the constraint $\#C$: $\#S \Rightarrow \#S'$ being actual.

Notice that if we start with an internal, antecedent state $\#s$ of type $\#S$, that it means that there is an external, consequent state of type S', and that there are two ways to get from the former to the latter. We may first consider the external significance of the mental state, that there is a situation s of type S, and then apply the constraint C, to get the information that there is a situation s' of type S'. Alternatively, we can apply the constraint $\#C$ on a's cognitive activity to get from $\#s$ that there is a cognitive condition $\#s'$ of type $\#S'$, that is, we can observe a's "inference" from $\#S$ to $\#S'$. Then we can consider the external significance of $\#s'$ of type $\#S'$, that there is a situation s' of type S'. If everything is working properly, the results of going the two different ways agree. That is what we meant above by saying that attunement requires an agent's cognitive conditions to follow the constraint. This "following" is nothing but a very general form of inference, where a infers from the presence of a situation of type S, that there is a situation of type S'.

Inference

Inference is often connected with representational theories of mind, where it is taken to be an operation on mental representations. We do not think that inference is an operation on representations or necessarily involves representations in any essential way. As theorists, we are constructing representations of mental states, and we think that mental states are meaningful. We also think that humans are among the many kinds of animals that make inferences. We also realize that most humans construct and deal with representations, linguistic ones in particular, as an important part of their cognitive life. It may well be that some of these representations are mental in some fairly clear sense, as when I think over what I am going to say. And inference, the formation of belief, is often aided by perception of representations, including drawings, proofs, derivations of various sorts, and so on. None of this, however, is essential to inference. On the contrary, the ability to infer is presupposed by the ability to deal with representations in this way. In constructing a proof, for example, one has beliefs about the representations one writes down on paper or conjures up in one's mind which are based on all sorts of knowledge gained in the past. But when one sees a hot and sweaty person jogging in a jogging outfit and infers that she has been running, one's belief about representations have nothing to do with it.

We have been assuming that all the constraints in our diagram were actual, so that the agent's inferences produced information. Of course in reality things don't always go properly, even when the agent is properly attuned, and inference does not always result in information. Each of the four constraints involved in an instance of attunement is, in general, conditional, and the conditions may not be right. Inference leads to information only under conditions where the conditional constraints involved are all actual.

Consider the constraint that objects left unsupported fall. This constraint is not factual, although a conditional constraint—that objects left unsupported near the surface of the earth fall—*is* factual. It would not be correct, however, to use this conditional constraint to represent the beliefs of someone who would confidently apply the constraint anywhere. We are surprised the first time we are told what happens to objects left unsupported in outer space. We want to save the conditional constraint to represent the minds of those who have been through this experience, and understand the limitations of the very simple but nonfactual constraints that all earth-dwelling animals are attuned to. But if I see an object in my study that has been left unsupported after I bumped it, and I move suddenly to catch it, it seems only fair to admit that I knew that it was going to fall. How can we account for this if the constraint I am attuned to or believe in isn't factual?

Our original constraint is this:

$$C := \text{at } l_u: \text{Involves, } E, E'; \text{yes}$$

where

$$E := \text{at } \dot{l}: \text{unsupported, } \dot{a}; \text{yes}$$
$$E' := \text{at } \dot{l}: \text{falls, } \dot{a}; \text{yes.}$$

This won't quite do to represent the beliefs of an ordinary person, however, even aside from the question of knowledge. We believe of particular objects we see, or fear may be, unsupported that they will fall. We need the constraint-type, $C/\dot{a}$. Being attuned to C means that I am also attuned to each anchored instance of $C/\dot{a}$. When I see the book on my shelf that I am about to bump, $\dot{a}$ is anchored to it. I believe that if it is bumped, and left unsupported, it will fall. I *know* the constraint, that that book will fall if unsupported, *if* it is near the surface of the earth. If I am in my spaceship and lurch suddenly to grab it, feeling foolish as it floats harmlessly around the ship, I didn't know it would fall, because I didn't know that if left unsupported it would fall.

We want our representation of my state of knowledge, then, to give me knowledge of the particular constraints, of the type that characterizes my state of belief, which are anchored to objects near the surface of the earth. But we want to filter out those constraints of the type that are anchored to other objects. Those I will believe, but do not know.

To do this, we form a role, $\langle \dot{a}, NS \rangle$, where

$$NS := \text{at } l: \text{near surface of, the earth, } \dot{a}; \text{yes.}$$

We can now look at our constraint-type as an indexed constraint type. Thus understood, we can use it to represent knowledge:

$$\text{at } l: K_r, a, C/\dot{a}; \text{yes.}$$

We shall call the change from considering $\dot{a}$ as a normal indeterminate to considering it as a role as *tightening the index* on an event-type.

Generally, one's epistemic states correspond to one's doxastic states with tightened indices, where the roles correspond to the conditions with respect to which the constraints are factual.

COGNITIVE VERSUS COMPUTATIONAL STATES: A DIGRESSION

The machinery we have set up gives us a way of stating our version of Fodor's "formality condition" (Fodor, 81).[16] He argues that cognitive science is possible only if "mental computations" operate with "representations" stripped of any semantic content. So we might put this as the claim that the right level at which to do cognitive science is not with what we have called cognitive conditions, perceptions, and beliefs, but rather what we have called computational states, those characterized by schemata S in which only indeterminates appear.

In representing the cognitive states of the individuals in the above examples, we have chosen not to abstract over properties and relations in the same way that we have abstracted over individuals and locations. We could have abstracted over properties and relations as well, anchoring the indeterminate properties and relations to the actual ones. Then we would have been representing the cognitive conditions of the agents purely in terms of computational states. However, the kinds of explanation one has to give as to why various constraints come into play, and how they operate, how cognition is possible, are hard to find, for they seem intimately tied to the properties and relations involved. Indeed, in attempting to build computers that have anything vaguely resembling human cognitive capabilities, this has proven to be a major hurdle, one that must be overcome if AI is to succeed. But for naturalistic psychology, which recognizes the interdependence of the organism and the properties and relations that it individuates, there is no reason to make the move to computational states at all.

In some sense, neither particular relations nor particular individuals and locations are in the mind; they are all in the world. But the anchoring of mental states to relations occurs at the level of the species or community, while the anchoring of particular individuals and locations happens in the life of the individual. This is why abstraction to the level of cognitive states is so useful in Folk Psychology, and it would be unwise to abandon this useful level without fully exploiting it.

The picture that got us from ST and BO to S_r and B_r was that of an organism set in an environment to which its species had become adapted, with perceptual and other causal relations to particular individuals. The repertoire of mental conditions is what people have in common; the anchoring relations to different individuals and locations is how they differ. One might try to capture the relation of various mental states to properties and relations that characterize the environment of the species in the same way. This is analogous to a step we do take when discussing sentence types, where we have not only the varying connections to individuals and locations represented, but also the relation between expressions and relations. This may prove an interesting level of analysis for psychology if we can find significant uniformities across the relationship between particular mental conditions and the corresponding relations in the world. But that presupposes an understanding of the details which we don't yet have.

CHAPTER ELEVEN

Further Directions

We have traveled a long road but we are still far from our destination, a comprehensive theory of meaning. Even in the area of linguistic meaning, our treatment here omits many standard topics. We hope we have discussed enough topics and worked through enough details to convince the reader of the plausibility of three points: (1) that attention to situations and relations between situations is an important part of the study of meaning; (2) that the external significance of language, the power of statements made with efficient sentences to carry information about the world, is a key to unlocking the mystery of language, not only as it relates to the world but also as it relates to the mind; and (3) that the ecological approach, looking at people as living things among other living things in an environment full of information, can shed light on the special case of language.

The fundamental question that ties these points together is "What and where is meaning?" Since Descartes many thinkers have assumed that meaning was in heads of people. Frege found it necessary to locate meaning outside the head in a third realm. Putnam, Gibson, and Dretske have caused us to look for meaning in the world, in the interaction of organisms with their environment. This is what we mean by the ecological approach.

Situation semantics is more committed to this approach than are any of the particular theories we have put forward in trying to do it justice. It has come to feel very much like a road that has to be followed home, taking its own course. We want to end this book by making a few speculative remarks about some twists, turns, and straightaways that we suspect are ahead. Most of what we say will be more in the line of research suggestions than of detailed exposition.

SPEECH ACTS

In recent years there has been a sharp conflict between those following Austin, who see a theory of linguistic meaning as grounded in speech acts, and those following Tarski, who favor the approach of truth-conditional semantics. Since we have learned much from both traditions, it is not surprising that we believe both sides have positive things to say about linguistic meaning. The meanings of expressions in a language *are* derived from the meanings of the linguistic events of which they are parts. But the communication of information is a fundamental speech activity, and the capacity of language to carry information is a key to understanding what it contributes to the multitude of activities of which it plays a part. Assertions are the central case and truth *is* a central property of assertions that carry information. Thus knowing how to do things with words and knowing the conditions in which a sentence can be truly asserted are both important parts of what a speaker knows about his language.

We think that situation semantics can form the basis of a formal account of linguistic activity that encompasses both views. We do not present such a comprehensive theory here, although we have ambitions, or at least dreams. In this section we want to pay attention to two kinds of speech act, asserting and questioning. The discussion of assertions has the modest goals of showing how the methods of Chapter 10 allow us to go back and remedy some of the defects in our treatment of assertions in Chapters 6 and 7, how some of our conceptions connect with interesting issues in current linguistic theory, and how these conceptions can be used to formulate a central conjecture that underlies our point of view. The much more speculative discussion of questions builds on the same conjecture.

Asserting

In discussing assertions, we will focus on the verb ASSERT. We have in mind the ASSERT of indirect discourse, to be distinguished from the direct discourse ASSERT with its quotation marks. Thus we have in mind only the odd-numbered sentences in this list:

(1) JONNY ASSERTED THAT HE WOULD FEED THE DOG.

(2) JONNY ASSERTED, "I WILL FEED THE DOG."
(3) GALILEO ASSERTED THAT THE EARTH MOVES.
(4) GALILEO ASSERTED, "THE EARTH MOVES."

The main verb phrases in the odd-numbered sentences represent a quite different strategy for classifying assertions than do the verb phrases in the even-numbered sentences. In direct discourse, agents are grouped by the efficient sentences used; in indirect discourse they are grouped by the situations described by their assertions. The contrast corresponds to one we have found with each of the attitudes, but with this difference: Efficient cognitive conditions are recognized implicitly in natural language in talk of beliefs, ideas, images, and perceptions, and implicitly in the way attitude reports are used in explanation, but natural language doesn't provide a mechanism for directly referring to such things. With assertions, however, the efficient communicative entities are explicitly recognized and referred to with quoted sentences. We exploited the relationship between direct and indirect discourse in Chapter 6 to get our semantic theory started. We relied implicitly on our understanding of what makes the assertion of an efficient sentence, in particular cirumstances, true. Now we want to put some of the facts we relied upon to start our theory back into the theory itself.

A simple model of verbal communication. A guiding strategy in working out our theory (though it probably isn't evident from its presentation so far) has been to focus on the pick-up of information by perception and its transfer by verbal communication. In our own thinking we have focused on seeing and saying with the conviction that if we could get that much right, we would be well on the way to understanding other attitudes.

Surely the most basic sort of communicative act is the transfer of information, linguistic or otherwise: smoke signals, an affirmative nod of the head, a gesture, and so on. Our paradigm of communication is a linguistic event u that involves a speaker a_d, an auditor b_d, and a common location l_d. The event has the following rough structure:

(a) At l_d: a_d and b_d are attuned to the constraints C_L of a common language L.
(b) At l_0: a_d has the information that φ.
(c) At l_1: a_d asserts (in L) that φ.
(d) At l_2: b_d hears a_d assert that φ at l_1.

(e) At l_3: b_d has the information that φ.

Here $l_0 \preceq l_1 \preceq l_2 \preceq l_3$ and all are sublocations of l_d.

There are three points that need to be made immediately. The first is that it is the flow of information, not the transfer of knowledge or belief, that we are after here. The issues of whether a_d really believes that φ in (b), or whether b_d believes that φ in (e) are separate from that of the flow of information. Newscasters (and newspapers and computers) often have information and make assertions that allow us to pick up information, without themselves ever bothering to (or being able to, in the case of newspapers and computers) believe or disbelieve what they are asserting. And it is certainly possible for me to have information without believing it. We *usually* assume that people believe what they are asserting, and we often believe what we hear, but ASSERTS THAT is an attitude quite different from KNOWS THAT or BELIEVES THAT. It does not indirectly classify cognitive conditions of the agent, but rather classifies communicative events, acts of asserting.

The second point to note is that there is no sense in which each of these steps necessarily follows from the one before. Rather, in a typical case of verbal communication, (a), (b), and (c) hold, (a) and (c) cause (d), and this, with (b), in turn causes (e) to hold.

The third point to note, a point we have made over and over but one that is obscured by the use of "that φ", is that it is neither the meaning of the sentence nor the meaning of the cognitive conditions of the agents that is preserved in the move from (b) to (e). Some philosophers have thought that the main difference between direct and indirect discourse is the difference between reporting which sentence was used and providing a translation of it into the reporter's language. On this view, the embedded sentence could be different from the sentence actually produced but would have to have the same meaning. This view doesn't survive once the efficiency of language is taken seriously and artificial restrictions on the sorts of examples that are considered are lifted. If you and I are talking and you assert, "You are wrong," I do not accurately report your utterance by saying, "You asserted that you are wrong." I have to say, "You asserted that I was wrong." The sentence embedded in my accurate report has a different meaning from the sentence you used:

YOU ARE WRONG,

I WAS WRONG

do not mean the same thing on *any* reasonable theory of meaning.

For the same reason, it is not sameness of cognitive state or property that is preserved. When I see that Joe is eating my pancake and tell him that he is eating my pancake, I start out in a condition characterized by S_r and E:

E: = at $\dot{b}$: pancake, $\dot{t}$; yes
        eating, $\dot{t}'$, $\dot{t}$; yes
        belongs-to, $\dot{t}$, $\dot{i}$; yes

with $\dot{t}$ anchored to the pancake and $\dot{t}'$ anchored to Joe.

By saying what I do, I don't want Joe to be in the visual condition E, or the belief condition E . The condition I want Joe to be in is:

E: = at $\dot{b}$: belongs-to, $\dot{t}$, $\dot{i}$; no
        belongs-to, $\dot{t}'$, $\dot{c}$; yes

where $\dot{t}$ is anchored to the pancake and $\dot{t}'$ is anchored to me.

Our account (a)–(e) does not spell out what the constraints C_L of a language look like, or provide a semantics for ASSERTS THAT that squares with its use in communication. About the former we shall have more to say below. To motivate our treatment of ASSERTS THAT, let us pause to discuss the treatment of the closely related attitude SAYS THAT from our earlier paper.

SAYS THAT: *Our old approach.* In the article "Situations and Attitudes" (Barwise and Perry, 81a), we thought of SAYS THAT as reporting utterances by focusing on their interpretations. When Joe says to Jim, "You are wrong," the interpretation of his utterance is that Jim is wrong. This is the same as the interpretation of the embedded statement in Jim's report, "Joe says that I am wrong." The idea was that

a SAYS THAT φ

is true, just when a_d says some sentence ψ that has, relative to a_d's context, the same interpretation that φ has relative to the reporter's context.

We are still fond of this simple idea. It accounts for the phenomena we noted in the last section, fits nicely with our emphasis on external significance, and serves as a paradigm for our thinking about cognitive attitudes. Our two paradigms were seeing$_n$ and this treatment of saying.[1] But there are serious problems with it.

One problem is that the interpretation of a statement, the class of events described, is a proper class and not a set. Our old theory forces us to take saying to be a relation to such a proper class, which violates our fundamental methodology. In the case of the other attitudes, we found a cognitive support for the attitudes, and factored them into efficient cognitive conditions and settings. It seems that this should be possible for saying too. We factor it into the use of a sentence in a setting, itself factored into discourse situation and connections. Indeed, it was by extending this picture—of saying as factored into a relation between an agent and an efficient sentence anchored in a larger setting—that led us to the idea of efficient cognitive states in the first place.

But this picture doesn't remain so simple when subjected to analysis. A theme of this book is that meaning is a relation between events supported by constraints. For cognitive states we have built up indexed event-types and schemata within the theory of situations and seen the meaning of such states as residing in constraints. These are all sets. But our theory of linguistic meaning falls short of the mark. As we have worked out the theory of the meanings of sentences, they are in theory constraints but are in fact relations between events—proper classes of pairs of events. For the purposes of Part II these proper classes did not appear within situations, so their use was legitimate. But our old theory of saying used them in an illegitimate way, as constituents of events described by the attitude "says that." Oddly enough, then, even though we have a theory of linguistic meaning and a theory of the attitudes, we are not ready to present a theory of the linguistic attitudes that integrates the two. That will await the working out of a conjecture that we state below.

Another problem with our old theory was that it was much too literal because it focused too narrowly on language, missing the extent to which attitude reports provide indirect classification of cognitive situations in general, and communication in particular.

In the first place, as we have seen, producing a sentence with the interpretation P is not enough to say that P. One must intend to convey the information that P. The requisite property of the speaker might be brought in through structural constraints, but now we think of this strategy as being the wrong way around. One of the reasons we have switched from SAYS to ASSERTS is that it avoids this problem. Asserting that φ involves intending to convey the information that φ in a way that just saying that φ doesn't always. Another reason for the switch is that while asserting is a communicative activity that typically involves the use of language, it needn't be. It is even more obvious with asserting than with saying that one often asserts something without producing any expression at all.

In the second place, the old account didn't leave enough room for the exploitation of shared knowledge of the world that goes on between a speaker and listener. Where the speaker and listener are both in touch with the same constraints, what is said can go far beyond the interpretation of the statement actually made. When I asked Joe if he wanted more pancakes, his nodding (with his mouth full) meant that he did. And that is why Sarah, taking pity on him, said, "Joe says that he does want some more pancakes." Focusing so narrowly on language misses the extent to which attitudes like "says that" and "asserts that" are used indirectly to classify communicative events.

But, most important, our old proposal seems misleading in respect to the true dependence relations. In a sense what one says depends on the sentences one utters and their interpretation. After all, one chooses them for just that reason. But what a sentence means also depends on what people in a linguistic community use it to say. Ultimately, what an expression means is determined by how people use it to say things, even though, on each occasion, what they say, using it, depends on its meaning, as already established.

Indirect classification of assertions. Communicating information requires a repertoire of efficient communicative actions. Examples are nodding and shaking the head, pointing, and uttering declarative sentences. When I asked Joe whether he wanted pancakes, and he nodded, his nodding meant that he did want them. Sarah fairly said later that he had said that he wanted them. Yet Joe's nodding at some other time could mean something entirely different. When I asked the student where the bookstore was, his pointing meant that it was in that direction, but of course the same gesture has been part of acts that meant countless other things. And the efficiency of the use of sentences has been a main theme of this book.

Reports of what a person asserts, then, like reports of what a person believes or knows, indirectly classify the person by the interpretation of meaningful properties. But, unlike these cases, the meaningful properties include some overt activity, suitable to being voluntarily produced, and to being recognized by others.

We can classify these properties with schemata, as we do cognitive conditions. We shall let A_r be a relation to indexed event-types. With this at our disposal, we can factor our model (a)–(e) of a communicative event u into efficient communicative actions and anchor:

(a) at l_d: attuned-to, a_d, C_L; yes

$$\text{attuned-to, } b_d, C_L; \text{yes}$$

(b) at l_0: *inf*, a_d, S; yes

$$\text{of, } \dot{x}, f(\dot{x}); \text{yes}$$

(c) at l_1: A_r, a_d, S; yes

$$\text{of, } \dot{x}, f(\dot{x}); \text{yes}$$

(d) at l_2: *inf*, b_d, E; yes

$$\text{of, } \dot{x}, f(\dot{x}); \text{yes}$$

$$\text{of, } \dot{t}, a_d; \text{yes}$$

$$\text{of, } \dot{l}, l_1; \text{yes}$$

where

$$E: = \text{at } \dot{l}: A_r, \dot{t}, S; \text{yes, and}$$

(e) at l_3: *inf*, b_d, S'; yes

$$\text{of, } \dot{x}, g(\dot{x}); \text{yes}$$

where $S[a_d, l_1, f] = S'[b_d, l_2, g]$. This is all rather formal, so we illustrate various aspects of it below. For now we simply point out that the last shift, from the schema S, a_d's context and f to the schema S', b_d's context and g, captures the idea that the objective content of the utterance from a_d's context with a_d's connections must match the objective context of b_d's state from his context relative to g.

Connective Links and Anchors

Let us look at a very simple example of the above to see more clearly what is happening. Suppose I say, "Helen is in New York," and suppose that I know it to be true. Suppose you hear me say this, so that you know that I have asserted that Helen is in New York. So you now have the information that Helen is in New York. Suppose further that you know me to be a trustworthy fellow and so come to know that Helen *is* in New York.

The interesting case here is where you have never heard of Helen before. After this exchange of information you have a concept of Helen. It is a meager one, no doubt, and you wouldn't be able to recognize her or say much about her. But you have become anchored to Helen through this linguistic event. You are now able to go on and inform someone else that Helen is in New York. And it may be possible for them to identify which Helen you are talking about better than you can—for example, if they saw me tell you and knew that Helen was my friend.

The relevant step here in our model of communication is the one from (c) to (d). Let

$E := $ at $\overset{.}{b}$: in, $\overset{.}{a}$, $\overset{.}{b}$; yes

and let me be j and you be k. Then the crucial step is:

(c) at l_1: A_r, j, E; yes

   of, $\overset{.}{a}$, Helen; yes

   of, $\overset{.}{b}$, New York; yes

(d) at l_2: inf, k, E'; yes,

where

$E' := $ at $\overset{.}{l}$: $A_r, \overset{.}{t}, E$; yes

   of, $\overset{.}{a}$, Helen; yes

   of, $\overset{.}{b}$, New York; yes

   of, $\overset{.}{l}, l_1$; yes

   of, $\overset{.}{t}, j$; yes.

Already at this step you have information about Helen, namely that I have asserted something about her. The use of the same formal individual in (c) and (d) captures the connecting link between you and Helen, the fact that you have information about her, a link established by your hearing me say something about her.[2] Now consider that there is (we hope) more than one of you reading this book. You are all anchored to Helen by the previous discussion. If we were representing both the discourse and the belief conditions to which it gives rise, this would be indicated by the same discourse indeterminate being linked to various ideas you have formed of Helen by reading this. The important thing to remember is what is real and what isn't. Helen is real, and so is the common link between various readers and Helen. It is this uniformity that is captured by the common indeterminate $\overset{.}{a}$. There is no sense in which $\overset{.}{a}$ is, or is in, your "representation" of her.

These connective links are very important for understanding anaphoric relations in discourse. Consider the following conversation:

A: Stan convined me that the traditional notion of logical form is silly.

B: Really? Stan told me that Cantonese food is bad for the brain.

Ordinarily, it would be quite odd if the second person's use of Stan did not designate the same Stan as the first person's use of the name. That is, sometimes in conversations it is quite clear that an *NP* is being used to designate the same individual that an earlier use of that *NP* or some other *NP* is being used to designate. Similarly with tense:

> Sarah is going to the store.
> Yes, I saw her riding her bike on Channing.

It would be inappropriate if the second speaker's 'saw' were not connected to a sublocation of the location connected to the first speaker's extended location.

The crucial point is that the relation we spot between the utterances in each pair is not that they actually are connected to individuals or locations which, as a matter of fact, are the same (or suitably related). Rather, it is that they are supposed to be. Suppose the first conversation had been embedded in a larger discourse in the following way:

> A: I met a very convincing man named Stan the other day too; I wonder if the Stan I met is the one you know.
> B: Well, maybe we can figure it out.
> A: Stan convinced me that the traditional notion of logical form is silly.
> B: Stan told me that Cantonese food is bad for the brain.
> A: No one with such sensible ideas about logical form could have such crazy ideas about Chinese food.
> B: You are right. They must be different Stans.

A's argument isn't a very good one, and there might well be just one Stan involved here. Then the two uses of STAN are in fact anchored to the same individual. But this is not to say that the conversation constrains them to be co-anchored. The interpretation of the conversation leaves it open whether or not they are co-connected, and, of course, the conclusion reached in the conversation is that they are not.

We call singular *NP*'s *anaphorically connected* when they are constrained to be connected to the same individual. Anaphoric connections are relations between uses of *NP*'s and other connectible items. We distinguish between anaphoric and co-anchored connections. In more traditional terminology, it is the difference between a pronoun having another *NP* as antecedent, and merely being co-referential with it. Anchored connections are between *NP*'s, etc. and individuals, locations, etc. in the world. Being anchored to the same individual is not sufficient for two *NP*'s to be anaphorically connected, as the above example shows if A and B are in fact talking about the same Stan. (It is also not necessary in that sometimes *NP*'s are not anchored at all, as we will see.)

What establishes the anaphoric constraint between two expressions? This is similar to the question what establishes that successive images are visually linked, that successive words are part of a single sentence, or that successive sentences are part of a single message. For our purposes, the important point is that there are such relationships, and that users of language are more or less good at picking it up. We don't try to analyze it (though we do not mean to suggest that it is unanalyzable, or that it would not be worthwhile to work on this problem.) The precise "phenomenology" of anaphoric connection has proved to be a challenging and interesting problem, as the vast literature on the topic shows. Unfortunately, there is no more reason to suppose that this semantically crucial property could be interestingly analyzed using the sorts of techniques suited to semantics than to suppose that the phonetic properties of two utterances of the same word (also a semantically crucial relation) could be.

We think event-types can be used to give a semantic account of discourse, with the formal individuals used to individuate anaphoric connections. Indeed, we think that event-types probably provide the right level of analysis to study the relationship between situation semantics and Kamp's discourse representation structures (Kamp, 79). But that goes beyond the scope of this book.

Fictional individuals. Discourse can be unanchored. Suppose we are sitting at a table in a restaurant eavesdropping on a conversation about Herman at the next table, and let us suppose that we believe what we hear. The fact that you and I are linked is captured by having the same indeterminate in representing our ideas and beliefs. But what if, unknown to us, the conversation is between two philosophers who have read Dretske's book and are discussing his example. There is no real Herman. Now what? Well, all it means is that there is no anchor. There is no *coe* described by their conversation, but there are event-types so described, with an indeterminate in them, the same one used to represent our ideas and belief.

This is the beginning of a long account one might give about fictional discourse and "fictional individuals." We do not think there are such things. There is no Santa Claus. Still, there is objective content to our talk of Santa Claus, as when I say, "Joe believed that Santa Claus gave him his bike," and there are concepts that embody our ideas of Santa Claus; there are connective links across the culture between various uses of SANTA CLAUS. But the concepts that embody these ideas are not concepts of any real individual. A promising line of research would be to use the tools of this book to construct fictional objects as certain abstract uniformities across concepts, much as one starts with the real numbers and constructs imaginary and complex numbers from them.

Questions

English has distinct terms for sentences and statements, but it does not make the same distinction when we turn to questions. We use the same word QUESTION for the speech act of asking a question as we do for the efficient sentence that is used in the speech act. To create a distinction we will use "Question" for the speech act and "question" for the sentence, and hope for the best when the word comes at the beginning of a sentence.

What are the meanings of Questions and what are the meanings of questions? In a very real sense, Questions are quests—quests for information—which use questions for implements. The (event) meaning of a Question is that the questioner wants some information. A YES/NO Question,

"Is Helen in Palo Alto?"

for example, seeks a truth value to get at some information. A WHO Question,

"Who is over there?"

seeks information about an individual. A WHERE Question,

"Where is Peter?"

seeks information about a location, a WHEN Question, about time. Thus the information in a Question is that the speaker is after certain specific forms of information.

The meaning of a question, on the other hand,

IS HELEN IN PALO ALTO?

WHO IS OVER THERE?

WHERE IS PETER?

is less clear. It has to be a uniformity across Questions, and across other kinds of speech acts, like assertions that use questions—say embedded questions—as in

"John knows who is standing over there."

A fairly standard proposal for dealing with the meaning of questions is to identify the meaning of a question with the set of propositions that constitute answers (or true answers) to the question (Karttunen, 78). As should be obvious by now, we must reject this proposal, since on our account propositions are, in general, proper classes and so are not members of sets and are not suitable to play any causal role. Yet there is something right about the idea. It seeks a uniformity that is important to understanding questions.

In keeping with the idea that the meaning of a question is a uniformity across the meanings of Questions that use it, we propose the solution to the similar problem we had with the classification of type of events. In fact, we propose to use event-types (and, more generally, schemata) as the meanings of questions. A YES/NO question will have a meaning that is an event-type or schema with a truth-value indeterminate TV. The meaning of a WHO-question will be a schema with an individual indeterminate, and so on. The insight that the meaning of a question has something to do with the possible answers is still present, for there are all the ways to anchor the indeterminate, and when asked on a particular occasion there are all the ways to anchor it which give you a factual situation.

We will go into this proposal in more detail in our paper, "Fragments of Situation Semantics."

TENSE, ASPECT, MODALS, CONDITIONALS

Critics are bound to complain that we have not treated many of the most basic topics usually treated in a first logic course. First-order logic, for example, is often formulated in terms of three basic primitives, sentence negation, the (material) conditional, and the universal quantifier. None of these basic topics from logic is treated explicitly in this book. Similarly, one of the success stories of philosophical logic has been the analysis of necessity, possibility, and other modal notions in terms of "possible worlds." We have not discussed this, either. Even our sympathetic colleagues find it frustrating that there is so little common ground on which to compare situation semantics with more traditional approaches.

If situation semantics is a road to a realist theory of meaning, as we intend it to be, then surely the topics that traditionally go under the above names will lie along that road somewhere. But there is certainly no guarantee that they are going to appear in the same order they appear on more traditional roads. We are keenly aware of the gaps in our theory but have found that certain topics should not be rushed. If the road from A to D goes through B before C, we have to get to B before we get to C.

In this regard it is instructive to look at a stinging criticism leveled against Austin's situation-based theory of truth (Austin, 79), a theory that has played an important role in guiding our own thought. In an article for the Tarski Symposium, Benson Mates compares Austin's theory with Tarksi's and finds the former seriously lacking because it does not give an account of so simple and basic a matter as modus ponens—that from the truth of φ and the truth of ψ whenever φ, one can infer the truth of ψ.

Suppose I state truly on some occasion or other, that whenever it is raining the streets are wet, and suppose also that my earlier statement, that it was raining, was true. Then it ought to follow that if, when I stated that it was raining I had also stated that the streets were wet, I would have made another true statement. But when one tries to work this out via *the [Austin] definition, one immediately gets stuck. What is "the historic [actual] state of affairs" with which the demonstrative conventions correlate my statement that whenever it is raining the streets are wet, and how is this historic state of affairs related to the historic states of affairs referred to in my other two statements? [Mates, 74, p. 395]*

Mates's objection, a good one, pointed to a real gap in Austin's theory. But the objection does not show that Austin's ideas are incoherent, as one might suppose from the general tone of Mates's article, but only that there is work to be done to flesh them out. That is part of what we have attempted to do in our theory of situations. It seems pretty clear now that the statement "It is raining" describes a certain simple state of affairs:

in s: at l: raining; yes.

The second statement, "Whenever it is raining the streets are wet," describes a more abstract state of affairs, a constraint:

C: at l_u: involves, E_1, E_2; yes

where

E_1: = at $\dot{l}$: raining; yes
$\qquad$ street, $\dot{b}$; yes
E_2: = at $\dot{l}$: wet, $\dot{b}$; yes.

Now suppose that there are also some streets in *s*, say

> in *s*: at *l*: street, *b*; yes
>   street, *b'*; yes.

If *s* and *C* are both factual, since factual constraints are respected by the facts, *s* must be part of some larger actual event *e*, such that

> in *e*: at *l*: wet, *b*; yes
>   wet, *b'*; yes.

Given our theory of event-types and constraints, Mates's objection is no longer a serious one. But if we had been determined to figure out modus ponens before we had the theory of event-types, we would have had some rough going.

To be fair to Mates, he saw the need for the kind of theory we have been discussing:

We need a sort of "algebra" of historic states of affairs . . . so that we can tell how historic states of affairs that are correlated with complex sentences and statements are related to those correlated with the sentences and statements that are their constituents. Otherwise, so far as I can see, we shall not even be able to establish, on the basis of Austin's definition of truth, the validity of the very simplest types of inference, e.g., of "if it is true that S *and it is true that if* S *then* T, *then it is true that* T."

In this section we want to discuss some of the topics mentioned earlier and how they might fit into the project at hand. To those who are sympathetic the discussion might generate ideas to be worked out, but to the skeptics they will probably be infuriating.

Tense and Aspect

One of the most serious deficiencies in this book—one we have tried to work around—is the very limited account we give of tense, treating only deictic uses of the present and past tenses by having spatiotemporal locations assigned directly to tense markers by speaker connections. Our excuse is that things are hard enough as they are without getting lost in the subtleties of tense and aspect.

In general, it seems that progressive tense markers are used deictically, but that the perfect is used quantificationally. That is, if I say

> (1) JACKIE WAS BITING MOLLY,

I must refer to some specific past occasion, but if I say

(2) JACKIE HAS BITTEN MOLLY,

I am referring to a present time (it's the present perfect) and quantifying over spatiotemporal locations that precede it. To treat this, we would have the connections assign a present location l and let the meaning of the perfect existentially quantify over $l' \prec l$. And if I say

(3) JACKIE HAD BITTEN MOLLY,

I refer to some past location l ($= c(\text{HAD}) \prec l_d$) and quantify over yet earlier locations $l' \prec l$. All this is very reminiscent of Reichenbach's "reference time" and "event time." Indeed, we think that Reichenbach (47) had many important insights that were ahead of their time and can be built into situation semantics.

By contrast, we think that what is usually called the "simple present" is not simple at all. Ordinarily, if one heard Joe say

JACKIE BITES MOLLY

it would be given a "habitual" reading, that biting Molly is something Jackie does nowadays. This reading can be captured by having the connections pick up a wide present location and then quantifying over locations that overlap it. Cooper (82) has studied the "reporter's use" of the simple present and suggests that it is used to refer to the discourse location itself.

Cooper (to appear) has also studied ways that different kinds of verbs, statives, activities, achievements, and accomplishments correspond to different kinds of structural constraints on the related properties and relations. This makes some important refinements in our analysis of verb phrases, and also suggests constraints that need to be stated directly in terms of one type of event precluding another, rather than having precluding be entirely derivative from involving, as we have done.

We have not mentioned the future "tense" in the book. Are future tense statements made about particular future situations? Are they true or false now in virtue of what future situations are already actual? We do not think this is the way the future works in English. In fact, the English auxiliary system treats the future WILL as a modal, along with other modals like MUST, MIGHT, CAN, SHOULD, and the like.

Modals and Conditionals

If there has ever been a simple theory that was obviously inadequate, it is the analysis of conditionals in terms of the material conditional. Mates's example above is a case in point, for it would usually be treated in first-order logic using a conditional, and the truth would amount to nothing more than that there happen to be no places in space-time where it is raining and the streets are not wet.

Mates's example was interpreted above as the statement of a nomic constraint. So, too, modals and conditionals are often used to describe constraints of various kinds. For example, the future WILL is often used in this way. Suppose an earthquake engineer examines the building and asserts:

This building will fall down in the next 6.5 quake.

Has the engineer referred to (or quantified over) the future? Is what she said true at the time she said it in virtue of there either not being a future actual 6.5 quake or being a future actual situation where there is such a quake and the building is falling down? Common sense says "no." Imagine that the construction team is brought in and reinforces the building. Along comes a 6.5 quake and the building does not fall down. Was the engineer wrong? Should we sue her for giving a false report? It seems more reasonable to say that she was describing conditional constraints: that, the building being in its present condition, and a 6.5 quake present at i, the building will collapse at some nearby $i' \succeq i$.

Similarly with other modals, like SHOULD, CAN, MUST, etc. What are we doing with

CHILDREN SHOULD OBEY THEIR PARENTS

if not stating some kind of conditional social or moral constraint?

Sentence Negation

Here is one of the places where we suspect that in Chapters 6 and 7, emphasizing the MO_C relations between events, rather than the underlying conventional constraints C themselves, has distracted us from a solution to a vexing problem. In general, constraints allow events to contain both positive and negative information, to show us that certain options are open and certain are precluded. By focusing on the situations described by an utterance, we have neglected those precluded by the utterance. This is one of the reasons the conjecture in the next section is challenging.

General Noun Phrases

We have treated only singular *NP*'s in this book for three reasons. One is, as we mentioned earlier, their importance in the history of semantics and logic. The second is that general *NP*'s like EVERY

MAN, EVERY MAN THAT OWNS THIS BOOK, NO PHILOSOPHER have two uses. They can be used to make assertions about particular situations, as in

EVERY LINGUIST IS EATING TOMATOES

NO PHILOSOPHER IS EATING TOMATOES

but they can also be used to state constraints, as in

NO ONE EATS IMAGES OF TOMATOES

EVERY MAN IS MORTAL.

The second sort of use is more interesting, since to develop the semantics to the state where we can give a formal treatment of these requires us to use event-types and schemata much more fully in the interpretation of arbitrary phrases. And this, too, is related to a fundamental conjecture, which we state below.

Actually, singular *NP*'s can also be used to state constraints, as in

The president of the U.S. must be a citizen of the U.S.

These are functional uses of the *NP*, and a detailed treatment of them must likewise be postponed.

A third reason for separating singular and general *NP*'s as we have is that even if we ignore the uses of *NP*'s to state constraints, there is a significant difference in the semantics of the two sorts of expressions. Whereas it makes perfectly good sense to refer to a man *b* either as Terry *the* man from Ithaca, or as Terry *a* man from Ithaca, it makes no sense to refer to him as every man from Ithaca or as no man from Ithaca:

TERRY, A MAN FROM ITHACA, IS SLEEPING ON THE BEACH.

*TERRY, EVERY MAN FROM ITHACA, IS SLEEPING ON THE BEACH.

*TERRY, NO MAN FROM ITHACA, IS SLEEPING ON THE BEACH.

The idea is that general *NP*'s are not interpreted as relations between situations and individuals, the way singular *NP*'s are interpreted, but as relations between situations and sets X_σ of individuals. For example,

$$d, c \llbracket \text{NO DOG} \rrbracket X_\sigma, s$$

just in case the set X_σ provided by the setting (often the extension of a verb phrase) doesn't contain any dog in s.

Another well-known difference between singular and general *NP*'s that must be accounted for is the difference in ability between the two to serve as antecedents of pronouns in other sentences.

JACKIE$_1$ WAS BARKING AND SHE$_1$ WAS SCRATCHING.

(A DOG WITH FLEAS)$_1$ WAS BARKING AND SHE$_1$ WAS SCRATCHING.

*NO DOG$_1$ WAS BARKING AND SHE$_1$ WAS SCRATCHING.

*EVERY DOG$_1$ WAS BARKING AND SHE$_1$ WAS SCRATCHING.

Our account of this runs roughly as follows. If a singular $NP\ \alpha_1$ is an antecedent for SHE$_1$, then the interpretation

$$d, c [\![\alpha_1]\!] a_\sigma, e$$

constrains $c(\text{SHE}_1)$ to equal a_σ, if defined. However, the proper setting for a general $NP\ \beta_1$ is not an individual but a set X_σ of individuals. If the NP is to serve as the antecedent of SHE$_1$, then $c(\text{SHE}_1)$ must be allowed to vary over individuals. A consequence is that for

$$d, c [\![\beta_1]\!] X_\sigma, e$$

to hold, $c(\text{SHE}_1)$ must be undefined, in order to give it the requisite flexibility to vary over individuals.[3] A consequence of this will be that general NP's cannot serve as antecedents of pronouns in other conjuncts or disjuncts, the way singular NP's can.

A FUNDAMENTAL CONJECTURE

We now return to a deficiency in our theory of linguistic meaning hinted at several times earlier in this chapter. The conception underlying our attitude toward linguistic meaning is that sentences provide ways of asserting, hence ways of communicating information about situations. This means that sentences should have meanings based on constraints between types of events, utterances, and described situations. In our formal theory we have not captured these constraints themselves, but rather the *MO* relations between situations they give rise to.

If our basic picture is correct, we should be able to present the theory in terms of constraints as relations between schemata of the kind developed in Chapter 5. Our basic conjecture is that this is possible. Establishing this conjecture will involve using event-types and schemata in a much more fundamental way in the interpretation of noun phrases, verb phrases, and all other categories.

We want to isolate this conjecture, since it is implicit in much that we have said about languge in this book. But we cannot prove it here for three reasons. First, there is a practical matter. We have not developed our theory of schemata and constraints as fully as we would need even to treat the meaning of the simple sentences we discuss in this book. Second, to carry out the appropriate inductive proof, we would need a formal definition of the set of sentences we were dealing with, and at the relatively informal level of presentation in this book that is not possible. It does seem possible for the fragments presented in the appendixes, but would be extremely tedious.

There is a more important difficulty, though, which is just that— difficulty. The conjecture we have formulated is a very bold one. Abstract as they are, schemata are sets of event-types, finite sets under the most reasonable interpretation of our metatheory. And our constraints are finite sets of facts relating schemata. It is not at all clear how they can capture all the meanings that natural language can provide. We seem forced to adopt the view that the kinds of things that *seem* to lead us into the infinite are really higher order uniformities to which we are attuned. The presumably finite nature of humans and other natural organisms, faced with organizing limitless reality, forces organization around such uniformities. Whether or not this conjecture can be confirmed, we are confident that the constructions formulated in the attempt to do so will contribute to the unraveling of the mysteries of thought and language.

HIGHER-LEVEL ATTUNEMENT

During the seventeenth century man became aware of the power of his own rationality and its uses in harnessing the power in nature to change the world in fundamental ways. Looking for the hallmark of this rationality—what it is that sets man off from other living things—it was perhaps natural to seize on language, the ability to do things with words. In writing to Princess Elisabeth, Descartes declared that it was the mystery of human language more than anything else that convinced him of the spiritual, nonmechanistic nature of man (Descartes, 37).

We believe that western thought took a seriously wrong turn under the influence of Descartes, one that reflects a dangerous arrogance in man's attitude toward the rest of reality. The Cartesian view of mind and meaning has shaped the way we view logic, science, and the world. In particular, it has helped us to ignore or misunderstand fundamental issues about the nature of freedom within a constrained environment, hence what it means to tamper with the basic conditions under which life has evolved.

Humankind's cognitive conditions and activities are part of the causal order. The species, with its system of conditions, represents a solution to the problem of survival within an ecological niche. The solution may be virtually permanent, as with bugs, or successful for an enormously long time, as with dinosaurs. But when conditions change to such an extent that the constraints to which the species is attuned become inadequate for its survival, there is either change in the species or, as in the case with dinosaurs, extinction. Within the past fifty years the distinct possibility has arisen that the cognitive conditions and activities that have seemed to form a solution to the problem of survival of our species may have taken on a life of their own, unrelated to the survival of the species, one that has led to developments that threaten the demise not just of the species but of life itself. We hope that putting humankind's cognitive activities back in the context of a world full of life and meaning might aid in some small way in understanding the gravity of the situation. It seems unlikely that a book as specialized as this one can make a significant difference, but we can dream.

There is a story that in one of the early seminars on Montague Grammar, a student asked Barbara Partee and Terry Parsons "What is the meaning of life?" The answer was put on the board:

^ *life*',

an expression in Montague's intentional logic that denotes a function from possible worlds to life on those worlds. It would have been a good joke if it didn't strike one as all too close a *reductio ad absurdum* of man's whole search for meaning. It seems to us that the ecological approach has more to say, because it shows the interdependence of meaning and organisms attuned to and creating regularities in their environment. The systems of cognitive conditions and activities of individuals of our species and other similar ones are meaningful, relative to the nomic and conditional constraints on which the design is based.

Among the things we are attuned to is the attuned activity of other organisms. An unattractive example is the vulture, who recognizes that the activities of a lion below mean a good chance of carrion for lunch. The lion's activities, in chasing an antelope, are themselves an instance of attunement. Humans are incredibly well attuned to the meaning of the activity of fellow members of their species. Language and common-sense psychology are intertwined complex and articulate developments of this capacity. They build on an innate capacity of our species for seeing the activites of others and ourselves as parts of complex patterns, a capacity for indirect classification and interpretation.

Communication exploits this higher-level attunement. The organism engages in activity, because of the effect it will have on other organisms, which are attuned to the meaning of what the organism does. When I make belligerent, threatening or conciliatory gestures toward my foe, I do so because I know that he will get information from my activity. He will learn of my intentions because he takes my activity as meaningful. And in engaging in this activity with the intention of affecting his beliefs and actions, I am attuned to his attunement to the meaning of my actions. In these ascending levels of attunement lies much of the information that shapes the life of language-using organisms. The world as we know it is the world as it lies at the end of the chains of information that terminate in our experience, the product not only of our immediate environment, but of generations of humans that, whatever their differences, are bound by the cooperative enterprise of language.

Language is a wonderful thing, and it may well be the hallmark of what it means to be human. It is certainly a powerful tool for understanding and affecting others and the wider world. But it is not a mystery different in kind from other conditional constraints on reality which give life meaning, both for ourselves and for the other forms of life with which we share our planet. Only by beginning to understand the meaning of the constraints that reality puts on man and his uses of rationality and power, we can hope to ensure the continuation of life and the meaning it recognizes in the world about it.

ON THE ROAD HOME

It was when I said,
"There is no such thing as the truth,"
That the grapes seemed fatter.
The fox ran out of his hole.

You . . . You said,
"There are many truths,
But they are not parts of a truth."
Then the tree, at night, began to change,

Smoking through green and smoking blue.
We were two figures in a wood.
We said we stood alone.

It was when I said,
"Words are not forms of a single word.
In the sum of the parts, there are only the parts.
The world must be measured by eye";

It was when you said,
"The idols have seen lots of poverty,
Snakes and gold and lice,
But not the truth";

It was at that time, that the silence was the largest
And longest, the night was roundest,
The fragrance of the autumn warmest,
Closest and strongest.

WALLACE STEVENS

Appendixes

References

Notes

Index

Determiner-Free Aliass

In the appendixes to Chapters 6 and 7 we present an Artificial Language for Illustrating Aspects of Situation Semantics, or "Aliass" as we have come to call it. Aliass has more of the structure of English than any other artificial language we know, but it does not pretend to be a fragment of English, or any sort of "logical form" for English. It is just what its name implies and nothing more. We present it to give a feeling for the way a situation semantics of English might be described. In our second book, *Situation Semantics,* we plan to present a situation semantics for a reasonably extensive fragment of English.

Dealing with an artificial language has several obvious advantages. First, we can choose which aspects of English to reflect and which to ignore. Second, since it's our language, no one can say that we've got the semantics wrong. And third, we can completely ignore syntactic intricacies that cannot be ignored with a natural language.

Here we won't present all of Aliass, but only the parts that illustrate topics from Chapters 6 and 7 of this book. The particular part of Aliass discussed in this appendix, Determiner-Free Aliass, reflects only topics discussed in Chapter 6.

SEMANTIC FEATURES

Usually artificial languages are defined by presenting an inductive definition of a set of expressions and a parallel definition of the semantics. The definition is given in such a way that no expression has more than one syntactic derivation and each is assigned a unique meaning. The reader of the section on ambiguity and logical form will not be surprised that our definitions do not take this form. Our description of Aliass generates not just syntactic expressions, but syntactic expressions with associated semantic features. These features are relevant for semantic interpretation in that they represent various ways the expression can be used. That is, the semantic features are our candidate for the extra parameter needed to disambiguate ambiguous expressions.

Consider, for example, the sentence:

(1) JACKIE WAS BITING MOLLY AND SHE WAS EXCITED.

The Aliass expression that comes closest to this in meanings is:

(2) (JACKIE BITING$_w$ MOLLY) $\wedge$ (x_1 EXCITED$_w$)

(The w's are past tense markers.) Sentence (1) is ambiguous; it can be used in three distinct ways. It can be used with SHE having either JACKIE or MOLLY as antecedent, or with SHE used to refer directly to some female. So we design Aliass so that (2) is generated with different semantic features to reflect these three ways that (1) can be used. For example, (2) is generated with the semantic features corresponding to uses where x_1 has JACKIE, MOLLY, or nothing as antecedent. ("$x \in AF(\alpha)$" should be read "α is (or contains) an antecedent for x".):

(3) $AF(\text{JACKIE}) = \{x_1\}$, $AF(\text{MOLLY}) = 0$
(4) $AF(\text{JACKIE}) = 0$, $AF(\text{MOLLY}) = \{x_1\}$
(5) $AF(\text{JACKIE}) = AF(\text{MOLLY}) = 0$.

When we are thinking of an expression like (2) associated with semantic features as in, say, (4), we will indicate this as in:

(6) (JACKIE BITING$_w$ MOLLY$_1$) $\wedge$ (x_1 EXCITED$_w$)

Note, however, that (6) is *not* an expression of Aliass, but rather a convenient, informal way of representing expression (2) generated with semantic features (4).

To reiterate, the reader should think of the definition below as an inductive definition not just of the set of expressions α of Aliass, but of a set of pairs $\langle \alpha, W \rangle$ where α is an expression and W is a list of associated semantic features:

$SCat(\alpha)$, $Var(\alpha)$, $Tense(\alpha)$, $AF(\alpha)$.

As indicated, $AF(\alpha)$ is the set of variables that have antecedents in α. $Tense(\alpha)$ is the set of tense markers that occur in α. $Var(\alpha)$ is the set of free variables of α. But what is $SCat(\alpha)$?

In general, the meaning of an expression α of Aliass is a relation $[\![\alpha]\!]$ between discourse situations d, connections c, settings σ, and described courses of events e. Just what is supplied by σ depends on what semantic features are associated with α. For example, if α is a singular *NP*, then the setting must provide an individual a. If α is a verb like KICKING, the setting must provide individuals a, b, a location l and a truth value $i = 1$ or 0, depending on whether the utterance contains the expression, say, WAS KICKING or WASN'T KICKING. To get a uniform treatment of meaning, we assign to each expression α a "semantic category," $SCat(\alpha)$, a set of indeterminates (roles, in most cases) and we take settings to be anchors on the semantic category of α.

Thus we distinguish indeterminates, $\dot{a}$, $\dot{b}$, $\dot{l}$, and a truth-value indeterminate $\dot{tv}$ to have special roles. The special role of $\dot{a}$ is to provide the subject, that of $\dot{b}$ to provide the direct object. $SCat(\alpha)$ will always be some subset of this set of indeterminates. A *setting for* α is an anchor σ defined on $SCat(\alpha)$. And the *meaning of* α is a relation

$$d, c [\![\alpha]\!] \, \sigma, e$$

(to be defined below) on discourse situations d, connections c, settings σ for α and *coe*'s e. If σ is a setting, we use abbreviations a_σ for $\sigma(\dot{a})$, l_σ for $\sigma(\dot{l})$, etc. The notation "$[\![\alpha]\!]$" used above suppresses the dependence of meaning on the particular features W associated with α. We will introduce specific conventions below to disambiguate this notation when necessary.

THE LEXICON

The lexicon of determiner-free Aliass has only three sorts of expressions, relation symbols (*RS*'s), individual terms (*IT*'s), and tense markers (*TM*'s). The lexicon comes with an interpretation function $\mathcal{g}$ that associates objects with some of these items. More specifically:

L1. *RS*: There are unary relation symbols R^1, S^1,... with $SCat = \{\dot{a}, \dot{l}, \dot{tv}\}$, and binary relation symbols R^2, S^2,... with $SCat = \{\dot{a}, \dot{b}, \dot{l}, \dot{tv}\}$. If R^1 is unary, then $\mathcal{g}(R^1)$ is a primitive property r and the meaning of R^1 is determined by:

$$d, c [\![R^1]\!] \, \sigma, e \text{ iff } \langle r, a_\sigma, tv_\sigma \rangle \in e(l_\sigma)$$

If R^2 is binary, then $\mathcal{g}(R^2)$ is a binary relation r and the meaning of R^2 is determined by:

$$d, c [\![R^2]\!] \sigma, e \text{ iff } \langle r, a_\sigma, b_\sigma, tv_\sigma \rangle \in e(l_\sigma).$$

L2. *IT*: There are individual terms of three kinds, all with *SCat* = $\{\dot{a}\}$. First is a first-person pronoun I whose meaning is given by

$$d, c \llbracket I \rrbracket \sigma, e \text{ iff } a_\sigma = a_d, \text{ the speaker in } d.$$

Second are variables $x_1, x_2, \ldots$ that function as third person pronouns. Their meanings are defined by:

$$d, c \llbracket x_n \rrbracket \sigma, e \text{ iff } a_\sigma = c(x_n).$$

Third are names $J, M, \ldots$. In spite of all we have said in the chapter to show it is a mistake, we assume that $\mathscr{s}$ assigns to each name, say J, some individual $j = \mathscr{s}(J)$ in A, and define the meaning of J by:

$$d, c \llbracket J \rrbracket \sigma, e \text{ iff } a_\sigma = j.$$

L3. *TM*: There are tense markers $n_1, n_2, \ldots$ (present tense) and $w_1, w_2, \ldots$ (past tense), with $SCat = \{\dot{l}\}$. Their meanings are given by:

$$d, c \llbracket n_j \rrbracket \sigma, e \text{ iff } l_\sigma = c(n_j) \text{ and } l_\sigma \circ l_d.$$
$$d, c \llbracket w_j \rrbracket \sigma, e \text{ iff } l_\sigma = c(w_j) \text{ and } l_\sigma \prec l_d.$$

A word of explanation for our treatment of names is surely in order, since we have made such a point of its being the wrong thing to do. A treatment of the proper use of ordinary names requires bringing in the attitudes, since to use a name properly to refer to an individual, the speaker must have the information that the individual has the name in question. Thus to do things really right would require that we bring in the attitude *inf* even at this elementary stage, which would distract from the features of Aliass which we want to bring out here.

THE GRAMMAR

The grammatical rules generate a collection of expressions with their associated semantic features, and assign meanings to them. A given expression α may well be assigned more than one meaning when it is associated with different features, since the features are intended to represent ways the expression might be used. Our aim is to give Aliass a structure that is similar enough to English to illustrate the specific points we have been making in a precise way. So, for example, we design Aliass to reflect facts about English like the following. The sentence (1) above can be used in three different ways. However, the sentence

SHE WAS EXCITED AND JACKIE WAS BITING MOLLY

can be used in only one way. It cannot be used with SHE having either JACKIE or MOLLY as antecedent.

Syntactic Categories

In addition to the three lexical categories of *RS*, *IT*, and *TM*, there are rules that generate and interpret Located Relation Phrases (*LRP*'s), Property Phrases (*PrPh*'s) that do double duty for both common nouns and verb phrases, Noun Phrases (*NP*'s), and Sentences (*S*'s). In stating the semantic rules for $d, c [\![\alpha]\!] \sigma, e$, we always assume that the triple d, c, σ is in the domain of $[\![\alpha]\!]$: this includes the assumptions that d is a discourse situation, that c is a connection defined on all the free variables and tense markers of α (i.e., $Var(\alpha) \cup Tense(\alpha) \subseteq \text{domain}(c)$), and that σ is a setting defined on all indeterminates in $SCat(\alpha)$.

S Rules

There are three *S* rules in Determiner-Free Aliass, corresponding to the formation of sentences from putting an *NP* in front of a *PrPh*, conjoining sentences, and disjoining sentences, respectively. The *SCat* of a sentence of Determiner-Free Aliass is always empty. Thus the setting coordinate is irrelevant for sentences. The rules for generating *S*'s follow:

S1: If α is an *NP* and π is a *PrPh* then $(\alpha\pi)$ is a sentence.
$SCat(\alpha\pi) = 0$.
$Var(\alpha\pi) = Var(\alpha) \cup (Var(\pi) - AF(\alpha))$.
$AF(\alpha\pi) = AF(\alpha) \cup AF(\pi)$.
$$d, c [\![(\alpha\pi)]\!] e$$
iff
there is a σ and a c' extending c such that $d, c' [\![\alpha]\!] \sigma, e$ and $d, c' [\![\pi]\!] \sigma, e$.

S2: If φ and ψ are sentences then $(\varphi \wedge \psi)$ is a sentence.
$SCat(\varphi \wedge \psi) = SCat(\varphi) \cup SCat(\psi)$.
$Var(\varphi \wedge \psi) = Var(\varphi) \cup (Var(\psi) - AF(\varphi))$.
$AF(\varphi \wedge \psi) = AF(\varphi) \cup AF(\psi)$.
$d, c [\![(\varphi \wedge \psi)]\!] e$ iff there is a c' extending c so that $d, c' [\![\varphi]\!] e$ and $d, c' [\![\psi]\!] e$.

S3: If φ and ψ are sentences so is $(\varphi \vee \psi)$. Its semantic features are defined just as for (2). Its meaning is given by:
$$d, c [\![(\varphi \vee \psi)]\!] e$$
iff
there is a c' extending c so that d, c' is in the domain of both $[\![\varphi]\!]$ and $[\![\psi]\!]$ and such that either $d, c' [\![\varphi]\!] e$ or $d, c' [\![\psi]\!] e$.

Some comments on these rules are in order.

1. Since tense markers are never bound in Aliass, we did not bother to make explicit the definition of *Tense*(α). It is always the union of all the tense markers in its constituents.

2. Note that because both *NP*'s and *PrPh*'s have $SCat = \{\dot{a}\}$, the quantification over settings σ in the first rule is really a quantification over individuals a_σ. Ignoring the binding of variables, it says that a situation e is described by ($\alpha \pi$) provided there is an a_σ that is denoted by the *NP* and has the property denoted by the *PrPh*.

3. In all three rules, pronouns free in the second constituent may have antecedents in the first, so not be free in the whole. The quantification over c' extending c is needed to take care of the pronouns free in the constituents but not free in the whole. Note that pronouns in the first constituent are never bound by the second.

Property Phrase Rules

There are three ways to form property phrases, from an *LRP*, from an *LRP* followed by an *NP*, and by conjoining *PrPh*'s. The rules are:

PrPh1: If π is an *LRP* with $SCat = \{\dot{a}\}$, then π is a property phrase with the same *SCat*, *Var*, *Tense*, *AF* and meaning as the *LRP*.

PrPh2: If π is an *LRP* with b in its *SCat* and β is an *NP*, then $(\pi \beta)$ is a *PrPh*.

$$SCat(\pi \beta) = \{\dot{a}\}.$$
$$Var(\pi \beta) = Var(\beta).$$
$$AF(\pi \beta) = AF(\beta).$$
$$d, c [\![(\pi \beta)]\!] \, \sigma, e$$
$$\text{iff}$$

there is an extension σ' of σ so that $d, c [\![\pi]\!] \sigma', e$ and $d, c [\![\beta]\!] \sigma'', e$; where $a_{\sigma''} = b_{\sigma'}$.

PrPh3: If π and π' are *PrPh*'s, then $(\pi \wedge \pi')$ is a *PrPh*.

$$SCat = \{\dot{a}\}.$$
$$Var = Var(\pi) \cup (Var(\pi') - AF(\pi)).$$
$$AF = AF(\pi) \cup AF(\pi').$$
$$d, c [\![(\pi \wedge \pi')]\!] \, \sigma, e$$
$$\text{iff}$$

there is a c' extending c such that $d, c' [\![\pi]\!] \sigma, e$ and $d, c' [\![\pi']\!] \sigma, e$.

Just to relate our notation to more common terminology, we

define the *extension of a property phrase* π in an event e (given d,c in the domain of $[\![\pi]\!]$) to be the set of things having the property in e, that is,

$$_{d,c}\,Ext(\pi, e) = \{a_\sigma \colon d, c[\![\pi]\!]\,\sigma, e \text{ for some } \sigma\}$$

NP Rules

There are two *NP* rules. One allows any individual term to be an *NP*. The second allows an *NP* to be an antecedent of a pronoun. This last rule affects only the *SCat* of the *NP*. The rules are:

NP1: Every *IT* is an *NP* with the same semantic features and meaning as the *IT*.

NP2: If α is an *NP* with assigned semantic features, and x_i is a variable, then x_i can be added to the *AF* of α. The *SCat* and *Tense* of α are unchanged. We represent the expression with its new semantic features by α_i. The meaning of the *NP* with its new associated features is

$d, c[\![\alpha_i]\!]\,\sigma, e$
   iff
$d, c[\![\alpha]\!]\,\sigma, e$ and if $c(x_i)$ is defined, then $c(x_i) = a_\sigma$.

LRP Rules

The last rule generates located relation phrases out of relation symbols, tense markers, and "~". It is:

LRP: If α is a relation symbol and t is a tense marker, then α_t and $\sim\!\alpha_t$ are *LRP*'s. In both cases
   $SCat = SCat(\alpha) - \{\dot{l}, \ddot{w}\}$,
   $Var = 0$,
   $Tense = \{t\}$, and
   $AF = 0$.

Their meanings are given by:
   $d, c[\![\alpha_t]\!]\,\sigma, e$
     iff
there is a σ' extending σ such that $\sigma'(\ddot{w}) = 1$, $d, c[\![\alpha]\!]\sigma', e$ and $d, c[\![t]\!]\sigma', e$.
   $d, c[\![\sim\!\alpha_t]\!]\,\sigma, e$
     iff
there is a α' extending σ such that $\sigma'(\ddot{w}) = 0$, $d, c[\![\alpha]\!]\,\sigma', e$ and $d, c[\![t]\!]\sigma', e$.

REMARKS

We conclude this appendix by working out an example and by stating some facts about the semantics of Determiner-Free Aliass.

Example

Consider the Aliass analogue of

JACKIE IS BARKING OR SHE IS SNEEZING

used with SHE antecedent on JACKIE:

$(\text{JACKIE}_1 \ \text{BARKING}_n) \lor (X_1 \ \text{SNEEZING}_n)$

This expression with associated features has a derivation in Aliass indicated by a tree similar to the first tree on p. 314. The only difference is that this sentence is missing the appositive ⟨A DOG⟩.

Let $\mathit{s}(\text{JACKIE}) = $ Jackie. Then the meanings of the various constituents of this expression are given below, working our way up the various branches of the tree. We indicate the relevant rule in brackets so that ⟨S2⟩ means that rule S2 has been applied, for example.

1. $d, c \, [\![\, \text{JACKIE} \,]\!] \, \sigma, e$ iff $a_\sigma = $ Jackie ⟨L2⟩

2. $d, c \, [\![\, \text{JACKIE}_1 \,]\!] \, \sigma, e$ iff $a_\sigma = $ Jackie, and if $c(x_1)$ is defined, then $c(x_1) = $ Jackie ⟨NP2⟩.

3. $d, c \, [\![\, \text{BARKING} \,]\!] \, \sigma, e$ iff ⟨L1⟩, $e(l_\sigma)$ (barking, $a_\sigma) = tv_\sigma$.

4. $d, c \, [\![\, \text{BARKING}_n \,]\!] \, \sigma, e$ iff a_σ is defined and there is an extension σ' of σ such that (3) holds with σ' in place of σ ⟨by LRP and PrPb1⟩,
   $l_\sigma = c(n)$,
   $c(n) \circ l_d$, and
   $tv_\sigma = 1$.
   In other words, iff
   in e: at $c(n)$: barking, a_σ; yes.

5. $d, c \, [\![\, \text{JACKIE}_1 \ \text{BARKING}_n \,]\!] \, e$ iff ⟨S1⟩ for some σ, (2) and (4), iff
      in e: at $c(n)$: barking, Jackie; yes,
   assuming that d, c are in the domain of the meaning of the sentence. In particular, if defined, $c(x_1) = $ Jackie.

6. $d, c \, [\![\, x_1 \,]\!] \, \sigma, e$ iff $c(x_1) = a_\sigma$ ⟨L2⟩

7. $d, c \, [\![\, x_1 \ \text{SNEEZING}_n \,]\!]$ iff
      in e at $c(n)$: sneezing, $c(x_1)$; yes
   This is similar to (5).

8. $d, c [\![(\text{JACKIE}_1 \text{ BARKING}_n) \lor (x_1 \text{ SNEEZING}_n)]\!] e$ iff $\langle S3 \rangle\ c(n)$ is defined and there is a c' extending c such that d, c' is in the domain of both sentence meanings and either (5) or (7) hold with c replaced by c'. The first requirement ensures that $c'(x_1)$ will be defined, and so it equals Jackie, so that the condition on e boils down to:

in e: at $c(n)$: barking, Jackie; yes

or

in e: at $c(n)$: sneezing, Jackie; yes

Truth and Statements

A *statement* $\Phi = \langle d, c, \varphi \rangle$ of Determiner-Free Aliass consists of a sentence φ with a set of associated semantic features, a discourse situation d, and a connection c defined on $Var(\varphi) \cup Tense(\varphi)$. The *interpretation* of such a statement is the collection

$$[\![\Phi]\!] = \{ e : d, c [\![\varphi]\!] e \}.$$

Let $\mathfrak{M}$ be a structure of situations. The statement Φ is *true* in $\mathfrak{M}$ if some $e \in [\![\Phi]\!]$ is actual in $\mathfrak{M}$. The interpretation of any statement of Determiner-Free Aliass is persistent (this follows from the following exercise), so we could equally well say that a statement is true if one of the e in its interpretation is factual, or, if the world w of $\mathfrak{M}$ is in its interpretation, provided there is a world of $\mathfrak{M}$, of course.

Exercise. Let α be any expression of Determiner-Free Aliass with semantic features *SCat, Var, Tense,* and *AF.* Let c and c' be connections that agree on *Var, Tense,* and *AF.* Let σ and σ' be settings for α that agree on *SCat.* Let d and d' be discourse situations with d a part of d' and let e and e' be *coe*'s with e a part of e'. Prove:

if $d, c [\![\alpha]\!] \sigma, e$, then $d', c' [\![\alpha]\!] \sigma', e'$

Corollary. The interpretation of any statement of Determiner-Free Aliass is persistent.

We present here a fact that we hinted above.

Proposition. Let P be a non-empty persistent collection of *coe*'s. Then P is not a set.

Proof. If P were a set, then it would be an object that could take part in *coe*. Take some property p like the property of being a set, and let e be in P. Assuming that P is a set, then e is part of an e' that has $\langle p, P, 1 \rangle$ in $e'(u)$. But then e' is in P, so we have a set P in its own transitive closure, which is impossible. $\square$

Strong Consequence

A statement Ψ is a *strong consequence* of statements $\Phi_1,...,\Phi_n$, which we write

$$\Phi_1,...\Phi_n \vdash \Psi,$$

just in case

$$[\![\Phi_1]\!] \cap ... \cap [\![\Phi_n]\!] \subseteq [\![\Psi]\!].$$

Notice that it is not required that the various statements have the same discourse situations or even the same speaker for this notion to make sense.

As we pointed out in Chapter 7, it does not really make sense to talk in general about the conjunction or disjunction of statements as another statement. This is especially true of disjunctions. A statement made using a disjunctive sentence is not the disjunction of two separate statements. So there is some danger of confusion when we write $(\Phi \vee \Psi)$ for $\langle d,c,(\varphi \vee \psi)\rangle$, as we did in Chapter 6. It should not be thought that we can take the disjunction of arbitrary statements.

With this notation we can state the following rather weak laws about Determiner-Free Aliass, which are about all we have left of propositional logic.

1. $\Phi, \Psi \vdash (\Phi \wedge \Psi)$

2. $(\Phi \wedge \Psi) \vdash \Phi$

3. $(\Phi \wedge \Psi) \vdash \Psi$

4. $\Phi \vdash (\Phi \vee \Psi)$

5. $\Psi \vdash (\Phi \vee \Psi)$

6. If $\Phi_1...\Phi_n \vdash \Psi$ and if each of $\Phi_1,...,\Phi_n$ is true in $\mathfrak{M}$, then so is Ψ.

Notice that (6) is not as trivial as it might look. Given the way that we have defined truth for statements, (6) depends on the fact that statements of Determiner-Free Aliass are persistent. For what we know from the truth of the Φ_i is that there are actual situations e_i described by Φ_i. But then there is an actual situation that includes each of these as a part, and so it is also described by each of the Φ_i (by persistence). Hence it will be described by Ψ. Statements of Singular Aliass, to be described in the next appendix, are not in general persistent. Since (6) is surely something that should hold, we must take some care in defining truth there.

The rather harmless-looking (4) and (5) fail when we add appositive uses of definite descriptions in the next appendix. And, as we have pointed out in Chapter 6, we do not have an arbitrary statement following from a contradiction.

Exercise. Add a new *NP* THAT and a new symbol MEANS to the fragment above so that you can form sentences

THAT MEANS φ

Work out the syntax and semantics needed. (Hint: You should add event indeterminates $\dot{e}_0$ and $\dot{e}_1$ and have the $SCat(\text{THAT}) = \{\dot{e}_0\}$ and $SCat(\text{MEANS}) = \{\dot{e}_0, \dot{e}_1\}$.)

APPENDIX TO CHAPTER 7

Singular Aliass

In this appendix we add determiners (*Det's*) to the language of the previous appendix to generate *NP's* which closely reflect the ways singular noun-phrases of English function. We treat both value-loaded and value-free interpretations of *NP's* and the expressions that contain them. We call the resulting part of Aliass *Singular Aliass.*

We will illustrate the syntax and semantics of this fragment with two sentences, (1) and (3) below, or rather, with their Aliass versions (2) and (4). To keep the notation a little simpler, we stick to examples in the present tense and so do not display the present tense markers in (2) and (4).

(1) THE DOG LOVES THE BOY WHO OWNS HER

(2) (THE DOG)(LOVES (THE (BOY $\wedge$ OWNS x_1)))

We treat the use of (1) where HER has THE DOG as antecedent, where THE DOG is used referentially, and THE BOY WHO OWNS HER is used attributively; see (5) below.

(3) JACKIE, A DOG, IS BARKING OR SHE IS SNEEZING

(4) (JACKIE ⟨A DOG⟩ BARKING) $\vee$ (x_1 SNEEZING)

Here SHE has JACKIE as an antecedent, so it is just like the sentence used as an example in the previous appendix with the addition of the appositive *NP* A DOG. We are interested in verifying that the semantics assigns a meaning to (4) which ensures that statements made with (4) can only be used to describe situations where Jackie is a dog, even if she is sneezing and not barking.

SYNTACTIC CATEGORIES

There is only one new syntactic category in Singular Aliass, that of determiner (*Det*). The main new rule allows one to form *NP*'s by combining a *Det* with a *PrPh*, as in:

THE (BOY ∧ OWNS x_1)

which means roughly what

THE BOY WHO OWNS IT

means in English.

We treat only two basic determiners, THE and A, though it is not difficult to extend the treatment to complex determiners, as in THE DOG'S, which is built from an *NP* and the possessive. We allow appositive uses of singular *NP*'s, as in

JACKIE ⟨A DOG⟩

which means roughly what

JACKIE, A DOG,

means in English.

Semantic Features and Settings

In addition to the indeterminates $\dot{a}$, $\dot{b}$, $\dot{l}$, and $\dot{\imath v}$ of the last appendix, we add a set indeterminate $\dot{X}$ and event indeterminates $\dot{e}_0$ and $\dot{e}_1$. σ is an anchor for $\dot{X}$ if $\sigma(\dot{X})$ is a set of individuals, written X_σ. σ is an anchor for $\dot{e}_i$ if $\sigma(\dot{e}_i)$ is a coe, written $e_{i,\sigma}$.

As in the case of Determiner-Free Aliass, the inductive definition below generates not just expressions, but expressions together with semantic features: *SCat, Var, Tense, AF,* plus a new feature *RS* (for "resource situation"). A setting for α is an anchor σ defined on *SCat* of α. Now, however, a *connection for* α is a function c defined on

$$Var(\alpha) \cup Tense(\alpha) \cup RS(\alpha),$$

mapping the event indeterminate $\dot{e}_0$ to a resource *coe* e_0 if $\dot{e}_0 \in RS(\alpha)$.

The following points may help to motivate the definition of the fragment, as well as to coordinate the appendix with the notational conventions of Chapter 7.

1. *SCat*(α) is a subset of the indeterminates listed above. The *SCat* of a singular *NP* will be either $\{ \dot{a} \}$ (for those that arise from individual terms, as in Determiner-Free Aliass) or of the form $\{ \dot{e}_i, \dot{a} \}$, for those involving a determiner. An *NP* with this *SCat* will constrain the course of events $e_{i,\sigma}$ and individual a_σ to fit the defining condition in

$e_{i,\sigma}$. To indicate an *NP* α with e_i in *SCat*(α) we write α^i, as in Chapter 7. Thus, for example, the fact that we are interested in uses of (2) where THE DOG is used referentially will be represented by (THE DOG)^0, the *NP* THE DOG with *SCat* = $\{\dot{e}_0, \dot{a}\}$.

2. In general, the situation e_1 described by a sentence can be constrained by *NP*'s in the sentence. We will represent this by having the sentence act as an antecedent for the *NP*. That is, if an *NP* α^i constrains the situation described by a sentence φ, we represent this by having the indeterminate $\dot{e}_1$ in $AF(\varphi)$. We will indicate that $\dot{e}_1$ is in $AF(\varphi)$ by writing φ^1, as in Chapter 7. The event indeterminate $\dot{e}_1$ plays the role of the situation described by a statement; so statements with attributive and appositive uses of singular *NP*'s need to have $\dot{e}_1$ in their AF.

3. Sentences may have event indeterminates in their *SCat*. However, *statements* will correspond to sentences with empty *SCat*. Event indeterminates in *SCat*(α) can get discharged in two ways:

1. the event indeterminate $\dot{e}_0$ may be shifted from *SCat*(α) to $RS(\alpha)$, representing *NP*'s of the form β^0 in α being used referentially, with resource situation $c(\dot{e}_0)$;

2. by constraining the situation described by some sentence.

Using the notational conventions just described, plus those of the last appendix, we may represent the expressions (2) and (4) with their intended semantic features by (5) and (6), respectively.

(5) [(THE DOG)$^0{}_1$(LOVES (THE BOY $\wedge$ OWNS x_1))^1]^1

(6) [(JACKIE$_1$ $\langle$(A DOG)$^1\rangle$ BARKING $\vee$ (x_1 SNEEZING)]^1

Additions to the Lexicon

As remarked above, the only new lexical items are the determiners THE and A with *SCat* = $\{\dot{X}, a\}$. A singular determiner has a meaning which allows one to relate an individual a_σ and a set X_σ as follows: a_σ is *an* X_σ if a_σ is in X_σ; a_σ is *the* X_σ if a_σ is the only thing in X_σ. To summarize these intuitions, we add the following lexical rule to the language of the previous section:

*L*4: The expressions THE and A are determiners. Their *SCat* is $\{\dot{X}, \dot{a}\}$. Their meanings are given by:

$d, c [\![\text{A}]\!] \sigma, e$ iff a_σ is in X_σ;

$d, c [\![\text{THE}]\!] \sigma, e$ iff a_σ is the unique thing in X_σ.

314

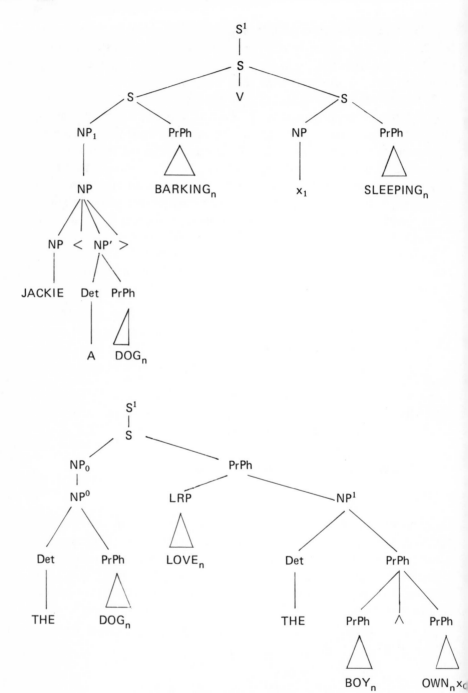

STRUCTURE TREES FOR (5) AND (6)

We are not going to treat determiners like EVERY and NO in this book, but if we did, they would be assigned *SCat* consisting of two set indeterminates $\dot{X}$ and $\dot{Y}$, as discussed in Chapter 11.

ADDITIONS TO THE GRAMMAR

There are two basic new ways to form expressions. One combines a determiner with a property phrase to form an *NP*. The other allows an *NP* to be used as an appositive relative clause to another *NP*. There is also a rule which adds $\dot{e}_0$ to the *RS* of an *NP*, corresponding to a value-loaded use. However, some of our earlier rules have to be modified slightly due to the possibility of having *NP*'s that contain free variables, and *NP*'s that serve as antecedents for variables that occur within them, as in:

[THE DOG THAT BIT THE BOY WHO OWNED HER₁]₁.

So we repeat the rules of the previous fragment, making changes that these new possibilities dictate. In defining the meaning of an expression α we always assume that d, c, σ is in the domain of $[\![\alpha]\!]$; that is, d is a discourse situation, c is a connection defined on $Var(\alpha) \cup Tense(\alpha) \cup RS(\alpha)$, and σ is a setting defined on $SCat(\alpha)$.

S Rules

There are four *S* rules in Singular Aliass, corresponding to the three in Determiner-Free Aliass, plus one that allows a sentence to serve as an antecedent for an *NP*. The rules for generating *S*'s follow:

$S1$: If α is an *NP* and π is a *PrPh*, then $(\alpha\,\pi)$ is a sentence.
$SCat = (SCat(\alpha) \cup SCat(\pi)) - \{\dot{a}\}$.
$Var = Var(\alpha) \cup (Var(\pi) - AF(\alpha))$.
$AF = AF(\alpha) \cup AF(\pi)$.
$\quad d, c [\![(\alpha\,\pi)]\!]\, \sigma, e$
$\qquad$ iff
there is a σ' extending σ and a c' extending c such that
$d, c' [\![\alpha]\!]\, \sigma', e$ and $d, c' [\![\pi]\!]\, \sigma', e$.

$S2$: If φ and ψ are sentences with e_1 in their *SCats*, then $(\varphi \wedge \psi)$ is a sentence.
$SCat = SCat(\varphi) \cup SCat(\psi)$
$Var = Var(\varphi) \cup (Var(\psi) - AF(\varphi))$.
$AF = AF(\varphi) \cup AF(\psi)$.

$$d, c \llbracket \varphi \wedge \psi) \rrbracket \sigma, e$$
iff

there is a c' extending c and a σ' extending σ so that
$d, c' \llbracket \varphi \rrbracket \sigma', e$ and $d, c' \llbracket \psi \rrbracket \sigma', e$.

S3: If φ and ψ are sentences with e_1 in their *SCats*, then $(\alpha \vee \psi)$ is a sentence. Its semantic features are defined just as for *S2*. Its meaning is given by:

$$d, c \llbracket (\varphi \vee \psi) \rrbracket \sigma, e$$
iff

there is a c' extending c and a σ' extending σ so that d, c', σ' is in the domain of both $\llbracket \varphi \rrbracket$ and $\llbracket \psi \rrbracket$ and such that either $d, c' \llbracket \varphi \rrbracket \sigma', e$ or $d, c' \llbracket \psi \rrbracket \sigma', e$.

S4: If φ is a sentence with $\dot{e}_1$ in its *SCat*, then φ is also a sentence with $\dot{e}_1$ transferred from its *SCat* to its *AF*. We abbreviate φ with these features as φ^1. The meaning of φ^1 is:

$$d, c \llbracket \varphi^1 \rrbracket \sigma, e$$
iff

for some σ^* extending σ with $e_{1,\sigma^*} = e$, $d, c \llbracket \varphi \rrbracket \sigma^*, e$.

Resource Situation Rule

RSR: If α is an expression of some category then you can transfer $\dot{e}_0$ from *SCat*(α) to *RS*(α). If we denote the expression with its new feature by α', then the meaning is:

$d, c \llbracket \alpha' \rrbracket \sigma, e$ iff

$d, c \llbracket \alpha \rrbracket \sigma', e$ where σ' is the extension of σ with $\sigma'(\dot{e}_0) = c(\dot{e}_0)$.

Property Phrase Rules

There are the same three ways to form property phrases in Singular Aliass as in Determiner-Free Aliass. The only changes have to do with *SCat*.

PrPh1: If π is an *LRP* with $\dot{b} \notin SCat$ then π is a property phrase with the same *SCat*, *Var*, *Tense*, *AF* and meaning as the *LRP*.

PrPh2: If π is an *LRP* with $\dot{b}$ in its *SCat* and β is an *NP* then $(\pi \beta)$ is a *PrPh*.
$SCat = SCat(\beta)$
$Var = Var(\beta)$
$AF = AF(\beta)$

$d, c [\![(\pi \beta)]\!] \sigma, e$
  iff
there is an extension σ' of σ so that $d, c [\![\pi]\!] \sigma', e$ and $d, c [\![\beta]\!] \sigma', e$.

*PrPh*3: If π and π' are *PrPh*'s, then $(\pi \wedge \pi')$ is a *PrPh*.

$SCat = SCat(\pi) \cup SCat(\pi')$
$Var = Var(\pi) \cup (Var(\pi') - AF(\pi))$.
$AF = AF(\pi) \cup AF(\pi')$
  $d, c [\![(\pi \wedge \pi')]\!] \sigma, e$
    iff
there is a c' extending c such that $d, c' [\![\pi]\!] \sigma, e$ and $d, c' [\![\pi']\!] \sigma, e$.

Remark. Given a property phrase π and a triple d, c, σ in the domain of $[\![\pi]\!]$, we define the *extension* of π in e by:

$_{d,c,\sigma}Ext(\pi, e) = \{ a_\sigma, \mid d, c, [\![\pi]\!] \sigma', e$ where σ' agrees with σ except possibly on $a \}$.

NP Rules

There are four *NP* rules in Singular Aliass, the two from Determiner-Free Aliass, one for building *NP*'s out of determiners and property phrases, and one for using a singular *NP* appositively.

NP1: Every *IT* is an *NP* with the same semantic features and meaning as the *IT*.

NP2: If α is an *NP* with assigned semantic features and x_i is a variable, then x_i can be added to $AF(\alpha)$. We use α_i to indicate the expression with its new features. The *SCat*, *Tense*, and *RS* of α_i are unchanged.

  $Var(\alpha_i) = Var(\alpha) - \{ x_i \}$.
  $d, c [\![\alpha_i]\!] \sigma, e$ iff there is a c' extending c so that
  $d, c' [\![\alpha]\!] \sigma, e$ and if $c'(x_i)$ is defined, then $c'(x_i) = a_\sigma$.

NP3: If δ is a determiner, π is a *PrPh* and $\dot{e}_i$ is one of the event indeterminates, then $(\delta \pi)$ is an *NP* with $SCat = \{ \dot{a}, \dot{e}_i \}$. We indicate this feature by writing $(\delta \pi)^i$. Its features *Var*, *Tense*, *AF* and *RS* are the same as those of π. Its meaning is:

  $d, c [\![(\delta \pi)^i]\!] \sigma, e$
  iff
there is an extension σ' of σ so that $X_{\sigma'} = {}_{d,c,\sigma}Ext(\pi, e_{i,\sigma})$ and
  $d, c [\![\delta]\!] \sigma', e$.

$NP4$: If α and β are NP's, and the $SCat$ of β is $\{\dot{a}, \dot{e}_1\}$, then $(\alpha \langle \beta \rangle)$ is an NP, all of whose features are the union of the features of the constituents. Its meaning is:

$d, c \, [\![\alpha \langle \beta \rangle]\!] \, \sigma, e$

iff

$d, c \, [\![\alpha]\!] \, \sigma, e$ and $d, c \, [\![\beta]\!] \, \sigma, e$.

LRP Rules

The rules for generating located relation phrases out of relation symbols, tense markers, and "$\sim$" are unchanged from the previous appendix, so are omitted.

REMARKS

We conclude this appendix in a manner parallel to the end of the previous appendix.

Examples

In discussing various constituents of Examples (5) and (6), we assume that $l = c(n)$ is a location overlapping l_d, and that $\mathcal{I}(\text{JACKIE}) = $ Jackie.

(1) $d, c \, [\![\text{THE DOG}^0]\!] \, \sigma, e$ iff $\langle NP3 \rangle a_\sigma$ is the unique dog in $\sigma(\dot{e}_0)$ at l. However, if we evaluate the same expression after RSR moves $\dot{e}_0$ from $SCat$ to RS, then we obtain, by RSR,

$d, c \, [\![\text{THE DOG}^0]\!] \, \sigma, e$ iff

a_σ is the unique dog in the resource situation $c(\dot{e}_0)$.

(2) The expression in (5) indicates a sentence with empty $SCat$. However, the first rule (working top down) that is applied is $S4$, so

$d, c \, [\![(5)]\!] \, e$ iff

$d, c \, [\![(\text{THE DOG})^0_1 (\text{LOVES} (\text{THE} (\text{BOY} \wedge (\text{OWNS } x_1))))]\!] \, \sigma, e$

where $\sigma(e_1) = e$.

That is, the situation described by the whole is picked up by the setting as the situation described, so it will be available when we get to the interpretation of the attributive use of the second NP.

(3) It is now easy to see why the appositive use of A DOG works out properly in (6). The situation described by the whole, the disjunction, is picked up by the setting and is available at the level of each disjunct, where the first constrains it to be one where Jackie is a dog.

Truth and Statements

A *statement* $\Phi = \langle d, c, \varphi \rangle$ of Singular Aliass consists of a sentence φ of Singular Aliass, with a set of associated semantic features, including $SCat(\varphi) = 0$; a discourse situation d; and a connection c defined on

$$Var(\varphi) \cup Tense(\varphi) \cup RS(\varphi).$$

The interpretation of such a statement is the collection $P = [\![\Phi]\!]$ of *coe*'s e such that $d, c [\![\varphi]\!] e$. We define strong consequence, $\vdash$, just as we did in the previous appendix. Truth, however, needs a more sophisticated definition. We have seen in Chapter 7 that there are two lines one could take on this matter. We pursue only one here, the one that follows Austin.

Let $\mathfrak{M}$ be a structure of situations. By a complete statement we mean a statement Φ such that $c(e_1)$ is defined. This is called *the situation referred to* by the speaker, and is denoted by e_d. A complete statement is *true* in $\mathfrak{M}$ if e_d is actual in $\mathfrak{M}$ and $e_d \in [\![\Phi]\!]$. Otherwise the statement is false. Notice that there are two ways for a complete statement to be false. One is where the situation referred to is not actual. The other is where it is not as described by the statement.

This raises an interesting possibility, namely that even in the case of persistent statements, the earlier definition of truth is too generous to the speaker. Suppose, for example, that I assert "Someone is sleeping" in my sleep laboratory, where I am referring to only that part e_d of the total situation e involving my assistants. The interpretation of my utterance is persistent, and there is an actual situation e described by it. But it might well be false of e_d. By the definition of the previous appendix, my utterance would count as true. By the definition given here, it would not be true.

Notice that with this definition of truth we do have the crucial fact relating truth and strong consequence mentioned in the previous appendix:

(6) If $\Phi_1, ..., \Phi_n \vdash \Psi$,

where the Φ_i and Ψ are complete statements, and if each of the Φ_i are true in $\mathfrak{M}$, so is Ψ.

References

Austin, J. L., 61. Truth. In Urmson, J. O. and Warnock, G. J., eds. *Philosophical Papers.* Oxford: Oxford University Press, 1961, pp. 117–133.

Barwise, Jon, 75. *Admissible Sets and Structures.* New York: Springer-Verlag, 1975.

Barwise, Jon, 81a. Some computational aspects of situation semantics. In *Proceedings of the 19th Annual Meeting,* Association for Computational Linguistics, 1981.

Barwise, Jon, 81b. Scenes and other situations. *Journal of Philosophy, 78,* no. 7, 1981, pp. 369–397.

Barwise, Jon, and Perry, John, 80. The situation underground. In Barwise, Jon, and Sag, Ivan A., eds. *Stanford Working Papers in Semantics,* Volume I. Stanford: 1980.

Barwise, Jon, and Perry, John, 81a. Situations and attitudes. *Journal of Philosophy, 78,* no. 11, 1981, pp. 668–691.

Barwise, Jon, and Perry, John, 81b. Semantic innocence and uncompromising situations. In French, Peter A., Uehling, Theodore E., Jr., and Wettstein, Howard K., eds. *Midwest Studies in Philosophy, 6.* Minneapolis: 1981, pp. 387–404.

Brandt, Richard, and Kim, Jaegwon, 67. The logic of the identity theory. *Journal of Philosophy, 64,* 1967, pp. 516–518.

Burge, Tyler, 73. Reference and proper names. *Journal of Philosophy, 70,* 1973, pp. 425–439.

Carnap, Rudolf, 42. *Introduction to Semantics.* Cambridge: Harvard University Press, 1942.

Castaneda, Hector-Neri, 66. 'He': A study in the logic of self-consciousness. *Ratio, 8,* no. 2, 1966, pp. 130–157.

Castaneda, Hector-Neri, 67. Indicators and quasi-indicators. *American Philosophical Quarterly, 4,* 1967, pp. 85–100.

Castaneda, Hector-Neri, 68. On the logic of attributions of self-knowledge to others. *Journal of Philosophy, 65,* no. 15, 1968, pp. 439–456.

Castaneda, Hector-Neri, 77a. Perception, belief, and the structure of physical objects and consciousness. *Synthese, 35,* 1967, pp. 285–351.

Castaneda, Hector-Neri, 77b. On the philosophical foundations of the theory of communication. *Midwestern Studies in Philosophy, 2,* 1977, pp. 165–186.

Chomsky, Noam, 72. Remarks on nominalization. In Jacobs, Roderick, and Rosenbaum, Peter S., eds. *Readings in English Transformational Grammar.* Boston: Ginn, 1972.

Chomsky, Noam, 81. *Lectures on Government and Binding.* Foris, 1981.

Church, Alonzo, 43. Carnap's "Introduction to Semantics." *Philosophical Review, 52,* no. 3, 1943, pp. 298–304.

Church, Alonzo, 56. *Introduction to Mathematical Logic.* Princeton: Princeton University Press, 1956.

Cooper, Robin, 82. Tense and discourse location in situation semantics. Presented at the Ohio Conference on Tense and Aspect in Discourse, May 1982.

Cooper, Robin, 00. Situation semantics, stages, and the present tense. To be published.

Culcover, Peter W., Wasow, Thomas, and Akmajian, Adrian, eds., 77. *Formal Syntax.* San Francisco: Academic Press, 1977.

Davidson, Donald, 67a. The logical form of action sentences. In Rescher, Nicholas, ed. *The Logic of Decision and Action.* Pittsburgh: University of Pittsburgh Press, 1967, pp. 81–95.

Davidson, Donald, 67b. Truth and meaning. *Synthese, 17,* 1967, pp. 304–323.

Davidson, Donald, 69. On saying that. *Synthese, 19,* 1969, pp. 130–146.

Davidson, Donald, and Harman, Gilbert, eds., 72. *Semantics of Natural Language.* Dordrecht: Reidel, 1972.

Descartes, René, 37. *Discourse on Method.* 1637.

Donnellan, Keith S., 66. Reference and definite descriptions. *Philosophical Review, 75,* 1966, pp. 281–304.

Donnellan, Keith S., 68. Putting Humpty Dumpty together again. *Philosophical Review, 77,* 1968, pp. 203–215.

Donnellan, Keith S., 70. Proper names and identifying descriptions. *Synthese, 21,* 1970, pp. 335–358.

Donnellan, Keith S., 74. Speaking of nothing. *Philosophical Review, 83,* no. 1, 1974, pp. 3–31.

Dretske, Fred, 69. *Seeing and Knowing.* Chicago: University of Chicago Press, 1969.

Dretske, Fred, 81. *Knowledge and the Flow of Information.* Cambridge: Bradford Books/MIT Press, 1981.

Etchemendy, John, 82. *Tarski, Model Theory, and Logical Truth.* PhD thesis, Stanford University, 1982.

Fodor, Jerry A., 81. Methodological solipsism considered as a research strategy in cognitive psychology. In his *Representations*. Cambridge: Bradford Books/ MIT Press, 1981, pp. 225–253.

Frege, Gottlob, 56. The thought: A logical inquiry. *Mind, 65,* 1956, pp. 289–311. Trans. A. M. and Marcelle Quinton.

Frege, Gottlob, 60a. On concept and object. In Geach, Peter, and Black, Max, eds. *Translations from the Philosophical Writings of Gottlob Frege.* Oxford: Basil Blackwell, 1960. Trans. P. T. Geach.

Frege, Gottlob, 60b. Function and concept. In Geach, Peter, and Black, Max, eds. *Translations from the Philosophical Writings of Gottlob Frege.* Oxford: Basil Blackwell, 1960. Trans. P. T. Geach.

Frege, Gottlob, 60c. On sense and reference. In Geach, Peter, and Black, Max, eds. *Translations from the Philosophical Writings of Gottlob Frege.* Oxford: Basil Blackwell, 1960, pp. 56–78. Trans. Max Black.

French, Peter A., Uehling, Theodore E., Jr., and Wettstein, Howard K., eds., 79. *Contemporary Perspectives in the Philosophy of Language.* Minneapolis: University of Minnesota Press, 1979.

Gee, J. P., 77. Comments on the paper by Akmajian. In Culcover, Peter W., Wasow, Thomas, and Akmajian, Adrian, eds. *Formal Syntax.* San Francisco, Academic Press, 1977, pp. 461–481.

Gibson, James Jerome, 79. *The Ecological Approach to Visual Perception.* Boston: Houghton Mifflin, 1979.

Goldman, Alvin, 70. *A Theory of Human Action.* Englewood Cliffs, N.J.: Prentice-Hall, 1970.

Goodman, Nelson, 61. About. *Mind,* 1961.

Grice, H. P., 57. Meaning. *Philosophical Review, 66,* 1957, pp. 377–388.

Grice, H. P., 75. Logic and Conversation. In Davidson, Donald, and Harman, Gilbert, eds. *The Logic of Grammar.* Dickenson, 1975.

Hintikka, Jaakko, 62. *Knowledge and Belief.* Ithaca: Cornell University Press, 1962.

Hintikka, Jaakko, 67. Individuals, possible worlds and epistemic logic. *Nous, 1,* 1967, pp. 33–62.

Hintikka, Jaakko, 69a. The logic of perception. In *Models for Modalities.* Boston: Reidel, 1969, pp. 151–183.

Hintikka, Jaakko, 69b. Semantics for propositional attitudes. In *Models for Modalities.* Dordrecht: Reidel, 1969, pp. 87–111.

Hintikka, Jaakko, 75a. Information, causality, and the logic of perception. In *Intentions of Intentionality.* Dordrecht: Reidel, 1975, pp. 58–75.

Hintikka, Jaakko, 75b. *The Intentions of Intentionality.* Dordrecht: Reidel, 1975.

Kamp, Hans, 79. Events, instants and temporal reference. In Bauerle, Weiner, Egli, Urs, and von Strechow, Arneim, eds. *Semantics from Different Points of View.* Springer-Verlag, 1979.

Kaplan, David, 69. Quantifying in. *Synthese, 19,* 1969, pp. 178–214.

Kaplan, David, 75. How to Russell a Frege-Church. *Journal of Philosophy, 72,* no. 19, 1975, pp. 716–729.

Kaplan, David, 77. "Demonstratives." Manuscript.

Kaplan, David, 79a. Dthat. In French, Peter A., Uehling, Theodore E., Jr., and Wettstein, Howard K., eds. *Contemporary Perspectives in the Philosophy of Language.* Minneapolis: University of Minnesota Press, 1979, pp. 383–400.

Kaplan, David, 79b. On the logic of demonstratives. In French, Peter A., Uehling, Theodore E., Jr., and Wettstein, Howard K., eds. *Contemporary Perspectives in the Philosophy of Language.* Minneapolis: University of Minnesota Press, 1979, pp. 401–412.

Karttunen, Lauri, 78. Syntax and semantics of questions. In Hiz, Henry, ed. *Questions.* 1978, pp. 165–210.

Kim, Jaegwon, 66. On the psycho-physical identity theory. *American Philosophical Quarterly, 3,* no. 3, 1966, pp. 227–235.

Kripke, Saul, 72. Naming and necessity. In Davidson, Donald, and Harman, Gilbert, eds. *Semantics of Natural Languages.* Dordrecht: Reidel, 1972, pp. 254–355.

Kripke, Saul A., 79. A puzzle about belief. In Margalit, A. ed. *Meaning and Use.* Dordrecht: Reidel, 1979.

Larson, Richard K., 83. "Restrictive Modification: Relative Clauses and Adverbs." PhD thesis, University of Wisconsin, 1983.

Lewis, David K., 66. An argument for the identity theory. *Journal of Philosophy, 63,* 1966, pp. 17–25.

Lewis, David, 79. Attitudes de dicto and de se. *Philosophical Review, 88,* no. 4, 1979, pp. 513–545.

Marcus, Ruth, 62. Modalities and intensional languages. *Synthese, 14,* 1962, pp. 303–322.

Mates, Benson, 74. Austin, Strawson, Tarski, and Truth. In *Proceedings of the Tarski Symposium.* American Mathematical Society, 1974, pp. 385–396. Proceedings of Symposia in Pure Mathematics, Vol. 25.

Meiland, J. W., 70. *Talking about Particulars.* New York: Humanities Press, 1970.

Michaels, C. F. and Carello, C., 81. *Direct Perception.* Englewood Cliffs, N.J.: Prentice-Hall, 1981.

Montague, Richard, 74a. *Formal Philosophy.* New Haven: Yale University Press, 1974.

Montague, Richard, 74b. English as a formal language. In Thomason, Richmond, ed. *Formal Philosophy: Selected Papers of Richard Montague.* New Haven: Yale University Press, 1974, pp. 188–221.

Montague, Richard, 74c. Universal grammar. In Thomason, Richmond, ed. *Formal Philosophy: Selected Papers of Richard Montague.* New Haven: Yale University Press, 1974, pp. 222–246.

Montague, Richard, 74d. The proper treatment of quantification in ordinary

English. In Thomason, Richmond, ed. *Formal Philosophy: Selected Papers of Richard Montague.* New Haven: Yale University Press, 1974, pp. 247–270.

Partee, Barbara Hall, 72. Opacity, coreference, and pronouns. In Davidson, Donald, and Harman, Gilbert, eds. *Semantics of Natural Language.* Dordrecht: Reidel, 1972, pp. 415–441.

Pendlebury, Michael, 80. "Believing." PhD thesis, Indiana University, 1980.

Percy, Walker, 75. *The Message in the Bottle.* New York: Farrar, Strauss, and Giroux, 1975.

Perry, John, 77. Frege on demonstratives. *Philosophical Review, 86,* no. 4, 1977, pp. 474–497.

Perry, John, 79. The problem of the essential indexical. *Nous, 13,* 1979, pp. 3–21.

Perry, John, 80a. Belief and acceptance. *Midwest Studies in Philosophy, 5,* 1980, pp. 533–542.

Perry, John, 80b. A problem about continued belief. *Pacific Philosophical Quarterly, 61,* 1980, pp. 317–332.

Perry, John, to appear, a. Castaneda and I. To be published.

Perry, John, to appear, b. Perception, action, and the structure of believing. Forthcoming, in a Festschrift for Paul Grice, ed. Richard Grandy and Richard Warner.

Putnam, Hilary, 75. The meaning of 'meaning.' In Gunderson, Keith, ed. *Language, Mind, and Knowledge.* Minneapolis: University of Minnesota Press, 1975, pp. 131–193. Minnesota Studies in the Philosophy of Science, Vol. 7.

Quine, W. V., 53. *From a Logical Point of View.* Cambridge: Harvard University Press, 1953.

Quine, W. V., 66a. Quantifiers and propositional attitudes. In his *The Ways of Paradox and Other Essays.* New York: Random House, 1966, pp. 183–194.

Quine, W. V., 66b. *The Ways of Paradox and Other Essays.* New York: Random House, 1966.

Quine, W. V., 66c. Three grades of modal involvement. In *The Ways of Paradox and Other Essays.* New York: Random House, 1966, pp. 156–174.

Quine, W. V., 66d. The scope and language of science. In *The Ways of Paradox and Other Essays.* New York: Random House, 1966, pp. 215–232.

Reichenbach, Hans, 47. *Elements of Symbolic Logic.* Berkeley: University of California Press, 1947.

Russell, Bertrand, 14. *Our Knowledge of the External World.* LaSalle, Ill.: Open Court, 1914.

Russell Bertand, 71a. *Logic and Knowledge.* New York: Capricorn, 1971. Ed. R. C. Marsh.

Russell, Bertrand, 71b. The philosophy of logical atomism. In R. C. March, ed. *Logic and Knowledge.* New York: Capricorn, 1971, pp. 175–281.

Saarinen, E., et al., eds., 79. *Essays in Honour of Jaakko Hintikka.* Dordrecht: Reidel, 1979.

Schilpp, Paul Arthur, ed., 44. *The Philosophy of Bertrand Russell.* Evanston, Ill.: Northwestern University Press, 1944.

Searle, J. R., 58. Proper names. *Mind,* 1958.

Shannon, Claude, 49. *The Mathematical Theory of Information.* Urbana, Ill.: University of Illinois Press, 1949.

Smart, J. J. C., 59. Sensations and brain processes. *Philosophical Review,* 1959.

Smith, Brian Cantwell, 82. "Reflection and Semantics in a Procedural Language." PhD thesis, Massachusetts Institute of Technology, 1982.

Strawson, P. F., 50. On referring. *Mind, 59,* 1950, pp. 320–344.

Urmson, J. O., 74. Criteria of intentionality. in Moravcsik, J. M. E., ed. *Logic and Philosophy for Linguists.* The Hague: Mouton, 1974, pp. 225–37.

Vendler, Zeno, 67. Causal relations. *Journal of Philosophy, 64,* 1967, pp. 704–713.

Wettstein, Howard, 76. Can what is asserted be a sentence? *Philosophical Review, 85,* 1976.

Wettstein, Howard, 81. Demonstrative reference and definite descriptions. *Philosophical Studies, 40,* 1981.

Wettstein, Howard, 00. The semantic significance of the referential-attributive distinction. *Philosophical Studies,* forthcoming.

Wilson, George, 78. On definite and indefinite descriptions. *Philosophical Review, 87,* no. 1, 1978, pp. 48–76.

Wittgenstein, Ludwig, 22. *Tractatus Logico-Philosophicus.* London: Routledge and Kegan Paul, 1922.

Notes

3. ABSTRACT SITUATIONS

1. At this point we are using the term "extensional relation" for those relations in $\mathfrak{R}$ that are uniquely determined by their extensions. More frequently in what follows we will use the term for "set-theoretic relation"—one that is identified with its extension. The reason for the distinction is that our set-theoretic assumptions are rather minimal, and the particular relations being discussed at this point probably cannot be identified with finite sets of ordered pairs. This point should become clear when we discuss our metatheory.

2. See, for example, Russell's (1914) construction of instants out of events. Hans Kamp has resurrected this idea and shown it to be applicable to the semantics of those portions of language which do not refer to precise points of space and instants of time. We follow this suggestion here. We take the three relations above as primitive, reflecting basic facts about locations which humans actually recognize in language, and use these relations to construct instants of time and points of space from locations (Kamp, p. 81). We will review this construction in our forthcoming book *Situation Semantics.*

3. This is also why we had to be careful not to identify the primitive extensional relations on locations with *sets* of ordered pairs. If we are to make such an identification, it would be with collections of ordered pairs.

4. The interested reader can discover all he needs to know about *KPU* by reading the first fifty pages of Barwise (75). We are not positive that *KPU* will, ultimately, prove the best suited for our purposes, but it is the best that is presently at hand.

5. Barwise (81,a,b), Barwise and Perry (80), and Perry (80b).

6. Whenever we have facts like $l \prec l'$ in a course of events e, the expression is short for in e: at $l_u : \prec, l, l'$; yes, where l_u is the universal location mentioned earlier.

7. This is meant to contrast abstract situations with real ones more than to take a stand on issues like the perception of abstract objects.

8. While our emphasis on events owes much to Davidson, our analysis is more in line with Brandt, Goldman, and Kim (Brandt and Kim, 67; Goldman, 70).

4. EVENT-TYPES

1. This works if one is using the axiom of choice. Otherwise the canonical representative is the set of all sets of minimal rank of a given size.

2. Actually, we make almost no use of the relation indeterminates in this book, and we will use $\dot{r}, \dot{r}', \ldots$ to vary over roles. We will also have occasion in the appendices to use some basic indeterminates we have not formally introduced. For example, for certain purposes it is useful to have a truth value indeterminate $\dot{t v}$, and a set indeterminate $\dot{X}$.

3. This notation is somewhat unfortunate since it violates our unwritten convention of using lower case letters to range over sets, upper case to range over collections that might not be sets. It seems better to stick with a form of "e" than switch to another letter, though. And it might be justified by the fact that our event-types are a way of abstracting that is an alternative to the formation of collections.

4. The reader may have noticed that event-types are defined in terms of indeterminates and indeterminates in terms of event-types, so what we actually have is a simultaneous recursive definition of the collections of event-types and indeterminates.

5. This is a recursive definition of what it means to be an anchor.

6. More precisely, e is a context for E wrt $\dot{r}_1, \ldots, \dot{r}_n$ if there is an anchor f for E in e such that any other anchor g for E in e agrees with f on $\dot{r}_1, \ldots, \dot{r}_n$.

5. CONSTRAINTS

1. In our earlier papers we made the opposite decision, or perhaps failed to think about it. Several people, including Ruth Marcus and Nuel Belnap, suggested that we should allow incoherent situations. If one keeps the classificatory nature of the project in mind, it seems the right thing to do.

2. It seems almost certain that the very existence of nuclear weapons means that many of the conditions humans rely on in this regard no longer hold.

3. We use "at l_u: involves, S, S'; yes" to denote the coe

at l_u: involves, E, S'; yes $\mid E \in S\}$

6. SENTENCE MEANINGS

1. In this book we consider only singular NP's, the kind that can be used this way, though they can also be used in other ways, as we'll see in the next chapter.

2. The reader might wonder why we put the setting provided by the other parts of the utterance on the right, with e, rather than on the left, with d and c. Mainly, its placement is an historical accident of our notation. But it does make things more symmetric.

3. This has a drawback that didn't dawn on us until fairly late in the final

draft of this book. When we deal with a constraint C, we have three important derivative notions, the domain MO_C, the relation Precludes$_C$, and the relation MO_C. Concentrating on the latter in the case of linguistic meaning sometimes obscures the importance of the former two.

4. This use of "co-indexing" should not be strictly identified with the co-indexing used by some linguists to indicate co-reference. We allow non-co-indexed NP's to be used so that they can (accidentally) co-refer.

5. Thus it seems that our strategy of describing the meaning of an expression φ in terms of the relation $u[\![\varphi]\!]e$, rather than describing the constraints themselves or describing all three associated relations, blocks the most straightforward treatment of sentence negation.

7. THE MEANING OF SINGULAR NOUN PHRASES

1. We call these terms semitechnical, because they are not used in situation semantics, only in our discussion of the rationale of certain parts of situation semantics, and in comparisons between it and other theories.

2. We could give an interpretation even more in the spirit of Russell's theory by replacing the second condition in our definition by one which builds the uniqueness constraint itself into e.

3. The way Donnellan makes the distinction, it also has to do with speaker intentions as well as connections and reference. We are claiming not that our value-loaded uses of definite descriptions capture everything that Donnellan wants to count as a referential use of a definite description, but that our value-loaded uses are a species of referential uses.

4. Even though Alice ter Meulen had encouraged us to examine the Partee puzzle, for some time we thought that all uses of definite descriptions could be accounted for simply as a matter of which of the various situations made available by an utterance were used as the argument of the function. Repeated questioning of this assumption by Helen Nissenbaum in connection with her work on the emotions finally made us realize that our theory accounts for the puzzles below only if we admit that properties of the function itself are sometimes described by the utterance.

5. To quote Austin exactly, "A statement is said to be true when the historic state of affairs to which it is correlated by the demonstrative conventions (the ones to which it 'refers') is of a type with which the sentence used in making it is correlated by the descriptive conventions" (p. 123).

6. We have in mind his treatment of ordinary names, not "logically proper names."

8. SEEING

1. For the time being we ignore the untensed construction with SEES$_n$.

2. Since, according to Frege's theory, reference is determined by sense, he also had to claim that the expressions in the embedded sentence do not have their usual sense.

3. This argument uses the idea of knowing something about someone, an idea that has been cast into doubt in recent philosophy (Goodman, 61). Indeed, it is taken as a great discovery that the very idea of a statement being *about* something is incoherent, that every statement is about everything. When unraveled, however, all the arguments for this remarkable claim come back to the slingshot and carry no weight for one who takes situations seriously.

4. Thus Davidson's theory of SAYS THAT is not innocent, according to our use of the term, even though we borrowed it from him.

5. In the Appendix to Chapter 6 we prove that no persistent proposition is an object.

6. A more extensive discussion of this distinction can be found in chapter 2 of Dretske (69) and in Barwise (81), on which much of this chapter is based.

7. It really isn't important that we call them sentences, as long as we do not deny that they are syntactic units with meanings as given in Chapter 6.

8. Again, we ignore settings when convenient.

9. ATTITUDES AS RELATIONS TO SITUATIONS

1. The subtlest statement of this sort of view is probably Kaplan (69).

2. We don't object to the use of "intuition" to describe the minimally theoretic reactions to various inferences, or even "logical intuition." The point is that it seems extremely unlikely, except in the case of naturally gifted logicians, that such intuitive judgments concern the form of the inference. They concern what one would say, and the use of metalinguistic variables in summarizing them doesn't get at some form they are really about, but merely provides a convenient format for summary.

3. The same considerations account for why unrestricted Existential Generalization fails in general. Because I know that the tallest spy is a traitor, it does not follow that I know of any particular person that she or he is a traitor. However, with primary SEE THAT the inference usually does go through.

RALPH SAW$_p$ THAT THE MAN WITH THE SCAR FELL DOWN.

does warrant the inference that there is a certain person and that Ralph saw$_p$ that he fell down.

4. Actually this definition is not quite what one wants in general, for it would claim that Melanie saw that no one was on the road when what Melanie was aware of was a small part of the road with no one on it. What we need, more generally, is that φ describes not just e but every e' of which e is a part. However, it follows from this definition that the only sentence φ for which one can see$_p$ that φ are those that are persistent—that is, whenever they describe some e they also describe every e' of which e is a part. For persistent φ the first and second definitions are equivalent. The reason for this will become clearer in the next chapter.

5. Notice that with the first form of belief, one has some tendency to suppose that if a believes that φ and a believes that ψ then a believes that φ & ψ. How-

ever, with the second this does not hold, as Scott Soames pointed out to us to convince us that the approach we take to belief would have to be modified to account for the second form of belief. For example, I may believe of each of ten horse races that I know the winner, since for each race there is a horse whose probability of winning I put high, say .8. But I do not believe that I know the winners to all the races, because the combined probability is too low.

10. REPRESENTING MENTAL STATES AND EVENTS

1. This example of indirect classification is borrowed from Helen Nissenbaum.

2. As Thomas Reid, the notable eighteenth-century critic of Locke would have put it, the image is a natural sign of the football seen.

3. The reason for not abstracting over properties and relations will be discussed in the section on computational states later in this chapter.

4. At the risk of disclosing something the reader may be skeptical about (or, worse, enthusiastic about for the wrong reasons), we note the similarity between the role frames of mind play in the representation of perception and the role of sentence types in the representation of utterances. Sentence types are, of course, a very abstract sort of entity. This commonplace is easy to ignore but it forces itself to the center of attention when one has to design a robot that can recognize speech or written zip codes, or figure out why someone with an excellent textbook knowledge of French is so helpless when confronted with the output of a native speaker. Uniformities across "tokens of the same type" are extremely abstract, although members of a linguistic community are very good at categorizing speech events in terms of them. Sentence types are artifacts of our common-sense theory of our own linguistic competence and behavior, entities that have a dual role, to represent the structure of speech and writing, on the one hand, and to represent reality by conveying information, on the other. In our theory of utterances, the connections between expressions used at locations and individuals really serve to anchor actual "tokens" to actual individuals; the expression types are playing the same coordinative role as the indeterminates in our representation of perception. Indeed, we shall claim shortly that sentences not only are analogous to our event-types but are, in fact, an instance of them.

5. To state this constraint fully would necessitate introducing event-type indeterminates and formalizing part of our theory of event-types and anchors in ways that would be counterproductive here.

6. This is an informal way of specifying some special roles.

7. We later restrict beliefs to events that preserve information, in a sense to be discussed.

8. In this book we are dealing only with ideas of things and places, not more complex ideas.

9. At this point, as is no doubt obvious, our account cannot be really satisfactory without being embedded in a much more comprehensive analysis of mind and action.

10. Computer analogies are as dangerous as they are seductive, of course, but we feel the main danger is simply that people will assume we understand how we describe computers better than we understand how we describe people (Smith, 82).

11. Implicit here is the assumption that the anchoring relation *of* is a partial function, that it does not assign two individuals to any one idea.

12. It should also be noted that on this account it does not follow that if a believes that φ and a believes that ψ, then a believes that φ & ψ. To some readers this will seem an advantage. Readers who find it a disadvantage will have to assume that there is a structural constraint on beliefs, that if

$$\text{in } e_0\text{: at } l\text{: } B_r, a, S_0; \text{yes}$$
$$B_r, a, S_1; \text{yes}$$

then

$$\text{in } e_0\text{: at } l\text{: } B_r, a, S_0 + S_1; \text{yes.}$$

13. As Richmond Thommason has emphasized.

14. This may require some softening of the position taken in Perry (83), although at this point the matter is entirely clear in the relevent part of our mind.

15. This is not to say that we disagree with Shannon's theory. On the contrary, we see the possibility of a general theory of information that treats both content and amount as very exciting; but we don't pursue it here.

16. Fodor gives only a negative characterization of his formality condition, but it seems to us that our positive construal goes to the heart of what he is after.

11.FURTHER DIRECTIONS

1. Note that if one take Davidson's idea of samesaying in "On Saying That" and subtracts all of the complications that arise from devotion to the slingshot and related arguments, this idea is immediately suggested. This is the essay in which Davidson's remark about recoverying one's pre-Fregean semantic innocence (which we quote whenever possible) occurs.

2. Another case of this phenomenon arises in the use of "*j*" in this example. Formally, we have let "*j*" be a name for me. You can refer to me by "*j*". But you may not know which of the authors wrote this part, and so be unable to give my ordinary name.

3. One possible exception would be if X_σ were a singleton. This may account for why some people can take a statement like "Every dog$_1$ was barking and she$_1$ was scratching" as describing a situation where there is a unique dog.

Index